Approaches to Teaching Petrarch's *Canzoniere* and the Petrarchan Tradition

Approaches to Teaching World Literature

For a complete listing of titles, see the last pages of this book

Approaches to Teaching Petrarch's *Canzoniere* and the Petrarchan Tradition

Edited by

Christopher Kleinhenz

and

Andrea Dini

The Modern Language Association of America

New York 2014

Library of Congress Cataloging-in-Publication Data

Approaches to Teaching Petrarch's Canzoniere and the Petrarchan Tradition / edited by Christopher Kleinhenz and Andrea Dini.
pages cm. — (Approaches to Teaching World Literature, ISSN 1059-1133 ; 129)
Includes bibliographical references and index.
ISBN 978-1-60329-136-1 (cloth : alk. paper) —
ISBN 978-1-60329-137-8 (pbk. : alk. paper) —
ISBN 978-1-60329-175-0 (EPUB) —
ISBN 978-1-60329-176-7 (Kindle)
1. Petrarca, Francesco, 1304–1374. Rime. 2. Italian poetry—To 1400—History and criticism. I. Kleinhenz, Christopher, editor of compilation. II. Dini, Andrea, editor of compilation.
PQ4480.P47 2014
851'1—dc23 2014016751

Approaches to Teaching World Literature 129
ISSN 1059-1133

Cover illustration of the paperback and electronic editions: *Francesco Petrarca*, by Andrea del Castagno. Circa 1450. Fresco on wood. Uffizi Gallery.

Published by The Modern Language Association of America
26 Broadway, New York, NY 10004-1789
www.mla.org

CONTENTS

This volume is dedicated to the memory of
Aldo S. Bernardo, dean of North American Petrarch studies.

PREFACE

The importance of Francesco Petrarca to medieval and Renaissance Italian literature and culture is both vast and well-known. Equally important is his formative influence on lyric poetry in Western Europe in the Renaissance. Petrarch's many, innovative works belong to a wide variety of literary genres and are crucial to our understanding of late medieval and Renaissance civilization.

Petrarch's *Canzoniere* represents the peak of artistic invention, summarizing and perfecting the preceding lyric tradition and providing remarkable examples for poets of subsequent generations to imitate and emulate. The *Canzoniere* is a collection of 366 poems, ordered and authorized by the poet in the codex Vatican Latin 3195. An earlier draft of numerous poems (Vat. Lat. 3196) allows us to view the inventive process as it unfolded during the revisions and eventual transcription into the final manuscript version (Vat. Lat. 3195). The evolution of this verse collection has been the subject of numerous scholarly investigations, just as the organizing principles of the *Canzoniere* have been the subject of much scholarly debate. Each of the 366 poems is a finely crafted and representative example of its genre and form, and Petrarch was a master poet who perfected the form of the sonnet and sestina and then passed on this poetic legacy to subsequent generations of Italian poets—the *petrarchisti*—and, mutatis mutandis, to later "petrarchizing" poets in Western Europe (England, France, and Spain), and to many others.

Given his importance and formative influence on Western lyric poetry, Petrarch is among the most widely taught medieval authors—with Dante and Boccaccio—in undergraduate humanities courses, across several disciplines (Romance languages, English, comparative literature), directly or indirectly, both in translation and in Italian. Given the extent of his literary production and the language of his masterpiece, presenting Petrarch to students is not a simple task.

Because lyrics are essentially imitative, the Italian lyric tradition as a whole and the Western love lyric in the Renaissance and beyond cannot be fully appreciated or investigated in their historical, stylistic, and thematic developments without an understanding of Petrarch's contribution to the formation of the canon of love poetry. The essays in this volume respond to the various needs that teachers of Petrarchism may have in characterizing that canon and in understanding the wide-ranging manifestations of Petrarch's legacy in subsequent literature and culture. The volume also attempts to bridge the pedagogical gap between those who study and teach Petrarch in Italian and those who focus on his legacy outside Italy.

The first section of the volume, "Materials," presents an overview of the extensive bibliography on Petrarch and Petrarchism. The essays in the second section, "Approaches," address a variety of pedagogical questions and techniques directed toward Petrarchism and the *Canzoniere*, taught in Italian and in English across very diverse curricula. Petrarch is a difficult author; indeed, readers often underestimate this fact because they think, in their initial encounter with the *Canzoniere*, that they have read and heard this all before. Their shock of recognition may be attributed to the ubiquitous presence of Petrarch's imagery and rhetoric in subsequent literature, to the extent that they believe they already know and understand him. We hope that this volume, by providing an overview of pedagogical approaches to Petrarch and his legacy, will help teachers in their quest to read, decipher, and appreciate his critically acclaimed poetry.

CK and AD

Part One

MATERIALS

Editions and Translations

The standard editions of Petrarch's *Canzoniere* are based either on the codex Vatican Latin 3195, partly written by Petrarch and, under dictation, by his secretary Giovanni Malpaghini, or on the diplomatic edition of this manuscript by Ettore Modigliani. As Mark Musa aptly points out in the preface to his 1996 translation and commentary of the *Canzoniere*, "Petrarch took no chance. He left us an autographed copy. . . . How lucky we are" (ix). Indeed, we are fortunate, since instructors and students alike do not have difficulty in finding the most authoritative modern edition. Nor do they have to spend large amounts of time over the indispensable (but often dry) philological commentaries, in search of a phantom textual truth embedded in possible textual explications, as they would in those cases where no autograph manuscript exists, as any student or instructor of Dante well knows.

The seven hundredth anniversary of Petrarch's birth, in 2004, gave rise to a multitude of conferences, studies, essays, and authoritative editions of Petrarch's works. Among these, Marco Santagata's revised 2004 Mondadori edition of the *Canzoniere* (a hefty volume [ccxvi and 1603 pp.] expanded on his already substantial 1996 edition [cxcvii and 1583 pp.]), is almost unanimously quoted by all instructors who use the Italian text without translations in English (or other languages). The year 2005 also saw the publication of the *Canzoniere: Rerum vulgarium fragmenta*, Rosanna Bettarini's two-volume Einaudi annotated edition (xcii and 1743 pp.), the fruit of over twenty years of research. In 2008 Giuseppe Savoca published another edition of *Rerum vulgarium fragmenta* for Olschki (xxvi and 668 pp.), which registers more than 5,200 lexical and orthographic differences (punctuation included) for almost half of the 7,785 verses of the collection. This edition also reproduces more than 900 sections and details from the original to allow the reader to verify some of the editor's philological decisions. A two-volume companion, *Concordanza del* Canzoniere *di Francesco Petrarca* (xxvi and 782 pp.), edited by Savoca and Bartolo Calderone, should also be kept in mind by instructors who want to work with advanced students in Italian on the *Canzoniere*'s thesaurus (see the essay by Madison Sowell in this volume). We indicate here the number of pages of the most authoritative tomes, since this information may play a role in the selection of a classroom text. Among the wealth of choices in editions and commentaries, however, several options are rendered impractical either by the sheer thickness of the volumes or by their cost (imported editions being the most expensive). The most recent and complete commentaries by Bettarini, Santagata, and Savoca, for example, are too pricey (and bulky) to be adopted in undergraduate courses that often devote a relatively small part of their syllabi to the *Canzoniere*. Nevertheless, instructors may wish to use these editions as their source of information on the collection and to choose to adopt paperback editions for courses involving an integral reading of the text. Instructors may also wish to profit from Savoca's edition to show students the reproductions from the original, in discussions of the philological consistency of the text or of the way an ancient text is persuasively edited in a modern edition. Savoca's edition is also accessible online through *The Oregon Petrarch Open Book* (*OPOB*; described in detail below in "Electronic and Audiovisual Resources").

There are several principal editions of the *Canzoniere* economically suited for the classroom: Gianfranco Contini's 1964 edition (annotated by Daniele Ponchiroli and preceded by the seminal yet arduous essay "Preliminari sulla lingua del Petrarca") was reprinted in paperback with an introduction by Roberto Antonelli in 1992 and accompanies Savoca's edition in *OPOB*; other serviceable editions include those by Ugo Dotti, Alberto Chiari, Raffaele Manica, Enrico Fenzi, Giovanni Ponte, Piero Cudini, and Guido Bezzola. The popularity of the edition by Giosuè Carducci and Severino Ferrari (1899) is due to at least two intertwined factors: its accessible and rather complete commentary housed in a slim, relatively compact volume and the general preference by instructors for a textual and stylistic examination of the *Canzoniere*, which undoubtedly remains the pivotal form of approach to Petrarch's verses in the original Italian. Sabrina Maffei has prepared a small selection of poems accompanied by a line-by-line paraphrase in modern Italian, with introductions and linguistic annotations. Her text could also be considered for introductory courses in Italian. (*OPOB* offers paraphrases into modern Italian by Cinzia Capon and "tweets"—summaries in no more than 140 characters—for each poem.)

Respondents to our survey indicate that they often prefer dual-language editions to the exclusive Italian text. Among English translations, Robert Durling's prose version, *Petrarch's Lyric Poems: The* Rime sparse *and Other Lyrics*, is the one consistently used by instructors. At the cost of sacrificing the integrity of the Petrarchan verse, Durling's edition is perhaps the best choice for courses in which students do not rely on a translation but possess a relatively good Italian proficiency that allows them to use the prose translation as additional help to untie the linguistic or structural knots of Petrarch's poems. Also among our survey respondents' favorite translations is Julia Conaway Bondanella and Mark Musa's selection in *The Italian Renaissance Reader* (22–59). This selection is adequate for introductory courses that include Petrarch but do not make the *Canzoniere* their exclusive focus. Other recent complete editions used are Musa's 1996 bilingual verse translation, *The* Canzoniere*; or,* Rerum vulgarium fragmenta, and David Young's English-only 2004 translation in blank verse, *The Poetry of Petrarch*.

Durling's manageable introduction (1–33) is also assigned to undergraduate students, often as the only critical source on Petrarch's poems. After a biographical section, Durling examines the role that Laura has in Petrarch's poetry (4–7), marks the collection's philological evolutions (7–11; he includes a repertoire of "vocabulary, images, structures," pedagogically useful for students and novice instructors alike [9]), explains the role that measures and numbers have in the collection (including metrical forms [11–18]), and finally dwells on the most relevant themes, love and memory (18–26) and metamorphoses (26–33). Durling's modular introduction lends itself well to section-by-section assignments, depending on the focus of each in-class segment of Petrarch's rhymes to be examined. *Rime sparse* (35–583) is sparsely annotated and is followed by "Poems excluded from *Rime sparse*" (586–89), by poems addressed to Petrarch (602–09), and by "Dante's *Rime petrose* and *Canzone montanina*" (612–35).

Musa's translation, on the contrary, is fully annotated (see "Notes and Commentary" 519–728) and seems to serve a different audience. His introduction (xi–xxxvi), which dwells more on the philosophical value of Petrarch's enterprise and consistently underscores the role of classical authors in the making of the book, may be well received by instructors and students who can spend a substantial portion of a course on the poems (perhaps a graduate class or seminar or an advanced undergraduate course). Musa's volume also contains two useful tables, showing the cyclic distribution of the poems (xii) and a selected chronology (xxxv–xxxvi), that can be used by students in advanced courses for an in-depth examination of the structure of the *Canzoniere*. The translated text (2–517) is also accompanied by a capital index (755–59) that cross-references all allusions in the text and the notes, together with all characters introduced and including relevant critical interpretations; this appendix is an invaluable research and pedagogical tool not to be neglected by the student or the instructor.

Other available translations in English include Anthony Mortimer's 2002 volume for Penguin; Musa's *Selections from the* Canzoniere *and Other Works* (1985), which also contains *The Letter to Posterity* and *The Ascent to Mount Ventoux*; and Frederic J. Jones's two-volume translation for the Troubador Italian Studies series (2000–01). A limited edition of J. G. Nichols's *Canzoniere* appeared in 2000, and *OPOB* offers an English translation by A. S. Kline (see also Kline, *Petrarch: The* Canzoniere).

Thomas P. Roche's hefty anthology *Petrarch in English* (2005) includes translations from the fourteenth century (Chaucer) to the twentieth century, including a coda with parodies and replays. Roche's volume might be more useful in a course on English Petrarchism than on Petrarch. But, as William Kennedy suggests in his essay on English Petrarchism included in this volume, there are otherwise many anthologies instructors should consider for a survey of British literature (Greenblatt et al.; Carroll and Hadfield; Hollander and Kermode) or for a majors' course on the English Renaissance (Rollins and Baker; Braden, *Sixteenth-Century Poetry*; Norbrook and Woudhuysen; E. Jones; Sylvester).

In Spanish, the two-volume, bilingual *Cancionero*, edited by Jacobo Cortines (1989), works well if used together with the unabridged, single-volume translation by Ángel Crespo (1995). *OPOB* reproduces the 1591 print edition of *Los sonetos y canciones del poeta Francisco Petrarcha*, translated by Enrique Garcés. In French, the more modern and textually closer translation by Gérard Genot (1969) can be accompanied by Ferdinand L. de Gramont's 1842 translation or the translation by Pierre Blanc published in a 1988 bilingual edition.

Otherwise (and especially when dealing with sixteenth-century French Petrarchism), a useful addition in *OPOB* is the 1555 edition of *Toutes les euvres vulgaires de François Pétrarquet*. *OPOB* also offers a partial translation in Russian, Osip Mandelstam's *Собрание сочинений в четырех томах*.

Required and Recommended Readings for Undergraduates

Respondents to our survey assign no secondary sources in Italian or English in undergraduate classes. Instructors reported limiting themselves to requiring Robert Durling's introduction to his translation as an overview of Petrarch's life and the general interpretation of the *Canzoniere*. Since most instructors advocate a close reading of the poems, avoiding in-class discussions of the various approaches to the *Canzoniere*'s structural interpretation as a macrotext allows instructors to engage with the texts at a more immediate, in-depth (albeit micro) level without sacrificing class time to something that is secondary or appropriate for advanced students. Even in students' written analyses, most instructors seem to prefer that students give their basic interpretations of the texts rather than quote from explications and annotations in books or commentaries that they may not fully understand. Overall, the results of our survey indicate that the instructors' emphasis is to avoid having students distracted from a close (lexical, stylistic, thematic) reading of the primary source.

When secondary readings are systematically assigned in advanced courses, instructors prefer selected articles to monographic studies. The survey results reveal a core of articles that touch on the main exegetic themes usually associated with interpretations of the *Canzoniere*: John Freccero's "The Fig Tree and the Laurel" is favored by most instructors, followed by Giuseppe Mazzotta's "Antiquity and the New Arts in Petrarch" and "The *Canzoniere* and the Language of the Self." The need for a structural interpretation of the text justifies the inclusion of Teodolinda Barolini's "The Making of a Lyric Sequence: Time and Narrative in Petrarch's *Rerum vulgarium fragmenta*." Other readings include excerpts from Ernest Hatch Wilkins's *Life of Petrarch*; Durling's "The Ascent of Mt. Ventoux and the Crisis of Allegory"; Albert Russell Ascoli's "Petrarch's Middle Age: Memory, Imagination, History, and the 'Ascent of Mount Ventoux'"; and Nancy Vickers's "Diana Described: Scattered Woman and Scattered Rhyme" and her (inter)textual investigation "Re-membering Dante: Petrarch's *Chiare, fresche et dolci acque*."

In courses focusing on Petrarchism, however, secondary readings (including monographic studies, which are not necessarily read in their entirety) become the rule; among the respondents' favorites are William Kennedy's *Authorizing Petrarch* and *The Site of Petrarchism: Early Modern National Sentiment in*

Italy, France, and England; Gordon Braden's *Petrarchan Love and the Continental Renaissance*; William Kerrigan and Braden's *The Idea of the Renaissance*; and Leonard Forster's classic study, *The Icy Fire: Five Studies in European Petrarchism*. For general studies on the concept of *imitatio*, our survey respondents suggest the following: Thomas Greene's *The Light in Troy*; Martin L. McLaughlin's *Literary Imitation in the Italian Renaissance*; and G. W. Pigman's "Versions of Imitation in the Renaissance." More specific analyses of works from the various national traditions include, for French literature, François Rigolot's *Louise Labé Lyonnaise ou la Renaissance au feminin*, Sara Sturm-Maddox's *Ronsard, Petrarch, and the* Amours, and Jean-Luc Nardone's *Pétrarque et le pétrarquisme*; for English Petrarchism, Heather Dubrow's *Echoes of Desire: English Petrarchism and Its Counterdiscourses* and Elizabeth Hanson's *Discovering the Subject in Renaissance England*. Italian instructors seem to focus more on Petrarch than on Petrarchism: the bibliography assigned in Italian usually includes Adelia Noferi's *Frammenti per i* Fragmenta *di Petrarca* and "Da un commento al *Canzoniere* del Petrarca: Lettura del sonetto introduttivo"; Franco Suitner's *Petrarca e la tradizione stilnovistica*; Mario Petrini's *La risurrezione della carne*; and Marco Santagata's *Per moderne carte. La biblioteca volgare di Petrarca*, *Dal sonetto al* Canzoniere. *Ricerche sulla preistoria e la costituzione di un genere*, and *I frammenti dell'anima. Storia e racconto nel* Canzoniere *del Petrarca*.

The Instructor's Library

Reference Works

The bibliography on Petrarch's *Canzoniere* and on Petrarchism is vast. The classic printed bibliography, although now limited in value, are the two volumes detailing the rich holdings of the Cornell University Library: the first compiled by Mary Fowler, *Catalogue of the Petrarch Collection Bequeathed by Willard Fiske*, and the second, *Petrarch: Catalogue of the Petrarch Collection in Cornell University Library*, which, through photoduplication of the card index, includes both the materials found in Fowler's catalog and more recent editions, translations, and critical studies. Joseph Fucilla's massive listing of contributions over a fifty-year period, *Oltre un cinquantennio di scritti sul Petrarca (1915–1973)*, has been supplemented by Piero Pieretti's "Bibliografia petrarchesca 1964–1973" and Luca Marcozzi's *Bibliografia petrarchesca: 1989–2003*.

In addition to the 2011 Savoca and Calderone *Concordanza* noted above, a two-volume concordance to the *Canzoniere*—*Concordanze del* Canzoniere *di Francesco Petrarca*—was published under the auspices of the Accademia della Crusca in 1971.

Victoria Kirkham and Armando Maggi have recently edited an invaluable reference work, *Petrarch: A Critical Guide to the Complete Works*, which provides an overview of each work, as well as a review of the scholarship. While a "Petrarch dictionary" does not exist, several fine reference sources to medieval and Renaissance culture contain valuable entries on Petrarch and related topics: Peter Bondanella and Julia Conaway Bondanella's *The Dictionary of Italian Literature*; Paul F. Grendler's *Encyclopedia of the Renaissance*; Gaetana Marrone, Paolo Puppa, and Luca Somigli's *Encyclopedia of Italian Literary Studies*; Joseph R. Strayer's *Dictionary of the Middle Ages*; Christopher Kleinhenz's *Medieval Italy: An Encyclopedia*; and Peter Brand and Lino Pertile's *The Cambridge History of Italian Literature*.

Biographies and Background Works

The standard biography is the detailed *Life of Petrarch* by Ernest Hatch Wilkins, whose focused studies of particular periods in the poet's life are also valuable (*Petrarch's Later Years* and *Petrarch's Eight Years in Milan*). A fine overview of Petrarch's life and works can be found in Thomas G. Bergin's *Petrarch* and in Kenelm Foster's *Petrarch: Poet and Humanist*; Morris Bishop's *Petrarch and His World* provides a more casual introduction to the poet and his times. Giuseppe Mazzotta's *The Worlds of Petrarch* provides a thoughtful investigation of Petrarch's thought, works, and personality, topics that Nicholas Mann also discusses in *Petrarch*. Two excellent biographies in Italian are Ugo Dotti's *Vita di Petrarca* and Marco Ariani's *Petrarca*. Antonio Enzo Quaglio's *Francesco Petrarca* provides a shorter treatment, and Raffaele Amaturo's *Petrarca* presents a concise biography with numerous anthologized selections from Petrarch's works. In addition to a synthetic biographical sketch, Roberto Fedi's *Francesco Petrarca* contains a short history of Petrarchan criticism. Two early, and now dated, accounts are H. C. Hollway-Calthrop's *Petrarch, His Life and Times* and James Harvey Robinson's *Petrarch, the First Modern Scholar and Man of Letters*. Edward H. R. Tatham's two-volume set, *Francesco Petrarca, the First Modern Man of Letters*, uses Petrarch's letters to situate the poet in the culture of Italy and Provence in the period from 1304 to 1347.

Several books provide a good overview of the medieval Italian background to Petrarch: Marvin B. Becker's *Medieval Italy: Constraints and Creativity* and John Larner's *Italy in the Age of Dante and Petrarch, 1216–1380* and *Culture and Society in Italy, 1290–1420*. Charles Trinkaus's *The Poet as Philosopher* situates Petrarch within the tradition of classical philosophy in the fourteenth century. The following studies provide an overview of the earlier Italian lyric tradition: Marco Santagata's *Dal sonetto al* Canzoniere; Mariateresa Cattaneo's *Francesco Petrarca e la lirica d'arte del '200*; Christopher Kleinhenz's *The Early Italian Sonnet*; Olivia Holmes's *Assembling the Lyric Self: Authorship from Troubador Song to Italian Poetry Book*; and Marianne Shapiro's *Hieroglyph of Time: The Petrarchan Sestina*, which studies this metrical form from Arnaut Daniel through Dante to Petrarch. David Thompson and Alan F. Nagel's *The Three Crowns of Florence: Humanist Assessments of Dante, Petrarca, and Boccaccio* is valuable for its account of the early success of these three authors.

Works on the Development of the Canzoniere

Two facsimile editions, one of an important incunable and the other of the autograph manuscript (Vat. Lat. 3195), have been published in the last decade: Rerum vulgarium fragmenta*: A Facsimile of the Valdezoco Edition (Padova 1472)*, edited by Gino Belloni, and the two-volume set edited by Belloni, Furio Brugnolo, H. Wayne Storey, and Stefano Zamponi, *Rerum vulgarium fragmenta: Codice Vat. lat. 3195*. Ernest Hatch Wilkins's *The Making of the* Canzoniere *and Other Petrarchan Studies* has for many years been considered the authoritative view on the development of the *Canzoniere*, a view that has been rightly challenged in more recent years. Peter Hainsworth's *Petrarch the Poet: An Introduction to the* Rerum vulgarium fragmenta provides an invaluable guide to the *Canzoniere*. Several studies in Italian merit attention, including Rosanna Bettarini's *Lacrime e inchiostro nel* Canzoniere *di Petrarca* and Umberto Bosco's *Francesco Petrarca*. Michelangelo Picone's edited collection of readings—*Il* Canzoniere*: Lettura micro e macrotestuale*—presents an insightful overview of the work, as does Serena Fornasiero's *Petrarca: Guida al* Canzoniere. Frederic J. Jones's *The Structure of Petrarch's* Canzoniere*: A Chronological, Psychological, and Stylistic Analysis* offers a very detailed account on the ordering of the *Canzoniere*. Sara Sturm-Maddox's *Petrarch's Metamorphoses: Text and Subtext in the* Rime sparse and her *Petrarch's Laurels* provide insightful readings of the *Canzoniere*, particularly with regard to the poet's adaptation of Ovidian sources. Dennis Dutschke's *Francesco Petrarca: Canzone XXIII from First to Final Version* provides a detailed investigation of the textual development of one of Petrarch's *canzoni* from its earlier version in Vatican Latin 3196 to its final state in Vatican Latin 3195. Belloni treats Renaissance commentaries on Petrarch's *Canzoniere* in *Laura tra Petrarca e Bembo*.

Collections of Essays

The celebrations surrounding the six hundredth anniversary of Petrarch's death in 1974 and the seven hundredth anniversary of his birth in 2004 resulted in many conferences, which in turn produced numerous collections of essays. The most important of these are Giuseppe Billanovich and Giuseppe Frasso's *Il Petrarca ad Arquà*; Aldo S. Bernardo's *Francesco Petrarca, Citizen of the World*; Aldo Scaglione's *Francis Petrarch, Six Centuries Later*; the *Convegno internazionale Francesco Petrarca*, sponsored by the Accademia Nazionale dei Lincei; Giorgio Padoan's *Petrarca, Venezia e il Veneto*; Fritz Schalk's *Petrarca,*

1304–1374: Beiträge zu Werk und Wirkung; Giuseppe Frasso, Giuseppe Velli, and Maurizio Vitale's *Petrarca e la Lombardia*; Teodolinda Barolini and H. Wayne Storey's *Petrarch and the Textual Origins of Interpretation*; Zygmunt Barański and Theodore Cachey's *Petrarch and Dante*; Dino Cervigni's *Petrarch and the European Lyric Tradition*; and Gino Belloni's *Francesco Petrarca, da Padova all'Europa*. Harold Bloom's *Petrarch* reprints several classic essays.

Essays

There are too many fine essays to list in this short space, but the following are especially important: Roberto Antonelli's "*Rerum vulgarium fragmenta* di Francesco Petrarca"; Robert M. Durling's "Petrarch's 'Giovene donna sotto un verde lauro'"; Thomas M. Greene's "Petrarch: The Ontology of the Self" and "Petrarch: Falling into Shadow"; Adelia Noferi's "Da un commento al *Canzoniere* del Petrarca: Lettura del sonetto introduttivo"; Marco Santagata's "Il Naufragio dei simboli (*R.V.F.* 323)"; and Aldo Scaglione's "The Structure of the *Canzoniere* and Petrarch's Method of Composition."

Petrarchism

For Petrarchism, Klaus W. Hempfer, Gerhard Regn, and Sunita Scheffel have compiled an impressive bibliography, *Petrarkismus-Bibliographie, 1972–2000*. Among the extensive bibliography on Petrarchism, the following volumes are especially important for the depth and scope of their analyses. For Petrarchism in Italy, Giacinto Spagnoletti's *Il petrarchismo*, Luigi Baldacci's *Il petrarchismo italiano nel Cinquecento*, and Bruno Porcelli's *Petrarca volgare e la sua fortuna sino al Cinquecento* stand out. Of special note for Petrarchism in Europe is *Il petrarchismo: Un modello di poesia per l'Europa*, edited by Loredana Chines (vol. 1) and Floriana Calitti and Roberto Gigliucci (vol. 2), as well as Pierre Blanc's *Dynamique d'une expansion culturelle: Pétrarque en Europe, XIVe–XXe siècle* and Karl A. E. Enenkel and Jan Papy's *Petrarch and His Readers in the Renaissance*.

Several works feature analyses of texts and authors from various national literatures. For English Petrarchism, see Martin McLaughlin and Letizia Panizza's *Petrarch in Britain: Interpreters, Imitators, and Translators over Seven Hundred Years*; the two volumes by Thomas P. Roche, Jr., *Petrarch and the English Sonnet Sequences* and *Petrarch in English*; Anthony Mortimer's *Petrarch's* Canzoniere *in the English Renaissance*; Stephen Minta's *Petrarch and Petrarchism: The English and French Traditions*; and Jack D'Amico's *Petrarch in England*, which provides pertinent texts from English authors from Wyatt to Milton. For Spanish Petrarchism, see Gregorio Cabello Porras's *Ensayos sobre tradición clásica y petrarquismo en el Siglo de Oro*, Mary Barnard's *The Myth of Apollo and Daphne from Ovid to Quevedo*, Joseph Fucilla's *Estudios sobre el petrarquismo en España*, and Ignacio Navarrete's *Orphans of Petrarch: Poetry and*

Theory in the Spanish Renaissance. For French Petrarchism, see the anthology *Les poètes français de la Renaissance et Pétrarque*, edited by Jean Balsamo.

Electronic and Audiovisual Resources

Texts and Studies

The third "crown" of Italian letters has finally found—like Dante and Boccaccio with the projects at Princeton University and Brown University—a digital room of his own. Since November 2011, the Web project *Oregon Petrarch Open Book* (*OPOB*) offers access to versions of Petrarch's *Canzoniere* (which on the site retains its original title, *Rerum vulgarium fragmenta*), ranging from the diplomatic Modigliani edition of 1904 to the 2008 critical edition prepared by Savoca. The *RVF* menu allows users to read Petrarch's text in different forms, media, and supports. The default text of the *OPOB* is the Savoca edition. (This text is under copyright and can be used only for research and consultation purposes; it cannot be copied or reproduced.) As of 2012, the section "Diplomatic Editions" includes only an excerpt from *Il* Canzoniere *di Francesco Petrarca* reproduced from the Vatican Latin 3195 manuscript and edited by Modigliani. The digital copy of this text was prepared by the University of Oregon Knight Library. "Manuscripts" is slated to include the codex. Queriniana D II 21, and "Incunabula" will include the *editio princeps* of the *Canzoniere*, published in Venice in 1470 by Vindelin de Spira (Inc. Queriniana G V 15). As of December 2012, "Bibliography" is still in progress, but specific bibliographies are available in different sections of the site. The options under "Apparatus" allow users to consult the different assets of the site: "Commentaries" includes the commentary by Alessandro Vellutello (1525); "Translations" makes available the sixteenth-century Spanish and French translations by Enrique Garcés and Vasquin Philieul, an English translation by A. S. Kline, and partial translations in Russian, Chinese, Japanese, and German; "Paraphrases" includes Italian paraphrases of all poems, aided by "Summaries" and "Tweets" (in Italian; some summaries are available also in English). "Rewritings" includes two examples from the contemporary Italian writer Gianni Celati (*Lunario del Paradiso*, 1978), prepared by Peter Kuon, and references to poems by Matteo Maria Boiardo, Luis de Góngora, and Francisco de Quevedo. "Archives," also under "Apparatus," provides an extraordinary, comprehensive database system for musical adaptations of the *Canzoniere* coordinated by Marc Vanscheeuwijck. The most useful function for instructors and students of Petrarch—and of Romance languages and comparative literature—may be the link "Compare poems and assets," which permits comparison of many versions of the original text in Italian and of different translations. Users have the ability to add selected elements of the apparatus to the base text, ranging from paraphrases, summaries, tweets, and commentaries. (Use of this feature should be especially encouraged for students dealing with the text in Italian.)

The University of Oregon's romance languages department also developed the first issue of *Humanist Studies and the Digital Age*, appropriately (and exclusively) available online. It contains the proceedings of the international symposium Francesco Petrarca: From Manuscript to Digital Culture, held in Eugene on 3 April 2010 (Hester, Lollini, and Middlebrook). The issue features a wealth of materials that instructors might benefit from when using *OPOB* or when preparing their courses on the *Canzoniere*. The first section, "Perspectives," presents essays that instructors of Petrarch and Petrarchism may wish to consider including in their advanced courses, such as Giuseppe Savoca's "Prolegomena to a New Lyric Petrarch in the Digital Future" (13–27); H. Wayne Storey's "Petrarch's 'Original' of the *Fragmenta* 1362–1558" (28–49); Robert M. Durling's "*Rerum vulgarium fragmenta*: From Manuscript to Print" (50–65); Massimo Lollini's "Return to Philology and Hypertext in and around Petrarch's *Rvf*" (66–79), which contains a theoretical history of the project behind *OPOB*; and Ronald L. Martinez's "Francis, Thou Art Translated: Petrarch Metamorphosed in English, 1380–1595" (80–108), which instructors can either use to supplement Kennedy's and Pollard's essays in the present volume or distribute directly to students of English Petrarchism. The article by Alicia de Colombí-Monguió, "Las visiones de Petrarca en la poésia hispánica y en la poética renacentista" (109–20), can supplement Leah Middlebrook's essay in this volume and be given to advanced students in Spanish. The section "Interventions" introduces analyses of Chaucer and Petrarch (121–27), the presence of Petrarch in seventeenth-century travel writing (128–35), the renegotiation of the Petrarchan code in seventeenth-century European Sapphic poetry (151–65), the representation of Petrarch in the eighteenth-century *Encyclopédie* (136–44), and, for his nineteenth-century critical success, Petrarch and Schopenhauer (170–79). Another section, "Projects," addresses the text of the *Canzoniere* and includes a study on the work's reception in later centuries.

With the notable exception of *OPOB*, however, accessing Petrarch in the age of the World Wide Web is not a simple feat. Students and instructors of Petrarch searching the Web have to sift through scores of results. Instructors should take the proverbial bull by the horns and provide their students with some guidance on what constitutes a good Petrarchan source on the Internet (or, more wisely, ask that they subscribe to *OPOB*).

As Paul Goring, Jeremy Hawthorn, and Domhnall Mitchell point out in "Guide to the Use of Electronic Media," designed for undergraduate students in literature courses, literature information online often limits itself to

> when a writer was born and died, what he or she wrote, and perhaps [to] a few standard excerpts from their works. Frequently, the pages are put there by fans—people who are interested in a particular writer, but who

> do not always have original or useful things to say about her or him. . . . [W]hat you will get is a brief biography taken from a printed text, a list of books, some photographs and perhaps a few short summaries. (113)

This scenario perfectly applies to material on most authors, including Petrarch, found on the Internet, thus limiting the scope of pedagogically relevant Web-based activities to approach his works: issues of copyright exclude (or *should* exclude) edited primary texts from appearing online (if not in severely shortened form), leaving space for fillers or rewriting of standard pieces of information from printed materials or links to secondary sources, mostly from the popular press. When primary texts appear in lengthier form, they often come from an undocumented source. Pertinence and reliability—the accuracy of content information, the soundness of the texts from a standard philological point of view, and so on—are always at stake.

We strongly recommend Goring, Hawthorn, and Mitchell to instructors who want to include electronic media in their courses. Their guide is an excellent aid in defining (and narrowing) students' Web searches, for it clearly illustrates how to browse the Web and evaluate primary and secondary sources, assessing issues of reliability, pertinence, and authority. Assigning the whole chapter will save instructors from having to explain basic concepts of what reading an electronic text means or how to conduct a successful search, allowing them to dedicate valuable class time to other topics. The chapter also plainly explains how to locate secondary sources using electronic databases, e-journals, and so on. For researching Petrarch, in addition to *JSTOR* and the *MLA International Bibliography*, instructors could alert students with a good command of Italian to the Italian-based *Italinemo*, directed by Marco Santoro. (In 2013, a search for "Petrarca" yielded 499 articles; "Canzoniere Petrarca" narrows the search to 118 articles, and "petrarchismo" yields 85.) The site, in operation since 2000, currently includes more than 100 literary journals, with more than 45,000 reviewed articles. Peter Sadlon's *Francesco Petrarch and Laura de Noves* is a comprehensive online source that houses texts, translations, manuscript illustrations, prints, and other related materials. This site, in English, is extremely clear and easy to navigate. Unfortunately, it is not necessarily among the first results of an Internet search for Petrarch on the Web; moreover, many of the links are extremely volatile, and, despite Petrarch's importance, there are relatively few reliable Web sites dedicated to the poet. For the student of Petrarch in Italian, the second-best electronic resource today, after *OPOB*, is *Italica*, a Web site on Italian culture and language hosted by Rai International, which houses a hefty section on Petrarch and the *Canzoniere*. Note that the home pages of the Italian and English editions—and the point of entry to several sections—do not look the same. We refer here to the site in Italian. The "Monografie" ("Monographs") section contains links devoted exclusively to the Rinascimento (the Italian Renaissance), whose page is broken down into sections on essays, monographs, witnesses, categories, works, iconography, and key words. The

"Saggi" ("Essays") section is most valuable, for it includes Amedeo Quondam's *Introduzione al Rinascimento* ("Introduction to the Renaissance"), with two chapters on Petrarch's view of Cicero's and Homer's contribution to literature ("Ritorno . . . Cicerone"; "Ritorno . . . Omero"), and Francisco Rico's very useful, comprehensive study "Francesco Petrarca," divided into forty-seven chapters following the chronology of Petrarch's life and works, eight of which are devoted to the *Canzoniere* (genesis, themes, tradition, language, style, metrics, etc.). We recommend Rico's online materials for instructors teaching graduate (or advanced undergraduate) classes in Italian. The schematic explanatory texts on stylistics and thematic aspects of the *Canzoniere* make this site pedagogically relevant: it is as if brief lectures in a rigorous yet highly accessible language are already given to instructors for immediate in-class use. In "Monografie," the works by Franco Pignatti—*Antichi e moderni* ("Ancients and Moderns") and *L'imitazione nel Quattrocento e nel Cinquecento* ("Imitation in the Fifteenth and Sixteenth Centuries")—contain, respectively, two chapters on Petrarch's relation to classical writers and his letters to Boccaccio on the concept of imitation. The "Parole chiave" ("key words") section contains the entry "*Canzoniere*: fasi redazione," in which the different drafts are described. This entry offers links to a description of several manuscripts—Vatican Latin 3196, Vatican Latin 3195, and Vatican Chigi L.V. 176—and the numbering of the last thirty-one poems in the *Canzoniere*.

If instructors merely wish to use (or to refer students to) an online text, the *Canzoniere* (ed. Contini, 1964) and the *Trionfi* in the original Italian can be downloaded from *Liber Liber*, edited by Roberto Gagliardi and Mirko Locatelli. Giuseppe Bonghi's *Progetto Petrarca* also gathers Italian and Latin texts together with critical selections from Francesco De Sanctis and from early biographies of Petrarch in Latin (e.g., those by Manetti and Bruni).

Audio Resources

Peter Sadlon's section on the *Canzoniere* on his site *Francesco Petrarca and Laura de Noves* has a dual-language text (with English translations by A. S. Kline) and the advantage of linking some of the texts to audio readings in Italian, taken from the audio library on *Il Narratore*, which offers free downloads of Italian literary texts. There are at least two audio CDs with readings of Petrarch's poems available. Recitar Leggendo Audiolibri offers *Petrarca*, Canzoniere, which contains thirty-five poems read by Claudio Carini. The CD *Petrarca e la letteratura italiana del XV e XVI secolo*, available through *Il narratore*, contains thirteen poems read by Moro Silo (1, 3, 35, 90, 126, 128, 129, 234, 267, 272, 310, 312, 365). Also available through *Il narratore* is the MP3 file "Francesco Petrarca—*Il Canzoniere* (poesie scelte)," read by Silo and featuring sixteen poems (1, 3, 16, 35, 61, 62, 90, 126, 128, 129, 234, 267, 272, 310, 312, 365). A fifty-eight-minute videocassette, *Il '300: Petrarca*, features the actor

Roberto Herlitzka reciting twenty-six of Petrarch's poems and was produced by Sampaolo Audiovisivi. Also useful are the pages devoted to Petrarch on *RSI Rete Due*, hosted by Radiotelevisione svizzera italiana, which include a reading and a commentary of five sonnets (9, 35, 180, 335, 364) by Giorgio Orelli, as well as three other audio files, two featuring discussions of the poet, by Antonella Anedda and Corrado Bologna, and one dedicated to music in Petrarch's age, by Giovanni Conti.

As for Petrarch's direct presence in music, in his essay for this volume Marc Vanscheeuwijck provides a selection of sixteenth-century musical settings by Luca Marenzio, Claudio Monteverdi, and Orlando di Lasso, Andrea Gabrieli, Giaches De Wert, and others. Vanscheeuwijck, in his role as a member of *OPOB*'s advisory board, maintains the site's expanded and detailed list of music and musical settings for Petrarch's *Canzoniere* (from "Apparatus," go to "Archives," then to "Music" or "Musical Settings"). Information on numerous musical settings of Petrarch's poems may be found on Emily Ezust's Web site, *The Lied, Art Song, and Choral Texts Archive*, which also includes Romantic versions by Franz Schubert and Franz Liszt. Silvia Ross's essay in this volume provides a list of songs by contemporary singers and songwriters that make use of what has come to be recognized as Petrarchan imagery.

Iconography

The section "Archives" on *OPOB* (under "Apparatus") hosts a growing section of images pertaining to 1, 16, 52, 66, 77, 78, 310, 366 (16, 77, and 78 have multiples samples). Sadlon's Web site includes a rich iconographic apparatus, divided among pictures of Petrarch, Laura, Petrarch and Laura together, and Petrarchan places, comprising paintings, sketches, and engravings, as well as statues, book covers, and stamps. Pictures of manuscripts and prints are included in the University of Pennsylvania's Web exhibition *Petrarch at 700*, which had its origin in an exhibition of books and manuscripts from the collections of Cornell University Library and the University of Pennsylvania Library. Another exhibition of materials relating to Petrarch was sponsored by the Beinecke Rare Book and Manuscript Library at Yale University in 2004 and is available online. The Web site of the Biblioteca Nazionale Centrale in Rome includes information on an interactive CD-ROM, *Un CD-Rom per Francesco Petrarca* (available for purchase), which contains two Petrarchan codices—Varia 3 (from 1444, containing the *Rime* and *Trionfi*) and Vittorio Emanuele 1632 (containing Cicero's *Tusculanae disputationes*, annotated in Petrarch's hand). Petrarch, now a pop-culture icon, was celebrated by Giovanni Cheli in his graphic novel *Franciscus, la vita del Petrarca a fumetti*, with illustrations by Lucia Cheli. The graphic novel could be used in introductory Italian literature courses, along with Petrarch's autobiographical texts. Giuseppe Frasso's *Travels with Francesco Petrarca* also offers useful illustrations of the places visited by the poet.

Part Two

APPROACHES

Introduction: The *Canzoniere* and the Petrarchan Tradition in the Classroom

Courses Taught

Undergraduate students typically read Petrarch's *Canzoniere* in survey and upper-level Italian courses on the literature of the Middle Ages and the Renaissance or specifically on the Italian lyric tradition. In translation, Petrarch is taught in general education courses on the same subjects or on Petrarchism, prompting instructors to go back and analyze the original source, as in sweeping Renaissance poetry overviews. Historical criteria structure the bulk of these undergraduate courses, but a thematic focus is sometimes possible.

In all cases, Petrarch is included as either a medieval or a Renaissance author: he might be discussed in classes covering Dante and Boccaccio (i.e., in surveys of the "three crowns" of Italian literature, either in Italian or English) or as the first writer introduced in a Renaissance course, especially if the focus is the Italian tradition. Otherwise, he is invariably included in courses on the Renaissance love lyric or among European Renaissance authors. Useful for understanding this ambiguous divide is Martin McLaughlin's essay "Petrarch: Between Two Ages, between Two Languages," which many instructors strongly suggest as recommended background reading for courses that address head-on where Petrarch might chronologically and philosophically belong.

Teaching modules on Petrarch's *Canzoniere* vary widely in length: from three one-hour lectures over the course of a week, to two weeks with eight classes of forty-five minutes each, to four weeks with twelve classes of seventy-five minutes each, to three hours a week for a whole semester. With the exception of courses that are advanced or that include Petrarch for the whole semester or quarter, simple arithmetic provides us with a clear picture of how much the *Canzoniere* (or even Petrarch *tout court*) is actually taught: despite Petrarch's importance as the founder of the Western love lyric, in the classroom this writer is seldom given the space he deserves. Dante and Boccaccio remain the authors privileged in courses on the Italian Middle Ages and Renaissance. The *Canzoniere*, as discussed below in "Approaches and Difficulties," is a problematic work to teach to an undergraduate audience. As a result, it suffers from a quantitative cut in the selection of texts being proposed and, as a direct consequence, from the time devoted to them in the classroom.

Upper-division courses that include Petrarch tend to be lengthier and concentrate on the *Canzoniere* (or on Petrarch and Petrarchism) as their sole object, sometimes even for the span of an entire semester. In such courses, students are often required to read other works by Petrarch (e.g., *The Letter to Posterity*, *The Ascent of Mount Ventoux*, the *Secretum*, a selection of letters, or the *Triumphs*).

Whereas Dante's *Comedy* might be read in whole or in part in courses ranging from surveys to seminars to undergraduate world literature classes, an in-depth reading of Petrarch's *Canzoniere* is confined to graduate Italian courses or to Italian courses for advanced undergraduate students. Because of its length and linguistic difficulty (despite its restricted vocabulary), the *Canzoniere* is very seldom read in its entirety: from as few as six poems to over a dozen as a rule in survey courses, to twenty or thirty poems in upper-division classes, to most or all of the lyrics in a handful of specialized courses.

When Petrarch is compared with other authors of the Renaissance in Italy, Spain, France, or England, the only poems generally introduced are the ones directly imitated—that is, poems whose original source can be directly used to discuss a Petrarchist poet's practice. These courses cover a range of topics: Petrarchism in the early modern world; dialogues of the French and Italian Renaissance; representing the early modern self, from Dante to Descartes; Petrarchism in English Renaissance literature; nature, gender, and sin in the Middle Ages and the Renaissance; desire and language in medieval and Renaissance literature, with a focus on the sonnet; Renaissance comparative literature; the Golden Age in Spain; and love profane and sacred in French literature.

Overall, Petrarch's *Canzoniere*, outside Italian major programs, is taught more in translation than in the Italian original. Many Italian programs also offer courses in translation that include Petrarch but not upper-level courses exclusively devoted to his work (as is the case for Dante's *Comedy* or Boccaccio's *Decameron*).

Respondents to our survey were unanimous in the way they require students to work on Petrarch. Because usually no secondary readings are assigned and a close reading of poems is the means by which Petrarch is discussed, students are seldom given research papers to write (with the exception of advanced courses studying the Italian original). Exercises concentrate on comments on the texts, through short papers and comparative readings; for example, students are invited to draw parallels between two or more poems by Petrarch or two or more poems by Petrarch and Petrarchists, especially if poems not previously introduced in class are the object of the *explication de texte*. Some instructors include weekly discussion boards (electronic forums) on course management systems to foster collective class discussions, while others prefer individual short answer (paragraph) work, particularly when students are dealing with Petrarch's style. Instructors seem to agree on short answer identifications (key terms, tropes or figures, dates, passages) and on essay-type questions. Sometimes instructors also require five-minute oral presentations of a lyric.

The diversity of assessments generally has one key element in common for undergraduate survey courses: *explication de texte* and short papers. Given the complexity of the *Canzoniere*'s language (and how difficult it is to present it to undergraduate students either in translation or in Italian), instructors point out that successful results as measured in assignments or exams derive more from student engagement with the text at a micro (i.e, thematic, stylistic, lexical) level than from complex or theoretical reconstructions of the work's overall meaning (i.e., a macro level).

Poems Taught

As our survey and the essays collected here attest, across languages and curricula—whether it be for a class on Petrarch in Italian or on English Renaissance poets or Spanish translations and interpretations of the *Canzoniere*—a core of twelve poems (eight sonnets, three canzoni, and one sestina) is the invariable selection to be taught as Petrarch's "greatest hits" (as one instructor labeled this choice): 1–3, 30, 35, 61–62, 90, 126, 134, 264, and 366. While this taxonomy discloses internal combinations of the most various sorts, the trend that generally emerges from the survey's results regroups the poems into three interesting clusters:

A
1 "Voi ch'ascoltate in rime sparse il suono" (sonnet)
90 "Erano i capei d'oro a l'aura sparsi" (sonnet)
126 "Chiare, fresche e dolci acque" (canzone)

B
3 "Era il giorno ch'al sol si scoloraro" (sonnet)
35 "Solo e pensoso i più deserti campi" (sonnet)
61 "Benedetto sia 'l giorno e 'l mese e l'anno" (sonnet)
134 "Pace non trovo e non ho da far guerra (sonnet)
366 "Vergine bella, che di sol vestita" (canzone)

C
2 "Per fare una leggiadra sua vendetta" (sonnet)
30 "Giovene donna sotto un verde lauro" (sestina)
62 "Padre del cielo, dopo i perduti giorni" (sonnet)
264 "I' vo pensando e nel pensier m'assale" (canzone)

Poems from group A are almost unanimously considered the most representative samples and are recurring choices in courses in the original and in English, French, and Spanish translations; those from group B are often taught in conjunction with the first group, as their direct corollaries (further illustrations of, or expansions on, Petrarch's love for Laura and its conclusion); instructors use poems from group C because they exemplify a specific poetic form (sestina or canzone) or a narrative point at the macro-textual level (and can be easily linked to previous selections already taught in class).

The selected poems are "representative of stylistic and thematic peculiarities of Petrarch's lyrical model," according to one survey respondent. Given

Petrarch's crystallized language, they include "the most recurring rhetorical figures" with regard to the canon of love poetry and to issues of narrative development within the collection. Invariably, this personalized anthology leaves out more of the *Canzoniere* than it includes. The instructors surveyed, however, provided sound rationales for their choices. Their selection always signals a pedagogical plan, while reflecting the objective of fair representation. Instructors tend to choose poems that can speak to students from more than the viewpoint of content (examples of Petrarch's love story, *si licet*, in the almost omnipresent form of sonnets); canzoni and sestine are included to provide a sense of Petrarch's life of forms, the embodiment of Petrarch's story *tout court* in its multiple poetic forms.

Our respondents identified the following possible teaching modules as having been successful in the classroom.

A book of songs and poetic forms: 1, 2, 3, 30, 34, 35, 61, 62, 90, 126, 134, 272, 310, 311, 364, 365, 366. This reading concentrates on love lyrics. "These poems give a good overview of the narrative sweep of the *Canzoniere*, as well as offering a nice mix of poetic forms (sonnet, sestina, canzone). They also afford the opportunity to look at how Petrarch represents contrasting emotions sequentially (e.g., 61 and 62)"; "One sestina is included to demonstrate the difficulty of such a metric system. In addition, one *ballata* presents this additional *modus poetandi*, in relation to the previous *ballate* of the Dolce Stil Novo."

Overview of major themes and poetic forms: 1–6, 10, 16, 22, 23, 27–30, 32, 35–36, 40–53, 61–62, 71, 112–14, 126–29, 132, 134, 149, 161, 196–98, 219, 264, 269, 272, 299, 323, 360, 366. This reading includes moral and political subjects (10, 53, 114, 128), which are usually avoided by many instructors.

Constructionism: Laura and Petrarch as poetic personas: Reading of 1, 16, 53, 119 as "self-conscious construction of [Petrarch's] poetic persona," followed by 62 (his "spiritual crises"), to finally address "Laura as poetic device" with 3, 23, 30, 90, 126, 129, 134, 264, 285, 323, 359, 362, 366.

Petrarch and history: moral and political poems: 7, 10, 17, 27, 40, 53, 103–04, 114, 128, 136–38. This reading attempts to analyze Petrarch's notion of history and political engagement as an integral part of his *Canzoniere*. Petrarch's political themes are not peripheral to the main story of unrequited love, since they "demonstrate the same melancholic feeling of having lost a beautiful past, and the pleasure of trying to recapture it in pieces through the activity of memory." The political canzoni also point out the difference between Petrarch and Dante's *poesia civile*.

Petrarch and the ethics of writing: 16, 20, 23, 77, 109, 127, 129, 149, 159, 268, 308, 339, 347, 362. An integral reading of the *Canzoniere* that privileges, for its global discussion and interpretation, otherwise neglected poems, seen through the lens of philosophy. This critical perspective, advocated in this volume by Massimo Lollini, is based on the notion of an ethics of writing, on how the notion of otherness in literature emerges in Petrarch's writings.

The following is a list of the poems taught, gleaned from course syllabi and answers to the survey: 1–6, 10–23, 27–30, 32, 34–36, 39–53, 59–62, 74, 77, 85, 90–92, 106, 109, 112–14, 118–19, 121–23, 126–29, 132–34, 136–37, 140, 149–50, 159, 164, 182, 185, 189–90, 196–99, 211, 219–20, 234, 248–49, 252, 263–64, 267–69, 272, 279, 285, 292–93, 297–98, 302, 308–11, 320, 323, 333–34, 339, 345–47, 353–54, 358–60, 362, 364–66. Instructors tend to use fewer than a third of the poems, concentrating on the first half (the "rime in vita") and only including a small sample from the second part ("rime in morte").

Approaches and Difficulties

The critical approaches instructors find most useful are based on a philological or close reading of the primary texts (in Italian or in English and other languages, if the *Canzoniere* is used to deal with Petrarchism in traditions other than Italian). Detailed textual readings of the poems (mostly at the thematic, stylistic, or lexical level, much less at the metric or prosodic level) are stressed, whether the original source (Petrarch) or its derivation (Petrarchism) is included in any teaching module.

Although believing it imperative to discuss Petrarch's contribution to the new language of love by deconstructing its components (i.e., by examining the linguistic and stylistic features of his lyrics), instructors concentrate first on the content of Petrarch's poems and on the range of interlocking themes that are proposed and then return to reassess any thematic interpretation in the light of what Petrarch's style and its linguistic features and forms seem to suggest. To ensure students' understanding of Petrarch's poems, instructors must read them for their plot first, clarifying what happens and (seemingly) why.

Many instructors alluded to the problem of student boredom in class, which sometimes led to their point-blank refusal of or disengagement from Petrarch, whose language is seen by the average student as monotonous, repetitive, and difficult to understand. This is not exclusively Petrarch's fault. Our respondents agreed that in working with undergraduates, the greatest challenge, with regard to *any* poetry, is to help them overcome their fear or antipathy toward poetry by enabling them to figure out what a sonnet or canzone is saying. To this end, many respondents have had their students rewrite a lyric in prose, reorganizing sentences in subject-verb-complement order, so that students can see that what they are reading is just sentences with words jumbled up. Texts are paraphrased line by line in modern Italian (when the original source is included) or in modern English when necessary (or directly in the modern equivalent of the language source, e.g., modern French or Spanish if poems are read in Renaissance or Golden Age translations). Analysis normally follows paraphrasis, and single poems (microtexts) are shown to students as belonging to the overall structure of the *Canzoniere* (macrotext), with the above-mentioned thematic approach generally privileged over any theoretical investigation.

Usually, the *Canzoniere* is presented as a daily, private journal written in poetic form, in which a person in love and desirous of a missing object struggles to find a balance between the dominant religious belief and his own passion. This type of unresolved rapport with the outside world and the constant attention that the poet pays to his own story can be traced in the precise chronology that Petrarch presents throughout the *Canzoniere*. For this reason, instructors might underline three structural features of the *Canzoniere*: its calendrical nature (the importance of numbers and sacred dates that are stressed by the texts); the Augustinian confessional ordering of the book; and the disjuncture between the confessional and biographical watershed in the work (*in vita* and *in morte*). The Augustinian framework (suggested by a few instructors and directly embraced by Welge and Lollini in their essays in this volume) seems to work in guiding students to examine a system of internal dichotomies: love for things of fortune versus eternal love; *uti* and *frui*; diversion and itinerary; pilgrimage and exile; and the necessary narcissism of confession and Petrarch's (re)construction of the (lyric) self.

In interpreting the *Canzoniere*, most instructors find it useful to introduce elements of the poetic traditions it renegotiates. For this reason, modules on Petrarch are normally preceded by an examination of the classical Latin tradition in medieval love poetry or by the study of Dante (especially the *Vita nuova*). The central theme in the *Canzoniere*—the antithesis of body and soul (or *eros* versus *caritas*)—can be presented while stressing the difference between Dante and Petrarch through the "donna-angelo" motif: while Dante incorporates Beatrice into the Christian tradition and reduces the danger of her eroticism, Petrarch is incapable of finding a place for Laura within Christianity, needing finally to marginalize her and substitute the Virgin for her. Another way to deal with the large questions of the relation between the spirit and the flesh, repeatedly underlined in the work, is to unpack the significance of Laura to Petrarch's larger appetite for fame. One approach used to discuss Petrarch's eroticism is to make students aware of how differently such concerns would be expressed today, stressing the subtlety of the emotions conveyed in the medieval love lyric. Petrarch's themes are then linked to love poetry in general, and even to modern love songs. When analyzing poems in which Laura is portrayed, some instructors try to elicit student discussion on the stereotyped, literary physicality of her representation, bringing the opposition of ideal/real woman (which today still constitutes a topic of interest) to the fore; students frequently respond with interest on the issue.

Although proposed approaches to the *Canzoniere* differ quite substantially at times, respondents to our survey and contributors to this volume were unanimous in emphasizing the many challenges that instructors face in teaching Petrarch, whether in the original Italian or in translation (or in the many incarnations of Petrarchism across languages). Problems are immediately twofold and interconnected: on the one hand, how to explain Petrarch's language (together with the stylistic and ideological corollaries of the poems' system of variants); on the other hand, how to present Petrarch's cultural and historical background, which lies at the core of his anxiety between earthly passion and religious devotion and becomes the ultimate cause of a continual hand-wringing embodied in the poems' reelaborations, elements that today's students often cannot comprehend.

Learning how to deal with Petrarch's language in the classroom becomes the most pressing concern. If taught in the original, especially in a survey course of Italian literature, one of the challenges stems from the epigonic role Petrarch assumes in the lyrical tradition stretching from the Provençal troubadours to Dante and Cino da Pistoia. A full exploration of Petrarch's *Canzoniere* would take into account non-Italian literary traditions, which can hardly be incorporated in a beginning literature course, as well as a substantial body of lyrical works in the Italian tradition, for which there is simply no time in a survey course. Whereas the second issue can be addressed in less traditional courses focusing on Petrarch, the multilingualism of medieval vernacular lyric—together with most of its Ovidian roots—can be seen as a pedagogical stumbling block. This volume contains a practical solution to these concerns in the section entitled "Teaching Petrarch's Literary Influences": the essay by Ilaria and Simone Marchesi and the essay by Simone Marchesi look at ways of incorporating effortlessly into the curriculum specific Petrarchan intertextual models and references, ranging from the Latin poetic canon to Dante (and these could also be used by courses teaching the work in translation).

Petrarch's ongoing process of finding the perfect lexical solution is often another problematic point in any teaching module. As indicated by most of the respondents, students usually consider the writing of a poem as immediate and impulsive, born of sudden inspiration. It is difficult for them to understand the Petrarchan concept of variants, of modifications continually brought to one's work, in a process to be always deemed inadequate and incomplete. Although Petrarch's works are sometimes seen as being created in a monotonous and repetitive linguistic and stylistic mode (Contini, "Preliminari"), the analysis of each single poetic text can demonstrate great complexity. Yet students find it hard to believe that Petrarch worked all his life on his poems to find the right line, the most satisfying written solution. Therefore, in the preparation of a course on Petrarch, it is necessary to consider first what contemporary students understand of poetry and of the process of writing poems. One recommendation is to shift away from the texts to the context, or to prepare the reading of the poems with extensive preliminary discussions on Petrarch's cultural and historical background (see the essays by Cachey, Alfie, and Welge in this volume). The challenge in the linguistic and stylistic presentation of Petrarch's poems can be somewhat lessened if students understand what it meant for Petrarch to write and to write of Laura. Contributors and respondents alike point to the usefulness of explaining Laura as a poetic construct and not as a person; of regarding the poet, the "I" of the poems, also as a literary construct, not to be identified with the historical Petrarch; and of presenting the *Canzoniere* as an overall conceit, a poetic game disguised as an autobiographical work. The hurdle of the students' initial impression of Petrarch's morbid humorlessness and unqualified self-pity (for an audience accustomed to the ubiquitous ironies of modern literary expression—especially when dealing with erotic matters) can be cleared by instructors willing to explicate the critical strategizing that conditions Petrarch's narcissistic pose. This approach might render students cognizant of the poet's demands in writing of Laura and ultimately allow them to come to terms with the follies, or even absurdities, of his persona, so that they may become better equipped to respond sympathetically and to grasp why Petrarch's poems would prove so overwhelmingly influential for his successors. (For the Petrarchan challenge to narrate Laura, see Lollini's essay in this volume, on alterity as the possible resolutive approach. For the evolution of Laura's figure within Petrarch's opus, see Bernardo's essay in this volume.)

When teaching Petrarch in translation, instructors do not find it difficult to convey the ideas Petrarch was interested in and the shift in intellectual inquiry he heralded; however, when it comes to the poems as works of literature, his allusions and wordplay are difficult to discern in English, and much of what Petrarch did on the level of individual words is often lost on students. (Durling's translation, for example, though brilliant, is in prose, which means it cannot capture the effects of sound in Petrarch's verbal elaborations [e.g., assonances, cadences, puns].) By necessity, instructors teaching Petrarch in translation underscore meaning over style or stylistic elaborations, although students still bristle at what they view as highly contrived comparisons in Petrarch's classical allusions or at what they call stereotypes or clichés (blond hair, ivory-white teeth, coral lips, etc.), wondering how Petrarch could have had such a long-lasting influence. Analyzing specific samples of contemporary popular music that make use of what we might call the topos of the *locus amoenus*, for example, can help students overcome their (first, superficial) reservation on Petrarchan language and of Laura's seemingly vague portrait (see the essay by Ross in this volume, which advocates using lyrics from pop music in the classroom to discuss the persistence of Petrarch's figurative language).

Notes on the Essays in This Volume

Petrarch's *Canzoniere*

The first essays in this volume address teaching Petrarch's *Canzoniere* (in the section subtitled "Design, Themes, Style") and are devoted to formalistic, thematic, prosodic, and lexical approaches, all seen as possible thresholds to its appreciation. Germaine Warkentin furnishes a systematic investigation of the frameworks or architectures that gather the *Canzoniere*'s scattered rhymes together. Petrarch left us little in the way of guidelines to the system by which, over four decades, he arranged his vernacular poems to produce a single work. In the succeeding six centuries, many ways of approaching the work's design and structure have been suggested. Warkentin's essay attempts to open up the various routes by which a student might investigate the design of the *Canzoniere*, laying open the critical and editorial approaches that over the centuries have attempted to deal with the various versions of this seemingly metamorphic work. The aim is to open both critical and methodological doors for students while encouraging constructive skepticism about the sometimes astonishing certitude with which critics of Petrarch have claimed to read the poet.

Central to Petrarch's inspiration and internal contrast between profane and spiritual love, human or heavenly glory, is Laura. Aldo S. Bernardo's essay follows the many embodiments of this figure in an overview that outlines Laura's evolution within Petrarch's opus. Instructors might find Bernardo's revisitation a useful background tool in discussions of what Simone Marchesi in his essay refers to as "the never-accomplished 'Beatricization' of Laura."

Christopher Kleinhenz's essay is an introduction to Italian prosody through examples directly drawn from Petrarch's lyrics. Divided into sections on meters, rhymes and rhyming techniques, and poetic forms, this overview is meant to provide instructors teaching Petrarch in the original Italian with the tools necessary for a technically oriented discussion of Petrarch's poetry. To complement this technical approach, Madison U. Sowell advocates the use of a concordance to Petrarch's *Canzoniere* as "a readily available and easily accessible tool for getting at the recurring words and images that characterize the poet's vocabulary and constitute the work's leitmotifs." Using a concordance, even in a class that analyzes just a single text, allows the *Canzoniere* to emerge as an organic corpus, facilitating a discussion of its restricted vocabulary and thus providing a possible springboard to an examination of Petrarchism. Christopher Martin presents a case study of canzone 126 in the *Canzoniere*, to provide a comprehensive entry to the poet's distinctive self-dramatization by delineating the ways that this lyric encodes signature features of the larger sequence.

The next section, "The *Canzoniere* and the Life," invites instructors to explore ways of incorporating Petrarch's historical and cultural background in the teaching of the *Canzoniere*. Theodore J. Cachey, Jr., offers a biographical account of Petrarch's life and works as characterized by a restless mobility for which no home is ever definitive, just as none of the major works was ever really finished. Using Petrarch's life as the means to understand his texts, Cachey considers the homology between two aspects of mobility that characterize the writer's life: geographic or topographic space versus textual space (or the place of the text) and geographic travel versus literary travel. Fabian Alfie's essay focuses on the historical and cultural roots of Petrarch's fundamental *dissidio* (profane versus spiritual love), which students usually find difficult to understand if not aptly discussed in the context of the various perspectives that medieval Christianity had on amorous relations between men and women. Petrarch's real-life or fictional love conflicts clearly emerge as part of a greater philosophical, cultural, and religious anxiety typical of the fourteenth century.

In his essay, Jobst Welge investigates how the rhetoric of solitude and privacy is reflected in the *Canzoniere* (as well as in post-Petrarchan lyric) and how the condemnation of love poetry in the *Secretum* can be read as Petrarch's critical engagement with the poetics of the *Canzoniere*. The essay demonstrates how this topic provides an opportunity to bring together Petrarch's moral-philosophical writings and his poetry, especially in a classroom context. Massimo Lollini considers several poems in the *Canzoniere* and examines the notion of an ethics of writing and of ethics as a point of intersection between philosophy and literature. His essay aims to help students and instructors realize the value of Petrarch's philosophy and poetry for contemporary cultural debates.

The next section, "Teaching Petrarch's Literary Influences," contains three essays that address head-on the *Canzoniere*'s classical Latin roots, Petrarch's Dantean appropriations (both conceptually and linguistically), and Boccaccio's *Decameron* as an additional (though often neglected) exemplary text to understand Petrarch's project with the *Canzoniere*. Ilaria and Simone Marchesi begin by indicating how "the two strains of Petrarch studies can fruitfully be brought together in a course that considers the vernacular project of the *Canzoniere* as animated by the same classicizing project as [Petrarch's own] Latin philological work." Such a comparative effort may provide students with an opportunity to study Petrarch's "strategy of reactivation of the classical poetic past," while, conversely, "a course on the Latin canon may use Petrarch's work as a summative case of an exemplary reader's response to the tradition." Simone Marchesi's essay on how to teach students to recognize Dante in Petrarch first explains how to use inventories of sources (lists of lexical borrowings, syntactic calques, rhythmic homologies, and thematic allusions) to offer "a philologically sound basis for evaluating the dialectics of imitation and emulation in which the *Canzoniere* engages its primary vernacular model" and then identifies "four main thematic clusters of divergences . . . in Petrarch's post-Dantean attitude: the reinterpretation of stilnovism, the never-accomplished 'Beatricization' of Laura, the treatment of political issues, and the redeployment of 'comedic' mythologems."

Complementary to the treatment of classical authors and of Dante is Laurie Shepard's essay on Boccaccio and Petrarch. Tradition has designated Petrarch's *Canzoniere* and Boccaccio's *Decameron* as opposite poles of fourteenth-century Italian literary innovation. If viewed from the perspective of language, theme, culture, or literary tradition, however, the two works present as many similarities as differences, of which Shepard provides a succinct overview.

The section "Teaching Petrarch through Music" treats Petrarch's lyric poetry in Western music, from the Renaissance to contemporary popular songs, and contains suggestions for musical settings and a selected discography. Music has brilliantly illuminated the *Canzoniere*'s aesthetic and ethical impulses. Exploring or assigning students to explore and present musical settings of specific lyrics in vocal or pop music makes Petrarch's lyrics accessible (particularly but not only to students of Italian) in familiar ways. Marc Vanscheeuwijck's essay is concerned with teaching polyphonic madrigals (e.g., those by Marenzio, Monteverdi) and also provides background information on the musical genre per se, together with specific listening activities and modes of discussion. The essay by Silvia Ross provides textual examples of pop songs and their parallels with specific poems in the *Canzoniere* along with examples of the manner in which contemporary songs can be read as reflecting canonical, consolidated Petrarchan themes.

The Petrarchan Tradition in Italy, France, England, Spain, and Russia and in the Comparative Literature Curriculum

The remaining essays are devoted to teaching the Petrarchan tradition and attest to the influential force that Petrarch had with his *Canzoniere* over early modern and modern Italian poetry (not to mention his controversial heritage for the novecento poetic production). Petrarch's legacy needs to be widely discussed in the Italian literature classroom, across introductory and specialized courses. The range of these essays includes discussions of Petrarchism from its inception to its necessary reevaluation in the contemporary context.

Michael Sherberg's essay begins the section "Petrarch and the Italian Tradition" and offers an overview of early Petrarchism in the Italian tradition, tracing it both in theory (Pietro Bembo) and in practice (e.g., in the poetry of Lorenzo de' Medici, Poliziano, Bembo, Giovanni della Casa, Michelangelo, as well as including the dissonant voices of such famous anti-Petrarchists as Francesco Berni). From Sherberg's reading of canonical authors, the section continues with the problems of canon renegotiation. Fiora A. Bassanese explores the difficulties facing women poets (Gaspara Stampa, Vittoria Colonna, Veronica Franco) writing in a culture imbued with imitation of a male model. These first two essays concentrate on Petrarchism up to and including the sixteenth century; the next essay, by Elisabetta Properzi Nelsen, focuses on the influence Petrarch had on the most representative voice of Italian Baroque poetry, Giambattista Marino. This study assists instructors and students in drawing useful parallels between Petrarch's style and later Italian poetic traditions.

Focusing on canzoni 53 ("Spirto gentil") and 128 ("Italia mia"), the essay by Elizabeth H. D. Mazzocco illustrates the influence, growth, and maturation of Petrarch's thoughts through the Renaissance and the Risorgimento. Manifesting itself in poems, treatises, and lyrics, his concept of "antica virtù" inspired a wide range of Italian intellectuals. In his examination of Petrarch's early-nineteenth-century fortunes and misfortunes, Andrea Dini proposes that instructors consider the problematic aspect of Petrarch's presence in post-Risorgimento Italian literature (usually read in negative terms as stifling) versus Dante's reemergence as the only deserving father of the Italian language. Dini provides instructors with strategies and tools to illustrate Petrarch's and Dante's legacy in Italian poetry while discussing the ideological implications of the rejection of the Petrarchan code and canon.

The volume continues with the section "Petrarch in a Comparative Context." Leah Middlebrook investigates the political, historical, and literary paths by which the *Canzoniere* arrived in Spain in the fifteenth century and the official introduction of Italianate "nueva poesia" into Spain by Juan Boscán, as well as the ensuing controversy that his poetry and that of Garcilaso de la Vega produced. The essay suggests ways of reading some Petrarchan poets such as Boscán, Garcilaso, Gutierre de Cetina, Francisco Medrano, Lope de Vega, Luis de Góngora, and Francisco de Quevedo. Deborah Lesko Baker looks at the Petrarchan tradition in France, exploring individual poetic voices and subjectivities fashioned by sixteenth-century French poets in response to Petrarchism's European fortunes. Her essay elaborates on the individual speaking subjects created by authors such as Maurice Scève, Louise Labé, Joachim du Bellay, and Pierre de Ronsard and provides examples of poems, images, and diction that have been particularly fruitful and interesting to students in the pursuit of this analysis.

Three essays address the Petrarchan tradition in England. In his essay on English Petrarchism, William J. Kennedy first outlines the alternatives in terms of anthologies, texts, and iconographic or musical sources to get students started in the study of the subject matter. He then provides instructors with seven modules that cover single authors (e.g., Philip Sidney, Edmund Spenser, John Donne, or Mary Wroth) or groups (e.g., Samuel Daniel, Henry Constable, Thomas Lodge, and Michael Drayton) across the sixteenth and seventeenth centuries. Tanya Pollard's essay concerns the teaching of Petrarch in courses on Shakespeare or English Renaissance literature, in which key Petrarchan tropes such as the cruel mistress, wounds, attacks on eyes, speechlessness, or the blazon of female body parts are emphasized and used as an invitation for a closer exploration of the way some Shakespearean characters are conceived. Pollard's analysis dwells on the play *Twelfth Night*, "because of the range of types of allusions and their centrality to the play's core themes and because students tend to respond well to its combination of playfulness and dark humor." Edoardo Zuccato's investigation chronologically complements Kennedy's with an overview of the Petrarchan presence in English poetry from 1750 to the Victorian age, starting with Thomas Gray and two figures normally critically neglected as (Petrarchan) poets in their own right: Charlotte Smith and Mary Robinson. While recuperating authors and works that deserve a more careful reading as examples of British Petrarchism, Zuccato discusses at length the pro-Petrarchan or anti-Petrarchan positions of the Romantic poets, analyzing the motivations that bring Coleridge and Shelley to embrace Petrarch and Wordsworth and Byron to reject him. The essay continues with the examination of the Victorian approach to Petrarch, seen through the lens of Elizabeth Barrett Browning and Christina Rossetti's poetry.

Tom Dolack provides a compact overview of Russian Petrarchism and outlines the ways and the reasons through which Petrarch was recuperated in Russian literature from the mid nineteenth century on. Dolack offers numerous examples of texts that are translations or imitations of Petrarchan poems and that instructors of Russian literature courses or courses in comparative literature can use fruitfully to define the many incarnations of Petrarchism. The volume's final essay, by Christopher Livanos, explores Petrarch's *Canzoniere* in courses specifically designed from a comparative point of view. Given Livanos's emphasis on readings that privilege Petrarch's psychological introspection within Augustinian culture, this approach is complementary to those of Alfie, Welge, and Lollini, and all four essays might be read together.

Approaches to the Design of Petrarch's *Canzoniere*

Germaine Warkentin

Not all of us have the opportunity to explore the entire *Canzoniere* with students, whether in Italian or English, whether at the graduate or undergraduate level. Yet anyone who teaches even a single poem is prompted to think about its place in the whole collection—and if we are not so prompted, one of our students is bound to raise the subject. The self-sufficiency of the single Petrarchan sonnet or canzone, a tour de force of formal design, breaks down immediately before the first innocent questions: Who is the speaker? Who is Laura? Why is he so upset? Is there a story here? Why does she die? What happens to him in the end? The questions don't go away in the English literature classroom any more than they do in the Italian. And when the teacher is working with more than one sonnet or adds a canzone or sestina, the question of design is added to the mix. The title *Rerum vulgarium fragmenta*, "fragments in the language of ordinary life," prompts the questions, Why "fragments," when the collection has such evident coherence of vision? Why does Petrarch keep on using a rigid form like the sonnet? Why not more canzoni? What is a madrigal, and why are there so few of them? Why is the book divided into two parts? All these are questions about design, both of the individual forms that make up the book and about the book itself. The teacher's task is to encourage students to use one set of questions to explore the other.

No teacher should feel too guilty about not having a position on the final design of the work as a whole, because it may well be that the poet didn't have one either. Petrarch was one of the great geniuses of design in the history of European lyric, but he kept on revising his book of fragments until the final year of his life. This doesn't mean, however, that a joyous relativism has reigned when the problem arises of the formal structure of the whole collection. Despite Petrarch's chosen term *fragmenta*, the *Canzoniere* has been subjected to an amazing range of theories about its organization, with many critics insisting that they have produced the definitive solution of the problem yet differing from one another in important ways. What might the word *design* mean, both for single poems and the work as a whole? Linear elements like narrative and chronology provide one kind of architecture, but juxtaposing deliberately contrasted poetic forms provides another, and the creation of a network of related poetic motifs and allusions across the whole work a third. And what can we learn about how Petrarch actually developed the work in manuscript?[1] There's an open invitation here to look at the formal poetic structures available to Petrarch and his contemporaries, the status of vernacular poetry in the context of emergent humanism, the roles of numerology, manuscript studies, book history, biography, cultural studies, and even political history. There are many paths through the *Canzoniere*, and it is worth thinking about whether Petrarch might have intended it that way.

The *Canzoniere* is made up of 317 sonnets, 38 canzoni and sestine, 7 *ballate*, and 4 *madrigali*. The critical study of its design is complicated by the history of Petrarch's revision of the poems and the work, by our information about his manuscripts as Petrarch left them, and by the enthusiasms of later editors trying to resolve the difficulties raised by that legacy. Few historically important literary texts (and Petrarch's influence has been vast, even into the twentieth century) have appeared before us in so many forms. There's a parallel in Shakespeare; students sometimes learn about the version of *King Lear* known to eighteenth-century theatergoers that was rewritten to provide a happy ending, and today they may be presented with three different, equally valid, texts of the play. During the five centuries between Petrarch's death in 1374 and Pierre de Nolhac's 1886 demonstration (*Le* Canzoniere *autographe de Petrarque*) that a manuscript in the Vatican Library—Vatican Latin 3195—was the poet's part-autograph, not many readers of Petrarch were familiar with a version of the collection organized like the one we now read. And there's more: another Petrarch manuscript in the Vatican, Vatican Latin 3196, presents us with twenty pages of draft poems originating from different periods of the poet's working life, many of them heavily revised. If there are problems here, however, there are opportunities as well.

Manuscripts, facsimiles, and old editions are wonderful tools for the teacher, because students tend to assume that the printed poem on their anthology's clean white page is somehow the very poem itself, that the words on the page are directly accessible, without the shock that comes from encountering them mediated by some other form. So there is a healthy Brechtian defamiliarization that comes with looking at a poem's translation into another language, poring over printouts of the poet's manuscript revisions[2] or experimenting with a centuries-old edition with its editor's commentary framing the poem instead of sitting at the foot of the page. Studying the design of the *Canzoniere* is rich in such opportunities for many different kinds of students, from the undergraduate simply studying a selection of poems, for whom the vexed textual history of the *Canzoniere* may provide the exciting next step in a critic's education, to the increasingly expert graduate student faced (probably at first on microform) with texts ranging from the more than 160 editions before 1600 to the post-1886 classic editions by Giovanni Mestica (1896), Giosuè Carducci and Severino Ferrari (1899), Ettore Modigliani (1904), Ezio Chiorboli (1924), Gianfranco Contini (1964), Marco Santagata (1996), and Ugo Dotti (1996).

The first printed edition of the *Canzoniere* was published in Venice in 1470; preceding it lies a century of manuscript recopying, sometimes from sources without much authority. Even the many Renaissance printed versions were accompanied by elaborate commentaries that often disagreed with one another about the work's structure (Kennedy, *Authorizing*). Early editors sometimes reorganized the poems to suit themselves, and modern ones (even after 1886) have disagreed on where the two-part division of the poems should lie. The experiments of placing editions by Alessandro Vellutello (1525), Sebastiano Fausto da Longiano (1532), and Lodovico Dolce (1547) beside one another or comparing modern editions by Mestica and by Carducci and Ferrari (there is a crucial difference even there) illustrates how unstable the texts of Petrarch historically have been and with what tact we need to explore not only the criticism based on them but also the work of poets who were influenced by Petrarch. When we find the maker of a sonnet sequence allegedly imitating the *Canzoniere*, we quickly learn to ask what edition of Petrarch he or she was using.

How do we defamiliarize the Petrarchan page, and why should that provide a pathway into the problem of design? A useful method is to engage the students' interest in Petrarch's obsessive revising of his poems and of the work as a whole. We have facsimiles and transcriptions of the precious drafts in Vatican Latin 3196—available on interlibrary loan if not locally—that show us how much Petrarch worked over individual poems; for example on f.2r there is a much rewritten draft of poem 196, "L'aura serena," and on f.5v "'Che fai, alma?'" (150) shows the revision of an entire sestet (in its marginal *transcriptum*, Petrarch tells himself he has made a fair copy). Experiments like this bring the student into Petrarch's workshop, to his very desk, and to the ways in which, over more than three decades, he wrote, erased, and rewrote, all the while talking to himself in the margins of the page.

Two strategies have been shared both by early editors of the *Canzoniere* and by critics writing after 1886: the search for narrative and the search for chronology or biography. The telling of stories in poetry and the poet's self-presentation were problems Petrarch and his contemporaries (including those abroad, like Guillaume de Machaut and Geoffrey Chaucer) also addressed, although in ways very unlike ours. Students may begin by trying to read the collection as if it were a novel and will be frustrated by Petrarch's repetition of motifs, by the absence of realistic characterization, and by the work's apparent lack of closure. Interestingly, Petrarch was one of several generations of Provençal and Italian poets who did not produce examples of the romance (ancestor of the novel) but instead experimented with other means of unifying their highly sophisticated single lyrics into larger bodies (O. Holmes), the best-known example—intimidating for a poet of the next generation like Petrarch—being Dante's *Vita nuova*. Whatever the differences in their renderings, the core concept of such a work was that it represented the poet's personal collection, his book of songs. The titles used for Petrarch's collection suggest their own critical narrative: in the fifteenth century it was generally known (as it often is today) as the *Canzoniere*; in the sixteenth century the most usual title was *Il Petrarcha* (the poet literally identified with the fabric of his book); in the eighteenth and nineteenth centuries it was simply the *Rime*. The popular *Rime sparse*, alluding to the first line of the first sonnet and by inference to Petrarch's Latin title, was first applied to the collection by Chiorboli in 1924. Petrarch composed other works built up out of parts, such as his various collections of letters and, particularly relevant here, the Latin pastoral poems of the *Bucolicum carmen* (Mann, "Making"). The extensive writing on the architecture of Dante's *Commedia* and the frame of Boccaccio's *Decameron* (a work made up of separate parts, although in prose) suggests many opportunities for the analysis of design. Advanced students working on narrative might want to try comparing the fictive strategies of the *Canzoniere* with those of some medieval romances.

If the *Canzoniere* possesses the fictive power we assign to the modern novel, at the same time it exploits the variety offered by different lyric forms (Warkentin, "'Love's sweetest Part'"). And without being recognizably realistic in the modern sense, it does make use of the circumstances of the poet's productive life: the anniversaries of his falling in love (Dutschke, "Anniversary Poems"), his political vision (28, 128), and his struggles with "le dogliose rime / che son seguaci de la mente afflita: / qual fien ultime, lasso, et qua' fien prima?" 'these doleful rhymes, which are / The rag-tag creatures of my troubled mind. / Which should be last, ah me! And which come first?' (127).[3] Generations of critics have thus searched the *Canzoniere* for its biographical or perhaps chronological order, whether, like Nino Quarta, they were attempting to identify who Laura really was or, like Bortolo Martinelli (*Petrarca*), pressed on to consider the deeper question of the moral structure of the collection. Critics like Francesco Rico ("*Rime sparse*") and Santagata (*Frammenti*) have exploited Petrarch's biography in different but allied ways. Dating "Voi ch' ascoltate" in late 1349, Rico argues that in this period of Petrarch's intellectual and creative life the poet began to assemble the *Familiari*, the *Epistole metriche*, and above all the *Canzoniere* into integrated wholes, in each case dwelling on the dichotomy between scattered parts and spiritual integration. Santagata's *I frammenti dell'anima* is significantly subtitled "Storia e racconto nel *Canzoniere*" ("History and Narrative in the *Canzoniere*").

Students will nevertheless find that the very dispersedness of the work continues to pose a theoretical problem; it is possible (though it has been tried more often with his imitators than with Petrarch himself) to apply the extreme skepticism of poststructural theory to the apparent fragmentation of the collection, showing that the *Canzoniere* in fact subverts itself at every turn (Hainsworth, *Petrarch*). Here it is interesting to contrast Dante, for whom the scattered leaves of the book of nature would one day be collected into a single book (*Par.* 33: 85–87), with Petrarch's willed entry into the dispersedness of earthly experience. The scattered poems Petrarch tries to assemble direct his poetic powers not heavenward, to the contemplation of unity, but earthward, to the evocation of the diverse texture of the lived world. Is a deliberate structural dynamic created between the sheer diversity of the poems and a more linear temporal narrative (Barolini, "Making")? Does this make Petrarch the authentic precursor of the autoreflexive lyrics of his Renaissance and modern heirs (Freccero, "Fig Tree")? If so, the fragmentation of the collection becomes a powerfully controlled fiction, demanding not only a theoretical reading but one sensitive to cultural setting as well. One such context, entirely occluded by both Dante and Petrarch but pressingly addressed by modern feminists, has been the massively idealized portrayal of the lady beloved by the poet; Nancy J. Vickers, for example, has shown how Petrarch's imagery literally fragments the figure of Laura and what the legacy of that treatment was for later writers and for concepts of the female ("Diana").

Numerological critics have taken a very different approach. Wilhelm Pötters, Frederic J. Jones (*Structure*), and Thomas P. Roche, Jr. (*Petrarch and the English Sonnet Sequences*), argue that, despite its apparent fragmentation, the *Canzoniere* was organized on a numerological pattern. To do so they reach deeply into the biblical world of Petrarch and other postclassical writers, citing the famous passage in the book of Wisdom, "thou hast ordered all things in measure and number and weight" (Wisd. 11). Numerological patterning is a documented feature of the music of the period, and there is little doubt that writers also exploited its possibilities. The 366 poems of the *Canzoniere* clearly suggest that Petrarch had a calendrical structure in mind, but during the more than three decades of the work's compilation he may have explored other possibilities as well. Critics still hypothesize the existence of an undivided collection of 1342 (Gorni), succeeded by the two-part collection initiated in 1349–51 copied by Boccaccio in the Chigi manuscript. Only in about 1366 did Petrarch determine that the two parts should be made up of a calendrical 366 poems (Wilkins, *Making*). At present, strict numerologists differ radically on what precisely the poet did to develop this structure and why. Students can be encouraged to explore this material yet recognize when the results become so rigid they exclude other features of design for which there is solid evidence (Warkentin, "*Infaticabile maestro*"). Was the conflict between the dispersed quality of fragmentation and the allure of a numerological order contrived by Petrarch?

What in fact was contrived by Petrarch? In all this diversity of critical approach, what guidelines can the student find in Petrarch's practice that will lead to a rich appreciation of his strategies of design? Petrarch begins the *Canzoniere* with a poem that presents the collection as *rime sparse*, scattered rhymes, an image figuring the disorientation medieval medicine regarded as typical of the effects of sudden passion on a lover (Wack), and he returns to the disrupting effects of love on his writing in later poems. That scattering, however, may have a double meaning, for the first three poems treat the onslaught of love from three different points of view, suggesting that traditional conceptions of narrative—at least those drawn from nineteenth-century fiction—simply aren't applicable here. (Today's student, used to the split screens and recursive storytelling of stylish movies and television dramas, may not be as surprised by this as we might think.) Furthermore, the opening poem belongs to a recognizable classical genre, the *excusatio*, which early readers would have encountered in Ovid (see, e.g., the poems beginning books 1 and 2 of the *Amores*) and the other Latin elegists that humanists like Petrarch were rediscovering. Amid this compositional variety, however, Petrarch made some careful choices; there are several poems in Vatican Latin 3196 that might well have appeared in the *Canzoniere* but were not selected. Finally, the revisions of individual poems in Vatican Latin 3196 and of the *Canzoniere* itself show that only someone who cared deeply about design could have worked so hard to revise, rework, and renew both his poems and his book; Petrarch was still changing the order of the last thirty poems a year before he died.

Other important features of Petrarch's poetic technique that have consequences for the design of the *Canzoniere* are his severely—and deliberately—limited poetic vocabulary, which is the basis of the powerfully cohesive style that unifies the apparent variety of the work, and the web of allusion to classical, biblical, and sometimes contemporary sources that links poem to poem even as the collection evolves (on the allusion to contemporary sources, see Santagata, *Per moderne carte*). If we keep in mind these features—commitment to the multiple poetic levels of his subject, textural variety and contrast, the exploitation of classical example and allusion, and the persistent investigation of design possibilities—we will have the keys to Petrarch's toolbox, if not the answer to everything it contains.

What are the features, if not of the design *of* the *Canzoniere*, then of design *in* the *Canzoniere*? Let's assume the most common situation of teacher and student, faced with a single sonnet. It's exciting to choose one of the most passionate ones—"Io sentia dentr' al cor già venir meno" (47) or "Lasso, ch' i' ardo et altri non mel crede" (203)—or one of those most often imitated by poets elsewhere, for instance "Chi vuol veder" (248), of which there are countless imitations or translations by later poets. A better point to begin might be with three sonnets linked by the most intricate filiations: poems 41–43, originating in some brief absence of Laura and as closely linked with one another as they are with the sonnets around them. A small, elegant grouping is created in which "the two outer poems thus embrace the inner one, creating a poetic order in the midst of narrative confusion" (Hainsworth, *Petrarch* 69). Are there other sonnet groupings that share this pattern or that are linked by patterns of their own? Is there a similar but more distant relation among 182, 183, and 184? If students think the sonnet form is rigid, they might find themselves fascinated by the sestina, which is really a kind of poetic computer game, although one with resonances unavailable to the aficionado of today's video games.

The careful internal and external structural relations Petrarch developed across sonnets like 1–3 and 41–43 are also evident in that most prestigious of early vernacular genres, the canzone; 30 is explicitly numerological, a climactic list of poets structures 70, and virtuoso variations on the topic of the lady's eyes draw together the canzoni known as the "three sisters" (71, 72, and 73), which are also linked—exceptionally—by the same rhyme scheme. Teaching the versification and genres of such poems is a staple of the repertoire of anyone working with Petrarch or Petrarchism, whether in Italian, French, or English. But they also provide a pathway into the larger question of the design of the *Canzoniere* as a whole. The Italian sonnet, for example, is characterized by its "turn," a break in the rhyme scheme that creates thematic and poetic contrast between the first eight lines and the last six. Is there a connection between the resources of this structure and Petrarch's decision to divide his collection into two parts, the second shorter than the first and contrasting powerfully with it? The student still grumbling about narrative might be induced to explore the effect "Standomi un giorno solo a la fenestra" (323) has on the reading of "Nel dolce tempo de la prima etade" (23), the later poem insisting, even in the face of the earlier and much greater one, on a now transformed way of seeing. So also "Italia mia" (128), the famous political canzone, returns to and reflects with expanded vision on the political themes of the earlier "O aspettata in ciel beata et bella" (28). Why doesn't one poem simply erase the other? What is the effect on the reader of the presence of both? In a collection that eventually assumed a calendrical structure, what kind of poetic time does such reenvisioning create?

Whatever our conclusions about the structure of the *Canzoniere* as a whole, it is evident that, in ways we are still working to comprehend, Petrarch skillfully built visionary theme into structural design and made design illuminate theme. Furthermore, his virtuoso repertoire for doing so remained secure throughout three decades of thinking and rethinking his collection. In the end, the most fruitful approach to the design of the *Canzoniere* may be as a powerful example of a lived, and indeed still living, experience of poetic craft.

NOTES

[1] See Wilkins, *Making*; Storey, *Transcription*; Rafti; Del Puppo and Storey; Storey, "Doubting"; Zamponi; and Warkentin, "*Infaticabile maestro*."

[2] See Del Puppo and Storey; Barolini, "Petrarch"; Storey, "Doubting"; and Zamponi.

[3] All quotations from the *Canzoniere* are from Cook's bilingual edition.

Petrarch, Laura, and the *Canzoniere*

Aldo S. Bernardo

After almost fifty years of studying and teaching Petrarch, I have come to the conclusion that he must be viewed as much more than a consummate lyric poet. Even a cursory examination of his life shows the extent to which he was involved in the international and national affairs of his day on both secular and religious levels. His acquaintance with most of the leaders of Europe is unparalleled by any poet or writer of his day. He was held in the highest esteem by popes, emperors, and other secular and religious leaders who often turned to him for advice. Nevertheless, his primary interest remained always the world of letters and learning from Greece and Rome to France, Italy, Germany, and even England. He truly qualified as citizen of the world.

Yet Petrarch's incredible knowledge, learning, productivity, and societal involvement pose a serious problem for the teacher dealing primarily with his Italian poetry. How could such a learned and active man have devoted so much of his life to writing endless poems about his love for a lady named Laura unless she represented in his mind more than sexual love? I found the answer by analyzing in depth the deliberate manner in which Petrarch developed and cultivated the image of his beloved from her birth to her death and beyond as he carefully structured his *Canzoniere*.

In Italy in Petrarch's day, two of his fellow Florentines, Dante and Boccaccio, were steering vernacular poetry and prose in new directions: Dante doing some very original things with religious poetry and Boccaccio with secular prose. Each, however, had steered his work in directions unappealing to Petrarch: Dante toward theological and dogmatic concerns, Boccaccio toward highly secular matters.[1] But, like his two contemporaries, Petrarch the lyric poet also followed in the footsteps of European developments in the love lyric of his day, using not only a ladylove as the basis of his inspiration but also the Italian vernacular as his chief mode of expression and current poetic forms as his chief building blocks. His lady likewise inspired him toward ever finer goals, but these were neither ultimate salvation, as with Dante, nor a questionable secular love, as with Boccaccio. One may perceive the difference in the names of the three ladyloves: Dante's Beatrice, whose name suggests a bestower of Christian blessings; Boccaccio's Fiammetta, the "little flame," who pines over her treatment at the hands of her lover; and Laura, who reflects the classical myth of Apollo and Daphne in which the lovely nymph Daphne escapes from the enamored Apollo. All three names are loaded, but Petrarch's Laura is the most ambiguous, containing some elements of both Beatrice and Fiammetta. Furthermore, all three writers produced a minor work that attempts to define their ladyloves. Dante, in *Vita nuova*, describes how Beatrice had entered his life and eventually became a driving force capable of leading one to a Christian salvation; Boccaccio, in *Elegia di Madonna Fiammetta* (*Amorous Fiammetta*) has Fiammetta describe her suffering after having been abandoned by her lover; and Petrarch, in *I trionfi* (*I triumphi*; *The Triumphs*), includes an epic framework that projects the figure of Laura as a humanistic ideal of virtue, beauty, and glory and is essentially an apotheosis of the beloved.[2]

While most of Petrarch's works that made him an international figure were written in Latin,[3] the two works that established him as a great lyric poet were written in Italian (although both bear Latin titles): the *Rerum vulgarium fragmenta* (known as the *Canzoniere* or *Rime*) and the *Triumphi*. Both dealt for the most part with the poet's love for a beautiful lady named Laura whose identity has never been successfully established, despite the poet's efforts in many of his Latin works to speak of her as a real presence (Bernardo, *Petrarch, Laura*, chs. 3–4). The *Canzoniere*, whose Latin title implies a collection of fragments in the vernacular, reflects a love poetry in the tradition of courtly love that had dominated the lyric poetry of southern France at the end of the eleventh century and influenced poets and writers throughout southern Europe, Germany, and England from the twelfth to the fifteenth centuries. Such poetry derived its popularity from its peculiar contradictory qualities reflecting erotic desire and spiritual aspiration: "[C]ourtly love is a doctrine of paradoxes, a love at once illicit and morally elevating, passionate and disciplined, humiliating and exalting, human and transcendent" (Newman vii). The tradition enabled Petrarch to depict his struggle to reconcile erotic desire and spiritual aspiration in an original and powerful manner, but with the help of another tradition that had proven popular in both the Latin and vernacular poetry and literature of the time—the use of allegory.

Allegorical poetry of love would usually turn the feelings, attitudes, and qualities associated with love into personified abstractions, which play the role of characters in a symbolic narrative illustrating most often the psychology of love. Thus, in the thirteenth-century French *Roman de la rose*, which became the standard for such poetry, we have young women representing qualities that contribute to the onset of love, such as idleness, mirth, gladness, courtesy, sweet looks, beauty, wealth, generosity, openness, and youth, while the symbolic rose becomes the object sought by the lover.[4]

Petrarch's interest in combining the traditions of courtly love and allegory in his Italian love lyrics was in part strongly influenced by his abiding interest in the work of the Roman poet Ovid, whose poetic masterpiece known as the *Metamorphoses* was highly popular among the more learned writers of the time. It is an epic poem composed of stories from classical and Near Eastern legend and encompassing world history from the formation of the earth, the emergence of life, the birth of mankind, and the evolution of man down to the times of Julius Caesar. Every story includes some kind of metamorphosis or change of shape of one or more of the characters. In the early fourteenth century a lengthy anonymous poem entitled *Ovide moralisé* attempted to reconcile Ovid's *Metamorphoses* with Christian doctrine through allegorical interpretation. Ovid also wrote other works dealing with the psychology of love that influenced Petrarch, such as *Amores*, *Ars amatoria*, and *Remedia amoris*, all of which had a direct influence on the evolution of courtly love.

Because of his poetic infatuation with the real or imagined Laura, Petrarch was particularly attracted to Ovid's tale of the god Apollo's love for the nymph Daphne. The story—in which Apollo, the god of light, music, manly beauty, art, medicine, and the sun, becomes a victim on Mount Parnassus when Cupid's arrow enkindles his love, while Daphne, a lovely river nymph, is a victim of another of Cupid's arrows, which curbs love—fired Petrarch's imagination. Apollo's desire to possess the unresponsive and fleeing nymph leads the god to give her desperate chase, only to find that her prayer to her father, a river god, to assist her escape resulted in her transformation into a laurel tree. Whereupon Apollo declares the tree to be his personal symbol of extraordinary achievement, the laurel crown henceforth to be awarded to those who excel in the creative, civic, or martial arts—and whence Daphne came to mean "laurel" in Greek. By adopting the myth as his inspiration, Petrarch hoped to make his love for Laura in his lyrics also reflect his almost lifelong desire for the glory of the laurel crown in poetry, thereby equating the drama of Petrarch and Laura with that of Apollo and Daphne (Bernardo, "Crux" and "Laura").

In keeping with the tradition of courtly love, Petrarch at a certain point in his life considered collecting his scattered poems into a carefully ordered collection. Although he had been writing love poems as early as 1327, it was not until between 1342 and 1347 (the year before Laura's presumed death from the plague) that he started selecting from his worksheets several lyrics written between 1336 and 1341. From the very inception of the collection, Petrarch projects an image of Laura that increases in ambiguity as the collection grows and eventually becomes a kind of labyrinth that causes the image to become almost evanescent. It is possible, nevertheless, to sense even in the opening of the collection's final form the basic qualities with which Petrarch wished to endow his image of Laura.

In the very first sonnet the poet apologizes for having spent so many years in pursuit of an earthly love. The second sonnet relates the many battles the poet had to wage in trying to avoid becoming, like Apollo, a victim of Cupid's arrows. In the third sonnet we learn that Petrarch's defeat at the hands of Cupid was the result of his being defenseless on first meeting Laura, since all his attention was concentrated on observing Good Friday. The fourth sonnet suggests a similarity between God's Son coming to earth in the humble setting of Judea rather than Rome and the humble birth of Laura. The fifth identifies Laura by name and establishes a clear connection among Apollo, Daphne, Laura, and the laurel crown of poets. The sixth poem reinforces the connection to Apollo by describing the poet's futile pursuit of his ladylove that ends at the "lauro onde si coglie / acerbo frutto" 'laurel where one picks a bitter fruit' (lines 12–13).[5] Endowing the Laura image early on with both classical and Christian overtones sets the stage for the remainder of the collection.

But perhaps the clearest way to see the evolution of Laura into a poetic icon is to examine, all too briefly, the various stages undergone by the collection as Petrarch throughout his life painstakingly organized it into its final form. The fascinating account of how and why the poet added or subtracted poems as the collection grew may be found in *The Making of the* Canzoniere *and Other Petrarchan Studies*, by the eminent American Petrarch scholar Ernest H. Wilkins, who in 1951 first succeeded in identifying nine stages of the collection. Through careful analysis of the actual worksheets, with their marginal notation and other markings, used by Petrarch, Wilkins identified fourteen poems as forming the nucleus of the first form. These included poems 34–36, 41–46, 49, 58, 60, 64, and 69, with 34 ("Apollo s'anchor vive il bel desio" 'Apollo, if the sweet desire is still alive') opening the collection (Wilkins, *Making*, ch. 11). In its embryonic form the collection thus opens with the name of Apollo, invoking him as the god of light and pleading that he clear the stormy atmosphere of the inclemency that is harmful to the laurel tree. From there follow poems 41–43, which describe the near-apocalyptic effects that result when the laurel is not in its natural state. Poem 45 shows how the elements are disturbed when Apollo fails to recognize that Laura is Daphne. In 44 Laura's image of a pitiless lady is built on a comparison with traits possessed by the Emperor Caesar and the biblical David, whereas 45 and 46 reflect echoes of the myth of Narcissus, and 49 contains an indirect allusion to the effects of Medusa. In 60 and 64 we find an intensification of the poet's involvement with the Laura-laurel motif. Poem 60 speaks of the way the laurel tree (Laura) had originally inspired him, but as time passed had become "obdurate" to the point of his wishing to see it wither. In 64 the poet expresses his conviction that his heart is the natural habitat for the laurel.

In the very first form of the collection, Laura's image is projected against a complex background of classical mythology and history, reflecting a wide spectrum of meaning symbolized primarily by the drama of Apollo and Daphne. Petrarch's initial concept of Laura was thus impregnated with what one scholar called "un'ebrezza pagana e apollinea" 'a pagan and Apollonian rapture' (Calcaterra 8; my trans.), while his songs to Laura were but reflections of his unceasing aspiration to achieve all that the laurel stood for since Greek and Roman times, or, perhaps better, since Apollo's proclamation of what the laurel would symbolize in Daphne's stead (Calcaterra, chs. 2–4; Wilkins, *Making*, ch. 2).

With the second form of the *Canzoniere* Petrarch starts adding an elaborate Christian framework to his love theme, dividing the collection into two parts, each introduced by a poem evaluating the effects of the love of Laura on the poet's moral and religious well-being. As Wilkins shows, in this second form what is now known as poem 1 opened part 1, and poem 264 opened part 2. Both poems were written in 1347, the year before the deadly plague of 1348. This division gives credence to the common knowledge that between 1335 and 1342 Petrarch underwent a spiritual crisis resulting from a more intimate acquaintance with the church fathers, especially Saint Augustine. This may be seen in the types of works he wrote between 1342 and 1348 in which he apparently sought answers to the crisis: the *Secretum*, the *De viris illustribus*, the *Africa*, and the *Rerum memorandarum libri*, all with classical overtones, and the *Psalmi penitentiales*, the *De otio religioso*, and the *De vita solitaria*, with clearly religious tones. Thus the two poems (1 and 264) opening the two parts of the collection reflect the same crisis, poem 1 describing the collection as a series of vain experiences that the poet now recants (in retrospect), and poem 264 defining the recantation as practically impossible. Laura's image thus becomes even more complex as the poet makes us feel both its serious dangers and its inescapable fascination and appeal.

Beginning with the third form, the *Canzoniere* begins to assume its official shape as a collection. Started in 1356 at the request of the ruler Azzo da Correggio and completed in 1357–58, it contained about 170 poems and retained the division into two parts, the first containing about 142 poems, the second about 29 poems (Bernardo, *Petrarch, Laura* 291; Wilkins, *Making* 153). By placing Laura's death in the year of the plague, 1348, Petrarch was inspired by a new image of Laura. As one critic put it, Laura underwent a spiritual transformation, from a pagan Daphne who inspired the poet to sing of a human love and beauty in pursuit of the laurel crown to a guide to the Christian heaven in the tradition of Dante (Calcaterra 14–17). In poem 142, which closes this form, we find evidence of this transformation. Like the collection itself, the first part of this poem analyzes the poet's lifelong relationship with the desired laurel and his devotion to the "belle frondi" 'beautiful leaves,' reflecting the effects wrought on him by the Daphnean Laura. The second part describes how age and the passage of time are beginning to teach him another road to heaven, one that offers true fruit, not just "fior et frondi" 'flowers and leaves.' He now seeks "Altr'amor, altre frondi et altro lume, / . . . et altri rami" 'Another love, other leaves, and another light . . . and other branches' (lines 37–39), implying a clear turning away from the Laura-laurel image and toward the Christian God and Christian heaven that are significantly described in terms of "frondi" and "rami." Although this description reflects a blurring of the original Laura image, it does not indicate its abandonment.

The clearest analysis of the Christian superstructure that seemed to pervade Petrarch's thinking at this time may be found in chapter 7 of Carlo Calcaterra's *Nella selva del Petrarca*. There Calcaterra shows that just as Petrarch had tied his love for the live Laura to the classical account of Apollo and Daphne, so he now ties the dead Laura to the passion of Christ by setting his first meeting with her on a Good Friday that fell on 6 April and her death ten years later on an Easter Sunday that fell on the same date. With painstaking research, Calcaterra also shows how for Petrarch the date of 6 April (*feria sexta aprilis*) represented the true day of Christ's crucifixion, regardless of the movable occurrence of Good Friday. The date was also traditionally associated with the day on which man was created and Adam sinned. What is more, Petrarch linked the date with other important events in his life, such as the start of his attempted epic, the *Africa*, and his coronation on the Capitoline Hill on Easter Sunday 1341 in the presence of the entire Roman Senate. By then placing the date of Laura's death on an Easter Sunday, he was consciously making a connection with the Christian drama of the redemption and implying Laura's enjoyment of divine grace and her resurrection in Christ. This enabled him to sing of 6 April as marking his liberation from earthly passion and his preparation for a resurrection in Christ. In short, Laura had captured him on the day of Christ's passion and had freed him on the day of the Resurrection. His love of Laura could thus be viewed as both a Parnassus and a Calvary.[6]

In the fourth form we find poems that reflect a distinct attempt to redefine Laura as both a beautiful lady and a heavenly guide (294–303). In lamenting Laura's death, the poet describes the great loss that had been suffered not only by him but by the entire world now that it has become clear that her beauty is inextricably fused with her great virtues. In 302 we see Laura taking the poet by the hand in the heaven of Venus and explaining how her only desires are his presence and the return of her body. This encounter is reminiscent of Dante, yet different in that Laura seems to have retained her humanity, as the poet realizes that she had resisted him on earth for his own good ([Zingarelli] 1324n). While Laura is obviously not completely humanized, the theme of the guide to a heaven where human qualities are not looked on disparagingly is clearly present.

With the fifth form it becomes clear that Petrarch intended to divide the collection into two distinct parts, the first containing poems pertaining to a live Laura, the second (except for the three introductory poems) to a dead Laura. The fusion of the two is now reflected in poem 318, in the depiction of Laura as a new laurel with its roots firmly implanted in the poet's heart. She has become part of his very being and an internal rather than an external stimulus—a real spirit rather than flesh. Yet the new image still partakes of classical as well as Christian elements. Although the dead Laura now enjoys the eternal sight of the Christian God, in 228 she has left behind echoes of human ideals and aspirations that had marked her while still alive: "fama, honor, et vertude et leggiadria, / casta bellezza in habito celeste" 'fame, honor, and virtue and charm, chaste beauty in celestial habit' (lines 9–10). The subsequent four poems continue this desperate attempt to fuse the classical and the Christian Laura as the poet continues adding poems to both parts.

It is in the seventh form that we sense the start of the end of the poet's long journey toward an image of the beloved pictured as both earthly and eternal. In poem 351 Laura is defined as "fior di vertú, fontana di bellezza" 'flower of virtue, fountain of beauty' and assumes a greater complexity with such phrases as "casto amore" and "somma cortesia, sovrana honestate" 'chaste love, highest courtesy, highest chastity' (lines 7, 2, 6). In 353 (originally 365), however, we find the poet succumbing to a grief greater than that of a nightingale's at the realization that Laura is dead. The poem reflects the darkness of hopelessness. But with the series 351–53, which was originally intended to precede 366 (the final poem added in the sixth form), we find a new light and a new hope appear.

Although it had become clear to the poet that the mortal Laura must be abandoned, he sees a way to save her immortal qualities without breaking all ties with the human. A lady had once existed who not only possessed all Laura's qualities but had done for mankind what the poet felt Laura had done for him: provided the link between the human and the divine. As the mother of God, Mary was the epitome of human potentiality and the inspiration for a new and final song that characterizes her as "bella . . . saggia . . . pura . . . gloriosa" 'beautiful . . . wise . . . pure . . . glorious' and finally as "stabile in eterno . . . humana . . . unica et sola" 'stable for eternity . . . kindly . . . single, sole.' She alone can end his grief over his attachment to "poca mortal terra caduca" 'a bit of deciduous mortal dust' by recommending him to her Son, "verace / Homo et verace Dio" 'true man and true God.' After all, it had been on the very day of her Son's passion and death that Petrarch had started along the path of a love that had ultimately taught him where true salvation lies. It was the Virgin who had really made it possible for man, and hence for Laura and her lover, to regain paradise lost. She possessed the epitome of those very qualities that the poet had worshipped in Laura: beauty, purity, goodness, and eternal glory. It is furthermore interesting to note that the opening verses of the poem depict the Virgin as reflecting the image of a lovely lady whose dazzling beauty had so appealed to the sun that it now shares this brilliance with her. This opening seems to echo once again the drama of Daphne and Apollo (the god of the sun), who in poem 188 and elsewhere is depicted as "Almo Sol" 'Life-giving sun,' who first loved the (laurel) branches that the poet alone now loves. By equating the Virgin with Laura and the sun (God) with the drama of Apollo and Daphne, the poet seems successfully to fuse the mortal and immortal Laura who had inspired him to pursue both the laurel crown (glory) and Christian salvation.

To achieve this transformation, however, Petrarch toward the end of his life had to juggle at some length the order of the last thirty poems of the collection (Bernardo, *Petrarch, Laura* 60–63). Although he desired to end the collection with an impressive religious climax by introducing a tone of repentance through the reordering of the last thirty poems, one can also detect a wavering as to whether it was necessary to turn his back on his beloved Laura in order to turn to God. The reordering of the last thirty poems reflects the same indecision and wavering seen in the manner in which the poet added poems to the two parts throughout his life. These mirrored the poet's changing perspective of his beloved and his moral dilemma in the face of his unrequited love: Laura as myth representative of the loftiest human ideals constantly balanced by Laura as living Christian witness for man, a perspective visible only to the man endowed with the necessary vision to perceive it. Petrarch's inability or unwillingness to grasp why the myth was dangerous and should have been discarded leaves the reader with the impression that Petrarch's book of songs has no real closure and reflects a yearly cycle of 366 days constantly repeating the poet's love dilemma in the manner of a diary reporting an endless love firmly implanted in classical and Christian roots.[7]

NOTES

[1] For details concerning the life and times of Petrarch, Dante, and Boccaccio, see Wilkins, *Life* and *History*; Bishop, *Petrarch*; Bergin, *Petrarch* and *Dante*; Branca, *Boccaccio*.

[2] For an analysis of Petrarch's *I trionfi*, see Bernardo, *Petrarch, Laura*; for distinctions among Dante's *Vita nuova*, Boccaccio's *Fiammetta*, and Petrarch's *I trionfi*, see Bernardo, "Dante."

[3] For a listing of all Petrarch's works, see Wilkins, *Making* xiii–xvii. For a listing of English translations of Petrarch's works, see Durling, *Petrarch's Lyric Poems* 638–41.

[4] See Boase and Bornstein; Barney; and Beer. For an extended study of the allegorical tradition in the Middle Ages, see Lewis, *Allegory*. For an overview of the main stylistic and thematic ingredients constituting the *Canzoniere*, see Durling, *Petrarch's Lyric Poems* 1–3. For an interesting example of Petrarch's use of allegory in one of his letters, see Durling, "Ascent."

[5] Citations from the *Canzoniere* in this essay follow Zingarelli's edition and Durling's translation.

[6] In his 1974 study "The Calendrical Structure of Petrarch's *Canzoniere*," Roche gives further evidence of the degree to which a Christian superstructure can be seen as pervading the *Canzoniere*, showing how the placement of poems reflects significant holidays of the Christian calendar.

[7] Further development of the image may be found in Petrarch's prose letters, letters in verse, *Coronation Oration*, *Secretum*, and *Bucolicum Carmen*; see Bernardo, *Petrarch, Laura*, chs. 3–4. Different interpretations of the role played by the laurel tree in Petrarch's poetry may be found in Freccero, "Fig Tree," and Durling, "Petrarch's 'Giovene donna.'" For interpretations by Italian critics of the Petrarch-Laura-Apollo theme, see Bernardo, *Petrarch, Laura* 1–25.

Petrarch's Lyric Poetry: Prosody, Rhymes, Forms

Christopher Kleinhenz

Petrarch's name has become virtually synonymous with the art of poetry, with stylistic excellence, and with the Italian sonnet, often termed the Petrarchan sonnet.[1] Just as we may easily understand, in retrospect, how these identifications were made, we should also note that Petrarch's poetic brilliance has blinded many students and scholars to the fact that the Romance lyric tradition in which he is a major luminary had, by his day, been in existence for some two centuries and was certainly not lacking in great and innovative poets. This is not the place for discussion of the pre-Petrarchan tradition, except to note its existence and its impact on Petrarch, who drew amply from this rich store of poetic materials. Petrarch acknowledges his literary predecessors, as, for example, in the "Trionfo d'Amore" ("Triumph of Love," lines 31–57), where the narrator views those souls conquered by love, naming in the long procession numerous poets from previous epochs: Dante, Cino da Pistoia, Guido Guinizzelli and Guido Cavalcanti, Arnaut Daniel, Folquet de Marseilles, and Jaufré Rudel, among others. By mentioning the names of the major love poets in the Romance tradition, Petrarch is able to trace, in broad strokes, the rise and development of the lyric tradition from its origins in Provence to his Italian contemporaries, Sennuccio del Bene and Franceschino degli Albizzi.

Petrarch also pays homage to his lyrical forebears in poem 70 of the *Rerum vulgarium fragmenta* (the *Canzoniere*)—the canzone "Lasso me, ch'i' non so in qual parte pieghi"[2]—where, in the final verse of the first four strophes, he incorporates the incipit of four earlier and well-known canzoni by Arnaut ("Drez et rayson es qu'ieu ciant e 'm demori" [line 10]), Cavalcanti ("Donna mi priegha, per ch'io voglio dire" [line 20]), Dante ("Così nel mio parlar voglio esser aspro" [line 30]), and Cino ("La dolce vista e 'l bel guardo soave" [line 40]). And we should not be surprised to find that, in the fifth strophe, the last poem cited in the sequence is one of his own from the *Canzoniere*—"Nel dolce tempo de la prima etade" (23)—and this is the final verse of the poem (line 50). Even while acknowledging the achievements of other poets, Petrarch succeeds in having the last word. In many ways, he sees himself as both the last in the long line of love poets and the first in the new lyric tradition that he was forging.

This essay serves as an introduction to Italian prosody through examples drawn from Petrarch's lyrics, thus providing instructors with the guidance necessary for a technically oriented discussion of his poetry.[3] It is divided into three sections, the first dealing with meters, the second with rhymes and rhyming techniques, and the third with poetic forms. But first some background on these topics is necessary.

Although versification in the Italian vernacular began in the late twelfth and early thirteenth centuries,[4] it was only with the lyrics of the Sicilian school that we see the rules of prosody being applied regularly, and in the products of these practitioners of the poetic art we may observe the beginnings of the Italian literary tradition. The written rules of versification and prosody appear around the turn of the fourteenth century, and the first and most important author to leave us his thoughts on the subject is Dante Alighieri.[5] In his incomplete work *De vulgari eloquentia*, Dante has two major goals: to identify which dialect would best serve as a sort of national literary language for Italy and, once the characteristics of this language are determined, to answer the question of how it should be used in poetry. This language would be, according to Dante, "illustre, cardinale, aulicum, et curiale" 'illustrious, cardinal, courtly, and curial' (1.17.1; my trans.), and it would be the proper medium for refined lyric poetry written on the three subjects worthy of treatment in the high or tragic style: prowess in arms (*salus*), love (*venus*), and virtue (*virtus*) (2.2.7). From the poets whom Dante cites in his treatise, we may observe the rich variety—in form and content—that characterized the first century of Italian literature.

Lyric poetry in Italy was initially based on earlier metrical forms, such as the canzone, from the Occitan *canso*; sestina, from the Occitan *coblas retrogradadas*; *tenzone*, from the Occitan *tenso*, although in Italy the sonnet was incorporated as the basic strophic unit; and *discordo*, from the Occitan *descort*.[6] Some popular forms were indigenous to Italy—*strambotto*, *ballata*—while others came into being as new artistic inventions, such as the sonnet and madrigal. Polyphonic music in France and Italy (the *ars nova*) influenced the development of the *caccia* and the refinement of the madrigal.

In *De vulgari eloquentia* Dante devotes the second of a projected four books to the art of the canzone, which is, in his view, the most noble poetic form, the best vehicle for treatment in the high, tragic style of the three most worthy topics. The other two major forms—the *ballata* and sonnet—are described as more appropriate to the "middle" style of poetry (2.4.1) and were to be discussed in the two final books of the treatise; these books, if they were ever composed, have not survived. Imitating the troubadour Arnaut, Dante composed the first sestina in Italian. Other lyric forms—such as the madrigal, *caccia*, and *frottola*—made their appearance only in the fourteenth century.

Italian Prosody

Early Italian poetry imitated the themes and forms of the earlier Occitan and Old French traditions, and medieval Latin rhythmical verse exerted a strong formal influence on all the nascent vernacular lyrics. Italian metrics are based both on the number of syllables and on the position of the major accent in the verse, and of these two the placement of the major stress is the determining factor in the definition of the various meters.

The hendecasyllable (*endecasillabo*),[7] by all standards the most excellent of meters, is determined not by the number of syllables in the line, which would normally be eleven, but by the occurrence of the major stress (`) on the tenth syllable. Further, the *endecasillabo* is composed of two hemistichs of uneven length, a septenary (*settenario*, determined by the major stress – ´ – on the sixth syllable) and a quinary (*quinario*, determined by the major stress – ´ – on the fourth syllable). The manner of division in the verse has also given rise to the distinction between an *endecasillabo a maiore*, where the septenary precedes:

e del mio va-neg-**giár** ver-go-gna_'l **frùt**-to
1 2 3 4 5 **6** 7 8 9 **10** 11
(Petrarch, *Canzoniere* 1.12)

and an *endecasillabo a minore*, where the quinary precedes:

in sul mio **prí**-mo gio-ve-ni-le_er-**rò**-re
1 2 3 **4** 5 6 7 8 9 **10** 11
(1.3)

Given that the position of the accent determines the nomenclature, a hendecasyllable can have as few as ten syllables (*endecasillabo tronco*):[8]

quan-do pos-so, mi spe-tro_e sol mi **sto**
1 2 3 4 5 6 7 8 9 **10**
(105.19)

Or it can have as many as twelve (*endecasillabo sdrucciolo*), with the understanding that the primary stress in the line is always on the tenth syllable:

mi veg-gio_an-dár ver la sta-gion con-**trà**-ri-a
1 2 3 4 5 6 7 8 9 **10** 11 12
(168.10)

Sometimes, to achieve the proper scansion of a verse, contiguous vowels must be elided to form a single syllable. Thus, to obtain the correct number of syllables, poets and readers alike must employ synaloepha (i.e., the vowels are elided between words):

ma ben veg-**gio_or** sì có-m**e_al** po-pol tùt-to
1 2 3 **4** 5 6 7 8 9 10 11
(1.9)

or syneresis (i.e., the vowels are elided within a single word):

del va-**rio** stí-le_in ch'**io** pian-go_e ra-giò-no
1 2 **3** 4 5 6 7 8 9 10 11
(1.5)

On other occasions contiguous vowels must be pronounced separately as individual syllables in order for the verse to scan, whether using dialoepha (i.e., the vowels occur between words):

a **voi ar**-ma-ta non mo-strar pur l'ar-co
1 2 3 4 5 6 7 8 9 10 11
(3.14)

or diaeresis (i.e., the vowels occur within a single word, and the first vowel is marked with raised dots [¨]):

al ve-ra-ce_o-r**ï**-**e**n-te,_o-v'_el-la_è vol-ta
1 2 3 4 **5** **6** 7 8 9 10 11
(28.15)

The septenary is the second most popular meter among thirteenth- and fourteenth-century poets. Petrarch's canzone "Chiare, fresche e dolci acque" (126) is composed of a mixture of septenaries and hendecasyllables:

Chia-re, fre-sche_e dol-**ci_àc**-que
1 2 3 4 5 **6** 7
(line 1)

In this same composition we find an example of a *settenario sdrucciolo*:

dol-ce ne la me-**mò**-ri-a
1 2 3 4 5 **6** 7 8
(line 41)

In *De vulgari eloquentia* Dante indicates that verses with an odd number of syllables are preferred by the early poets, and we find examples of verses with nine (*novenario*, determined by the major stress on the eighth syllable), five (*quinario*, accent on the fourth), and three (*trisillabo*, accent on the second) syllables in the earlier lyric tradition. Of these shorter meters, Petrarch infrequently uses only the *quinario* and then only for internal rhymes, as, for example in the concluding poem of the *Canzoniere*, "Vergine bella":

che scon-si-**gliá**-to — a te vèn per con-sì-glio
1 2 3 **4** 5 6 7 8 9 10 11
(366.26)[9]

He also does so in canzone 135, "Qual più diversa e nova":

ma più nel **tém**-po — che ma-don-na vì-di
1 2 3 **4** 5 6 7 8 9 10 11
(line 90)

Rhyme, Rhyming Techniques, and Rhyme Schemes

In the Italian language, rhymes are exact, and, to rhyme, words must be identical from the major stress to the end of the word. Designations of rhymes and their meters follow the terminology given to individual words depending on whether the stress is on the penultimate syllable (a *parola piana*, e.g., *dolòre* / *amòre* [1.6–7]). Thus an *endecasillabo piano* would conclude with a *parola piana*, as in virtually all of Petrarch's verses.

Early Italian lyric poets incorporated a number of rhyming techniques. In derivative rhyme (*replicatio*) the words have the same etymon (e.g., *piace* / *dispiace* [21.3, 7]). In rich rhyme (*rima ricca* or *rima cara*) unusual word forms are used instead of their more common ones, such as *cibo* / *bibo* ("bevo") / *describo* ("scrivo") / *delibo* (193.1, 4, 5, 8). In equivocal rhyme (*traductio*) the word appears to be the same, but the meaning changes from verse to verse (e.g., *passo* ["step"] / *passo* ["I pass"], as presented in Giacomo da Lentini's sonnet "Lo giglio quand' è colto"). In Petrarch's *Canzoniere* we find a few examples of this verbal play: *amo* ("I love") and *amo* ("hook") (*Canzoniere* 257.4–5); *sole* ("alone") and *sole* ("sun") (222.1, 5); and *legge* ("law") and *legge* ("reads") (222.9, 12). The sonnet "Quand'io son tutto vòlto in quella parte" (18) provides a good example of this poetic practice, in the sense that all the rhyme words—*parte*, *luce*, *morte*, *desio*, *sole*—are either equivocal or identical:

Quand'io son tutto vòlto in quella parte
ove 'l bel viso di madonna luce,
et m'è rimasa nel pensier la luce
che m'arde et strugge dentro a parte a parte,
i' che temo del cor che mi si parte,
et veggio presso il fin de la mia luce,
vommene in guisa d'orbo, senza luce,
che non sa ove si vada et pur si parte.
Cosí davanti ai colpi de la morte
fuggo: ma non sí ratto che 'l desio
meco non venga come venir sòle.
Tacito vo, ché le parole morte
farian pianger la gente; et i' desio
che le lagrime mie si spargan sole.

Only two poetic forms are fixed:[10] *terza rima* (*rima incatenata*), which Dante invented for the *Comedy*[11]—ABA BCB CDC DED—and the sestina, discussed below. All other poetic forms have multiple possibilities for their rhyme schemes, as well as the number of verses in the strophes and the number of strophes in the poem. A couplet—AA—is termed *rima baciata*, while an alternating pattern is *rima alterna*: ABABAB. Other varieties of patterns are inverted rhyme (*rima invertita*)—CDE EDC—and *rima incrociata* (or *rima abbracciata*)—ABBA; CDC CDC.

Poetic Forms

The Canzone

Lyric and narrative poetry integrate all the disparate elements noted above into a poetic whole, a unified metrical structure with particular verse forms and rules. In Italy the development of the canzone, which Dante considered the most noble poetic form, was influenced by the Occitan *canso*, the Old French *chanson*, and the German *Minnesang*. Petrarch included twenty-nine canzoni in the *Canzoniere*, and they are among his finest compositions. The following stanza from Petrarch's canzone "Vergine bella, che di sol vestita" (366) will serve as the basis for discussing the strophic structure of the canzone:

fronte	*first piede*	Vergine bella, che di sol vestita,
		coronata di stelle, al sommo Sole
		piacesti sí, che 'n te Sua luce ascose,
	second piede	amor mi spinge a dir di te parole:
		ma non so 'ncominciar senza tu' aita,
		et di Colui ch'amando in te si pose.
sirma		Invoco lei che ben sempre rispose,
		chi la chiamò con fede:
		Vergine, s'a mercede
		miseria extrema de l'humane cose
		già mai ti volse, al mio prego t'inchina,
		soccorri a la mia guerra,
		ben ch'i' sia terra, et tu del ciel regina.

The rhyme scheme of the thirteen-verse strophe is ABC BAC CddCEf(f_5)E. The standard practice for indicating rhyme scheme is to use capital letters for hendecasyllables and lowercase letters for septenaries; all other meters are identified with lowercase letters plus a subscript number to indicate its meter. In this poem, for example, the last verse's internal rhyme—f, a *quinario*—is indicated as follows: (f_5). Thus this strophe is composed of ten hendecasyllables, three septenaries, and a final *quinario* as an internal rhyme (always designated by parentheses). The basic division of most canzone strophes is bipartite, into *fronte* and *sirma*. In this example the *fronte* divides into two identical *piedi* ("feet") of three verses each—ABC BAC—and the seven-line *sirma* is undivided: CddCEf(f_5)E.[12] The passage from *fronte* to *sirma* also marks the change from one musical pattern to another, and this moment of transition is called the *diesis*, which refers both to the changeover and often to the first verse in the *sirma* that introduces the new harmony. Here the transition is effected through the repetition of rhyme C: *-ose* (*pose / rispose*).

Petrarch's canzoni usually have between five and seven strophes, all following the same rhyme scheme. Most of his canzoni are composed of *coblas singulars*, which means that each strophe has its own rhymes, unlike the very popular *coblas unissonans* in the Occitan tradition, in which the same rhymes occur in every strophe (see, e.g., poem 29 in the *Canzoniere*, "Verdi panni sanguigni, oscuri o persi").[13] Following another Occitan model, Petrarch engages in a poetic tour de force in poem 206, "S'i' 'l dissi mai, ch'i' vegna in odio a quella," which is based on just three rhymes—A (*-ella*); B (*-ei*); C (*-ìa*)—and incorporates the strophic structure of *coblas doblas*, by which the canzone proceeds by twos, with the first two strophes rhyming, then the next two, and so on. The strophic structure of this canzone is as follows: ABBA AcccA ABBA AcccA, BCCB BaaaB BCCB BaaaB, CAAC CbbbC CAAC CbbbC, and the rhyme scheme of the envoi is CbbA(a_5)C.

Sometimes, again following Occitan models, a canzone will conclude with an envoi (also called the *congedo*, *commiato*, or *tornada*),[14] which is metrically identical to the *sirma* or to a part of it (e.g., in the *Canzoniere*, the three-line envoi [71–73, 125, 126, 270, and 323] and the two-line envoi [29]).[15] In the envoi the poet often addresses the poetic composition and gives it specific advice or instructions (where it should go, with whom it should speak, what it should say, etc.), as we may see in 128:

Canzone, io t'ammonisco
che tua ragion cortesemente dica,
perché fra gente altera ir ti convene,
et le voglie son piene
già de l'usanza pessima et antica,
del ver sempre nemica.
Proverai tua ventura
fra' magnanimi pochi a chi 'l ben piace.
Di' lor: "Chi m'assicura?
I' vo gridando: Pace, pace, pace."

The Sestina

The troubadour Arnaut Daniel invented the sestina, and, in imitation of Arnaut, Dante introduced this particular type of canzone into Italian literature. Also known by the descriptive phrase *retrogradatio cruciata* (which refers to how the rhymes "cross over" first from the end and then from the beginning of the stanza), the sestina has six stanzas of six verses each plus a three-line envoi. In technical terms, the sestina is a tour de force, for the same six rhyme words are used throughout the poem, and the rhyme scheme follows a rigid permutation, whereby, at the end of the six stanzas, the pattern is ready to repeat itself. Unlike a standard canzone, the sestina has no division within the stanza between *fronte* and *sirma*. Petrarch wrote nine sestine in the *Canzoniere*;[16] "Giovene donna sotto un verde lauro" (30) demonstrates the intricate set of changes the rhymes follow over the course of the composition. The six rhymes—A (*lauro*); B (*neve*); C (*anni*); D (*chiome*); E (*occhi*); F (*riva*)—are ordered according to the following pattern:

stanza 1	stanza 2	stanza 3	stanza 4	stanza 5	stanza 6
1 A	6 F	3 C	5 E	4 D	2 B
2 B	1 A	6 F	3 C	5 E	4 D
3 C	5 E	4 D	2 B	1 A	6 F
4 D	2 B	1 A	6 F	3 C	5 E
5 E	4 D	2 B	1 A	6 F	3 C
6 F	3 C	5 E	4 D	2 B	1 A

The envoi of the sestina uses all six rhymes, two per verse, but not necessarily according to any strict pattern. Petrarch also invented the double sestina (e.g., "Mia benigna fortuna e 'l viver lieto" [332]), in which the permutations run through twelve six-line stanzas, instead of six, plus a three-verse envoi.

The *Ballata*

The distinctly Italian *ballata* (also called *canzone a ballo*) had its origin in the mid–thirteenth century. As its name suggests, it was intended as a song to accompany a dance. Because of this poetically "impure" state, Dante placed it lower than the canzone in the hierarchy of poetic forms but higher than the sonnet, which he apparently did not consider a serious form because of its brevity. The metrical form of the *ballata* follows that of the canzone with two important exceptions: every *ballata* begins with a refrain (*ripresa* or *ritornello*), which in performance would be repeated after each stanza, and a link through rhyme always exists between the refrain and each stanza, through the repetition of one or more rhymes of the *ripresa* at the end of each stanza. Petrarch composed seven *ballate* in the *Canzoniere*, including 59, "Perché quel che mi trasse ad amar prima":

refrain		Perché quel che mi trasse ad amar prima, altrui colpa mi toglia, del mio fermo voler già non mi svoglia.
stanza 1	*first piede*	Tra le chiome de l'òr nascose il laccio, al qual mi strinse, Amore;
	second piede	et da' begli occhi mosse il freddo ghiaccio, che mi passò nel core,
	sirma (undivided)	con la vertú d'un súbito splendore,

		che d'ogni altra sua voglia sol rimembrando anchor l'anima spoglia.
stanza 2	*first piede*	Tolta m'è poi di que' biondi capelli, lasso, la dolce vista;
	second piede	e 'l volger de' duo lumi honesti et belli col suo fuggir m'atrista;
	sirma (undivided)	ma perché ben morendo honor s'acquista, per morte né per doglia non vo' che da tal nodo Amor mi scioglia.

The rhyme scheme of this refrain is YxX, and that of the stanza is Ab / Ab // BxX. Rhyme X (*-oglia*) is the link between refrain and strophe and provides the metrical and musical transition to the refrain, which would then be repeated. *Ballate* are several in kind, and their names are determined by the number of verses in the *ripresa*: a four-verse refrain indicates a *ballata grande*, a three-verse refrain is a *ballata mezzana* (the example given above), a two-verse refrain is a *ballata minore*, a one-verse refrain is a *ballata piccola* (a one-verse refrain with a meter shorter than an *endecasillabo* is termed a *ballata minima*), and a refrain with more than four verses makes the poem a *ballata stravagante*. Of Petrarch's seven *ballate* in the *Canzoniere*, four are *ballate grandi*, and three are *ballate mezzane*.

The Sonnet

The invention of the sonnet has been attributed, with good reason, to Giacomo da Lentini, a notary attached to the imperial court of Frederick II Hohenstaufen in Sicily.[17] Various attempts have been made to trace the origin of this fourteen-line composition: it may have resulted from the fusion of two *strambotti* (eight-line popular poems in *endecasillabi* in alternating rhyme with a curtailing of the second stanza to six verses); it may represent the attempt to achieve mathematical perfection in terms of Pythagorean harmonies; it may have resulted through imitation of the canzone strophe; or it may simply be the result of a felicitous inventive moment on Giacomo's part. Whatever the sonnet's origin, its basic fourteen-line form was fixed from the beginning as a bipartite composition consisting of an octave (or two quatrains) in alternating rhyme ABABABAB and a sestet (or two tercets) in a variety of schemes (CDCDCD and CDECDE are the most common), all hendecasyllables. Later on in the thirteenth century a new form for the octave was invented—ABBAABBA—and this became the preferred pattern. Numerous rhyme schemes were devised for the sestet—CDEEDC, CDCCDC, CDEDCE, and so on. What emerges is a sense of versatility and flexibility within the artificial restrictions of the fourteen-line composition. Indeed, this short metrical form provided a sort of proving ground for poets, who were eager to test their poetic abilities within these limits.

Early on, the sonnet became the vehicle for poetic correspondence in *tenzoni*, in which one poet would write a sonnet on a particular topic (generally on love but also on moral issues) and send it to another, requesting that poet's views on the subject. The addressee would then respond, generally *per le rime*, that is, using the same rhymes and rhyme scheme as those in the original sonnet.[18] A few of Petrarch's sonnets in the *Canzoniere* would appear to have been, originally, part of a *tenzone* or exchange of sonnets, such as "Geri, quando talor meco s'adira" (179), in which Petrarch responds to a sonnet by Geri de' Gianfigliazzi, as well as those sonnets addressed to Orso dell'Anguillara (27 and 98), to Pandolfo Malatesta (104), to Sennuccio del Bene (112–13), and to Stefano Colonna (10).

Despite the large number of formal transformations of the sonnet in the first century of its existence,[19] Petrarch used only the pure, fourteen-line form for the 317 sonnets in the *Canzoniere* and almost always the ABBA ABBA rhyme pattern for the quatrains;[20] the tercets display a variety of rhyme schemes: CDE CDE; CDC CDC; CDE DCE; CDC DCD; CDD DCC; CDE EDC; CDE DEC. A prime example of his expertise with the sonnet form is "Solo et pensoso i più deserti campi" (35), in which Petrarch speaks of the constant presence of love, even in the most solitary places (rhyme scheme ABBA ABBA CDE CDE):

> Solo e pensoso i più deserti campi
> vo mesurando a passi tardi e lenti,
> e gli occhi porto per fuggire intenti
> ove vestigio uman l'arena stampi.
>
> Altro schermo non trovo che mi scampi
> dal manifesto accorger de le genti;
> perché ne gli atti d'alegrezza spenti
> di fuor si legge com'io dentro avampi;
>
> sì ch'io mi credo omai che monti e piagge
> e fiumi e selve sappian di che tempre
> sia la mia vita, ch'è celata altrui.
>
> Ma pur sì aspre vie né si selvagge
> cercar non so ch'Amor non venga sempre
> ragionando con meco, et io co llui.

In another sonnet (134; rhyme scheme ABAB ABAB CDE CDE) Petrarch presents his anguished amorous state through a series of oxymorons, and this served as the model for centuries of imitations:

> Pace non trovo, e non ho da far guerra;
> e temo, e spero; et ardo, e son un ghiaccio;

e volo sopra 'l cielo, e giaccio in terra;
e nulla stringo, e tutto 'l mondo abbraccio.

Tal m'ha in pregion, che non m'apre né serra,
né per suo mi ritèn né scioglie il laccio;
e non m'ancide Amore, e non mi sferra,
né mi vuol vivo né mi trae impaccio.

Veggio senza occhi, e non ho lingua, e grido;
e bramo di perir, e cheggio aita;
et ho in odio me stesso, et amo altrui.

Pascomi di dolor, piangendo rido;
egualmente mi spiace morte e vita:
in questo stato son, donna, per vui.

Most critics agree that Petrarch's most important contribution to the lyric tradition lies in his great success with the sonnet form. His sonnets are praised for their precision, compactness, graceful symmetry, vibrant musicality, noble sentiments, and intimate tones. In the sonnet form Petrarch was able to capture the lyrical quality of his desires and aspirations, express his internal conflict between love and reason and his simultaneous quest for earthly glory and spiritual salvation, and compress the rhetorical intensity of moral and political invective. Indeed, in the crystallization of the sonnet form and the concomitant thematic elevation and stylistic refinement in the lyrics of Petrarch we may note the origin of and motive behind the literary current known as Petrarchism, which spread throughout Europe in the Renaissance.

The Madrigal

The fourteenth century witnessed the birth and development of other lyrical forms, among them the madrigal, the *caccia*, and the *frottola*. Perhaps modeled on the strophe of the *ballata*, the madrigal usually consists of two three-line *piedi* based on three or four rhymes and a final rhymed couplet (or two), all in hendecasyllabic meter. Petrarch wrote four madrigals in the *Canzoniere*; the first is 52:

Non al suo amante più Dïana piacque,
quando per tal ventura tutta ignuda
la vide in mezzo de le gelide acque,

ch'a me la pastorella alpestra et cruda
posta a bagnar un leggiadretto velo,
ch'a l'aura il vago e biondo capel chiuda,

tal che mi fece, or quand'egli arde 'l cielo,
tutto tremar d'un amoroso gielo.

The rhyme scheme begins as *terza rima* and concludes with a rhymed couplet: ABA BCB CC. The rhyme schemes of Petrarch's other madrigals are as follows: ABA CBC DED E (54, "Per ch' al viso d'Amor portava insegna"); ABC ABC DD (106, "Nova angeletta sovra l'ale accorta"); and ABB ACC CDD (121, "Or vedi, Amor, che giovenetta donna").

As the foremost lyric poet of the fourteenth century, Petrarch demonstrated his talents and versatility and became for all practical purposes one of the most influential literary geniuses who ever lived. His impact on the subsequent lyric tradition was profound and wide-ranging, both temporally and spatially. Most of his imitators knew his poetry in its original shape, and thus, to teach the works of Petrarch and the Petrarchists, we should be able to navigate to some degree these same linguistic and cultural waters.

NOTES

[1] This is perhaps a misnomer, for, during the period of its origins (the early thirteenth century), the sonnet possessed certain formal and thematic characteristics that anticipate its subsequent development in Italy: diversity of subject matter, formal and thematic divisions within the structure, and general artistic sophistication. Indeed, the excellence of the Petrarchan sonnet may be viewed, in large part, as the fulfillment of those elements that were present in the sonnet ever since its invention.

[2] I follow Santagata's edition of the *Canzoniere* for all the examples given in the text.

[3] On Petrarch's metrics, see Praloran; Pulsoni; Soldani; and Zenari.

[4] The earliest examples are the *Ritmo Laurenziano*, the *Ritmo su Sant'Alessio*, the *Ritmo Cassinese*, and the famous canticle of Saint Francis of Assisi (*Cantico delle Creature* or *Laudes Creaturarum*). In all these works we recognize the attempt to write poetry according to certain metrical principles, but the poems do not, generally, reflect strict adherence to rules of rhyme and rhythm, for their metrical structure lacks uniformity.

[5] Other early metrical treatises are Francesco da Barberino's *Documenti d'amore*, Antonio da Tempo's *Summa artis rithimici vulgaris dictaminis*, and Gidino da Sommacampagna's *Trattato dei ritmi volgari*.

[6] These terms are derived from Occitan primarily but also from Old French and Middle High German. Much of the terminology used to describe early lyrical forms and metrical techniques is drawn directly from Occitan, formerly called Old Provençal, since that was the language of the first troubadours. In the early Italian lyric tradition, poets often imitated certain structural techniques from their Occitan predecessors. For example, it was common among the troubadours and, to a lesser degree, the early Italian poets—but not in the lyrics of Petrarch—to have a *canso* in which the rhymes of all the strophes are the same (*canso unissonans*; see, in Petrarch's *Canzoniere*, poem 29, "Verdi panni sanguigni, oscuri o persi") or in which the strophes were joined through *coblas capfinidas* (the joining of two strophes through repetition of a word or phrase from the last line of the preceding strophe in the first line of the following strophe) or *coblas capcaudadas* (the linking of two strophes through repetition of the rhyme of the preceding strophe as the initial rhyme of the subsequent strophe).

[7] Most scholars trace the origin of the hendecasyllable to the decasyllable of Old French and Occitan.

[8] This terminology follows that used to indicate the position of stress in words, i.e., oxytone (*parola tronca*), paroxytone (*parola piana*), and proparoxytone (*parola sdrucciola*). These rhyme words—*sto* and its mate, *no* (line 1)—are the only examples of *versi tronchi* in Petrarch's poetry.

[9] In Italian poetry internal rhymes are indicated either with a long dash or with an extended space between the internal rhyme and the following word, thus:

che sconsigliato — a te vèn per consiglio

or

che sconsigliato   a te vèn per consiglio.

[10] One popular meter, the eight-line *strambotto*, admits to two basic forms that are designated according to the presumed place of origin: the so-called *ottava siciliana*, with the rhyme scheme ABABABAB, and the *ottava toscana* (or *ottava rima*), ABABABCC.

[11] Following Dante's great model, poets composed didactic, allegorical poetry—dream visions and the like—in *terza rima*. Petrarch used *terza rima* for the *Trionfi*, Boccaccio for the *Amorosa visione*, and Fazio degli Uberti for *Il Dittamondo*.

[12] Sometimes, but never in Petrarch's poetry, the *sirma* is divided into two equal parts, or *volte*.

[13] In the early lyric tradition it was not uncommon to find the *cobbola* (*cobla* [Occitan "stanza"]), an isolated stanza of a canzone, which stands thematically and metrically on its own, following the Occitan tradition of *coblas esparsas* ("scattered strophes").

[14] Almost all of Petrarch's canzoni in the *Canzoniere* have an envoi, with the exception of 70 and 105.

[15] For example, Petrarch's canzone "Vergine bella" has the envoi CddCEf(f_5)E, which follows the rhyme scheme of the *sirma*, including the internal rhyme:

Il dí s'appressa, et non pòte esser lunge,
sí corre il tempo et vola,
Vergine unica et sola,
e 'l cor or coscïentia or morte punge.
Raccomandami al tuo figliuol, verace
homo et verace Dio,
ch'accolga 'l mïo spirto ultimo in pace.
(lines 131–37)

[16] For a study of the Petrarchan sestina, see Shapiro, *Hieroglyph*.

[17] For the history of the sonnet in Italy, see, among many others, Kleinhenz, *Early Italian Sonnet* and "Petrarch"; Santagata, *Dal sonetto*; and Wilkins, "*Invention*."

[18] In addition to this epistolary use, the sonnet became the basic strophic unit in sonnet cycles (known as *corone di sonetti*), which were composed on such subjects as the days of the week and the months of the year (e.g., those by Folgore da San Gimignano) and on longer narratives (e.g., *Il Fiore*, which has been attributed to Dante and presents a greatly abbreviated version of the Old French *Roman de la rose* in 232 sonnets).

[19] In the thirteenth century the sonnet underwent a number of formal transformations in the hands of adventuresome poets who expanded in various ways the seemingly rigid fourteen-line structure. For example, *sonetti caudati* ("tailed sonnets") have additional verses (one, two, or three) tacked on at the end (e.g., ABBA ABBA CDC DCD D or ABBA ABBA CDC DCD EE). Other extended forms include the following: the *sonetto*

doppio ("double sonnet"), the *sonetto doppio caudato* ("double tailed sonnet"), the *sonetto rinterzato* ("triple sonnet"), and the *sonetto raddoppiato* ("redoubled sonnet"). The *sonetto doppio* was invented by Pucciandone Martelli ("Signor sensa pietansa, udit'ho dire") and consists of twenty verses with *settanari* added after verses 1, 3, 5 and 7 of the octave and after verses 10 and 12 of the sestet (e.g., AaBAaB AaBAaB CDdE CdDE). The *sonetto doppio caudato* follows the form of the *sonetto doppio* with the addition of extra verses forming the tail (e.g., AaBBbA AaBBbA CdDD DdDC EE). Guittone d'Arezzo invented the *sonetto rinterzato* (e.g., "O benigna, o dolce, o graziosa"), which is very similar to the *sonetto doppio*, except that its twenty-two verses have an additional two *settenari* in the sestet (e.g., AaBAaB AaBAaB CcDdC DdCcD), thus giving greater emphasis to a rhyme by repeating it in the *terzine*, the sestet. The *sonetto raddoppiato* is true to its name in that it has twenty-eight verses, twice the number of the standard sonnet (e.g., ABAB ABAB ABAB ABAB CDE CDE FGH FGH [or CDCDCD EFEFEF]). Another variation on the basic sonnet form was invented by Guittone d'Arezzo but brought to perfection by the Florentine rhymer Monte Andrea; this is the sixteen-verse sonnet, with a ten-line first part (e.g., ABABABABAB CDCDCD).

[20] Petrarch uses the pattern ABAB BAAB for only one poem (295), ABAB BABA for three poems (210, 260, 279), and ABAB ABAB for ten poems (56, 79, 134, 187, 280, 281, 307, 310, 311, 318).

Using a Concordance to Teach Petrarch's *Canzoniere*

Madison U. Sowell

For the Italian and comparative literature courses in which I teach Petrarch's *Canzoniere* and its influence on later Italian lyrics or world literature, a concordance proves a readily available and easily accessible tool for getting at the recurring words and images that characterize the poet's vocabulary and constitute the work's leitmotifs. These repeated words, often involving wordplay, and images, often involving variations on a theme, require our attention for two basic reasons. First, only as students comprehend the extent and usage of these terms and concepts do they begin to grasp the breadth and artistry of the *Canzoniere* as an organic corpus. It is one matter to analyze a single Petrarchan sonnet, madrigal, sestina, or canzone in isolation from its fellow poems; it is another to interpret that poem as one of 366 carefully juxtaposed lyrics, each of which in turn is made up of individual word-images placed in intricate patterns. Second, these very *parole* and *immagini*, so well known to centuries of frustrated lovers and devoted writers, fostered the complex phenomenon of Petrarch's *Nachleben*—the subsequent imitation of his style that we call Petrarchism. While Petrarchism is hardly limited to imitations of wordplays and adaptations of conceits, Petrarch's restricted vocabulary (narrow compared with Dante's, for example) nevertheless played a central role in the diffusion of Petrarchan influence across the Alps and around the globe.

I introduce the theoretical and practical uses of concordances in the classroom by inviting students to consider the article "Computer-Aided Lexicography: Indexes and Concordances," written by my colleagues Randall L. Jones and Steven P. Sondrup. Among the many points made, these emerge as most germane: a concordance, especially one that includes rather extensive context, "brings to light new uses of words, points out unusual frequency, and shows how the author uses specific words to produce unusual effects" (491). Unusual frequency, I point out, can be a word used only once in a corpus (an example of hapax legomenon) or an uncommon word used much more frequently than one might expect. Furthermore, "[a]lmost at a glance it can be determined whether a significant lexical item tends towards rather general usage or toward comparatively restricted application, whether it has a relatively rich series of associations or typically a narrow focus" (501). A concordance thus holds out the possibility of "scientific" (i.e., rational or at least statistical) support for a student's "hunch" that a particular term or concept is being highlighted by the poet or contains seminal meaning. Finally, "[b]y using concordances to examine co-occurrences of words and ideas, to untangle complex referential and symbolic networks, and to trace involuted patterns, even the most opaque of . . . poems may be coaxed to yield up new insights" (503). In other words, a student who experiences difficulty in grasping a poem's meaning may turn to key words, such as those found at the beginning of a line or in rhyme position, and use a concordance to see if they are being used uniquely or as part of a larger network in the poetic corpus as a whole.[1]

Although all the students in my upper-division Italian course can easily read modern Italian, many find that Petrarch's fourteenth-century Tuscan initially poses various problems for their comprehension. In my comparative literature courses, only a few of my students are fluent in Italian. In both cases, therefore, I use Robert Durling's *Petrarch's Lyric Poems*, a bilingual edition that presents a literal prose translation in English facing the original on each page. More often than not, I have found that this ready access to a translation encourages rather than discourages students to peruse the Italian original. Having the Italian so accessible certainly facilitates my own in-class references to the original and fosters student use of a concordance to research pertinent questions and intriguing hypotheses regarding the frequency and location of terms in the *Canzoniere*.

The Petrarchan concordance that I place on reserve in the university library is the exhaustive two-volume *Concordanze del* Canzoniere *di Francesco Petrarca*, produced by the Accademia della Crusca. This particular Petrarchan concordance, unlike its predecessors, is not limited solely to key terms and phrases but includes even words presumably less endowed with lexical value ("meno ricche di valori lessicali" [xiii]). It also provides what is called a concordance line—a fairly ample context for each word, including the complete verse in which the researched term appears and, when necessary for clarity, enough of the preceding or succeeding verse to clarify how the term functions grammatically and what exactly is being said. For those who prefer an online approach to word searches, at least two possibilities have become available in recent years. Students with little to no knowledge of Italian probably can accomplish individual word searches most quickly using Wikisource's electronic edition of the *Canzoniere*, which uses Gianfranco Contini's edition, *Canzoniere (Rerum vulgarium fragmenta)*. Anyone comfortable working in an Italian-only environment definitely should consult the IntraTex–Èulogos SpA version, which also uses Contini's text and contains a concordance as well as a frequency list and an alphabetical listing of hapax legomena.

I give my students, including those with limited Italian, various assignments that require the use of a concordance. One is to find examples of hapax legomena and then determine through consultation of etymological dictionaries how many of these unique terms are neologisms, or words created by Petrarch for a particular context and purpose. As a model for how to interpret such a word that doubles as a neologism, I refer students to my own article on the word *nembo*, "'The Jingling Sound of Like Endings': Genesis and Evolution of the *Grembo-Nembo-Lembo* Rhyme." Another assignment has students locate all references to the name Laura. Some initially retrieve only the four times that her name per se appears, in but three poems (239.8, 239.23, 291.4, and

332.50), but more astute students quickly realize that allusions to and variations on her name occur throughout the corpus of the *Canzoniere* and, most notably, include *l'aura*, meaning "the breeze,"[2] as well as *l'aure*, *l'aurata*, *l'aurate*, *l'aurato*, *l'aurea*, *l'aureo*, *l'auro*, *l'aurora*, *laurea*, *laureto*, *lauri*, and, of course, the famous *lauro* (the laurel tree of Apollo and Daphne renown). Interestingly, students often cannot fail to notice that the half-dozen entries that immediately precede the name *Laura* in the alphabetical concordance are *laudare*, *laudate*, *laudato*, *laudati*, *laude*, and *laudi*. This discovery invariably leads them to other puns on the name of Petrarch's beloved and to poem 5 ("Quando io movo i sospiri a chiamar voi"), with its play on the syllables of *Lau-re-ta* (Laureta), a Latinate variation of the French *Laurette*.

In the case of *l'aura*, even a cursory glance at the references raises questions in the student researcher's mind. What is the thematic connection among poems 194 ("L'aura gentil che rasserena i poggi"), 196 ("L'aura serena che fra verdi fronde"), 197 ("L'aura celeste che 'n quel verde lauro"), and 198 ("L'aura soave al sole spiega et vibra"), which are grouped together and each of which begins with *L'aura*, the pronunciation of which is indistinguishable from the name *Laura*? Or how do the multiple occurrences of *l'aura* in poem 239, the only poem that contains two citations of the actual name Laura, support the *l'aura-Laura* metamorphic connection? Similarly, why does the poet juxtapose *l'aurora* and *l'aura* in the same verse in poem 223 and then again in poem 239? How does such wordplay support the widespread Ovidian theme of metamorphosis in the collection of poems as a whole?

Exercises using a concordance need hardly be limited, however, to variations or plays on the name Laura. Typically Petrarchan conceits provide another rich source of study. For example, tracing the many references to fire (*foco*) and either ice (*ghiaccio*) or snow (*neve*), to heat (*caldo*) and cold (*freddo*), or even to summer (*estate* or *state*) and winter (*inverno* or *verno*) invariably reveals why the phenomenon of Petrarchism relies so heavily on such antithetical pairs when it comes to describing the effect of love on the unrequited lover. These antitheses are, in a word, commonplace in the *Canzoniere*. A concordance can document just how often and where precisely these pairings of opposites occur. Do they occur more regularly in the first part, *in vita di Laura*, or in the second, *in morte di Laura*? Do they evolve or do they remain static? To what parallel images are they juxtaposed? These are the types of questions that students who learn to make use of a concordance on a regular basis are forced to address.

While the benefits of knowing how to use a concordance are many, perhaps the most salubrious aspect of teaching students to consult such a tool is that it provides them with a method for approaching the text but does not impose on them any one interpretive strategy. Students remain free to approach Petrarch's poems from viewpoints as diverse as linguistics, historicism, structuralism, postmodernism, and gender-based theories. A concordance, used sagaciously, simply supplies good grist for the interpretive mill, allowing students to see patterns that otherwise might be difficult to discern. In the case of Petrarch's

Canzoniere, a work whose 366 poems were carefully selected, honed, arranged, and rearranged over decades, it is incumbent on the alert reader to seek out the patterns of word usage (and, therefore, image usage) in as methodical and efficient a manner as possible. To accomplish this task, the concordance remains an essential tool.

NOTES

[1] Other articles that I have found useful for understanding and teaching the varied uses of concordances in classroom settings include Koubourlis; Raben; and O'Keeffe and Farr (which focuses on TESOL applications but nonetheless contains practical instruction for how to read concordance lines).

[2] Following are the instances of *l'aura* in the *Canzoniere*: 52.6, 79.3, 80.7, 90.1, 109.9, 112.4, 113.10, 127.83, 129.69, 133.14, 142.5, 143.9, 159.6, 194.1, 196.1, 197.1, 198.1, 212.2, 217.6, 223.12, 227.1, 239 (lines 1, 16, 27, 36, 37), 246.1, 270.31, 278.4, 279.2, 286.1, 320.1 , 323.16, 327.1, 332.46, 356.1, 359.16.

"Parole Estreme": *Canzoniere* 126

Christopher Martin

Despite his reputation as the innovator of a distinctively modern lyricism, Petrarch can appear on first contact an altogether remote and outlandish figure. The poet made a career out of alienating the very readership he so ambitiously courted, a point that serves as perhaps the supreme oxymoron subtending his *Canzoniere* as a whole. The only thing he feigns to desire as much as our sympathy is our distance: neither a welcoming nor easily intelligible pose. My experience of introducing Petrarch's work to undergraduates, both in broad surveys of European literature and in advanced-level seminars, has taught me how even the most generous first-time readers often collide with what they regard as his maddeningly solipsistic temperament and find themselves confused if not antagonized by an arrant self-pity infusing the verses. Efforts to address these matters preemptively, moreover, have further sensitized me to how determinate an instructor's strategic entrance into the sequence will prove to the class's subsequent receptivity. With this in view, I want to make a case for the often neglected canzone "Chiare, fresche et dolci acque" ("Clear, cool, sweet, running waters"), poem 126, as a useful starting point for discussion of the *Canzoniere*, however abbreviated or expansive a treatment one's schedule might permit. Portentously advertising itself as the agonized lover's "parole estreme" 'last words,' the poem steers conveniently between extremes available in two other well-worn inroads, the first sonnet's compressed prefatory performance and 264's protracted spiritual contortions. "Chiare, fresche et dolci acque" concentrates its lyric energies in a splendid encapsulation of the larger sacred and secular issues informing the *Canzoniere* while unfolding the multivalent and unorthodox self-image that Petrarch crafts to embody these. In so doing, its sixty-eight lines present a full yet uniquely economized chance for students to confront those challenges that may initially threaten to obscure the poet's impressive achievement.

The correct answer to my standard lead-in question about what precisely happens in canzone 126 is, of course, nothing. On its surface, the poem offers no more than a sustained, lyrical apostrophe to the landscape once graced by Laura's presence. It begins with the poet enjoining the river, the vegetation, and the very air, "date udienzia insieme / a le dolenti mie parole estreme" 'listen all of you together / to these my mournful, my last words' (lines 12–13).[1] Unlike the running waters, however, the lover remains fastened in place, expressing to the end his somber regard for the deprivation that isolates him: "Se tu avessi ornamenti quant' ài voglia, / poresti arditamente / uscir del bosco et gir infra la gente" 'If you had all the beauty you desired, / you could with boldness leave / the wood and make your way among mankind' (66–68). But to provoke consideration of just how deceptive this immobility may in fact be, I have students chart the stanzas' temporal shifts, an exercise that better focuses the lyric's psychological restlessness. From the vantage of a static present (stanzas 1 and 6), they observe, Petrarch's speaker projects fantasies of a bittersweet future (stanzas 2 and 3) inspired by his memory of a definitive past event (stanzas 4 and 5). What had at first appeared a stalled performance that fails to attain significant closure even within its delimited scope opens into a sophisticated mental itinerary that forsakes spatial movement in favor of emotional transport. This discovery serves to alert readers immediately to the kind of interior relocation demanded by the poet, for whom landscape becomes an extension and function of his own psychology.

I turn next to discussion of what memory involves for the poet, whose recollection of a singular past experience endows the poem's setting with such profound meaning. Though no longer present, Laura continues to animate the setting through the agency of his memory, and a specific act of remembering connects the opening movement with the fifth stanza's abrupt but spectacular tableau. Petrarch glosses his initial address to this place formerly inhabited by the beloved with line 5's parenthesis "con sospir me rimembra," which Mark Musa renders "I sigh to think of it" and Robert Durling translates more literally "with sighing I remember." This remark arches over to line 41's invocation of the specific day in question as "dolce ne la memoria," one which the speaker "sweetly call[s] to mind." As if to substantiate this claim, the fourth stanza summons one of the *Canzoniere*'s most beautiful visual passages:

> Da' be' rami scendea
> (dolce ne la memoria)
> una pioggia di fior sovra 'l suo grembo,
> et ella si sedea
> umile in tanta gloria,
> coverta già de l'amoroso nembo;
> qual fior cadea sul lembo,
> qual su le treccie bionde
> ch' oro forbito et perle
> eran quel dì a vederle,
> qual si posava in terra et qual su l'onde,
> qual con un vago errore
> girando parea dir: "Qui regna Amore." (40–52)

> Falling from gracious boughs,
> I sweetly call to mind,
> were flowers in a rain upon her bosom,
> and she was sitting there
> humble in such glory
> now covered in a shower of love's blooms:
> a flower falling on her lap,
> some on her golden curls,

like pearls set into gold
they seemed to me that day;
some fell to rest on ground, some on the water,
and some in love-like wandering
were circling down and saying, "Here Love reigns."

Literally spectacular in its design, this pivotal one-sentence reverie highlights Petrarch's descriptive powers as it confirms his mastery of love poetry's graphic conventions. Students who otherwise react adversely to the sterility of idealized Petrarchan love find their skepticism challenged, I have repeatedly witnessed, by the lines' undeniably lush sensuality. Moreover, the sexual longing that infuses the passage sweetens the surrounding melancholy, from which it seems to emerge organically. In this way, the stanza efficiently illustrates what William Kerrigan and Gordon Braden identify in their outstanding treatment of Petrarch's English legacy as the *Canzoniere*'s defining impulse, a transmutation of sustained erotic frustration into great poetry (see the chapter "Petrarch Refracted: The Evolution of the English Love Lyric" [157–89]). If anything, time's passage and the absences it occasions enhance those pleasures that the lover imaginatively experiences afresh. As surely as Petrarch reinvents motion as emotion, he links this psychological restlessness intimately to the human capacity for highly individuated memory. It is Petrarch's ability to honor and capture the common idiosyncrasy of the lover that at once justifies his obsession with the placid yet vacant landscape before him and acclimates readers to the revitalized interiority they will encounter throughout the collection.

Beyond illuminating or validating for students Petrarch's capacity as a love poet, conversation about these recollected details can foreground the conflict between memory and forgetfulness that further complicates his poetic stance. I next draw attention to the way that the premium placed on memory jars against an awareness, expressed in the final extended stanza, of how Laura's "divine" appearance affected him:

Così carco d'oblio
il divin portamento
e 'l volto e le parole e'l dolce riso
m'aveano, et sì diviso
da l'imagine vera,
ch' I' dicea sospirando:
"Qui come vann' io o quando?" (56–62)

And her divine behavior,
her face and words and her sweet smile
so filled me with forgetfulness
and so divided me
from the true image,

that I would sigh and say,
"How and when did I come here?"

The temporal synthesis that Petrarch features in 126 simultaneously presages the spiritual collapse threatening so many of the poems. Questions about what constitutes "l'imagine vera" 'the true image' to which he here refers (God's image? the prosaic reality of his fallen, worldly surroundings? a humbler, demythologized self-image more conducive to his spiritual well-being?) conventionally spark some of the liveliest discussion. Whatever conclusion the students reach, they unavoidably come to perceive how the landscape transforms from a shelter or *locus amoenus* to a scene of spiritual hazard. The enraptured recollection comes at the expense of a piety Petrarch suppresses (however tenuously) to sustain his vision. Early interrogation of this essential dividedness adequately sets up the class for the binaries of denial and affirmation that will strain the sequence throughout.

Where the selectively remembered details and sensations betray the apostasy toward which Laura tempts her lover, the second and third stanzas' postmortem fantasy casts this spiritual crisis in high relief. As it translates memory into anticipation, the second stanza quietly but unmistakably subverts religious orthodoxy. Misdirecting his reflections on mortality, the obsessed lover takes solace in hopes that "la carne travagliata et l'ossa" '[his] poor belabored flesh and bones' may come to rest nowhere else but here (26). Contemplation of one's own death should inspire the believer with a willingness to resign the temporal realm; Petrarch's fantasy, by contrast, looks ahead to a time when the poet will find release from worldly torment only through deeper physical integration—interment—with the locale he here romances. We see how removal from the setting, even amid the prospect of having his soul "torni . . . al proprio albergo ignuda" 'return to its home naked' (19), is what he most fears. Making his spiritual peace contingent on the precise placement of his remains in this world, he literally grounds his eternal happiness in the soil of a profanely sanctified terrain.

I next invite the class to evaluate the extent to which the ensuing stanza compounds this risky confusion of earthly and divine. The prospect of his own demise carries the lover forward imaginatively to an even more distant future, when "a l'usato soggiorno / torni la fera bella et mansueta" 'to the well-known place / the lovely animal returns, and tamed' (28–29), in which he adopts his former role as grieving subject. Such a turn positions the poem's ostensible object, the mistress, as a key topic for discussion. Laura, whose name signifies the coveted laurel of poetic fame, contrasts Dante's less equivocal model of Beatrice; yet why should the character who undergoes virtual apotheosis in the poem be cast simultaneously as a beast, albeit a "lovely" one? The dehumanization suggested by the Italian *fera*, which Musa translates "animal," invariably excites critical reaction, even from those students familiar with the tropes of courtly love lyric that Petrarch had inherited. Durling's more tonally accurate "the lovely, gentle wild one" helps but hardly disables the image's harsher inflections for either the speaker or the lady. I point out to the class that Dante had used the term *fiera* in reference to the predatory beasts that block the pilgrim's path in the *Inferno*'s opening canto and ask if we can recognize any connection between these wild animals and Laura. Where Beatrice dispatches Vergil to rescue Dante, Petrarch's lady confounds promises of destruction and redemption in a distinctly modern fashion. Her feral cruelty, domesticated in his vision by her guilty regret, empowers him, however much he professes to rely on her "mercé m'impetre / et faccia forza al cielo" '[to] win for me some mercy / and force open the heavens' after his death (37–38). Unlike Dante, Petrarch mingles sentiments of despair and hope within his paradoxical beloved to crystallize the definitive experience of one who, by poem's end, professedly finds himself "credendo esser in ciel, non là dov' era" 'thinking I was in Heaven, not where I was' (63).

The third stanza's revenge fantasy turns the tables on Laura, who (the poet dreams) discovers her error of taking his devotion for granted. At the same time, it trains attention on the blatant self-pity that typically compromises readers' sympathies. I present the lines as an opportunity to examine what Petrarch hopes to attain by exposing to our ironic gaze this confession of a defeated lover, who takes bittersweet delight in the spectacle of the other's belated affection:

> Tempo verrà ancor forse
> ch' a l'usato soggiorno
> torni la fera bella et mansueta
> et là 'v' ella mi scorse
> nel benedetto giorno
> volga la vista disiosa et lieta,
> cercandomi, et—o pieta—
> già terra infra le pietre
> vedendo, Amor l'inspiri
> in guisa che sospiri
> sì dolcemente che mercé m'impetre
> et faccia forza al cielo,
> asciugandosi gli occhi col bel velo. (27–39)
>
> And there will come a time, perhaps,
> that to the well-known place
> the lovely animal returns, and tamed,
> and there where she first saw me
> that day which now is blessed
> she turns her eyes with hope and happiness
> in search of me, and—ah, the pity—
> to see me there as dust
> among the stones, Love will
> inspire her and she will sigh

so sweetly she will win for me some mercy
and force open the heavens
drying her eyes there with her lovely veil.

Should students find the sentiment maudlin (as they typically do), I suggest that their distaste is not anachronistic. In all likelihood Petrarch's contemporaries would have judged such fantastic reveling in the trivialities of this world even more harshly than we do. If the poet deliberately flirts with our disdain here, I propose, he does so because he wishes to expose the insidious delight we take in self-pity. Much like the illicit sex that his rarified passions displace, self-pity threatens the subject with social scorn and self-loathing yet (for all our denials) remains an intensely pleasing sensation of which all are guilty. Petrarch stands almost alone in his bold willingness to confront us, at his own expense, with our very human propensity for this emotion. The reflex displayed so candidly in 126 returns us to one of the initial sonnet's announced hopes that "ove sia chi per prova intenda amore / spero trovar pietà, non che perdono" 'in anyone who knows love through its trials, / in them, may I find pity and forgiveness' (1.7–8). From the outset, the shame inspired by his worldly infatuations sparks a hunger for "pietà" that—as the rest of the sequence will unfold with distinctively Petrarchan ambivalence—proves as powerful as any other appetite and begs (in turn) for its own brand of sympathetic "perdono."

I end up by circling back to the expression "mie parole estreme," to ask the class what they think Petrarch means by casting his lament in 126 in such terms. Does he intend these as dying words? Since we know the poet will carry on to say a great deal more on the subject, what do we make of the hyperbole if this is the case? Does he alternatively regard the poem as his uttermost statement about his love for Laura? If so, what might privilege the particular sentiments expressed here? Do we detect any more ironic intimations about the extreme or overstated nature of his plight? This last prospect opens an important critical window on an understanding of the Petrarchan lover's propensity for a subtly comic self-regard. The poet appears aware of how the extravagance of his imagined plight opens him not only to spiritual dangers threatened by any worldly attachment but also to his audience's ironic response. He dares to look ridiculous before us, candidly disclosing the absurdity to which love has reduced him. In this manner, he forces the question of whether "anyone who knows love through its trials" can escape indictment. And no sooner does his self-indulgence arouse our contempt or amusement than the sheer lyric beauty of his work checks our impatience with his excess, discovering the way such fantasy fires poetic inspiration. The potential for a more facetious self-characterization significantly qualifies Petrarch's reputation as a writer who takes himself far too seriously. By undermining the speaker's posture, the gestures in 126 present a figure that is more approachable, less alien and alienating.

Since undergraduates often meet and react to Petrarch as some version of not-Dante, 126's neat elucidation of how the *Canzoniere* supplants Dantesque narrative with fragmented but no less kinetic lyric microdramas proves significant. However well the temperamental space dividing Petrarch from Dante discriminates medieval attitudes from the hallmarks of early modernity, such comparison usually does not play to the junior poet's advantage. *The Divine Comedy*'s dynamic forward movement and vast dramatis personae, things altogether absent from Petrarch's sequence, sustain us through the allegorical journey's most breathless and conceptually rugged moments. Understanding of the *Canzoniere*'s progress, by contrast, demands appreciation of the curious energy released within the stationary moments that the speaker repeatedly enacts. No lyric in the sequence captures this energy more perfectly than canzone 126, in which Petrarch collapses Dante's spiritual oppositions in the character of Laura and turns the pity experienced by the *Comedy*'s pilgrim inward. Dante had toured the underworld to grasp precisely what he has been saved from, before he can appreciate what he has been saved for (Nohrnberg 76). Petrarch mentally revisits scenes of frustrated erotic rapture, such as the one recalled in 126, to understand better what he has relinquished, and at what price. It goes far to exemplify what I have characterized elsewhere as the difference between Dante's elevation of his *commedia* to a divine level and Petrarch's adoption of a poetic stance "more absurdly secular in its orientation, and thus 'comic' in a more distinctively modern sense of the term" (79).

It makes better sense, in my experience, to travel outward to poems like sonnet 1 or canzone 264 from the basis of canzone 126. The opening poem expresses anguish over the prospect of having become a *favola*, or idle talk of the crowd, but the recollected scene of 126 explicitly displays the poet as a fashioner of his own story, fully in progress. In like manner, the keenly articulated spiritual crisis of 264 finds a more placid yet no less ominous configuration in 126's reverie. The poem shows us what the lover's world looks like from within, providing a firmer sense of what impulses entice him toward the spiritual torpor he risks. Whoever claims the last word in classroom debate about the poet and his work, "Clear, cool, sweet, running waters" sounds an appropriate first note in any critical discussion of this enigmatic and elusive writer's legacy. By itself or at the entry to any broader discussion of the sequence, canzone 126 displays Petrarch's art—and Renaissance lyric generally—at its best.

NOTE

[1] English quotations from the poems refer to Musa's translation for Oxford University Press, the edition I assign in the survey courses I teach at my home institution. In my seminars I use Durling's bilingual edition, with facing-page translations, from which I cite the Italian text in this essay.

THE *CANZONIERE* AND THE LIFE

The Life and Works as Journey

Theodore J. Cachey, Jr.

Students can easily relate to Petrarch's life and works as an itinerary of travel, living as they do in an age of global tourism, characterized by constant and wide-ranging mobility, both virtual and real. One way to begin to establish the basic parameters of the itinerary and to enter on the path is by conducting a review of Petrarch's life and works accompanied by a visual tour of some of the Petrarchan sites. Many of the highlights can be conveniently accessed through the black-and-white photographs in Giuseppe Frasso's *Travels with Francesco Petrarca*, one of the most useful and suggestive of the volumes published at the time of the celebration of the sixth centenary of Petrarch's death in 1974. An initial meeting or two can be organized around the discussion of a detailed chronology (an excellent one is available in Santagata's edition of the *Canzoniere*) and the slide presentation of selected images derived from Frasso's volume, including Petrarchan popes, manuscripts, piazzas and palazzi, mountains, hills, rivers and streams, frescoes, tombs, codices, autograph annotations, drawings, and maps. As the point of departure for a course on Petrarch's vernacular lyric, an illustrated review of his life and works ideally ought to capture something of their internal rhythm, which oscillated between movement and stasis, between forward progress and rest (like the progress of the slides in the projector), and which expressed an unstable equilibrium between the author's lifelong aspiration to achieve a state of rest and his no less pressing desire for forward movement. The goal of these initial class meetings is for the students to recognize that the journey is not simply an external conceit for the course but an essential part of its subject matter. In fact, the model of the itinerary as an open-ended series of departures and arrivals represents a signature structure at the heart of Petrarch's life and works. As students progress on the path of the course, this notion will be important for achieving a dynamic understanding of the making of the *Canzoniere* and the *Triumphs*. These works in progress were the sites of reiterated departures and arrivals over many years, interrupted only by the death of the author, at which point the works departed on a journey to posterity that has yet to reach its final destination.

Because of time constraints, inevitably, the presentation of the iconographic apparatus and the chronology has to be somewhat limited. I focus on the early life, using as commentary Petrarch's autobiographical writing in the *Familiares* and *Seniles*. Petrarch's father, Ser Petracco, along with Dante, was exiled from Florence, and thus Petrarch was born in exile in Arezzo. In *Familiares* 21.15, Petrarch shares his recollection of Dante with his father in Pisa when he was seven and introduces the critical theme of the relationship between Dante and Petrarch, which will return repeatedly in the discussion of the *Canzoniere* and the *Triumphs*. But the vital point to grasp about the transition from Dante to Petrarch is their very different relations to home and to place. The exiled Dante longed for home and always aspired to homecoming, both to Florence to receive the laurel crown and to God, by means of the kind of spiritual return enacted by the *Commedia*, whereas Petrarch, born in exile, had no home to return to. In effect, his life and works can be interpreted in the light of the "homeless" or originally expatriated state of his point of departure. From this perspective, his insistence on marking his birthplace in Arezzo as a touristic site in his letters can appear a quaint form of compensation (*Seniles* 13.3). Yet students might consider that Petrarch's fashioning his autobiographical writings as an open-ended itinerary and his obsessive preoccupations with establishing his connections to place (even, as Ceserani has noted, in the invention of his own name, from Petracco to "petra" "arca," the stone tomb or monument) represent responses to his originally expatriate and estranged status. For Petrarch, literature came to represent a compensatory home through which he constructed his place in the world.

The ideas of writing as a place in which "the man who is without a home finds a place to live" (Adorno 87) and of life as a nomadic itinerary are not critical concepts anachronistically projected by postmodern readers on to Petrarch's life and works. The second part of the introduction to the course is dedicated to illustrating this point and is focused on the discussion of selected letters from Petrarch's Latin epistolary. These discussions develop alongside continuing conversation about the chronology of the life and works that I invite students to continue to investigate according to the accounts of the life by Ernest Hatch Wilkins (*Life of Petrarch*) and Ugo Dotti (*Vita di Petrarca*). Depending on the time available, selections from the Latin epistolary can vary, but canonical elements include the dedicatory letter (1.1), the "Ascent of Mount Ventoux" (4.1), Petrarch's tour of Roman ruins (6.2), and the unfinished "Letter to Posterity." This selection might be considered standard for any Petrarch course, even one primarily dedicated to the vernacular lyric, but students should be encouraged to explore independently his Latin epistolary, his underread and underrated masterpiece, beyond these few letters. The ongoing discussion of the chronology of the life and works can serve the purpose of stimulating the curiosity of the students in this respect. In addition to the fascinating and wily letter on Dante to Boccaccio (*Familiares* 21.15), other letters readily recommend themselves for consideration, including those rich in biographical information, such as the letter to Guido Sette (*Seniles* 10.2), or otherwise important for Petrarch's idea of tradition, like those addressed to the classical authors that close out the *Familiares* or the letters to Boccaccio throughout the epistolary, including those that conclude the *Seniles*.

But the dedicatory letter to the epistolary (*Familiares* 1.1) is particularly useful for revealing the way in which Petrarch conceived of his life and his writing as interrelated and complementary journeys. Moreover, within the context of the chronological review of the life and works, the dedicatory letter, written in January 1350, is an ideal text for focusing attention on what is widely considered the key turning point in Petrarch's career between 1348 and 1353. In fact, it was following the death of Laura and of his patron, Cardinal Giovanni Colonna, in 1348 that Petrarch entered into a period of existential crisis. He spent five years undecided between France and Italy, wandering between the cities of north-central Italy and Provence, until the definitive departure from France for Italy and eight years of homesteading in Visconti Milan, beginning in 1353. Significantly, it was during this diasporic interval that Petrarch conceived and began in earnest the work of gathering together the "fragments of my soul," as he wrote in the *Secretum* ([Quillen] 147; this work was also composed or at least substantially rewritten between 1348 and 1353), into the major books of his maturity. These included the prose epistolary collections in Latin (ending with the unfinished "Letter to Posterity") and the *Canzoniere*, whose proemial sonnet, also dated around 1350, marks the beginning of the conceptualization of the collection of lyrics as a book, in structural and chronological parallel with the dedicatory letter to the *Familiares*. The project of these books that preoccupied Petrarch for the rest of his life represented a response to a period of existential and spatial uncertainty during which he sought to establish his place in the world by literary means.

In preparing for the discussion of the dedicatory letter to the *Familiares*, I ask students to identify passages that draw attention to the project of gathering the fragments of the life into books that were undertaken at this time (including allusions to the *Canzoniere* and the *Epystolae*) and to illustrate Petrarch's use of figures related to the journey theme. I invite them to attempt to interpret these instances as programmatic not only for the *Familiares* but also for Petrarch's life and works as a whole. For example, the allusion in the first paragraph to the journeys of merchant travelers to the East, powerless to recover what has been lost in the plague, places that kind of travel in implicit opposition to the literary journey on which the author is about to embark. Like Boccaccio's contemporary *Decameron*, Petrarch's epistolary collection is designed to accomplish a form of literary recuperation and recovery after the apocalypse, leading to a revitalization of culture.

Petrarch next likens himself to a wanderer arranging his belongings in little bundles in preparation for the journey and to a tired traveler looking back from the vantage point of having concluded the journey. Paradoxically poised between departure and arrival, the similes capture Petrarch's existential state along the itinerary of his life, where every point of arrival is a point of departure, and also describe the journey of writing as looking backward on the past at the same time that it moves forward. Petrarch's signature theme of shipwreck is also introduced in the letter, albeit implicitly, when he compares the destruction of many of his letters with the technique of prudent navigators in high seas who unload even precious cargo to remain afloat. Unlike Dante, who attributed shipwreck to Ulysses to distinguish between his own divinely ordained journey and that of the Greek hero, Petrarch appears in the dedicatory letter to the *Familiares* to accept his Ulysses-like destiny (and the inevitability of shipwreck). Thus his epistolary project represents not a heroic journey on the high seas according to the "ship of the poem" trope Dante used in the *Commedia* but a response to the experience of shipwreck. Finally, it is important to draw attention to the passage where Petrarch styles his writing as both a journey that will continue as long as he lives and a "place" of rest: "Only then will I no longer feel this obligation and will have to consider this work ended when you hear that I am dead and that I am freed from all the labors of life. In the meantime I shall continue along the path I have been following, and shall avoid any exits so long as there is light. And the sweet labor will serve for me almost as a place of rest" (13).[1]

The discussion of other texts from the epistolary can develop further, as time permits, the themes introduced by the dedicatory letter related to the figure of the life and works as journey. *Familiares* 3.1 and 4.1 might be considered in tandem as constituting a textual and territorial gateway at the beginning of the epistolary that defined the parameters of the Petrarchan journey between the geotopographical limits of Thule, the most distant island in the west, and the top of Mt. Ventoux (Cachey, "Petrarchan Cartographic Writing"). Petrarch inaugurates the modern genre of archaeological tourism in his letter on the sites of Rome (*Familiares* 6.2), which can be profitably read and discussed in conjunction with critical work ranging from Thomas Greene's "Petrarch and the Humanist Hermeneutic" to Michel de Certeau's "Walking in the City." The unfinished "Letter to Posterity" (*Seniles* 18.1) represents the culminating fragment of the work in progress. In fact, according to the premises of Petrarch's project of autobiographical writing, the work had to end without an ending: how could the author write the itinerary of his life through to the end of his own life? The letter begins by evoking instead the journey of the author to posterity that is as open-ended and ongoing as the unresolved state in which the interrupted ending of the letter captures Petrarch, at the height of the crisis period of his life, shuttling back and forth between France and Italy, "incapable of staying still, and not so much with a yearning to see again what I had seen a thousand times, as with an effort to cope with stiffness—as sick people do—by a shift of position" (2: 679).[2]

It is Petrarch's characteristic restlessness, his continual oscillations between the poles of movement and stasis, that can serve as a framework for a third and final part of the introduction to the course, focused on the preliminary presentation of the vernacular lyric works, the *Canzoniere* and the *Triumphs*, particularly of their complex, not to say tormented, compositional histories within the context of the life and works. As Wilkins wrote insightfully in his *Life of Petrarch*:

> Petrarch never felt constrained to finish one work before beginning another. There was indeed in his nature a certain restlessness—frequently shown in his changes of residence and his thoughts of still other changes—that manifested itself, in his literary activity, in a turning from one to another of the works that he had on hand at a given time, or in the undertaking of an entirely new work. As a result of this readiness to shift his attention from one task to another, he ultimately left several works unfinished, among them both the *De viris* and the *Africa*. (19)

The history of Petrarch's life and works, in terms of the dynamic described by Wilkins, can be further illustrated and explored through a general consideration of the chronology of life and works in their spatial dimension together with selected letters from the epistolary, highlighting the author's preoccupation with establishing his place in the world, from the first surviving work written in honor of his mother, the *Breve Pangiricum defuncte matri* (*Epystolae*, bk. 1, letter 7); to the obituary note on the death of Laura, which he wrote on the verso of the first guard leaf of his manuscript of Vergil; to the *Testament*, in which he anxiously attempts to predispose the site of his burial place ("if I should die in Padua . . . I should wish to be buried in the church of S. Agostino . . . if, however, in Rome, either in the church of S. Maria Maggiore or in St. Peter's" [Mommsen]).

For it is from this spatial perspective on the life and works that the study of the making of the *Canzoniere* and the contemporary composition of the *Triumphs* can be approached as something more than a dry exercise in historical philology. From this vantage point it becomes possible to recognize how the underlying compositional rhythm of the construction of these books corresponds to the same unstable tension between Petrarch's desire for rest and his desire for forward movement. There is not the space in this context to undertake a detailed presentation of the compositional histories of the works. A handy synthesis of the nine forms of the *Canzoniere*, as first established by Wilkins in *The Making of the* Canzoniere, is available in the pages dedicated to the *Canzoniere* in Remo Ceserani and Lidia De Federicis (1067–68). Wilkins's scheme can be contrasted with that of Marco Santagata, found at the beginning of his edition and commentary ("Le redazioni" ccvii). Santagata, in *I frammenti dell'anima*, gives great emphasis to the first published form of the book, the Correggio (which was prepared for Azzo di Correggio between 1356 and 1358, while Petrarch was in Milan), and interprets the subsequent forms in terms of a progressive resolution of the ideological incongruities present in that first redaction, believed to have consisted of poems 1–142 in the first part and poems 264–92 in the second. The forms of the *Canzoniere* that follow the Correggio represent a series of departures and arrivals that reflects the author's desire to achieve some form of ideological and formal resolution or state of rest or, alternatively, his resistance to closure and the desire to continue the journey. Almost immediately following the publication of the Correggio form, the book was reopened and poems were added to both parts. The subsequent Chigi form (1359–63), whose first part ended with the shipwreck poem "Passa la nave mia" (189), reflects both a new departure for the book and a moment of crisis in its ideological setting (Cachey, "From Shipwreck to Port"). Petrarch's restlessness, his refusal to consider any arrival to be definitive, is thereafter documented not only in his revisions of individual poems but also in the series of redactions or forms of the book. The changes extended even to the renumbering of the last thirty-one poems in the autograph Vatican manuscript, which had already been copied, at the very end of his life, as he was completing the "Triumph of Eternity," whose final "hoc placet" ("this pleases me"), the marginal annotation the author often made to signal his satisfaction with a revision, dates from the poet's last days.

From the late 1350s forward, likely in relation to Boccaccio's exhortations to Petrarch that he should give due consideration to the greatness of the poetry of Dante, Petrarch began to focus his energies especially on the vernacular lyric. Despite his protestations about the insignificance of his vernacular poetry, which he famously described as *nugellae* ("trifles" [*Seniles* 13.10; my trans.]), Petrarch wrote little or no more Latin poetry after this time (the *Africa* having been set aside) and turned his attention to the *Canzoniere* and the *Triumphs*. In this respect, the chronology of Petrarch's life and works after the fateful meeting with Boccaccio in 1350 reflects the latter's influence on Petrarch in the vernacular realm, a reversal of Petrarch's influence on Boccaccio, who, according to a commonplace of the literary historiography, turned primarily to Latin works after coming into contact with Petrarch. Be that as it may, after his discussion of Dante with Boccaccio, Petrarch appears to have attended to his vernacular poetry with renewed focus and energy (Cachey, "Between Dante"). In fact, the history of the *Canzoniere* parallels the compositional history of the Dantean *Triumphs* in an intriguing and contrapuntal manner from the late 1350s forward, the date from when Petrarch's work on the *Triumphs* is continuously recorded by the manuscripts until to his death. One can speculate about the complementary development of these works in progress along parallel and contrapuntal paths. On the one hand, the stasis of the calendar-like circular structure of the *Canzoniere* concludes with Petrarch's repudiation of Laura in favor of the Virgin, while, on the other hand, the linear and forward-moving march of the *Triumphs* culminates in the resurrection of the glorified body of Laura in the "Triumph of Eternity." The reading of the vernacular lyric works to be undertaken in the course pursue further this dialectic of stasis and movement forward, exploring how the inner rhythm of the journey of Petrarch's life and works inspires and informs their making, their significance, and their art.

NOTES

[1] Quotations from *Familiares* follow Aldo S. Bernardo's translations (*Letters on Familiar Matters* [1975–85]).

[2] Quotations from *Seniles* are from the translation by Aldo S. Bernardo, Saul Levin, and Reta A. Bernardo (*Letters of Old Age*), unless otherwise noted.

Love and Misogamy in the Age of Dante and Petrarch

Fabian Alfie

My contribution was inspired in part by a student's interjection—"What's this guy's problem?"—during the discussion of poem 264 in Petrarch's *Canzoniere*. This took place during the fall 1999 semester, when for the first time in my career I was teaching the course ITAL 250A: Italian Literature in Translation: The Middle Ages. The course deals with the masterpieces of medieval Italian literature: Dante's *Vita nuova* and *Inferno*, in their entirety; selections from Petrarch's *Canzoniere*; selections from Boccaccio's *Decameron*; and numerous lesser works, including the poetry of the Sicilian poets, the *dolce stil novo*, and selected letters by Saint Catherine of Siena. The course is part of the general education offering at the University of Arizona and, as such, can fulfill a requirement for students of all different majors. Hence, while many of the students in the class were quite adept at discussing poetry—either because they had taken other literature classes or had some previously undiscovered talents or interests—others were not, and they struggled at times to keep up with the material. Clearly the student who raised the question about the poet fell into the latter category, but that is not to suggest that he was ignorant or uninterested. On the contrary, his question highlights an obvious difference in popular and literary culture between the fourteenth century and the start of the twenty-first century. When I taught the class in later semesters, I made a point to address the core issue of the student's interjection, and I found that doing so led to a deeper understanding of Petrarch and his subject matter.

My experience teaching Petrarch in ITAL 250A forms the basis for the present discussion. But before I continue, I would like to establish a point of comparison by referring to another class. The University of Arizona also offers a general survey of Italian literature, ITAL 400A, conducted entirely in Italian and intended for Italian majors possessing some familiarity with literary studies, however scanty at times. In this class, we also read and discuss Petrarch, but in the original Italian, and thus I dedicate much class time to reading Petrarch's poems and clarifying his difficult language. I also ask the students to analyze his style both phonologically and lexically. To achieve the former, I put the students into groups and ask them to circle all the voiced, unvoiced, or geminate consonants in a sonnet by Petrarch and a passage from Dante (*Inferno* 32); the students can then compare the very different styles of two masterful poets. To address Petrarch's lexicon, I ask students to keep track of the terms that are repeated from one poem to the next and to see which patterns develop. Both exercises serve to illustrate Petrarch's stylistic achievements. The students can see how Petrarch develops a melodious, mellifluous style by avoiding geminates and unvoiced consonants (i.e., /p/, /t/, /k/, /f/, /s/). The students also experience

Petrarch's highly selective vocabulary, which omits terminology that might possess unwanted connotations or undertones. His Latinate lexicon avoids anything that suggests the plebeian or unseemly. In ITAL 400A, I close the section on Petrarch by asking the students to listen to Guillaume Dufay's musical version of 366 from the *Canzoniere*, "O vergine bella," thereby illustrating how the poet influenced other artistic forms.[1] In short, in ITAL 400A, I can capitalize on the students' knowledge of Italian and background in literature to address some of the fundamental issues surrounding Petrarch's poetry.

In the general education course, I adopt Robert M. Durling's translation of the *Canzoniere*. I do not rule out entirely the techniques used in ITAL 400A; I play Dufay's music, for instance, and I ask the students to examine the phonology of Petrarch's style even though they might not understand Italian. Given the limitations of using a translation, however, the students in ITAL 250A do not come away from the class with the profound understanding of Petrarch's language that comes from a firsthand experience of it. Furthermore, in rendering intelligible each particular lyric, the translator sometimes translates the same term differently in each poem. Thus a study of Petrarch's lexicon in English translation does not yield the same results as a study of Petrarch's original, since the lexicon of the English translation is much broader. Without being able to rely on the students' familiarity of Italian, I cannot explore the poet's aesthetics in ITAL 250A. What the poet says becomes the primary, almost exclusive focus of the class, but how he expresses himself in his verse virtually falls by the wayside. Students are required to keep abreast of the subtle gradations of Petrarch's meaning as they move from one love poem to the next, and the course runs the risk of becoming a microanalysis of the poet's ever-changing views on love rather than a discussion of finely honed poetry.

Let us return, then, to the context of the student's interjection. Early in the semester, we had discussed the *Vita nuova*, and Dante's "little book" served as the backdrop for the reading of Petrarch's *Canzoniere*. During the analysis of the *Vita nuova*, I continually highlighted Dante's use of religious and ecclesiastical terminology. At the same time, I tried to postpone for as long as possible revealing that Dante's "controlling metaphor," to use Charles Singleton's words, was a comparison of Beatrice with Christ (22). I wanted to allow Dante's radical ideology to dawn gradually on the students, paralleling the way that Dante slowly informs his readers of Beatrice's angelic nature. Later in the semester, I reviewed much of Dante's amorous philosophy in the *Vita nuova*, in particular his treatment of Beatrice as an objective correlative for God, divine love, or theology. Before the student posed the question that opens this essay, we had discussed many of Petrarch's well-known poems. I had made a point of noting the language similar to that of Dante's *Vita nuova* but also of illustrating how Petrarch casts it as problematic. I had demonstrated the growing tension between the poet's love for Laura, in all her symbolic guises, and his love for God. The tension, known among Italian criticism as the *dissidio*, comes to the foreground in 264 and predominates in the second half of the lyric collection. We had come to the point in the class when we saw that Petrarch calls into question Dante's amorous ideology, when the student raised his hand and asked the question, which from a certain perspective has a great deal of legitimacy: Why all the hand-wringing about being in love with Laura? Why would being enamored create difficulties for a man of faith? Today, loving another human being frequently does not interfere with one's relationship to God.

On reflection, the student's question made me understand that a crucial element of Dante's *Vita nuova*, and by extension Dante's "vitanovistic" language, has been lost over the years. That missing element forms a component part of Petrarch's critique of the *dolce stil novo*. Some two centuries have now passed since the Romantic poets adopted and reworked one of the central tenets of Dante's work. Because of their influence, many contemporary readers find nothing amiss in Dante's comparison of Beatrice with the transcendent. Not only has such a trope become a commonplace of nineteenth- and twentieth-century literature, but it also has entered the general vocabulary of everyday life. Numerous popular songs, for example, employ the metaphor of the beloved woman (or man) as having a divine provenance: "Earth Angel" (the Penguins), "You're an Angel" (Madonna), "Like a Prayer" (Madonna), "(She Moves in) Mysterious Ways" (U2), to name only a few. For many modern readers, Dante's comparisons of Beatrice with the divinity seem normative, almost banal. Yet in the culture of the late thirteenth and early fourteenth century, Dante's literary treatment of Beatrice was shockingly innovative. The so-called anti-stilnovism of the comic poets of the age, such as Cecco Angiolieri, posed the implicit question of the legitimacy of Dante's language (Marti 100–19). In fact, for Bartolomeo Sermartelli's *princeps* edition of the *Vita nuova*, published during the sixteenth century, the Inquisition was still offended by Dante's audaciousness and required the removal of all religious terminology applied to Beatrice.[2] The student's inquiry, about how loving Laura might jeopardize the poet's salvation, was the logical application of a modern perspective to the medieval text. From the student's standpoint, Petrarch was fretting over seemingly trivial matters. But from the point of view of medieval culture, the situation was reversed. Petrarch's concerns echoed those of the predominant teachings of the age. It was the compromise affected by Dante's *Vita nuova* that constituted the new and unorthodox. In other words, the general culture has come full circle and now treats Dante's "strange" text, to paraphrase Harold Bloom, as normal (*Western Tradition* 72). From the modern viewpoint, Petrarch's *dissidio* seems unnecessary, perhaps neurotic, whereas Dante's fusion of religious and amorous vocabularies has lost the power to surprise readers.

With the realization inspired by the student's blunt, although by no means irrelevant, query, I approach the question of Petrarch's *dissidio* from a historical-cultural perspective. Now when I now teach ITAL 250A, I anticipate the discussion of Petrarch's inner conflict by introducing some key concepts. I work in the notion, elaborated by Alastair Minnis, that during the Middle Ages, a writer could not be an *auctor* and currently in love; at the very least, the author needed to be out of love to be acceptable (181). Minnis's perspective helps explain why Petrarch speaks in his authorial voice only after Laura has passed on (e.g., 1). When the students thoroughly understand Minnis's outlook, I then open up the class to a general discussion of why passion might undercut a writer's authority among the general readership of the Middle Ages. The conversation is usually productive; students have proffered structural comparisons with a conversion narrative and cited exemplars such as Saint Augustine of Hippo. Minnis's conclusions lay the groundwork, therefore, for a general, albeit simplified, overview of medieval thought about the proper relations between men and women.

The first lecture given during the portion of the syllabus dedicated to Petrarch does not, in fact, address Petrarch at all. Rather, I provide the historical background to the question of love. Given the influence of the church authorities on the issue, the cultural ethos of thirteenth- and fourteenth-century Christianity was skewed toward a severe, conservative perspective. At least a week beforehand, I place Ralph Hanna and Traugott Lawler's edition of *Jankyn's Book of Wikked Wives* on reserve in the library. This anthology and translation of numerous misogynistic texts includes Saint Jerome's *Adversus Jovinianum*, Theophrastis's *Liber de nuptiis*, and Walter Map's *Dissuasio Valerii*. I divide the class into three groups and assign readings from the anthology to each of the groups. I want the students to be familiar with classical and medieval misogynist literature before examining Petrarch's poetry. When the time comes, I ask for volunteers to provide overviews of each of the major works, and the students are frequently surprised to see how remarkably similar the misogynist texts were. To cite R. Howard Bloch, it was as if the misogynists all spoke with the same mouth (2–3). My point is not to treat specific antifeminist writers but to view antifeminism as a central component of the history of Western culture and literature.

I dedicate the lecture to the emphasis placed on misogyny in some strands of medieval thought. Katharina Wilson and Elizabeth Makowski label the description of women's horrible natures in the attempt to ensure monastic celibacy as "misogamous" (1). Misogamy indelibly characterized the medieval theological discourse about relationships between the sexes. In the minds of many religious thinkers, the only licit relationship between men and women was no relationship at all. I begin the lecture by citing 1 Corinthians 7.9, which reads in part, "it is better to marry than to burn." I then explain that for centuries it was interpreted not as an endorsement of marriage but as the condemnation of human weakness. As John Chrysostom glossed the biblical passage, it is also better to be blinded in one eye than in both, but that is not to say that blindness is good. During my discussion, I primarily consider Jerome's *Adversus Jovinianum* as exemplary of medieval misogyny. I provide a general synopsis of the work, in comparison with the others assigned to the students. I also underscore

Jerome's intentions in the text of dissuading other men from leaving the monastery by marrying or falling in love. Although there is some reason to interpret *Adversus Jovinianum* as satiric, it also may have been read straightforwardly and formed the basis of a lengthy tradition of misogynistic literature (Hanna and Lawler 17–18).

I then point out that the negative conception of all interactions between the sexes became more complicated later in the Middle Ages. When the vernacular literature of love developed in the eleventh and twelfth centuries, conservative elements within Catholicism applied the church fathers' condemnation of sexuality to the poetry of passion. D. W. Robertson, Jr., for example, interprets Andreas Capellanus's *De amore* not as a straightforward treatise on loving properly but as the moral condemnation of amorous literature (400). As Alexander Joseph Denomy writes, "It is impossible to reconcile the tenets of Courtly Love with the commandments of God, with the Divine Will as interpreted by Saint Paul, with the teaching of Christ and of His Church" (27). This discussion is not intended to suggest that the culture of the Middle Ages was monolithic, or that all thinkers shared all the concepts about women or about love as incompatible with Christianity. Rather, I want to show how the promulgators of vernacular amorous literature found themselves on the proverbial horns of a dilemma: on the one hand writing about love, while on the other trying to follow the teachings of the church. It would be mistaken, however, to view misogamy as strictly about enforcing the brothers' chastity; instead, it employed women as metaphoric for all worldly attachments (Cassell 354). Given how Petrarch treats Laura as a polysemous symbol, now representing a young woman and now representing worldly literature and poetic fame, the expansive understanding of misogamy appears relevant.

Once the greater historical movement of misogamy is understood, then the writings of the great thinkers of ITAL 250A suddenly take on a new and different tenor. Dante's *Vita nuova*, for example, is cast in an entirely new light. Instead of giving the appearance of a firmly doctrinal text, it seems more tenuous, like the uneasy reconciliation of two possibly incompatible belief systems. The uncertainty underlying Petrarch's *dissidio*, furthermore, comes across as the further destabilization of Dante's youthful work. Laura cannot be a true stand-in for God or theology, because worldly love was the deviation from authentic religious veneration. By foregrounding the question of misogamy, Petrarch's *dissidio* ceases being the insecure reflections of a troubled individual. It is, rather, the symptom of a period in transition, when the older notions of Christian asceticism were beginning to cede to a valorization of worldliness. Petrarch understood the teachings of the authorities of the age, which required the renunciation of earthly attachments, but he cast himself as unwilling or unable to follow them. By directly addressing the historical question of misogamy, I feel I more fully address the student's question. The problem was not unique to Petrarch; rather, it was the anxiety of an entire society.

NOTES

[1] I typically have the students listen to the version of Dufay's song recorded by the Early Music Consort of London, directed by David Munrow.

[2] For a description of Sermartelli's *princeps* edition, see Michele Barbi's edition of the *Vita nuova* ("Manoscritti" lxxix).

Solitude and Inwardness: Approaching the *Canzoniere* through *De vita solitaria* and the *Secretum*

Jobst Welge

While teaching at the University of California, Santa Barbara, in 2003, I chose to introduce a seminar on early modern subjectivity, entitled Representing the Early Modern Self, with the figure of Petrarch. I began with a representative selection of poems from the *Canzoniere*, a very short excerpt from *De vita solitaria*, and a reading of the *Secretum* before moving on to later forms and genres of self-representation, including selections from Cardano, Luther, Montaigne, and Descartes, as well as some examples of early modern visual self-representation, including the famous 1500 self-portrait by Dürer. A close look at the self-portrait shows that its pose of inwardness and self-absorption is inevitably an effect of performance and display—which helps illustrate the same point with regard to Petrarchan self-representation in the *Canzoniere* (but where it is perhaps less immediately visible for students). The various exhibits present students with examples of late medieval or early modern subjectivity, autobiographical texts in a broadly conceived sense that all speak, through their historical transformations, to the contrast between body and soul and to the rhetoric of inwardness versus strategies of exterior self-(re)presentation. For instance, our discussion of Petrarchan solitude in the *Canzoniere* and *De vita solitaria* provided a useful platform for our later reading of Montaigne's *De la solitude* (*Of Solitude*). Students were thus able to see that the dialectic of interiority, withdrawal, and literary communication is not just a Petrarchan idiosyncrasy but a central theme of early modern humanism.

I do not hesitate to insert Petarch into a broad framework of early modern literature and culture. Whatever stance we take with regard to the period problem of the Middle Ages and Renaissance, Petrarch undeniably plays a prominent part in it. His writings offer the possibility of early modern subjectivity, which cannot be understood, I would argue, without taking into account the historical transformations of the rhetoric of inwardness that is so pervasive in the Petrarchan corpus. If we bring Petrarch into contact with later (but also earlier) notions of inwardness, it is not necessarily to claim him as the inventor of the modern self—a notion against which Timothy Reiss has argued, claiming that the whole rhetoric of private and public, as well as of inner and outer, is anachronistic with regard to Petrarch's time, since in this context every private utterance is inevitably a social one, especially in the case of the *Familiares* (*Mirages* 327). I concur with Reiss that the terms *private* and *public* are associated with an incipient modernity and need to be carefully employed in the late medieval context of Petrarch. In the same vein, inwardness and solitude are deceptive categories for Reiss, who prefers to speak of the intermingling of the contemplative and the social, the personal and the civic, the ethical and the political. Again, I agree with Reiss that terms like *solitude* and *inwardness*—part of Petrarch's own vocabulary—should be understood not in an essentialist sense but rather as part of a complex constellation where different impulses and requirements are negotiated. In fact, to Reiss's opposing categories I would add the terms *inwardness* and *authority*, for Petrarchan, humanist authorship continuously performs the self against the claims of literary, religious, and political authority. Somewhat contrary to Reiss, however, I believe that an analysis of the Petrarchan rhetoric of inwardness can help us understand the powerful "subjectivity effect" generated by Petrarch's work (Fineman). Students can be referred here to the now canonical, accesible study by the philosopher Charles Taylor, *Sources of the Self*, which dedicates a chapter to Saint Augustine as one of the most influential contributors to the discourses of Western inwardness. While recent studies on early modern literature have made important contributions to the study of the rhetoric of inwardness (e.g., Eisaman Maus; Berger), the role of Petrarch in this context, precisely through his idiosyncratic adaptation of the authority of Augustine, has not yet been sufficiently recognized.[1] In the following, I would like to indicate, however briefly, that Petrarch's moral-philosophical texts can be strategically used to illustrate the complex of solitude, inwardness, and authority and, by implication, how these matters can be brought to bear on the *Canzoniere*. Having isolated the key concepts of solitude and inwardness in the *Canzoniere*, we can then see how the same categories of Petrarchan authorship are discursively employed in the prose works, which in turn will illuminate aspects of the poetry.

Let me first recall that the opening poem of the *Canzoniere* makes evident that the individual poems to follow may be subsumed under the overarching theme of self-difference:

> Voi ch'ascoltate in rime sparse il suono
> di quei sospiri ond'io nudriva 'l core
> in sul mio giovenile errore,
> quand'era in parte altr'uomo da quell ch'i' sono. (lines 1–4)
>
> You who hear in scattered rhymes the sound of those sighs with which I nourished my heart during my first youthful error, when I was in part another man from what I am now.[2]

These lines hint not only at a partial, or halfway, conversion (taking into consideration also the concluding poem, which contains a prayer to the Virgin as a renunciation and transfiguration of the cult of Laura), they also invoke, with the very first word, a second person ("Voi"), an audience, which is clearly differentiated from the not so frequent "voi" (e.g., in 3 or 5) that refers to Laura. In other words, the discourse of solitude, so characteristic for Petrarch ("Solo et pensoso" [35]), also has a public or social dimension (as Reiss would have it). Indeed, the sestet of the first poem begins by making explicit an interrelation between public and self, as well as a relation that the self has with itself, as it were: "Ma ben veggio or sì come al popol tutto / favola fui gran tempo, onde sovente / di me medesmo meco mi vergogno" 'But now I see well how for a long time I was the talk of the crowd, for which often I am ashamed of myself within' (lines 9–11). If in the preceding lines the lyric self wants to share his experience with others, these last lines speak of the fact that this self had already been seen as an object by others, which in turn leads to an interior self-objectification, wonderfully expressed through the doubly reflective, anaphoric words. The opening poem, then, exemplifies the general phenomenon of lyrical self-reflexivity, of self-difference, as well as the characteristic coexistence of self-repentance (the "youthful error," the "vane speranze" 'vain hopes' [6]) and poetic self-affirmation (implicit, for instance, in the poetics of a "vario stile" 'varied style' [5]) and self-authorization in the face of an intimate public. In this regard, as we will see, the poem resonates in particular with the last scene of the third book of the *Secretum*, where Franciscus parts ways with Augustinus, and returns to his literary work. The *Canzoniere*, as well as the tradition of love lyric on which it builds, rests on the notion of temporal development as connected with liturgical and confessional forms, yet in Petrarch the memory of these forms, and especially the invocation of a postconversion perspective in the opening sonnet, only serves to dramatize the sense of poetic self-circularity, where growing temporal distance with regard to the beloved object and the eternal presence of remembrance intersect (Stierle 649). Starting with a close reading of the opening poem, then, students will come to see that the relation between interiority and a public, between self-abnegation and self-affirmation, is constitutive of Petrarch's writing—the *Canzoniere* as well as his other works. Especially for purposes of teaching, the categories of solitude and inwardness provide a useful thread to discuss Petrarch's writing.

"Solo et pensoso": **De vita solitaria**

During the years 1342–43, Petrarch retreated to the place of Vaucluse, near Avignon, where he wrote not only a dialogue of spiritual self-investigation, the *Secretum* (*De secretu conflictu mearum curarum*), but also *De vita solitaria* (*On the Solitary Life*). *De vita solitaria* is a self-apologetic treatise in which Petrarch polemically opposes the solitary, forest-dwelling life of the poet to the self-alienating, active city life of courtly or clerical service, emblematized by the symbolic places of the sylvan Vaucluse and the "Babylonian" Avignon, respectively (*Canzoniere* 136). The text is informed by medieval monasticism (the second part contains long collections of hagiographic exempla) and by the classical ideal of secular *otium*, which entails a legacy already much more complex than simply advocating a retreat from the active life.

In *De vita solitaria* the retreat from the public life is said to lead to spiritual fulfillment, but it is also described as the ideal condition for literary production: "Vacuitatem vero seu vacationem dici mavis literarum atque artium fontem esse" 'To be absent or free . . . from affairs is the source of literature and the arts' (76).[3] Not only is Petrarch writing about solitude, but writing and solitude are identified with each other, so that solitude becomes a place of conversation in a Ciceronian sense: "Sunt enim quibus solitaria vita morta gravior sit et mortem allatura videatur. Quod precipue literarum ignaris evenire solet, quibus si confabulator desit, quid secum, quid ve cum libris loqui valeant non habent, itaque muti sunt. Equidem solitudo sine literis exilium est, carcer, eculeus" 'There are those for whom solitude is more threatening than death, graver than death. This happens to those ignorant ones, who, without interlocutors, are not capable of talking to themselves, or to books, and therefore remain mute. Solitude without culture is certainly an exile, a jail, and a torture' (47). In fact, one of the interesting dimensions of the text is the strategy of literary self-doubling that resonates with the "me medesmo meco" of *Canzoniere* 1, or the role of Augustinus as a controlling witness of the self's discourse in the *Secretum*. While Petrarch explicitly distances himself from the technique of creating a "testis imaginarius" 'imaginary witness,' a notion advised by Epicurus and in Seneca's *Letters to Lucilius* (letter 25), his Christianization of this technique (Christ as a true witness) ultimately amounts to the same strategy of interiorized self-observation.

On the one hand, Petrarch describes his writing as an "interventionist" kind of literature that ultimately aims at the moral improvement of society by claiming, "Volo solitudinem non solam, otium non iners nec inutile, sed quod e solitudine prosit multis" 'he wants a nonsolitary solitude, an *otium* neither sterile nor uselesss, a solitude that can be useful for many' (1.270, 272). On the other hand, Petrarch rejects Cicero and other writers of the Roman Republic, by fully adopting the Augustinian perspective of the city of God. He defends a stance of spiritual inwardness against the ornamental, external dimension of rhetorical culture. Thus he criticizes Cicero, whose desire to derive glory from oratory pushes him inevitably into the public realm: "Est illud oratoribus singulare et proprium ut pro magnitudine ingenii magnis urbibus ac populorum frequentia delectentur, solitudines execrentur, iudiciorumque silentium adversentur atque oderint" 'It is peculiar and characteristic of orators that they take pleasure in large cities and in the midst of the crowd, in proportion to the greatness of their own talents. They curse solitude, and hate and oppose the silence required for decisions' (250). While the life in the urban crowd is generally rejected, Petrarch at one point seems to endorse the Senecan notion that solitude might also be achieved metaphorically: "[S]ed ita ut, siqua me necessitas in urbem cogat, solitudinem in popolo, atque in medio tempestatis portum michi conflare didicerim, artificio non omnibus noto sensibus imperitandi ut quod sentiunt non sentiant" 'But if some circumstance should push me towards the city, I know how to create solitude in the midst of the crowd, a haven in the middle of a tempest, by using a system not known to all: to control the senses in such a way that they don't feel what they feel' (52).

Even *De vita solitaria*, the Petrarchan text most directly concerned with the question of solitude, then, sees itself as ultimately promoting civic welfare. Drawing on monastic ideals of eremitic seclusion, Petrarch represents these ideals as ultimately unattainable for himself. His portrayal of the solitary life appears no longer as the ideal of a religious community or institution but as a viable practice for individual, secular readers. The text was dedicated to Philippe de Cabassoles in 1366, the proprietor of the Vaucluse territory, who had visited Petrarch twenty years earlier during his state of solitude. The figure of Cabassoles, constantly invoked throughout the text, is appealed to as a friend, a double of the Petrarchan self. Petrarch remarks at the end of the treatise, "eam me solitudinem laudasse, non que unum etiam, sed que turbas fugit" 'I realize that I have exalted the kind of solitude that flees from the multitude, not the one which also flees from a friend' (304). Petrarch is thus a pioneer for practices of solitude that are no longer tied to transindividual communities; he transforms solitary life from a normative ideal into a subjective principle. The condition of solitude is bound up with the practice of writing. The quasi-monastic ideals espoused in *De vita solitaria* are thus more than the other of Petrarchan humanism; they also suggest the model for it. Even brief selections from this text (especially the opening pages) will alert students to the fact that "communication in solitude" is for Petrarch not only a lyric sentiment ("solo et pensoso") but a concept that draws on both ancient Stoic as well as Christian ideas of self-observation in order to model a sense of inwardly based authorship.

"Con l'Occhio Interno": Inwardness and Authority in the Secretum

In contrast to the somewhat repetitive format of *De vita solitaria*, the *Secretum* is an astonishingly vivid text to which, in my experience, undergraduates respond well.[4] The text is best read in its entirety; otherwise, it can be difficult for students to gauge its complexity and contradictory nature. If selections need to be made, I recommend focusing on the first and the third parts (the second book concerns the somewhat more abstract question of the freedom of the will). Like the opening poem of the *Canzoniere*, the *Secretum* depicts the conflict between a present subject and its personal past, in a form that is at the same time confessional interrogation, autobiography, and humanist dialogue. It thus can be read as a kind of extended gloss on the rhetoric of conversion in the opening sonnet (as, in a different way, the well-known letter from the *Familiares*, the "Ascent of Mount Ventoux" [4.1]). Moreover, the Petrarchan self finds itself poised between different authorities, Christianity and humanism, which have to be negotiated with each other but which cannot always be reconciled.

A reading of the *Secretum*, then, helps bring to the fore these conflicts of the Petrarchan psyche; it serves to emphasize, now from a prosaic, discursive perspective, the importance of the conversion model for Petrarch, as it is embodied by Augustine's *Confessions*.

The *Secretum* is a text that assumes a paradoxical relation to authority: more than any other text by Petrarch it challenges the values of his literary career with the model of religious conversion. At the same time, however, it provides a shrewd defense of his humanist project and thus becomes a text of literary self-authorization. The *Secretum* is a three-day-long conversation between the voices of Augustinus and Franciscus, whose relation to the historical Augustine and Petrarch is far from straightforward (e.g., Franciscus might be a former version of Petrarch at the time of writing), as Francisco Rico has shown in an authoritative, fascinating study (*Vida*; see also Wojciehowski). The very title of the work alludes in part to the secret location of the Milanese garden to which Augustine had withdrawn during his conversion experience (*Confessions* 8). The rhetoric of privacy makes the *Secretum*, which was never published during Petrarch's lifetime or explicitly referred to in his other writings, indeed appear as a secret and somewhat more personal text in contrast to his other familiar, semipublic writings. Yet some critics have argued, rightly, I think, that Petrarch's self-conscious and highly sophisticated use of literary subtexts (or even the form of the Ciceronian, public dialogue) should be taken as evidence that this private text is always already conceived for a reader (Kahn). Nevertheless, the possibility that this might not be the case, that the text might be entirely private, provides an illuminating contrast with the *Canzoniere*, where this is obviously not the case. At the same time, the paradox is that all secretive communication is necessarily dialogical. The presence of Augustinus illustrates the point that a spiritual self-exploration is in need of an authoritative center, an interiorized authority, regardless of how far Franciscus is willing to cede to this authority.

The literary form of the dialogue is intimately connected with the question of ethics, a debate about the right form of life. Canzone 264 ("I' vo pensando") is perhaps the poem of the *Canzoniere* where this dialogical or even psychomachic tension within the self is most visible and can be most directly compared with the form of the *Secretum*. In this poem Petrarch dwells on the eternal battle of wills and suggests that the right path and the voyage toward it are always betrayed by deviation, by a return to the sinful state of desire in which his contrary inclinations, the "duo nodi" 'two . . . knots' of love and glory, keep him (line 83). The division of the will produces the duplication of voices, leading to a sort of inner dialogue: "L'un penser parla con la mente, et dice: / —Che pur agogni? onde soccorso attendi?" 'One thought speaks to my mind and says: "What are you yearning for still? Whence do you expect help?"' (19–20). Similarly, the *Secretum* invokes the moral image of the *bivium* from the *Aeneid* and relates the dialogical opposition of two different directions with the framework of religious conversion. Yet if the *Confessions* provided a paradigmatic perspective that was organized around the destruction of a former self—and that was crucially based on the difference between the self as subject and as object of autobiographical discourse—Petrarch, in the words of John Freccero, "is turning Augustine against himself, making sin the principle of individuation" ("Autobiography" 16). In the third and last book, where Augustinus reproaches Franciscus for his pursuit of the two destructive chains of "amor et gloria" 'love and fame' (16),[5] the discussion comes to the topic of Laura, and hence the *Canzoniere*. Franciscus at first insists that his love for Laura is entirely spiritual and thus not sinful. Yet, as Augustinus presses on, Franciscus admits that this spiritual love would not occur without the help of physical beauty. The whole passage indicates a crisis of the Dantean concept of female beauty as a conduit toward the divine. This problem might be related to a moment in the second book where Augustinus recalls the fable of Narcissus (see also *Canzoniere* 45) to remind Franciscus that the care for outward appearances does not go beyond the fragility of the earthly body: "Exterioris cutis contentus aspectu, oculos mentis ultra non porrigis" 'If you stop at the exterior aspect of the skin, then you will never direct inwards the eyes of the intellect' (60). Franciscus admits his sin, as required by the generic conventions of the confessional dialogue, and hovers here and elsewhere between contrition and self-affirmation. The thematic of the third book, then, can easily be related to the complex of Laura in the *Canzoniere*: the self-reflecting circularity of Petrarchan poetics, where the desire for Laura is inseparable from the desire for the poetic laurel. The end of the last book holds the decision to convert in suspension. Augustinus asks Franciscus to abandon his pagan literary projects (notably, the Latin epic *Africa*), but Franciscus wants to finish them anyway. While the earlier books saw Franciscus giving in to the criticism from his revered master, the last book culminates with the self-affirmation of the writer Petrarch. The possibility of becoming another Franciscus, while not directly renounced, is deferred beyond the boundaries of the book. The confessional dialogue foregrounds Petrarch's tendency to convey an impression of psychological inwardness by exhibiting self-contradictions.

The conflicted, dialogical presentation of the *Secretum* will help students recognize this principle in the *Canzoniere*, where secular love (Laura) and literature (the laurel) emerge likewise from an interior conflict. Thus students will better understand and appreciate the peculiar fragmentary structure of the *Canzoniere* and its loosely confessional character, including the final substitution of Laura by the Virgin. Specifically, students may analyze how canzone 264 stages the conflicting interior voices of the poetic self and how certain poems of the *Canzoniere* (e.g., 127 and 129), especially in the later sections (350–66), depart from a dematerialized image of Laura and foreground the process of thought and interior vision: "ché più bella che mai con l'occhio interno / . . . la veggio" 'for more beautiful than ever I see her with my internal eye' (345.12–13). Moreover, to encounter Petrarch simultaneously as an Italian lyric poet and as a Latin humanist—to see the doubling of the authorial self into different voices and genres and the dialogical nature of the *Canzoniere*—will help show that the more or less public rhetoric of inwardness and solitude are central categories for the emergence of Petrarchan authorship and of authorship generally.

NOTES

[1] Students new to the topic might most immediately profit from the survey essay by John Martin, "Inventing Sincerity, Refashioning Prudence."

[2] All quotations from the *Canzoniere* are from the bilingual edition by Robert M. Durling.

[3] All quotations from *De vita solitaria* are from Bufano's edition; all translations from the work are my own. For an older English translation, see Zeitlin's *The Life of Solitude*.

[4] For this undergraduate class I have used, in the absence of better alternatives, the very affordable translation by J. G. Nichols. As much as this widely available, popular edition should be welcomed in principle, more could be wished for than a mediocre, barely three-page introduction and the complete absence of explanatory notes or commentary. The *Secretum* is a fascinating and complex text not least because of its intertextual references.

[5] All quotations from the *Secretum* are from Dotti's edition; all translations are my own.

Petrarch and the Ethics of Writing and Reading

Massimo Lollini

Writing means to adventure into the future.

(Pontiggia, *Contemporanei* 58)

Why Teach Petrarch? Why Read the Classics?

In academia nowadays it is not possible to take for granted the need and necessity of reading the great authors of the past. Thus I always start my courses asking myself, Why teach Petrarch? I ask my students, Why read the classics? These two questions are interrelated and suggest the need to find a good motivation for making the effort to read something difficult, far away from ourselves, and written in a language different from our own. A first answer to these questions could be Italo Calvino's idea that "a classic is a book that has never finished saying what it has to say" (128). This answer implies that there is an actual and modern value in ancient and medieval texts and that it is wrong to think of the past as something dead and alien.[1] Giuseppe Pontiggia suggests that a classic is "contemporary to the future," that an artist always writes not only to create a living text but also to give birth to something that is projected into the future, beyond the historical perspective, something that may overcome the limits of the present (*Contemporanei* 58; "Contemporaneità" 128–32). I would offer two important examples of this artistic projection into the future, one from Dante and the other from Petrarch.

Dante constructs the final vision of the *Divine Comedy* to give to the "futura gente" a glimpse of the divine glory:

> O somma luce che tanto ti levi
> da' concetti mortali, a la mia mente
> ripresta un poco di quel che parevi,
> e fa la lingua mia tanto possente,
> ch'una favilla sol de la tua gloria
> possa lasciare a la futura gente. (*Paradiso* 33.67–72)

> Oh Light Supreme that art so far uplifted above mortal conceiving, relend to my mind a little of what Thou didst appear, and give my tongue such power that it may leave only a single spark of Thy glory for the folk to come.[2]

Dante conceives his poem and poetic vision on a vertical scale, as a contribution to the knowledge of the divine, offered to those to come. Petrarch appeals to the future in a different way; his scale is "lateral" (Greene, "Flexibility" 249) and, to a certain extent, oblique, as one understands reading his famous *Posteritati* (*Lettera ai posteri* [ed. Villani]; *Letter to Posterity* [trans. Robinson]). Notwithstanding the intention of giving an idealized portrait of himself, Petrarch shows here that he has to offer to the future not the vision of divine wisdom but the account of his life full of inquietude, "sins," and incertitude. For Petrarch the wisdom that one can achieve coming of age and maturing is always human and never completed. In *Letter to Posterity*, he also speaks of his love for the ancients that moves him to reject the present age and to continually attempt living in spirit in other ages. Petrarch points here to the mysterious presence of the future in the present and to the alterity of an element in his life and intellectual research always resistant to current human understanding.

I begin my course on Petrarch by having students read *Letter to Posterity*, which demonstrates how the poet was aware that the ancient classics were to him contemporary to the future. In this letter the founder of humanism suggests that the *humanae litterae* and the ancient manuscripts were important to him not just for their actual value, for their ability to help the understanding of the present age, but also and above all for the difference that they represented, for their not yet fully developed and understood meaning. Petrarch, too, considers himself a classic, the first of the modern classics, and in this perspective it is important for us to ask ourselves, as we would when reading any other classic, Are we contemporary to Petrarch? In other words, in our reading and interpretation, are we addressing and keeping alive that projection into the future that the classics conceal as a treasure?

Ethics, Literature, and Alterity

Hans Robert Jauss developed an interesting notion of the alterity and modernity of medieval literature, drawing in part on C. S. Lewis's *The Discarded Image*. This approach provides a good historical and cultural background to the literature of the Middle Ages and Renaissance. The idea of a medieval model and mind-set that eventually was dismissed by modernity helps us understand the medieval difference and alterity that enable a full appreciation of medieval texts as they were conceived and read. I argue, however, that this kind of alterity conceived as historical distance is not peculiar to the so-called Middle Ages but is also present in any identifiable historical period, including ancient times. In teaching ancient and medieval texts I do not erase that historical alterity, but neither do I amplify it.

Instead of reducing the classics to their historical dimension, I attempt to prepare students to appreciate how these texts challenge the given historical context. To do so I introduce an ethical notion of alterity that involves both the author and the reader, since ethics is the field in which the notion of otherness and alterity is articulated and discussed. There are at least three aspects of this notion that I consider when I teach Petrarch. First, there is the otherness of the love experience in its encounter and tension with the language, an infinite experience that the poet wants to hold and crystallize in the written text. Second, there is the otherness of time, death, and eternity that the human subject cannot entirely embrace and describe in writing. Finally, I point to the otherness of the writing subject that discovers itself always incomplete and changing, inside and outside itself, in the encounter with the other and the external environment.

This multifaceted idea of alterity is at the core of Petrach's *Canzoniere* (*Rerum vulgarium fragmenta*) and developed throughout his literary production. It emerges in key moments as a philosophical reflection on writing, as an ethics of writing, which is an ethics of a subject aware of his own limits and conditions.[3] I teach a monographic course for undergraduate and graduate students based on a close reading and critical reassessment of Petrarch's great poetic work, addressing in a new perspective its relevance to the formation of lyric and love discourse within the context of Italian and European literature and philosophy. I teach the *Canzoniere* both in Italian, using Marco Santagata's edition, and in English, using Robert Durling's translation. I focus on the question, Is Petrarch simply inventing a new conventional, erotic, and poetic language, or is he also concerned with alterity and ethics? The most popular image of the founder of modern lyric is the portrait of a contradictory and divided human being, unable to resolve the moral tensions that lacerate his soul. Here I complicate this portrait by suggesting that in addition to the irresolvable moral tensions in Petrarch we find a significant ethical awareness of the limitations of human subjectivity, as it manifests itself in writing, in human representations and knowledge.

As a philosophical introduction to the *Canzoniere*, I have the students read Petrarch's *De sui ipsius et multorum ignorantia* (ed. Fenzi; *On His Own Ignorance and That of Many Others* [trans. Nachod]) and, as a fundamental complement to it, the *Triumphi* (*Trionfi* [ed. Pacca and Paolino]; *Triumphs* [trans. Wilkins]). The idea of the ethics of writing developed by Petrarch allows me to call for an ethics of reading his works, based on the idea of alterity outlined above. In our attempt at understanding the writer we should keep in mind that the "other," as Emmanuel Lévinas writes, "is not a being we encounter, but a relationship with the future and infinity" (79). The face-to-face meeting—be it a real-life situation or a metaphorical and mental construction triggered by reading a literary text—is not a relationship of full presences, both on the part of the writer and the reader, but a relationship with the mystery of the future, the very presence of the future in the present.

This ethical approach to reading and teaching Petrarch takes seriously his aspiration to create something that would live beyond his intention and control, a classic that would become contemporary to the future. Calvino writes that the classics are the books of which we usually hear people say, "I am rereading" and never "I am reading" (125). Thus I call my course Rereading Petrarch's *Rvf* precisely because I want to suggest the idea that this text cannot be exhausted with just one reading. I focus my analysis more on the subject position in the text than on the text's formal aspects, and I conceive my course as an introduction to Petrarch's *Canzoniere* with the hope of starting a relationship with a text that the students may cultivate throughout their lives.

Even though the philosophical notion of subjectivity is developed only later in Western culture, I show its emergence in Petrarch as an ethics of writing and reading. I insist on Petrarch's influence, particularly on the formation of the European philosophical tradition and on European notions of identity and of autobiography.[4] Petrarch's implied notion of subjectivity is much broader and more complex than that of Descartes. Whereas the French philosopher will conceive a human subject based on reason and the present time ("I think, therefore I am"), Petrarch introduces an idea of subjectivity also founded on human affections, such as love and friendship, and practices, such as writing and reading. Petrarch's idea of subjectivity is ethical as long as it remains open to the past and the future, becoming aware and able to accept all the incertitude and limitations implied in the human condition. On the contrary, Descartes's subject will be interpreted in modernity as an autonomous subject that finds in itself a principle of certitude, legitimizing any sort of scientific and political endeavor.[5]

On His Own Ignorance *and the Primacy of Ethics*

In the first part of the course we read in the original and in translation some of Petrarch's autobiographical letters and prose works written in Latin. I have already mentioned *Letter to Posterity* and *On His Own Ignorance*. Also, I have students read *Rerum familiarium libri* (*Letters on Familiar Matters*) 21.12, in which Petrarch presents his life as a model of humanism.[6] Several main themes of the letter recur in the *Canzoniere*: the impermanence of time; the idea of life as navigation and travel and the parallel idea of the human being as *viator*; the necessity of focusing one's life on cultivating one's own soul through reading and writing (Petrarch reads and writes everywhere, even when riding a horse); the study of literature and moral philosophy as a life project that cannot be interrupted in old age; and the affirmation that the humanist does not fear death and instead lives his life as already completed (*peracta*), neglecting material things and concentrating on the cultivation of the soul. This last idea, which comes from Seneca's *Letters to Lucilius* (32.5), allows me to introduce Stoicism, one of the philosophical sources of Petrarch.

We continue the discussion of Petrarch's philosophical sources by reading *On His Own Ignorance*, where the poet declares his love for Cicero and Plato as models of ancient wisdom, which in part he wants to synthesize as a form of Christian humanism. This text shows more than any other not only how Petrarch opened the road to Erasmus's ideas but also how he was aware of the limits of humanism (Rico, *Sueño*). Petrarch renewed the ancient meaning of philosophy as a way of living with practical implications that were neglected by medieval scholasticism. Starting from the twelfth century, philosophy was taught in the university as an exegesis of Aristotle and was considered on the same level as the liberal arts of the quadrivium. Moreover, in antiquity philosophy included a discussion of religious matters; scholasticism broke this tradition and considered philosophy as servant to theology. Petrarch played an important part in reestablishing the ties between the two disciplines, claiming a decisive role for ethics (Hadot; Domański).

In *On His Own Ignorance* Petrarch rejects the professionalization of philosophy and argues that what really matters is how one lives. Developing a Christian idea of love, modeled after John and Augustine, Petrarch, on the one hand, holds that in this life it is not possible to know God fully. On the other hand, he argues that the only way to know God on earth is to love: "In this life it is impossible to know God in His fullness; piously and ardently to love Him is possible" (105).[7] Professional philosophers such as the four Aristotelians who, Petrarch reports, accused him of being ignorant cannot exhaust the search for God understood as love. *On His Own Ignorance* is his reply, in which he argues that this search is open to everybody capable of loving: a farmer and a fisherman may not be able to understand all the subtleties of the concept of divine love, but they may prove to be much better than intellectuals in turning the concept of love into a real practice, and this is what really matters (71–79). Petrarch concludes that "it is better to will the good than to know the truth," because, whereas the search for truth has no justification in itself and can trigger human arrogance and pride, to will the good is always valuable (105). Here Petrarch comes very close to the basic idea of "ethics as first philosophy" that has been developed in our time by Lévinas (Peperzak, *Ethics*). In this perspective Petrarch underlines that Aristotle must be considered not only a great thinker but also a man with all the limitations implied in the human condition (*On His Own Ignorance* 107).

Ancient philosophy becomes important for Petrarch insofar as it anticipates some elements of Christian philosophy, along the lines of Augustine's argument in *The City of God* (bk. 8). Like Augustine, Petrarch quotes Paul to explain that the ancient philosophers were able to understand before the Christian era some elements of God because "the invisible things of him from the creation of the world are clearly seen, being understood by the things that are made, [even] his eternal power and Godhead" (85).[8] Socrates and Plato are the philosophers who came the closest to Christian ideas because they abandoned their epistemological approach to nature and, inspired by the idea of divine good, turned their attention to moral and practical life. Petrarch holds that ancient philosophers were unable to look for real happiness without the help of divine revelation and the idea of the immortality of the soul introduced by Christianity. Yet Petrarch, like Augustine, believes that human beings can only find complete satisfaction in their love for God after death, since at no other point can they find rest and real happiness. Until then the Christian is doomed to be a traveler (*viator*) in exile.

On His Own Ignorance plays a pivotal role in undermining the foundations of Aristotelian theology and medieval scholasticism. Petrarch keeps alive the genuine philosophical search precisely in this idea of exile, which may be considered a Christian adaptation of Plato's definition of the philosopher as *atopos*, someone unclassifiable, out of place, who neglects material possessions and superficial knowledge and lives a virtuous life in search of a divine wisdom.[9] Indeed, Petrarch thinks of himself as *peregrinus ubique*, a "stranger everywhere," because fortune forces him to travel from one country to another without a land in which to rest: "Nullaque iam tellus, nullus michi permanet aer; incola ceu nusquam, sic sum peregrinus ubique" 'And no land or air persists to me for living or breathing; I do not belong to any place, as I am foreign everywhere' (*Epystole*, bk. 3, letter 19, lines 15–16; my trans.). He found this idea of exile and foreignness especially in Paul (2 Cor. 5.6) and Augustine (*De vita beata* 1.1–3). In this perspective Petrarch acknowledges his Socratic and Christian "ignorance," stressing human "imperfection" and becoming aware of the inquietude of the human condition and the limits of human knowledge (*On His Own Ignorance* 65–66).

These ideas are a good preface to the *Canzoniere*, where Petrarch continues his ethical search for truth. He never claims to possess it and points to the methodological problems implied in this search and the ways in which it emerges in the living experience of human consciousness. Useful here is the *Secretum*, composed of three imaginary dialogues between Petrarch and Augustine, who speak in the presence of Lady Truth. Throughout the dialogue Lady Truth remains silent, precisely to show how for Petrarch the search for truth and wisdom is never ending. This work reflects his sense of inner crisis and depression, which even Augustine's wise counsel is not able to resolve. In the *Secretum* Augustine is an austere figure created by Petrarch to reproach his *accedia* and material desires. In the *Canzoniere*, however, Augustine will become the emblematic and inquiet figure of Western spirituality, the one who confesses and comprehends his sins as part of his journey to God (Courcelle).

Petrarch's Ethics of Writing and the Canzoniere

Petrarch's reflection on writing is multifaceted and widespread throughout his works. Armando Petrucci's *La scrittura di Francesco Petrarca* is still an excellent introduction to Petrarch's ideas on writing as a graphic and cultural revolution.[10] Petrarch started the humanist tendency to abandon the Gothic script widespread in Northern Europe to recuperate and renew the Roman *littera antiqua*, creating the premises for humanist cursive writing, with rounded letters joined together.[11] Indeed, the style that we nowadays call italics can be considered an imitation of Petrarch's handwriting. Moreover, Petrarch was aware of the decisive and substantial role of writing in cultural production, to the point of identifying it with the creative activity of the humanist (Petrucci 63). I emphasize Petrarch's fundamental contribution to the idea of writing as the ontology of the self and as the crucial principle of individuation in human knowledge.

In crucial moments of the *Canzoniere* Petrarch's reflection on writing becomes an ethical awareness of the particularities, contingencies, and limitations of human identity and knowledge. It is through writing and reading that Petrarch understands how the divine sign in the human creature implies not only the ontological structure of the self but also its frailty and weakness, which he expresses in his poetry conceived as the language of *mutabilitas*. In the following examples from the *Canzoniere*, Petrarch's ethics of writing discovers a many-sided and complex alterity.

The Representation of Laura

Writing for Petrarch is a fundamental means to pursue his psychological inquiry and autobiographical project. Poem 129 in the *Canzoniere* describes the poet "in guisa d'uom che pensi et pianga et scriva" 'like a man who thinks, weeps and writes' (lines 50–52).[12] Petrarch presents his poetry as linked to a sort of love martyrdom; through writing he wants to testify to the sighs, the anxieties and perturbation of desire. Criticism attentive only to this dimension and to the level of rhetorical and literary representation has recognized in Petrarch's poetry two faces of Laura. On the one hand, there is the cruel and antagonist Laura, object of a desire that cannot be satisfied and that deprives the lover of his faculties, making him a slave to passion (23.69, 76.3, 83.13). On the other hand, there is the angelic Laura, the woman who brings salvation to her lover, following the tradition of *stilnovismo*. Indeed, starting from canzone 70, Laura assumes a supernatural quality, which helps the lover purify his feelings and uplifts him to love as *caritas* (Santagata, *Frammenti*).

In addition to this level of representation, there are also rare moments in the *Canzoniere* in which Petrarch develops an ethical reflection on the face of Laura and on her irreducible alterity to his writing. The recognition of this ethical dimension does not lead either to identify a third face of Laura or to emphasize the theme of the ineffability of the face of Laura. Instead, the ethics of writing in the *Canzoniere* shows how the writing subject is aware of not being present in his fullness in the text and how he problematizes the object of his representation within the act of writing without resolving it. The poet reaches a great awareness on this point:

> Da poi più volte ò riprovato indarno
> Al secol che verrà l'alte belleze
> Pinger cantando, a ciò che l'ame et preze,
> Né col mio stile il suo bel viso incarno. (308.5–8)

> Since then I have often tried in vain to depict in song for the age to come her high beauties, that it may love and prize them, nor with my style can I incarnate her lovely face.

The lovely face of Laura that Petrarch portrays with his mind (129.29) and wants to praise in his poetry tends to emerge in his writing within a Platonic and Christian vision of the soul. The most striking feature of Laura's face is what Petrarch calls "l'aria del bel viso" 'the gentle breeze' (149.3), the spiritual element that constitutes the unique character of Laura's face, the living breath of air, the pneuma of the soul. Elsewhere "l'aria del bel viso" becomes "l'aura" as a further homage to the beloved, to her spiritual identity, which is invisible and has its "form" in the soul (Segre):

> L'aura soave che dal chiaro viso
> Move col suon de le parole accorte
> Per far dolce sereno ovunque spira
> Quasi un spirto gentil di paradiso
> Sempre in quell'aere par che mi conforte,
> Sì che 'l cor lasso altrove non respira. (109.9–14)
>
> The gentle breeze that moves from her bright face with the sound of her wise words, to make sweet fair weather whenever it breathes, like a spirit of Paradise always in that air seems to comfort me, so that my weary heart breathes easy nowhere else.

After Laura's death it will become apparent to the poet that her lovely human face has something divine, which in a Christian perspective will manifest itself completely only after the resurrection of the flesh.

> Oimé, terra è fatto il suo bel viso
> Che solea far del Cielo
> Et del ben di lassù fede fra noi!
> L'invisibil sua forma è in Paradiso,
> disciolta di quel velo
> che qui fece ombra al fior degli anni suoi,
> *per rivestirsen poi*
> *un'altra volta et mai più non spogliarsi,*
> *quando alma et bella farsi*
> *tanto più la vedrem quanto più vale*
> *sempiterna bellezza che mortale.* (268.34–44; my emphasis)
>
> Alas, her beautiful face has become clay, which was wont to give testimony among us of Heaven and the happiness up there! Her invisible form is in Paradise, set free from the veil that here shadowed the flower of her years, *to be clothed with it again another time, and never to lose it, when*

> *so much the more kindly and beautiful we shall see her become as eternal beauty is higher than mortal.*

Petrarch holds here a Platonic and Christian vision of the face of the other. He thinks that the individual soul is ineffable, having its origin in the world of ideas (159.1–4). This notion is reinforced by the awareness of the inadequacy of writing to render that face in its proper terms. The ineffability of the individual soul for Petrarch is not only a religious creed or a rhetorical and literary topos but also an ethical concern related to a philosophical approach to the problem of writing.

The reflection on writing constitutes the extraordinary element of Petrarch's poetic experience, which precisely for this element is able to open itself to an ethical dimension. In crucial moments Petrarch does not assimilate and efface the love object of his writing by reducing it to a conventional love discourse. In those moments Petrarch questions the subject position as well as the process of objectification made by an omniscient subject:

> Onde quant'io di lei parlai né scrissi,
> ch'or per lodi anzi a Dio preghi mi rende,
> fu *breve stilla d'infiniti abissi:*
> *ché stilo oltra l'ingegno non si stende*;
> et per aver uom li occhi nel sol fissi,
> tanto si vede men quanto più splende. (339.9–14; my emphasis)[13]
>
> Thus whatever I spoke or wrote about her, who now before God returns me prayers in exchange for praises, was a *little drop from infinite depths for one's style does not extend beyond one's wit*, and though one has his eyes fixed on the sun, the brighter it is the less he sees.

In this poem Petrarch points to writing as the fundamental practice allowing one to think of the subject and his truth. Moreover, he does not hypostatize the activity of writing and moves beyond simple self-reflection. Writing for him is not a neutral technology capable of registering his emotions and the movements of his desire. By saying that the "stilo," the individual style expressed in writing, does not extend beyond the human mind, Petrarch recognizes how individual consciousness and human reason created through writing cannot transcend the practice that makes them possible. In this way he realizes also that the individual and subjective wills cannot exhaust the search for truth. The presence and the alterity of the face of the other tend to condition the construction of the subjectivity and cast the subject's rationalistic impulse to know and possess his object in an ethical light, which poses the problem of transcendence. The stage of writing moves from the interiority of the writing subject to the disclosure of the face of the other. Petrarch understands that transcendence and infinity as he perceives them in the face of Laura cannot be reduced to a gnoseological or theoretical problem, solvable through vision and the metaphor of light. Petrarch transforms that "infinite depth" into an ethical problem, which alludes to an original signification, to an enigma that can be solved only partially through charitable love.

The Representation of the Love Experience

The alterity and infinity that Petrarch discovers in the face of Laura return in the representation of his love's experience in which he discovers himself to be inhabited by a force and a desire that he cannot control (35). The macrotext of the *Canzoniere* is an autobiography based on a moral reflection focused on presenting an ideal image by mixing fiction and reality. Nonetheless, the fictive and artificial elements convey Petrarch's most intimate intellectual and moral convictions. The most significant moments in this architecture imposed a posteriori on the work are sonnet 1 and the last sequence of poems, from 361 to 366, that announce the physical and spiritual transformation of Petrarch.

In the opening poem, "Voi c'ascoltate in rime sparse il suono" ("You who hear in scattered rhymes the sound"), Petrarch presents his love experience as a "giovanile errore" 'youthful error.' As Augustine makes clear, the entire life of the Christian is a sacred desire to see God, to become similar to him. Since human reason is not adequate to fulfill this desire, Augustine advises the Christian to stick to the safest boat that can help navigate through the tempest of life: the *lignum crucis* (*In Joannis Evangelium Tractatus*, tractatus 2, ch. 2, column 1390). The image of the *lignum crucis* comes back in Petrarch's *Canzoniere*, where nevertheless the poet laments being in "frale barca / . . . in alto mar senza governo" 'a frail bark, without a tiller' (132.10–11).[14] The last poem of the *Canzoniere*, which includes a prayer to the Virgin Mary, reinforces the necessity of clinging to divine love, through the mediation of the "madre, figliuola et sposa" 'mother, daughter and bride' of Christ in preparation for death (366.47).

However, the terminal point of love and *caritas* can find a full expression only in a face-to-face vision of God as confirmed by Paul (1 Cor. 13). The poetic imagination of Petrarch can conçeive this meeting only as an extension of human love made possible by the mediation of the other, the charitable intervention of the beloved, as in sonnet 362, "Volo con l'ali del pensiero al cielo" ("I fly with the wings of thought to heaven"), where the poet imagines Laura taking him before God to contemplate the face of God and that of the beloved: "Menami al suo Signor. Allor m'inchino / Pregando humilemente che consenta / Ch'i' stia a veder et l'uno et l'altro volto" 'She leads me to her Lord; then I incline myself, humbly begging that He permit me to stay to see their two faces' (lines 9–11).[15]

This poetic vision confirms that for Petrarch only the love for the other, even in spiritual form, allows the vision of God on earth. This is the last stage of Petrarch's poetic and intellectual research: the transformation of love into the most important substance of human vision and thought. Petrarch considers love not as a mythopoetic hypostasis but as an element of the alterity that inhabits human conscience. The human soul presented by Petrarch in the last sequence of the *Canzoniere* is neither the winged soul of Plato that aspires to a purely contemplative dimension nor the mystic soul aspiring to an immediate union with God. On the contrary, it is a soul still in love that thinks of itself in relation to the other and that through the mediation of the other—seen as a human being (Laura), Christ, or the Virgin Mary—aspires to a renewal necessary to express the love for God. The erotic element, the "giovanile errore" in the last poems of the *Canzoniere*, is dismissed but not erased: it is still a crucial part of Petrarch's autobiography.

The Representation of Time, Death, and Eternity

Petrarch's reflection on time confirms that he introduces a notion of human subjectivity deriving from ontology as well as from an ethical discourse open to the transcendence of the self. The poet is aware of the strict interconnection linking writing to time and tries in different ways to evade the notion of a crystallized subjectivity, related to the hypostasis of the present that the writing process tends to create. Petrarch considers death a "refugio" 'refuge' (*Canzoniere* 331.63), something that creates the possibility of evading the hypostasis of time and opens the perspective of eternity, of a different kind of temporality that disrupts the present moment of the human subject writing in solitude.

For this aspect it is crucial to read the *Triumphi* in conjunction with the concluding poems of the *Canzoniere*. Following Augustine and developing a Christian notion of eternity and resurrection, Petrarch in his "Triumphus eternitatis" situates the human search for authenticity in the *intentio* directed toward the eschatological time (*Trionfi* 67–69; Augustine, *Confessions* 9.10, 24), in which there will be neither present nor future but only being. For Petrarch, the triumph of eternity will only be possible in the moment of the final judgment and of the resurrection of the flesh, whereas the Christian notion of eternity emphasizes not the infinite postponement of the eschatological future but the irruption of the eternal in the present, the link between the past and the future without which time would not be possible. For both Dante and Petrarch, Christ bears witness precisely to the possibility of the encounter of eternity with time. Both poets see figures of Christ in their beloved and tend to interpret their own life sub specie aeternitatis following the Augustinian model. Among the many examples in the first and second part of the *Canzoniere*, poem 338 is the most telling. Here Petrarch states that Laura's death represents for the world a loss comparable to that caused by the death of Christ. Petrarch reinforces this association by referring to Laura what Saint John writes of Christ: "That was the true Light, which lighteth every man that cometh into the world. He was in the world, and the world was made by him, and the world knew him not" (John 1.9–10).

Laura's death makes Petrarch think of eternal life:

> Pon freno al gran dolor che ti trasporta,
> ché per soverchie voglie
> si perde 'l Cielo ove 'l tuo core aspira,
> dove è viva colei ch' altrui par morta
> et di sue belle spoglie
> seco sorride et sol di te sospira. (268.67–72)
>
> Rein in the great sorrow that transports you; for excessive desire will lose the Heaven where your heart aspires, where she is alive who seems dead, and she smiles to herself at her beautiful remains and sighs only for you.

The seed of eternity is born out of the meditation on the death of Laura. Faith in the resurrection of the flesh makes the poet believe in the possibility of reuniting with her. She will reappear to him in the glory of her beauty. To reach this moment the poet knows that he has to die as well and that moment will be in time but also paradoxically outside time: it will be a moment of extreme passivity of the human subject. Before that moment the poet's ethical reflection points his meditative attention and responsibility to the death of the other and recognizes the unavoidable relationship to her, the necessary intersubjective dimension of human life.

Petrarch worked for decades on the *Canzoniere*, following an ideal of infinite perfectibility that could be interrupted only by death.[16] Had he lived a few more months, we would have had a different version of his major work (Scaglione, "Structure"). For Petrarch the search for meaning in human life is destined to be open-ended and not to exhaust itself in writing. Thus he realizes that poetry is powerless before the Christian perspective of the eternal life opened after physical death; that is why the laurel as symbol of poetry is literally broken by an overwhelming power. This happens above all in the "canzone delle visioni," poem 323, one of the richest and most complex poems of the *Canzoniere*. I recommend having students read this poem in the last part of the course because it confirms that Petrarch conceives his search for truth and reality as an ethical rejection of idolatry and serene recognition of death as opening to the eternal. Although poetic symbolism is destroyed in a tragic atmosphere, Petrarch depicts here Laura's death as "lieta" 'happy' and "secura" 'confident' (line 72; Santagata, "Naufragio"). Reading Petrarch focusing on his ethics of writing helps us understand him outside the conventional images of the divided self and unrequited lover. This approach is admittedly partial but nevertheless necessary to keep alive his humanistic spirit as having both deep roots in the past and a fundamental projection into the future. Through weekly exercises, mostly comments on the primary texts, class discussions, and personal papers, students as well as instructors are invited to realize that the future may visit our classroom.

We can become contemporary to Petrarch, if in following his humanism we keep considering that writing and reading are ethical activities, as long as they leave the door open to the unexpected, to the interruption of the economy of the same made possible by the encounter with the other.

NOTES

[1] Boitani has stressed the alterity and modernity of medieval texts, including Petrarch's.

[2] All quotations from Dante's *Divine Comedy* are from Bosco and Reggio's edition and from Singleton's translation.

[3] Mazzotta addressed the complexity of Petrarch's self and its ethical implications: "The fragmentation and solitude of self . . . are the reverse side of a self as a knot of roots inextricably bound in a bundle of contradictory relations" (*Worlds* 84). Questions of style and composition are crucial to Petrarch's understanding of the self, and they embody what Mazzotta calls "an ethics of writing" (92). For a philosophical notion of ethics of writing, see Sini.

[4] For a general overview on this subject, see Reiss, *Patterns*; Tripet.

[5] Struever has shown how Petrarch is removed from a purely self-reflexive discourse: "To be sure, if the virtue of modern ethics is a specially rigorous reflexivity, an acutely critical self-consciousness, Petrarch is disappointingly pre-modern" (31).

[6] I use the 2005 Italica reprint of Bernardo's translation in class.

[7] To understand Petrarch's position, see 1 John 4.12: "No man hath seen God at any time. If we love one another, God dwelleth in us, and his love is perfected in us" ("Deum nemo vidit umquam. Si diligamus invicem, Deus in nobis manet, et caritas eius in nobis perfecta est" [*Multilingual Bibles*]). See also Augustine, *In Joannis Evangelium Tractatus CXXIV* (tractatus 7, ch. 10), in which Augustine argues that God is invisible to human eyes and that we need to look for him through our heart, because God is love.

[8] Romans 1.19–20. The Vulgate text reads as follows: "[Q]uia quod notum est Dei, manifestum est in illis. Deus enim illis manifestavit. Invisibilia enim ipsius, a creatura mundi, per ea quae facta sunt, intellecta conspiciuntur sempiterna quoque eius virtus, et divinitas" (*Multilingual Bibles*).

[9] See *Thaetetus* (172c–177c) and *Symposium* (214e–222b) in Cooper's edition of Plato's works; see also Domański. Even though Petrarch did not have access to these texts by Plato, he was familiar with the Socratic idea of the philosopher, as *On His Own Ignorance* attests. On Petrarch and medieval Platonism, see Gentile; Garin.

[10] For a broader historical contextualization, see also Stock.

[11] Petrarch criticized the calligraphic principle—the effort to write beautifully and ornamentally—that made the Gothic style difficult to read and to understand. Petrarch's use of graphic styles such as the semi-Gothic in different literary contexts started a graphic revolution that was completed only in the fifteenth century by Florentine humanists such as Coluccio Salutati (Petrucci 68–73).

[12] Italian quotations from the *Canzoniere* are from Savoca's edition, as digitized in *The Oregon Petrarch Open Book*; English quotations from the *Canzoniere* follow Durling's translation.

[13] Here "stilo" alludes not only to style but also to stylus as an instrument for writing or pen.

[14] See *Canzoniere* 62.13–14: "reduci i pensier vaghi a miglior luogo, / rammenta lor come oggi fusti in croce" 'lead my wandering thoughts back to a better place, remind them that today you were on the Cross.'

[15] Petrarch expresses here an original poetic vision, considering that on the theme of the beatific vision he shares Benedict XII's ideas as expressed in the bull "Benedictus Deus," which defines the *immediate intuitive vision of God* as the soul of the just having no faults to expiate. This face-to-face vision would be completed with the resurrection of the flesh (see *Rerum familiarium libri* 12.9). On the general problem of the beatific vision from the scholastic disputes to Benedict XII, see Trottmann; on the problem of the beatific vision in Petrarch's *Triumphi*, see Bertolani.

[16] On the *Canzoniere*'s genesis and composition, see Wilkins, *Making*; Barolini, "Petrarch." On the structure and method of composition, see Scaglione, "Structure." For a more recent approach based on a textual interpretation of the *Canzoniere* that takes into account the evolution of the text from manuscript to print and digital editions, see my "Return to Philology" and the digital humanities project *Oregon Petrarch Open Book*.

Petrarch's Vernacular Poetry and the Latin Poetic Canon: The Poetics of Classical Philology

Ilaria Marchesi and Simone Marchesi

In recent studies on Petrarch's monumental literary corpus, a sharp line seems to divide the writings of scholars interested in his prehumanistic, philological products and of those concerned with the study of his vernacular poetry. With the perhaps sole exception of the *Secretum*, Petrarch's choice of bilingualism has been treated as an indication of the existence of two independent cultural projects. On the Latin side, Petrarch has appeared as a writer deeply interested in recuperating and reviving—in essence, in reproducing—classical literary genres.[1] On the side of the vernacular, he has been treated as responding to a range of cultural solicitations, from his responsive reevocation of the Provençal poetic tradition to the subtle dialogue with Dante's lyric and epic poetry.[2] The two strains of Petrarch studies can fruitfully be brought together in a course that considers the vernacular project of the *Canzoniere* as animated by the same classicizing project as the Latin philological works. Marco Santagata has most recently championed this reading by arguing, in what could with profit be used as a general reading principle, that Petrarch approaches his Latin and vernacular projects from essentially the same standpoint—namely, activating "il grande mito del ritorno alle origini come passaggio necessario per far nascere il nuovo" 'the great myth of the return to the origin as the necessary step to engender the new' (Introduzione xliii; our trans.).[3] Just as Petrarch's *Familiares* (*Rerum familiarum libri*) looks to Cicero's collections of letters and his *Africa* looks to Lucan and Vergil as models, Santagata argues, so too the *Canzoniere* may be shown to have a Latin antecedent that it endeavors to revive. There are several possible avenues of approach to the classicism of the *Canzoniere*, each passing through a precise set of texts and illuminating one aspect of Petrarch's wide-ranging involvement with the classics.

The rationale behind the idea of teaching Petrarch's poetry in relation to the classical Latin poetic canon is that such a comparative effort may provide students with an opportunity to study from a double point of view the self-reinforcing mechanisms of a tradition in its making. A consideration of the Latin poets, included early on in a syllabus focusing on the *Canzoniere*, may offer a suitable departing point for an analysis of Petrarch's strategy of reactivation of the classical poetic past. Conversely, a course on the Latin canon may use Petrarch's work as a summative case of an exemplary reader's response to the tradition. The work of a classicist, Petrarch's *Canzoniere* may both shed light on the phenomena that led to the formation and organization of their past and, in turn, be illuminated by them. Petrarch, in his selective citation from and strategic recombination of a body of writing to which he laid claim, may be shown to have initiated the transmission to the modern West of what T. S. Eliot will call, in his modernist code, "these fragments . . . shored against my ruins" (*Waste Land* [line 431]). The study of Petrarch's work contains an implicit philological thrust from the past of the canon toward the present of the book, and the *Canzoniere* can be understood against the background of its sources—the complex array of the Latin antecedents with which it resonates and to which it responds. Yet, in redeploying the Latin poetic canon in his lyric poetry, Petrarch may be shown to have rediscovered and exploited precisely the mechanisms that had been integral to the formation of the canon he transmits. In this light, the study of his work contains an additional hermeneutical dimension, reaching from the present of the book to the past of its sources: produced by an attentive and innovative reader of the classics, the *Canzoniere* helps focalize on the internal dynamics of canonization of its Latin antecedents.[4]

Getting the Past Reborn: The Philological Roots of Vernacular Poetry

Petrarch's sense that his vernacular poetry could be presented as the reproduction from a distance of a genre already established in the classical past was based on the notion that accentual poetry had indeed existed even in antiquity—an idea that he was able to elaborate by exploiting a gloss to Vergil by Servius, which he could read in the commentary to the *Georgics* (Servius, *Ad. Georg.* 2.385–86, as annotated in Petrarch's own manuscript, the Virgilio Ambrosiano, on f. 31v [qtd. in Feo, "Petrarca ovvero l'avanguardia"]).[5] That the existence of accentual poetry constituted a matter of reflection for Petrarch can be seen in the recurrence of the theme in the programmatic opening letter of the *Familiares*. Here he provides the outline of his poetic production according to a tripartite division: Latin verse, Latin prose, and vernacular verse. Regarding the third partition, Petrarch notes that the genre of rhythmic lyric, "[q]uod genus, apud Siculos, ut fama est, non multis ante seculis renatum, brevi per omnem Italiam ac longius manavit, apud Grecorum olim ac Latinorum vetustissimos celebratum" 'which has been reborn in recent times and spread throughout Italy and beyond, had once been used by the earliest Roman and Greek poets" (*Familiares* 1.1.6; our trans.).[6] The theoretical importance of Servius's gloss can hardly be overestimated. As Petrarch interpreted it, Servius's comments came to solve a literary-historical problem that had plagued previous theorizations of vernacular classicism, most notably Dante's. According to the brief sketch of the history of poetry that Dante first develops in *Vita nuova* 25, Dante thought that vernacular (love) poetry had been born about one hundred fifty years before in Provence and had from there migrated first to Sicily and finally to continental Italy.[7] It was into that novel tradition that he intended to inscribe his work as a vernacular poet. Without the help of Servius, Petrarch was going to be constrained by the same system of dichotomies that had forced Dante to keep distinct in all his works the discussion of his classical (mostly epic) models from that of his near-contemporary (mostly lyrical [i.e., erotic]) antecedents.[8]

Beyond the authorial theoretical awareness that can be extracted from the interplay of the Vergilian glosses and Petrarch's witness, his classicizing project has a wider reach. Petrarch should, in fact, be credited with elaborating a coherent (if metaphoric) theory of imitation that applies to both Latin and vernacular writings. Petrarch's second letter to Boccaccio may prove useful here. In the context of the qualified praise Petrarch lavishes on his secretary Giovanni Conversini, the author distinguishes between servile (and sterile) regurgitation of verbal material extracted from classical texts and a mediated (and fruitful) redeployment of their concepts and figures. The result of imitation, he states, should not be the collection of the "flowers" of alien poetry but the production of one's own "honey" (*Familiares* 23.19). Measuring these theoretical pronouncements against the imitative and allusive practice of the *Canzoniere* might prove a beneficial exercise for students who, as nonmedieval readers, are trained to appreciate the genial originality of modern texts more than the carefully plotted intertextual strategies of classical and classicizing poetry.

The Limits and Dynamics of the Tradition: Petrarch's List of Favorite Books

An autograph note on folio 58v in one of Petrarch's own manuscripts (Paris Latin 2201) offers a record of books, the heading of which reads, "Libri mei peculiares. Ad reliquos non transfuga sed explorator transire soleo" ("These are my favorite books: I only explore the others not seeking refuge in them," an adaptation of a statement from Seneca's *Epistulae morales* 2.5; as qtd. in Milde). Animated by a strong classicizing drive, the list that follows bears witness to an extremely personal taste, both in the choice of texts and in the order of presentation. At the top there are philosophical and rhetorical writings by Cicero, philosophical works by Seneca (together with his tragedies), and Boethius's *Consolatio philosophiae*. Then come the Latin historians, followed by the ancient poets, grammarians, a treatise on dialectics, and works on astrology. At the end, four works by Augustine are listed: *De civitate Dei*, *Confessiones*, *De orando Deo*, and the *Soliloquia* (Milde 230; see also Ullman). Most fruitful for a reading of the *Canzoniere*, the section on ancient poets may be used to give the sense of Petrarch's poetic canon: the catalog is opened by Vergil, followed by Lucan and Statius (representatives of the leading genre of epic); next comes Horace, representing lyrical poetry with his *Carmina*; and the list is capped by Ovid's *Metamorphoses* and by Juvenal, who stands for the genre of satire.[9]

To gauge the peculiarity of this brief catalog, a good exercise is to compare it with Dante's more limited classicizing canon, as it is laid out in *De vulgari eloquentia* 2.6.7. Dante's catalog comprises Vergil, Ovid of the *Metamorphoses*, Statius, and Lucan. The first element of divergence is the purpose of the list: Dante is offering to the would-be poet a catalog of *idonei auctores*, prescriptively recommending them for linguistic and stylistic imitation; Petrarch records the result of a personal, even idiosyncratic, life choice in a descriptive mode.[10] The second striking difference is the plurality of genres that Petrarch surveys in contrast to Dante's monochord epic canon of regular poets. Even when Dante opens up the catalog in *Inferno* 4.88–90 by listing Homer, Vergil, Ovid, Horace, and Lucan, the only real addition to the school of poets will be Horace, who enters its ranks specifically as the author of the *Satires*.[11] Whereas the *Comedy* appears interested in vindicating its identity as an epic poem with an added moral (satiric) component, Petrarch delineates his canon with a more varied spectrum of genres in mind and with the significant difference of choosing Horace as a lyrical rather than satiric poet.

The detail of Horace's inclusion might bear further interpretive weight. In addition to being the unchallenged teacher of poetics as the revered author of the *Ars poetica* (some principles of which resonate in the *Canzoniere*), Horace is the poet on whose example Petrarch imports a principle of variety into his book, thus breaking away from the vernacular tradition as defended, for instance, by Dante in *Vita nuova* 25. Like the *Canzoniere*, Horace's *Odes* are a composite book, containing in a very calculated structure erotic, symposiac, political, and even occasional poems. As Santagata notes, Petrarch does not shy away from composing extraerotic poems and including them in the *Canzoniere*: the book is made up of thirty-nine texts not directly related to its central love story.[12] A consideration of Horace's model might help add a different dimension to the habitual medieval terms of comparison for the structure of the book—if it is true, that is, that Guittone d'Arezzo's collection acted as the model for a bipartite (erotic and penitential) structure of the *Canzoniere* together with the split structure and double register of Dante's *Vita nuova*, it is probably in Horace that Petrarch could find a classical example of varied themes (and the varied style) deployed in a single volume of lyrical poetry.[13]

The Epistle on the Ascent of Mount Ventoux: Livy's Lesson in Hermeneutics

Familiares 4.1 is a third possible text that might be used to frame a discussion of Petrarch's classicism in comparison with two of his romance precursors: Dante and the *Roman de la rose*. The letter articulates more clearly than other loci in Petrarch's works a theory of interpretation that contrasts two opposite modes of conceptualizing literary history and associates philological and typological reading strategies to the hermeneutical methods required by the texts of Livy and Augustine. A reading of the letter could bring to the fore the circumstance that, even if it culminates with the reading of an Augustinian passage, the text starts as an exercise in philology, with Petrarch holding before his eyes the narrative of a different climb—one recounted by Livy (Robbins; Ascoli). Livy's *Ab urbe condita* is not a text that Petrarch chose at random to begin his report of the ascent. The Roman historian was a highly charged antecedent whose evocation at the outset of the epistle functioned as a signpost for a cultural enterprise of constructing the past as different from the present: different and utterly "other." The establishment of Livy's text was the recognizable monument of Petrarch's philological work and the cultural locus in which Petrarch articulated sharp historical distinctions between the irretrievable ancient Roman past and his own age.[14] By balancing each other, the two reading scenes encapsulated in the epistle may be represented as organized in a polarized opposition, and their juxtaposition may be used to elicit a sense of difference between typological and philological readings. The former exercise produces typological literary objects, the singularity of which is overcome by their equivalence to distant realities; the latter produces philological objects that maintain their singular status even when brought into contact with distant equivalents (T. Greene, *Light* 104–11; Freccero, "Fig Tree").

The otherness of the past signaled by Livy in the letter extends to Petrarch's sense of poetic tradition: both the epistles he addresses to classical poets (*Familiares* 24.10–12, which might also serve as a starting point for the same discussion) and the poems in the *Canzoniere* that directly address questions of literary genealogy (166, 186, 187, and 247) mark the same discontinuity.[15] The core notion that these texts help confirm is that Petrarch strategically avoids inscribing himself not only into the epic canon, as it was delineated by Dante in *Inferno* 4, but also into the more traditional elegiac-erotic lineage linking Catullus to Gallus, Tibullus, Ovid, Guillaume de Lorris, and Jean de Meun, as constructed by the God of Love midway through the text of the *Roman de la rose* (lines 10511–600). Petrarch's sense of the tradition does not rest on the notion of transmission but rather on that of imitation. It is based not on a genealogical metaphor and on the paradigm of *translatio* but rather on the notions of reactivation and discontinuity. It functions not according to a principle of inclusion but according to one of substitution, with the present reproducing rather than continuing the past.

The Primary Texts: Mythology, History, and Metapoetics

In the *Canzoniere*, there are three main areas in which Petrarch can be shown to rely on his audience's deep familiarity with the classical heritage. The first is, of course, mythological lore: some of the central myths of Petrarch's poetry are constructed using Ovidian material, and their effect cannot be gauged by readers who are not conversant in the language of mythology. Petrarch, however, could count on the fact that his audience was familiar with at least the basic lines of traditional Ovidian plots. The Apollo-Daphne myth, which structures a wide array of poems through thematic and etymological wordplay, and the more rare and refined treatment of the Actaeon story, as well the fundamental Medusa allusions and the metapoetic evocation of the Orpheus story, rely on widely disseminated literary and artistic texts.[16]

The three areas—mythology, history, and metapoetics—are not coextensive when it comes to their intended audiences. When Petrarch alludes to questions of style and literary history, he appeals to a restricted public, most likely his co-practitioners of poetry. The contrastive taxonomy of Greek and Latin prose and poetry writers offered in *Canzoniere* 247, for instance, employs as a vehicle the literary-historical topos of the geographic antonomasia, which requires a higher amount of ingenuity to be deciphered and a more thorough involvement with literary issues (cf. the sphragis poem of Ovid's *Amores* 3.15). The same could be said about some of the historical allusions, particularly those that target Livy's *Ab urbe condita*;[17] they are used to engage in a subtler dialogue with readers who share not only Petrarch's own deep knowledge but also his novel view of the Roman past. These implicit readers are philologists who are simultaneously demanded and constructed by the text.

Organized according to these three categories, the following are the most relevant poems containing allusions to classical matters.

> Mythology
> 5 (Apollo), 22 (Apollo), 23 (Apollo and Daphne, Phaeton and Cygnus, Mercury and Battus, Biblis, Echo, Actaeon, Jupiter and Danae, Egina, and Ganymedes), 24 (Apollo), 41 and 42 (Apollo, Jupiter, and Vulcan), 45 (Narcissus), 51 (Daphne, Atlas), 52 (Actaeon), 60 (Jupiter and Daphne), 78 (Pygmalion), 105 (Phaeton, in passing), 111 (Jupiter), 126 (Diana, obliquely), 130 (Leda, Helen, the Naiads and Driads [esp. lines 40–52]), 136 and 137 (Golden Age), 151 (Cupid), 155 (Jupiter), 179 (Medusa), 188 (Apollo), 193 (Jupiter, the ambrosia), 197 (Apollo, Medusa), 210 (the Parchae), 219 (Aurora), 225 (Jason, Paris), 254 (Ariadne, Callisto), 255 (Apollo and Daphne), 291 (Aurora), 296 (the Parchae), 306 (Avernus and Styx), 310 (Zephyr, Jupiter, Venus, Procne and Philomela), 323 (Eurydice), 325 (Jupiter, Apollo, Polyphemus, Mars), 332 (Eurydice and Orpheus), 366 (Medusa)[18]

Metapoetics
20 (Horace's *Ars poetica*; see also 293), 166 (disrupture of poetic genealogy), 186 and 187 (Vergil and Homer), 247 (poetic canon)[19]

History
Trojan cycle: 75 (Achilles: see also 164), 157 (Aeneas and Anchises, obliquely)
Roman history: 24 (Augustus), 44 (Caesar), 53 (virtuous Romans and Hannibal), 102 (Caesar, Hannibal), 103 (Hannibal), 104 (virtuous Romans), 128 (Roman conquest wars), 155 (Caesar), 177 (Caesar, obliquely), 262 (Lucretia)

In addition to passages more or less directly addressing classical matters, the *Canzoniere* also has a deeply engrained filigree of allusions to classical poetry that affects both individual poems and the structure of the book; the index compiled by Ilaria Marchesi (http://people.hofstra.edu/Ilaria_Marchesi/) lists relevant passages of *loci* openly imitating or obliquely alluding to texts of the Latin canon.[20]

NOTES

[1] On the philological culture of Petrarch, see Nolhac, *Pétrarque*; Bosco, "Petrarca"; Billanovich, "Tra Dante"; T. Greene, *Light*; and Velli.

[2] On the side of the vernacular production, see in particular the repertories by Scherillo (for Occitan poetry) and Trovato (for Dante). See also the broader picture sketched out in Bernardo, "Petrarch's Attitude," as well as in Santagata, "Petrarca" and *Frammenti* (esp. 24–39 and 185–209). See the remarkable collection of essays in Barański and Cachey.

[3] Detailed and valuable work in this area has been produced by Petrie (reviewed in Frasso, "Recensione"), as well as by Rizzo.

[4] For recent discussions of this theoretical framework, see Hardie, *Epic Successors* 1–18 and 101–16; Hinds 17–51; and Hardie, "Ovid."

[5] Feo was the first to draw attention to the innovative potential of this gloss ("Petrarca ovvero l'avanguardia" 10–11).

[6] All quotations from *Familiares* are from Rossi's edition.

[7] The distance between the two formulations can be measured by the different metaphors Dante and Petrarch use for the insurgence of vernacular poetry: what for Dante "*appeared* for the first time not too long ago" has for Petrarch been reborn in the past few generations. See Dante's *Vita nuova* 25.3.4 and *De vulgari eloquentia* 1.10.3 (on Provençal poets) and 1.12.2 (on the Sicilians).

[8] For negotiations around this dichotomy, see Barolini, *Dante's Poets*.

[9] On the exclusion of the elegiac genre from the catalog, a tradition that will lend several loci to the erotic component of the *Canzoniere*, see the texts Shapiro ("Petrarch") extracts from Petrarch's oeuvre (in particular, *Familiares* 9.4.10–16 and 24.4.9–10). See

also Dolla. The resistance has the force of a programmatic axiom (see Boccaccio, *Decameron* introd. to day 4 [33]).

[10] On authors "suitable for imitation," see Kaster.

[11] Horace had already appeared in *Vita nuova* 25—as the author of the *Ars poetica*—in the exemplary catalog of Latin poets ("Vergilio . . . Lucano . . . Orazio . . . Ovidio") who, having used figurative speech, authorize Dante's personification of love as *Amor*.

[12] Specifically, three invectives against the papal court (136, 137, 138), a series of political poems (27, 28, 53, 103, 104, 128), an exculpatory sonnet to Cardinal Giovanni Colonna (266), an invitation to Bishop Giacomo Colonna (10), and a few notes accompanying gifts (8, 9), correcting the news of the poet's own death (120), or containing individual advice to correspondents (7, 38). See Santagata, Introduzione xxxviii–xxxix.

[13] Other collections of varied texts were available in antiquity. In poetry, Catullus's corpus (the most authoritative antecedent for the many Latin collections of lyric and elegiac poems of Augustan age) displays the same alternation of tone, meter, and themes that will characterize Petrarch's. The example of the multiform correspondence set by Cicero (and of Pliny the Younger, if Petrarch had knowledge of its nine books of epistles, as poem 234 has suggested at least to Castelvetro, who linked it to *Epistulae* 5.7) might also have acted in favor of including the occasional poems surveyed above (Cherchi).

[14] See Billanovich, "Petrarch" and "Tito Livio." A recapitulation of the whole question can be found in Billanovich, *Tradizione* and *Livio*.

[15] Petrarch's imaginary correspondence with classical authors is available in Cosenza.

[16] For the Apollo-Daphne myth, see Sturm-Maddox, *Petrarch's Metamorphoses* 9–38, and *Petrarch's Laurels*; for Actaeon (with its Dantean and Boccaccian connections), see Branca, "Atteone"; for Medusa, see Foster, "Beatrice"; for Orpheus, see Mazzotta, "*Canzoniere*," and Migraine-George.

[17] See Billanovich, "Petrarch" 170–71, to whose philological analysis of 102 one might add 7.1–3 as alluding to Livy 33 and 27.11–12 as modeled on Livy 1.26.

[18] Special consideration should be given to three texts characterized by a blurring of the line between mythological and historical materials: they are the lists of examples of wrath, beauty, and ancillary love stories in 232, 260, and 325, respectively. The first poem names Alexander and Philip of Macedonia, Tydaeus and Melanippus from the Theban cycle, Silla and the Emperor Valentinian from Roman history, and Ajax from the *matière* of Troy; the second groups together Helen of Troy, the Roman matron Lucretia, along with Polyxena, Hypsipyle, and Argias; the third mentions Agamemnon, Achilles, Hannibal, and Lucretia.

[19] On canon formation in Ovid, see Tarrant 15–17.

[20] The index of parallel passage, keyed to each poem of the *Canzoniere*, is compiled, with additions, on the basis of four of the most classicizing commentaries to Petrarch's lyric poetry: Carducci and Ferrari, Scherillo, Dotti, and Santagata, whose ad loc glosses remain the best sources for a comprehensive sense of Petrarch's strategy of allusions to the classics.

Echoes and Mirrors: Dante's Shadow in Petrarch's *Canzoniere*

Simone Marchesi

In our teaching, it is often merely a matter of circumstances if we use Dante's presence in the *Canzoniere* to investigate Petrarch's texts or if we take advantage of the existence of an exceptionally gifted reader of poetry such as Petrarch to explore possible interpretations of Dante. Whatever our approach or the direction of the interpretive acts might be, a consideration of the Petrarch-Dante connection is inescapable. Readers of Petrarch cannot avoid becoming readers of his primary vernacular precursor, just as readers of Dante should not dispense with one of their most authoritative forefathers. In both cases, the pedagogical and practical issue is for the designer of the course to determine how much of Dante—and which of his works—students need to know to be able to grasp Petrarch's Dantean echolalia.

Of course, knowledge of Dante's complete poetic oeuvre (*Vita nuova*, *Rime*—especially the *Petrose*—and *Commedia*) would constitute an ideal backdrop, against which Petrarch's game of mirrors with his forerunner could be gauged.[1] But such a thorough acquaintance with Dante is unlikely in students in an undergraduate course on Petrarch, unless the course is designed as the final component in a sequence on the poetry of the Italian trecento. As a consequence, what follows contains some, admittedly idiosyncratic, suggestions of texts (and parts thereof) that have proved particularly helpful in establishing the main lines of Petrarch's redeployment of Dantean poetic material.

The basic tools for the study of the Petrarch-Dante connection on a textual level are three inventories of sources and a few scattered, more localized contributions, mainly in Italian. In chronological order, they are Hermann Gmelin's study "Das Prinzip der *imitatio* in den romanischen Literaturen der Renaissance" (98–173), Santagata's long article "Presenze di Dante 'comico' nel *Canzoniere* del Petrarca," and Paolo Trovato's *Dante in Petrarca* (to be combined with and balanced by Franco Suitner's *Petrarca e la tradizione stilnovistica*).[2] Taken together, these catalogs provide readers with a detailed and reasoned map of the interplay between Dante's poetic langue and Petrarch's lyric *parole*. They suggest some ways in which Petrarch was able to reclaim and distinguish his own poetic identity from his predecessor's in the practice of vernacular poetry.

The lists of lexical borrowings, syntactic calques, rhythmic homologies, and thematic allusions recorded by Gmelin, Santagata, and Trovato offer a philologically sound basis for evaluating the dialectics of imitation and emulation in which the *Canzoniere* engages its primary vernacular model. In particular, they show that, when it came to his lyric poetry, Petrarch needed to address a fundamental question: how not to be Dante. What kind of variation could he introduce into his poetry to distinguish it from the highly recognizable and highly authoritative model that Dante had established in the vernacular? For the sake of this exposition four main thematic clusters of divergences may be identified in Petrarch's post-Dantean attitude: the reinterpretation of *stilnovismo*, the never-accomplished "Beatricization" of Laura, the treatment of political issues, and the redeployment of "comedic" mythologems. For each of them, Petrarch may be shown to have introduced elements of variation on Dante's canonical treatment.

Petrarch's New Stilnovo

While, as Trovato's study shows, Dante's *Commedia* accounts for more of the influence on Petrarch than does his lyric poetry, Petrarch's reading of Dante was hardly limited to the epic poem. The paradigm Dante established with his most strictly lyric poetry—especially his canzoni—was an inescapable point of reference for the poet of the *Canzoniere*. Several lexical and thematic keystones of Petrarch's vernacular poetry originate in Dante and in the lyrical poets who have come to be called the *stilnovisti*. As points of entry into a discussion of Petrarch's thematic and stylistic redeployment of the lyrical model of *stilnovismo*, one may use two interrelated elements of strategic divergence: the subjective perception of time's passing and the attention to the geographic coordinates of the central love story.

Petrarch's novel use of time and space in his poetry can best be measured by reading *Vita nuova*, Dante's most stylized and delocalized work. Particularly significant are the initial sections, in which the sequence of encounters with Beatrice, marked from the beginning by the miraculous recurrence of the number nine, constructs a liturgical rather than a chronological progression (chs. 1–3, 19, and 23 [ed. Gorni]). In Dante's first *prosimetrum*, the passing of time affects less the psychology and physicality of the characters than the readers' understanding of their meaning in the action: Dante's love for Beatrice is the same at nine, eighteen, and beyond, but his understanding of that love is in perpetual evolution. Dante's achronic presentation of his experience of love is countered, on Petrarch's side, by an insisted recording of the progress of linear time (from the calendrical structure of the collection to the anniversaries marked by poems 212 and 221).[3] In Petrarch, the process is both felt subjectively and measured by the physical marks that it leaves on the protagonists' bodies (the time span of the love story is measured most precisely in 118, 145, 222, and 364). To illustrate vividly this crucial difference, one may contrast lyrics from *Vita nuova* with either the poems that hinge on Laura's potentially vanishing beauty (90, 267–68) or those that focus on the aging of the lyric self (122, 168, 295, and 315).

A similar exercise of contrastive reading may take the most extremely delocalized chapters of *Vita nuova* (4, 7, 13, 15, 17, 23, and 29) to serve as an apt counterpoint for the geographic precision of the Vaucluse landscape (deemed essential to the correct functioning of the love story as in the diptych in *Canzoniere* 116–17—to be compared with 279–81—or in 126), the extravagant travelogues from the Ardennes (176–77) or on the way to Rome (16–18 and 68–69), and the rhapsody on fluvial onomastics of poem 148 (reinforced by the closely related musing on the limits of vernacular geography and linguistics developed in 146). Dante's reticence in naming the unmistakable cityscape of Florence contrasts with Petrarch's indulgent mapping of a programmatically classicizing and antiurban landscape.

The "Beatricization" of Laura

The *Canzoniere* contains both poems that denounce the moral shortcomings of the poetic self and others that hint at the possibility of a positive spiritual resolution of the erotic experience. The latter is a tendency that will reach a provisionary apex in the vision of the enamored and reciprocating Laura set in the center of the unstable universe of the *Trionfi*. There, especially in "Triumphus mortis" 2.88–102, Laura will explain that her rejection of Petrarch's tokens of love was only for his moral benefit: her self-discipline was a pedagogical tool for the poet in love, his love only a trial and a training ground for the achievement of a higher spiritual good.[4]

Petrarch avoids the final conciliatory solution to the moral conundrum of the *Canzoniere*'s erotic dimension that he explores in the *Trionfi*. This phenomenon—one could perhaps call it the "Beatricization" of Laura—has limited impact on the collection, and the allegorical trial of *Canzoniere* 360, designed to adjudicate the Lover's complaint against Love, ends by returning no verdict. Both the vaguely neo-Platonic solution practiced in the angelology of *stilnovismo* and the more deeply analogical version advanced by Dante in the central chapters of his *Vita nuova* (esp. 15 and 17–18) remain beyond the reach of Petrarch's lyric poetry: Laura is neither an angel-like creature, who directs the poet's meditation toward God (as the closing stanza of Guinizzelli's "Al cor gentil" appears to suggest), nor unequivocally a miracle, a creature God has produced bypassing Nature, or allusively an analogue of Christ, as Dante's *Vita nuova* 17–18 would imply. In addition to the central sections of *Vita nuova* mentioned above, another area of Dante's oeuvre that may prove relevant to the definition of Beatrice's salvific nature and role in Dante's biography is the chapter on her death (first obliquely intuited, then experienced in the imagination, and finally inscribed into the *in morte* section of the book). Episodes from the *Commedia* are also pertinent, especially *Purgatorio* 30–32, in which one witnesses the return of a Christ-like, triumphant Beatrice, as well as *Paradiso* 31, with the Pilgrim's final prayer to her, an allocution conceived in the *dolce stil novissimo* that dominates the poem's last cantos. The interplay between these texts provides the clearest, final, and most explicit intimation of Beatrice's role.

By surveying the Dantean antecedents, students should gain a sense of how carefully Petrarch's book resists the temptation of casting Laura in the final, unambiguously redeeming function that first Guido Guinizzelli and then Dante had devised for the angel-like lady of their poems. This strategic decision in favor of the constant deferral of meaning has just as much poetic as ethical value: a strict patterning of Laura on Beatrice might have solved the spiritual dilemma, the Augustinian clash of spiritual and earthly affections, that nourishes the *Canzoniere*. In so doing, however, it might have also brought the *Canzoniere* into a dangerously close proximity with the traditional solutions advanced in other trecento erotic lyricists, shifting its patterns of imitation from the *danteggiare nuovo* to the *danteggiare tradizionale* (Santagata, "Presenze" 167), which the *Trionfi* will activate.

The Political Commitment

A new kind of intellectual, deracinated from the sociopolitical soil of the central Italian commune on which Dante had taken his first steps, Petrarch also shares little of his antecedent's political vision, especially when it comes to considering the intertwined history and balanced role of the two universal powers. Petrarch's Rome, for one, is an archaeological, essentially utopian, and not always unambiguously imperial ideal. His sketching of its history and value is utterly different from Dante's, and the *Canzoniere* leaves little room for Dante's contemporary, divinely preordained, and highly symbolical seat of the empire, as it emerges from both the historical survey of *Convivio* 4 and the sequence of the three cantos 6 in the *Commedia*. The "Roman-ness" of *Canzoniere* 28 and 53, in particular, is strikingly different from Dante's meditation on the continuity of past Roman institutions with the political alternatives of the present.

There is a greater proximity in tones and themes in the invectives against the corruption of the church, seen in Petrarch's poems deploring the "captivity" of the papacy in Avignon (136–38). Common biblical sources rather than an intentional strategy of allusion can be seen at work in this section of the *Canzoniere*, in which Petrarch's polemical voice comes closest to the peculiarly prophetic tone Dante adopts when discussing church matters. A survey of the *Commedia*'s treatment of successors of Peter may serve well the elucidation of Petrarch's "Babylonian sonnets"; at the very least, *Inferno* 19, *Purgatorio* 19, and *Paradiso* 27 should be included. The most complete discussion of Dante's stance on political issues may be found in his Latin *Monarchia*: his recurring accusations against the Donation of Constantine as the original sin of the modern church anticipate Petrarch's references to Constantine in *Canzoniere* 138.

The Common Mythologems

A subset of textual loci in Dante's *Commedia* appears to have exerted a particular fascination on Petrarch's poetic memory and mythographic imagination. As

Zanato has shown, three cantos have generated echoes scattered throughout the *Canzoniere*: *Inferno* 5, *Inferno* 13, and *Paradiso* 12. In addition to Zanato's treatment of the presence of Francesca, Pier delle Vigne, and Saint Francis in Petrarch's poetry, I would note a further mythologem of Dantean origin: Ulysses. Familiarity with the respective cantos may suffice for the first three figures, but to understand the larger spectrum of Odyssean resonances that are scattered throughout Dante's poem, students need to be exposed to other areas of the text beyond *Inferno* 26 (and possibly 27).[5] Given the ethical and metapoetic value that nautical metaphors assume in both Dante and Petrarch, some time should be spent on the invocation and address to the reader contained in *Purgatorio* 1 and *Paradiso* 2, respectively. It is from these passages that the uncanny shadow Ulysses's voyage casts on the poetic journey of Dante's poem may emerge. A parallel reading of Dante's and Petrarch's redeployment of the Ulysses myth might help students appreciate the gulf separating Dante's condemnation of (his own) Ulysses, in his relentless and hubristic quest for knowledge, from Petrarch's metapoetic meditation on the restlessness of his own existential wanderings and, just as important, on the ever-impending shipwreck of his book's poetic and spiritual enterprise (80, 132, 189, 235, and 323.13–24). Only in a Latin epistle, *Familiares* 21.15, will Petrarch allusively connect Dante's Ulysses to the biographical circumstances of what Boccaccio had presented to him as a *concivem doctumque satis pariterque poetam*,[6] but it is perhaps in Ulysses as a mirror image of both that Petrarch comes closest to facing Dante's mythology of the poetic self.

NOTES

[1] Aside from the lyrical character of the first two canzoni in *Convivio*, which have left minimal traces in the *Canzoniere* (Trovato 154–55), Petrarch does not seem to have been involved in a thorough study of the theorizing, prose-writing Dante.

[2] Knowledge of Italian and German, though useful, is not mandatory for the use of such works. Other contributions of more limited scope, but with no less insight, are Billanovich, "Tra Dante"; Contini, "Preliminari" and "Un'interpretazione"; Feo, "Petrarca"; Kuon; Orelli, "Dantismi"; Martinelli, "Dante"; Picone, "Riscritture"; De Robertis; and Zanato. Most recently and perhaps most comprehensive in their approach, see the essays collected in Barański and Cachey.

[3] On the underlying calendrical structure of the *Canzoniere*, see Roche, "Calendrical Structure"; Biancardi.

[4] Consideration of the *Trionfi*, perhaps Petrarch's most Dantean (and certainly most Boccaccian) work, is beyond the scope of this essay. Essential orientation may be found in Giunta; Eisner.

[5] On textual and thematic interconnections, see Fenzi 492–517; see also Cachey, "From Shipwreck" and "Place."

[6] Literally, "fellow citizen, quite learned, and equally a poet." The hexameter comes from Boccaccio's carmen "Ytalie iam certus honos," in *Carmina*.

Boccaccio and Petrarch

Laurie Shepard

Tradition has designated Petrarch's *Rerum vulgarium fragmenta*, or *Canzoniere*, and Boccaccio's *Decameron* as opposite poles of fourteenth-century Italian literary innovation. Each masterpiece requires prolonged study, but curricular constraints sometimes demand the presentation of the two works in a semester. In this essay I suggest ways in which the juxtaposition of the works allows students to appreciate more fully some of the complex moral questions that animated vernacular conversation in fourteenth-century Italy. The essay focuses on several interrelated topics that are essential to the understanding of both works but that can also serve as approaches to the less accessible *Canzoniere*. If taught in Italian, undergraduates will not be able to read the two works in their entirety, but the class could be taught using an English *Decameron* and a bilingual *Canzoniere*.[1]

Francesco Petrarca and Giovanni Boccaccio were friends; as the former observed, "Would that we might have lived together, for then we should have been but one mind in two bodies" (*Seniles* 5.3).[2] Attacked by critics, Petrarch turned to Boccaccio, his ideal reader and the man who understood his thought most profoundly (2.1). Their first encounter came in 1350, following the devastating plague, when both men were approaching maturity. This was the season of the two great vernacular works: part of the *Decameron* had already circulated at the time of their meeting, and Petrarch was organizing his vernacular poems.[3] Boccaccio would, apparently under the influence of his friend, devote much of the remainder of his activity as a writer to moral and ethical works in Latin. Petrarch, in a period of extraordinary creativity as a vernacular poet (Foster, *Petrarch* 7–8), was also at a turning point. Laura had died in April 1348, and the poet's infatuation long before its object. In this period Petrarch broke with the Colonna family, engaged in the politics of Rome, and in 1353 abandoned his refuge in the Vaucluse for Italy. He was beginning to edit and order his letters.

The two men met at the walls of Florence in October 1350, the *poeta laureatus* Petrarch assuming the role of master, Boccaccio that of disciple.[4] Their subsequent letters preserve a conversation about Italian poetry, the precepts of ancient and patristic moral philosophers, and the more pressing problem of how to lead a life of rectitude in an age characterized by rapid social, economic, and political transformation and by corruption and decadence. Vittore Branca contends that their friendship was "productive beyond any other in the history of letters" (*Boccaccio* 93).

Although the years of composition of the two masterworks only partially coincide with the years of friendship, the conversation between the two men raises questions that are pertinent to both texts. The *Decameron* and the *Canzoniere* are rooted in the problem of the virtuous life. Virtue is explored not merely as the opposite of sin; it is examined in relation to action and inaction and to the ultimate Christian virtue of humility or the abandoning of the will to God. Central to the problem of virtue is discernment and the significance of love: virtuous love, lust, and love's institutions, marriage and friendship. The meaning of time is the other question raised here: although innovative notions of time contour both works, they reveal profound differences in the crafting of the concept. The problem of time circles back to the question of virtue, to a moral reckoning that occurs daily and at the end of life.

In the *Decameron*, the exercise of the civic virtues of Aristotle (and Dante) determines outcomes of stories.[5] Many stories focus on the great civic virtue of magnanimity, which depends on an ability to read signs accurately and to think dispassionately. Boccaccio privileges an aristocratic life that allows fruitful leisure (but does not necessarily imply the intellectual intensity of humanist *otium* or the spiritual concentration of Christian contemplation) and promotes discernment and magnanimity. Ser Torello, the paragon of merchants in the *Decameron*, is introduced while out on a recreational hunt (day 10, novella 9, sec. 7), and Natan, the greatest prince, is first presented at rest (day 10, novella 3, sec. 12). The most significant example of this ideal is the *lieta brigata* ("joyful band"), which has retreated from the city of sin and death to the garden.

Magnanimity by the powerful is the other half of the *pronta battuta*, the brief, witty, defensive, and often corrective verbal response to a potentially compromising situation. The *pronta battuta* itself is an expression of civic virtue, and Pampinea's advice that women be concise (day 1, novella 10, secs. 3–4) reflects the Roman precept that a spare style implies a well-ordered mind, whereas the undisciplined speaker divulges a "foulness of the mind" (Parker 203). Among the most important civic lessons in the *Decameron*, this verbal instrument allows the weak to defend themselves and correct wrongdoing, but only when the powerful are not already blinded and deafened by sin. The counterexample to magnanimity is the ninth story of the sixth day, the importance of which is highlighted by its position in the *Decameron*, its setting in the spiritual heart of Florence, and by Elissa's introduction. Guido Cavalcanti, contemplative among the tombstones, responds to the aggression of Betto Brunelleschi with a *villania* ("insult") that demonstrates his superiority, punctuated by his athletic escape from Betto and the band, but which is neither magnanimous nor productive.[6]

Motivated by concerns about the merchant class's ability to govern, stories condemn impetuous actions. The merchant Bernabò, for example, acts impulsively on spurious evidence of wrongdoing when he commands that his virtuous and accomplished wife, Zinevra, be killed (day 2, novella 9). The *Decameron* is also full of cautionary tales about minds besmirched by avarice. Francesco Vergellesi, blinded by the vice, allows Zima to successfully corrupt his faithful wife before his very eyes (day 3, novella 5). Also tainted by avarice, the merchant brothers of Elisabetta fail to provide a dowry for her marriage; they kill her lover and do not notice that their sister's grief is consuming her life until alerted by a neighbor. In the end they feel compelled to flee (day 4, novella 5). Other vices also destroy lives: Prince Tancredi, spurred by arrogance, because his daughter has taken a lover of low social rank, and by jealousy, kills his daughter's lover and causes his beloved Ghismonda to commit suicide (day 4, novella 1, secs. 58–61). Lack of reflection and discernment, whether in a callow youth like Andreuccio da Perugia (day 2, novella 5), a mature businessman like Rinaldo d'Asti (day 2, novella 2), or even the impetuous Bernabò, is punished, but rarely as severely as sin.

The question of God's judgment of our lives is taken off the table in the first tale, when the worst of men, Ser Cepparello da Prato, becomes Saint Ciappelletto, against all logic: the human mind cannot fathom the ways of God. In the introduction to the ninth day, however, the author expresses his belief, with the caveat that this is only a human opinion, that the *brigata* would be saved, for anyone who encountered the youths, crowned by garlands of oak, would declare that they would not be conquered by death and that their deaths would be joyful (sec. 4).[7]

The *Canzoniere* is at once exemplary and deeply personal, and it rarely addresses questions of civic virtue.[8] Initiating his love story on Good Friday (poem 3), Petrarch establishes the thematic foundation of Christian sin and redemption, and the whole is structured by confessional, penitential poems like "I'vo pensando" (264), in which the poet laments his failure to surrender himself to "quelle pietose braccia" 'those merciful arms' (line 14).[9] He will not free himself from the two knots, his desire for fame (stanza 4) and his love for Laura (stanza 5).

It is difficult to define Petrarch's love for Laura as lust, the intense erotic response of characters in the *Decameron* tales, yet the *Canzoniere* returns continually to the central problem that the poet's love is not virtuous, and that it prevents him from following the steps of his brother and turning to God. Laura is the poet's lodestar in love (151), virtue (156), beauty (159), and happiness:

> Sì come eterna vita è veder Dio,
> né più si brama, né bramar più lice,
> così me, donna, il voi veder, felice
> fa in questo breve et fraile viver mio. (191.1–4)
>
> As it is eternal life to see God, nor can one desire more, nor is it right to desire more, so, Lady, seeing you makes me happy in this short and frail life of mine.

His mind is clouded; he confuses Laura with "the true image" (126). He has allowed himself to be deluded by her unparalleled beauty and virtue, a theme reiterated especially in the second half of the first part of the *Canzoniere* (160, 165, 173, 185, 188, 193, 215, 246). She is the new Eve, "senza par poi che l'addorno / suo male et nostro vide in prima Adamo" 'without an equal since Adam first saw his and our lovely bane' (188.3–4).

Memory embodies and perpetuates the struggle with virtue and discerning at the heart of the *Canzoniere*, and although the poet is conscious that the years have aged his muse (90), memory preserves his love laurel-green (126, 143, 156, 175, 190, 207). He makes only sporadic efforts to reclaim his free will from Love's dominion (1.14, 248.8).[10] Yet in this work inspired by Augustine's *Confessions*, "it is possible to trace . . . the outlines of a moral autobiography, however faint and uncertain as to details and dates" (Foster, *Petrarch* 65). Gradually the *Canzoniere* reveals the poet's liberation from the memory of beauty that has made him prefer his own illusion of happiness to the summum bonum and prevented him from turning to "quelle pietose braccia."

Like the *Decameron*, the *Canzoniere* concludes not with an assurance of salvation but with a petition, a prayer to the Virgin for assistance:

> Vergine, que' belli occhi
> che vider tristi la spietata stampa
> ne' dolci membra del tuo caro figlio
> volgi al mio dubio stato
> che sconsigliato a te vèn per consigilio. (366.22–26)
>
> Virgin, turn those beautiful eyes that sorrowing saw the pitiless wounds in their dear Son's sweet limbs, to my perilous state, who come dismayed to you for counsel.

The prayer expresses the desperation of the poet's dilemma; his life has been spent on praise of mortal beauty and vain prayers, and now he fears death (366.79–91).

An imperfect convergence of the *Canzoniere* and the *Decameron* occurs in the final novella of the latter, the unlikely tale of Griselda, a shepherd's daughter who abandons her will to her husband and lord, the cruel tyrant Gualtieri. Griselda finds the inner fortitude to prevail, with only a single, mild reproach (sec. 59), an act that helps the reader suspend disbelief just a little bit longer. The aging Petrarch wrote Boccaccio that he had committed the story to memory and rewritten it in Latin (*Seniles* 17.3). The appeal may have been Griselda's stoic suffering or her surrender of self, for which the poet yearned but unfailingly resisted. Petrarch's private idolatry of the creature whose beauty illuminated his memory and inspired his poetry meant that he could not, like the shepherd's daughter, forget himself. Although it holds pride of place, in the *Decameron* the novella is presented in an equivocal light: the behavior of Gualtieri is described as *matta bestialità* ("mad bestiality") at the beginning of the tale (sec. 3), and Dioneo gives the story a bawdy twist at the conclusion (sec. 69).

It is significant that the final tale of the *Decameron* tells of a marriage and a family. If Griselda's humility in the face of the brutality of her lord constitutes perfect love, a love modeled on the Virgin Mary or perhaps Job, the social and spiritual inequality of the union promised a marital nightmare in the context of the book. (In this case, of course, Griselda's superiority to her husband in spirit matches his superiority to her in rank.) Boccaccio advocates marriage between a man and a woman who are equals in spirit, and the *Decameron* exhibits deep disdain for acquisitive merchants who seek to "ennoble" themselves through marriage (day 3, novellas 4, 8; day 7, novella 8). The exemplary marriage, that of Ser Torello and Adalieta in the ninth tale of the tenth day, proposes a vision of love nurtured by equality and nobility of spirit, although it is a marriage between a merchant husband and a noble wife. A certain facile optimism prevails when tales conclude with a marriage that is born of lust, as in the fifth story of the fifth day.

The stories of the *Decameron* return continually to the question of friendship, the courageous and altruistic love that restores the ruptured bonds between men in a society that is radically corrupt (as the introduction relates), and hierarchical. Friendship premised on love or respect generates goodness: Saladino, sultan of Babylon, befriends the Jewish usurer Melchisedech after the latter extricates himself from Saladino's trap and is in turn enriched by Melchisedech (day 1, novella 3); the socially eminent Messer Geri Spina befriends the baker Cisti and enjoys both his wisdom and his fine wine (day 6, novella 2). In the second story of the first day, a friendship between a Christian merchant and a Jewish merchant leads to the conversion and salvation of the latter. When premised on communality of interests, as in day 4, novella 9, and day 7, novella 10, the fruits of friendship are not always so sweet. Intellectual equality unites Giotto and Forese da Rabatta (day 6, novella 5), and their friendship underscores the sterility of Betto Brunelleschi's offer of society to Cavalcanti (day 6, novella 9). Intended to be exemplary, the bond between Tito and Gisippo (day 10, novella 8) illustrates friendship as self-sacrificing, mutually beneficial, and the prerogative of males. The last point is contradicted by the *lieta brigata*, however, where the friendship that is most clearly articulated is that of Pampinea and Filomena.

Friendship is not absent in the *Canzoniere*: one of the compelling themes is the transformation of Laura in the second part of the work. Her spirit, in the guise of a loving companion, visits the poet and appeases his troubled soul. Marco Santagata argues that Laura's death was providential for the poet (*Frammenti* 18): although the poet expresses confusion and grief in a *planctus* written on the day he learned of her death—"Che debb'io far? che mi consigli, Amore?" 'What shall I do? What do you counsel me, Love?' (268.1)—he eventually resolves his dilemma. Unlike Dante, who saves Beatrice after death by glorifying her, or even unlike the Franciscus of the *Secretum*, Petrarch chooses a way that is entirely original in Italian letters (Santagata, *Frammenti* 214–17). Laura becomes a companion, "now . . . a mother, now . . . a lover" (285.9),[11] "a remarkable poetic achievement, and arguably Petrarch's finest," according to Kenelm Foster (*Petrarch* 45).

The question of time in the two works is also of interest, because it allows students to focus on changing attitudes toward time, morality, and mortality. In the plague year, those who survived were mindful of the time that remained to them, as seen in the *Decameron* (day 1, introd., secs. 55–58). Time management by the *lieta brigata* is communal, and even leisure hours become profitable. The text opens with a precise date (sec. 8); the flight from the city of death is set on a Wednesday morning, and storytelling, the principal activity of the *lieta brigata*, is designated to allow the *brigata* to enjoy the hours of the day when the sun is hottest (secs. 111–12). Days are set aside for personal hygiene and devotion (day 2, conclusion, sec. 6), and the decision to return to Florence is predicated on the number of days the *lieta brigata* has been away and the potential consequences of an absence of that length (day 10, conclusion, sec. 6). Excuses are made when a novella is particularly long (day 10, novella 9, sec. 4). The *ballate* and dances at the end of each day become a rhythmic, ritualized celebration of time, while back in the city of death, masses, funerals, and other sacred rituals marking time and mortality are haphazard occurrences.

Like virtue, time is personal and problematic in the *Canzoniere.* The whole is structured on principles of time, with a prefatory sonnet and one poem for each day of the year. Throughout the *Canzoniere* we encounter autobiographic poems like 23 or anniversary poems (30, 50, 62, 79, 101, 107, 118, 122, 145, 212, 221, 266, 271) that celebrate or curse the day the poet first set eyes on Laura. Yet envisioning Laura as a timeless beauty is a symptom of the poet's error of discernment (Foster, *Petrarch* 55), and the inclusion of these poems may be a strategy to counter the essential resistance to chronology in the *Canzoniere.*

Poetry plays with time. The euphony of "Chiare, fresche e dolci acque, / ove le belle membra / pose colei che sola a me par donna" 'Clear, fresh, sweet waters, where she who alone seems lady to me rested her lovely body' (126.1–3), may make our hearts skip a beat, but our brain is immediately engaged by the unexpected shift in tense from a dream-like present to an obsessive past:

> Quante volte diss'io
> allor pien di spavento:
> Costei per fermo nacque in paradiso.
> . . . .
> Qui come venn'io, o quando? (126.53–55, 62)
>
> How many times did I say to myself then, full of awe: "She was surely born in Paradise!" . . . "How did I come here and when?"

The poet seeking immortality achieves it through poetry (61.12–13), but he also invents it in his poetry. In sonnet 34 he creates a private space for Apollo and himself by joining in a metaphor the beloved ancient nymph and the temporal lady and then collapsing the metaphor into a simple gesture: "sì vedrem poi per meraviglia inseme / seder la donna nostra sopra l'erba, / et far de le sue braccia a se stessa ombra" 'Thus we shall then together see a marvel—our lady sitting on the grass and with her arms making a shade for herself' (lines 12–14). She is forever caught between time and eternity in a moment that unites poet and god. Colloquial rhythms in the next sonnet suggest a similar intimacy with Amor, the god who rules the poet's heart: "Ma pur sì aspre vie né sì selvagge / cercar non so, ch'Amor non venga sempre / ragionando con meco, et io co llui" 'but still I cannot seek paths so harsh or so savage that Love does not always come along discoursing with me and I with him' (35.12–14). With economy the poet reminds us that his beloved is subject to time, even if the changes are barely perceptible: "ed era il ciel a l'armonia sì intento / che non se vedea in ramo mover foglia, / tanta dolcezza avea pien l'aere e 'l vento" 'and the heavens were so intent upon the harmony that no leaf on any branch was seen to move' (156.12–14). The unseen movement of a leaf in the ambivalent line 13 becomes an intimation of mortality: "no one saw a leaf move on the branch." These few examples show Petrarch's manipulation of time in poetry, and how his desire to escape the confines of mortality through poetry is even more provocative and innovative than Boccaccio's reconstruction of time.

Remote and often difficult for twenty-first-century students, the *Decameron* and *Canzoniere* probe the meanings of our lives, the problems of living well, and the obstacles to discernment and salvation, and they slowly yield their lessons to the reader. The *Decameron* is civic and communal, the *Canzoniere* intensely personal, and their juxtaposition helps students understand the complexity of these and other questions on the minds of two fourteenth-century writers, thinkers, and friends.

NOTES

[1] Boccaccio's lessons are woven into his syntax, and this aspect of the work is inevitably lost in English translations. I recommend that the course begin with the *Decameron* and that students study the entire frame; days 1, 3, 6 and 10 in their entirety; and day 2, novellas 1–3, 5, 7–10; day 4, novellas 1, 2, 5, 7, 9; day 5, novellas 1, 4, 6, 8–10; day 7, novellas 1, 2, 4–6, 8–10; day 8, novellas 1–3, 6–10; and day 9, novellas 2–6, 8, 10. Citations in this essay are from Branca's edition of the *Decameron*.

[2] Thirty letters from Petrarch have survived, and four from Boccaccio. The translation of *Seniles* quoted from here is by James H. Robinson, reprinted from his edition and translation *Petrarch: The First Modern Scholar and Man of Letters* in Sadlon.

[3] In his edition of the *Canzoniere*, Santagata is judicious in his dating of the individual poems and also offers a useful schematic version of the evolution of the collection (clxxiv–cxc).

[4] Besides the brief encounters in Florence as Petrarch traveled to and from Rome in 1350–51, Boccaccio journeyed north to visit Petrarch four times: in Padua in 1351, Milan in 1359, Venice in the spring of 1363, and, finally, Padua in the summer of 1368. My thanks to Todd Boli for this chronology. For a discussion of the friendship, see Dotti 219–36.

[5] "According to Aristotle's definition, the active life is characterized by eleven moral virtues . . . : courage, temperance, liberality, munificence, magnanimity, love of honor, gentleness, affability, truth, good disposition, and justice" (Mezzadroli 866).

[6] My reading of the novella is based on Durling, "Boccaccio."

[7] Cristiana Fordyce suggested this reading to me. The image of the *brigata* crowned by oak leaves reverses the travesty of the first story, when Cepparello, the "old stump," or Adam, is mistakenly crowned with a garland when he becomes "Ciappelletto" in Bourgogne and a saint.

[8] Examples of the *Canzoniere*'s addressing traditional virtue include sonnet 7 and the seventh stanza of "Italia mia" (128).

[9] All readings are from Santagata's edition; all translations are from Durling's. Other penitential poems include the first sonnet and the prayer to the Virgin (366), which closes the work, as well as 32, 62, 80, 81,142, 189, and 355. Foster (*Petrarch*) is my principal guide in this reading of the *Canzoniere.*

[10] See also 173, 311, 323, 325.

[11] See also 279, 281, 284, 289–90, 302, 305, 336, 341–42, 343, 345, 359, and 362.

"Another Petrarch": Teaching Petrarch through Music

Marc Vanscheeuwijck

> Io so forsi parlare qual Musico, ma non armonizzare. Diremo dunque, secondo nostra sembianza, che il Marenzio (per parlar de' moderni) sia un'altro Petrarca.
>
> I can perhaps speak as a musician, though I cannot compose. We shall say then, in our view, that Marenzio (among the moderns) is another Petrarch.
>
> —Torquato Tasso, in Alessandro Guarini's dialogue *Il Farnetico savio, overo il Tasso* (Bizzarini 242)

That Petrarch's poetry is closely related to music is no news to anyone. Although the poet probably never meant his verse to be set to music, dozens of composers set most poems from Petrarch's *Canzoniere*, predominantly in the musical genre of the polyphonic madrigal, during the period 1520–1630.[1] Still, when music historians teach the madrigal, they most often address an audience of music majors, and they concentrate their efforts, first, on a quick demonstration of how composers translate the poetry into music, and, second, on the development of the genre throughout the late Renaissance. Most literary historians, on the other hand, limit themselves to illustrating a few poems by playing a musical setting of, say, "Zefiro torna" (*Canzoniere* 310) by Luca Marenzio or Claudio Monteverdi, confessing an inability to go any deeper into the music than to point out a few general ways in which meaning and expression are conveyed in the piece.

I suggest here approaches for nonmusicologist instructors who wish to present sixteenth-century madrigals on Petrarch's poems to a nonmusically specialized audience. The main challenge is that I cannot here provide either score or recorded examples to demonstrate how I proceed. But since the most obvious way to approach a discussion of such musical settings is through sound examples, I refer to specific pieces and provide a basic discography in an appendix.

Background on the Madrigal

I begin the class session on the madrigal by presenting the musical form's history, including a twentieth-century debate on the madrigal in comparison with other popular musical genres in sixteenth-century Italy. The madrigal, a musical genre flourishing from circa 1520 to circa 1630 in Italy, can be defined as a polyphonic secular composition written on any poetic text, for four or five unaccompanied solo voices. Its musical aim is to express as closely as possible the words and the general meaning of the text. For several decades after the publication of Alfred Einstein's three-volume *The Italian Madrigal* in 1949, the commonly accepted view on the development of the genre emerged from his assertion that

> The genesis [of the madrigal] is known: the transformation of the *frottola*, from an accompanied song with a supporting bass and two inner voices serving as "fillers" into a motet-like polyphonic construction with four parts of equal importance, can be followed as easily as the transformation of a chrysalis into a butterfly. (1: 121)

Much of what Einstein asserts here is debatable, but the most problematic aspect of his claim is that, to judge solely by printed materials, the *frottola*[2] ceased to exist around 1520 and that the madrigal began its development ten years later, leaving a gap that he calls an "artistic pause." Einstein and others also thought that the Petrarchist (and Bembist) movement was responsible for the poetic choices composers made in creating their madrigals.[3] Thus the madrigal was born from a new taste for more serious texts and free-verse forms set for unaccompanied voices in a more complex polyphonic texture with an increased equality between the parts. Such a learned polyphony called for the compositional techniques introduced in Italy by the *Oltremontani*, the composers from the Low Countries, Germany, and France who established themselves in the Italian courts throughout the fifteenth and sixteenth centuries (e.g., Philippe Verdelot, Jacob Arcadelt, Adrian Willaert, and later Cipriano de Rore and Giaches De Wert).

Iain Fenlon and James Haar were the first musicologists to challenge the "artistic pause" theory, on the basis of both a reconsideration of the cultural factors explored by Einstein and their study of *frottole* and madrigals transmitted not in printed sources but in manuscripts. They found that in the manuscript traditions, *frottole* continued to be produced into the early 1530s, and madrigals were already circulating before 1520, showing that the genres actually overlapped by at least a decade. Of great importance was also the fact that both genres rarely appeared in the same manuscripts: *frottole* and madrigals overlapped chronologically but never geographically or in musical or poetic style. The musical madrigal then became predominantly a genre cultivated in the Medici-dominated Florentine and Roman papal courts, whereas the various northern Italian courts continued to enjoy *frottole*. When Isabella d'Este, one of the great patronesses of such *frottole*, and her Mantuan court lost interest in the genre (during the 1520s) in favor of the poetry of the more academic Petrarchists, the madrigal began to be a favorite genre not only in Mantua but also in the other northern Italian courts (Fenlon and Haar 5–10). The development from *frottola* into madrigal is now no longer generally accepted as plausible, although it still is a point of controversy.

My proposed readings for the students oppose two important poles in this discussion: Fenlon and Haar introduce their monograph with a more subtle and elaborate description of what I have just summarized, whereas Dean Mace further develops Einstein's ideas, restricting the poetic choices of the madrigal composers from a Petrarchist to a Bembist interest.[4] Mace's main thesis is as follows:

> Since the madrigal cannot be explained logically as a "natural" development in the history of music, and since the use of polyphony with secular amorous verse has seemed an "aberration" to the principal historian of this form, does it not seem reasonable to understand the madrigal as the response of musicians to the new Bembistic reading of Petrarch? (74)

Listening to Madrigals

At this point, having introduced the problem, I proceed to illustrate a sixteenth-century method for listening to madrigals, which differs fundamentally from the way we listen to madrigals today. We often hear madrigals sung by choirs, although the genre was designed for solo performance (i.e., one voice per part), or we get to enjoy a two-hour concert with twelve to twenty compositions, in which one madrigal after another is performed. Having heard each piece once—and we are lucky if the original text (not just a translation) is provided in the program—we are then either looking at that text, missing many of the subtleties expressed in the music, or we enjoy the beauty of the sounds, not realizing how creative the composer has been in trying to express all the details in the poetry. If we manage to concentrate on both aspects of the composition, knowing that we will hear it only once, we end up either completely exhausted from the experience or frustrated with our inability to concentrate intensely for two hours. This is not the way madrigals were received in their original context.

Before the seventeenth century, when madrigals began to be a genre performed by virtuoso professional performers, they were often referred to as *madrigali da tavolino* ("table madrigals"). In the gatherings of the various academies of literati in Italy, poets, philosophers, composers, and other intellectuals often organized sessions in which various musical settings (by member composers) of a given poetic text would be compared for effectiveness in expressing the meaning of the words. After a discussion of the poetic text, four or five members of the assembly would sing one madrigal two or three times, so all could get well acquainted with the way the composer set the text (composite scores were not available, since singers sang from part books containing only one vocal line each). Subsequently, they discussed the compositional techniques used, and the piece was performed again and further scrutinized. The singers would then present another musical setting of the same text, and the same procedure was observed again. In short, the academicians could easily spend a three- or four-hour session listening in depth to and discussing no more than two or three madrigals.

I try to replicate this experience with my nonmusic students, but within an eighty-minute class session. Having chosen a short madrigal by Tomaso Cimello (c. 1500–c. 1580) on the *commiato* of the twenty-second canzone in Petrarch's *Canzoniere* (268.78–82), I begin with a short analysis of the text:

> Fuggi 'l sereno e 'l verde,
> non t'appressare ove sia riso o canto,
> canzon mia, no, ma pianto;
> non fa per te di star fra gente allegra,
> vedova, sconsolata, in veste negra.
>
> Flee the clear sky and greenery, do not approach where there is laughter and singing, my song, no, but where there is weeping; it is not fitting for you to be among cheerful people, disconsolate widow in black garments.[5]

Before listening to the musical rendition, I ask the students how they imagine a composer could express certain words musically. If they lack the verbal tools to describe compositional techniques, I offer some suggestions. For example, the verb *fuggire* ("to flee") could be expressed by fast upward or downward scales or by the musical device of *fuga* ("fugue"), in which the voices begin in staggered sequence and imitate one another's melodies in quick succession. I ask how "sereno" 'serene' and "verde" 'green' could be rendered in music, particularly when opposed to "pianto" 'weeping.' Even untrained listeners might come up with the contrast between consonant and dissonant harmonies (e.g., a wrenching sound on "pianto"). The last two lines of the stanza directly address the "disconsolate widow," admonishing her not to dwell "among cheerful people." An effective musical approach to these lines, breaking from the technique that up to this point has been predominantly imitative, is to have all the voices join and sing with equal rhythms, thus creating a homophonic or purely chordal texture. The contrast is strong enough to make these lines sound like an authoritative warning.

I give the students a few hints of this kind and ask them to focus on what strikes them most and what happens musically on specific words as they listen to the song. I then play the entire madrigal—using the compact disc *In Morte di Madonna Laura* (track 4), performed by the Huelgas Ensemble (and I invite the reader to get the recording and to follow along)—while they look at the text.[6] After briefly talking about the general mood of the music (fairly dark and sad), I walk the listeners through the broader structure of the piece: the first three lines are only sung once, with a slight cadence (the musical equivalent of a comma or period in a text) at the end of the first line, a stronger cadence at the conclusion of the second line, and a change of mood in the third line, again followed by a cadence. In moving to the fourth line, the composer connects the text swiftly but has the singers repeat the line and then sing the final line three times. In doing so, Cimello has clearly respected the poetic structure but at the same time clarified with musical means (through harmony, cadential formulas, and repetition) what in his view should be emphasized in the text. In other words, we already hear, just after one listening, how the music forces interpretation of the short verse in one particular direction.

In a second listening I look at the text again, glossing what the composer does, and I pause the recording after each line or even half line to call students' attention to a few simple compositional techniques, based entirely on what they hear (no score involved). *Fuggire* is indeed expressed through quick imitation (fugue) in the voices, but all singers come together in a consonant cadence on "verde." In the second line, "non t'appressare" 'do not approach' is imitative again, but the general pitch is higher, drawing greater attention from the listeners after the fairly neutral exordium. The singers use a closer imitation to express "appressare," and the first little melisma (melodic ornament) occurs appropriately on the word "canto" 'singing.' After a cadence on a major chord (expressing a happier mood), the contrast with the minor key that follows is quite strong, presaging the transition from "riso o canto" 'laughter or singing' to "pianto." The composer thus introduces what is to follow through a minor-key harmony and then produces a wrenching dissonance and elongated note values on "pianto." If time allows, I play this part of the madrigal again as a summary before moving on to the second section, in which the admonition is now direct and set in a chordal texture. Such a musical rhetorical figure (*noema*) is a conventional way to call listeners' attention to authority, and Cimello uses it with circumspection and efficiency. The importance of the warning is expressed in the repetition of the line, but Cimello also emphasizes the character of "allegra" 'cheerful' in his use of dotted, almost dance-like rhythms. A new contrast comes as "vedova sconsolata" 'disconsolate widow' is set on long notes in opposition to the quick syllabic setting of the previous line. The darkness of the widow's garments is expressed again in the minor-key harmony, long note values (i.e., slow rhythms), low pitches, and in the three iterations of the line, the last of which slows the overall rhythm down even more. In this particular performance, the Huelgas Ensemble then repeats the entire short madrigal, in which the soprano adds a few very tasteful improvised ornaments on "canto" and on "gente allegra" 'cheerful people,' thus helping create a stronger contrast to what follows. The repetition also provides an uninterrupted listening through which the students can put all the information they have received together.

In my experience a close listening of this sort makes listeners much more aware of what can happen in music and how effectively a composer can convey an interpretation of a poem through compositional choices. After this introductory listening exercise, one can pick another madrigal set to a poem from the *Canzoniere* or, even better, two different musical settings of the same poem, for comparative listening.[7] In taking the same approach to text and musical setting as I did for Cimello's "Fuggi 'l sereno," teachers will be impressed at how much their students will now hear in the madrigal.

After our intensive listening session, we return to our readings by Fenlon and Haar and by Mace for further discussion of Petrarchism and Bembism, approaching Bembo's doctrine of propriety and its accomplishment in vernacular poetry by use of the qualities of *gravità* ("gravitas") and *piacevolezza* ("pleasing quality") (Mace 69–70), addressing the question of how this propriety can be achieved through a musical setting of a poem. If we accept Mace's idea that the musical madrigal emerged in response to Bembo's theories (Fenlon and Haar 11), we still encounter the problem that Bembism flourished primarily in Venice, under the patronage of Domenico Venier, whereas the madrigal developed first in Florence and Rome, reaching the northern Italian courts only after the cultivation of the *frottola* had been abandoned.

But musical genres rarely develop as the result of a single major influence; rather, they develop from of a variety of tendencies. Certainly the Petrarchist movement was quite important in the 1520s, as Bembism would be a decade later. But there are several other factors to be taken into consideration: the increased number of *Oltremontani* immigrating to Italy at the time, thus introducing a taste for more complex polyphony; Adrian Willaert (*maestro di cappella* at San Marco in Venice from 1528 to 1562) was gradually establishing Venice as one of the most important musical centers in Italy; the *frottola* and the chanson began to be perceived as too limited in their expression, yielding to freer forms such as the madrigal that allowed an increase in experimentation, particularly in expressing the text; an interest in codifying new rules of composition, led by Gioseffo Zarlino, was growing, thus setting a basic theoretical framework inspiring composers such as Monteverdi to go beyond these rules; and strong cultural differences existed between the smaller northern Italian courts and the Duchy of Tuscany and the Papal States.

Interweaving a literary historical discourse with heightened appreciation for musical settings of Petrarch's poetry is in a way a Petrarchist act in its own right. We can teach students to identify and relish the devices and gestures composers used to communicate poems musically and do so without the specialized language of musicological analysis by cuing them to listen actively, as sixteenth-century listeners did. We should not overlook the musical settings of his poetry that continue to be composed and that offer an additional dimension to the teaching of Petrarch's poetry.

NOTES

[1] For a fairly exhaustive list of musical settings of poems in Petrarch's *Canzoniere*, see Culcasi (135–86).

[2] The *frottola* is a fifteenth-century soprano-dominated syllabic polyphonic closed-form secular (dance) song written on a variety of poetic forms, usually set for three or four vocal or instrumental parts. It flourished mainly in Florence and Rome, and important composers include Marco Cara and Bartolomeo Tromboncino.

[3] Within the concept of mannerism, Maria Rika Maniates explains *bembismo* as follows: "Although not all petrarchan poetry is manneristic, most mannerist verse, especially in the second stage of poetic development, is petrarchistic. Because Pietro Bembo initiated the fashion of petrarchism, this fashion is sometimes called *bembismo*. And because it flourishes at the same time and in the same centers as does early *maniera* in art, *bembismo* has been linked to Mannerism in poetry. We should further note that *bembismo* also coincides with the first phase of the polyphonic madrigal. Bembo's eclectic approach creates a norm of petrarchan imagery, a canon for imitation. Even though Bembo's aim is to rise above the triviality of previous petrarchism (*poesia per musica*), his emphasis on *maniera* inevitably becomes distorted in the hands of countless imitators" (66).

[4] To avoid overloading students with musically technical essays, I use Mace's "Pietro Bembo and the Literary Origins of the Italian Madrigal" and the short introduction to Fenlon and Haar's *The Italian Madrigal in the Early Sixteenth Century* (3–14).

[5] I am quoting from Durling's bilingual edition *Petrarch's Lyric Poems*.

[6] The CD, released by Sony Vivarte in 1991, can also be downloaded online at *Avax Home*, among other sites.

[7] Poems from the *Canzoniere* with more than one musical setting include "Zefiro torna e 'l bel tempo rimena" (310), by Luca Marenzio and Claudio Monteverdi; "I' vo piangendo i miei passati tempi" (365), by Andrea Rota and Giaches De Wert; and "Solo et pensoso i più deserti campi" (35), by Marenzio, Giaches De Wert, and Orlandus Lassus.

APPENDIX
MADRIGALS ON PETRARCH'S *CANZONIERE*

"Voi ch'ascoltate" (1): Giaches De Wert (1561), Sigismondo d'India (solo madrigal 1618). Hoste da Reggio (1554), Claudio Monteverdi (1640)

"Solo et pensoso" (35): Orlandus Lassus (1555), Luca Marenzio (1599), Giaches De Wert (1581)

"Nova angeletta" (106): Hoste da Reggio (1554), Luca Marenzio (1585), Benedetto Pallavicino (1579)

"Or che 'l ciel" (164): Sigismondo d'India (solo madrigal 1618), Claudio Monteverdi (1638)

"Oimè il bel viso" (267): Hoste da Reggio (1547), Luca Marenzio (1582), Claudio Monteverdi (1614)

"Zefiro torna" (310): Luca Marenzio (1585), Claudio Monteverdi (1614)

"Vago augelletto" (353): Andrea Gabrieli (1566), Giovanni De Macque (1576), Claudio Monteverdi (1614), Stefano Rossetti (1560), Giaches De Wert (1588)

"I' vo piangendo" (365): Andrea Gabrieli (1562 and 1587), Orlandus Lassus (1567), Padre F. Mauro de' Servi (1547), Andrea Rota (1592), Giaches De Wert (1561)

Promoting Student Understanding of Petrarch's *Canzoniere* through Popular Music

Silvia Ross

For teachers of Petrarch's *Canzoniere* (or any other medieval Italian work), one of the greatest challenges is rendering the text accessible to undergraduates and highlighting those issues that might still resonate with them today. Here I explain the reasoning behind and put forward some strategies for employing popular music as an instrument to make Petrarch's *Canzoniere* relevant to students and to help them understand and take ownership of concepts and stylistic features characteristic of his poetry. In my course The Italian Lyric Tradition, this approach functions in conjunction with more orthodox pedagogical methodologies, namely close textual analysis that emphasizes thematic, linguistic, and stylistic features of the poems of the *Canzoniere*. Using popular music therefore serves a complementary purpose in my teaching: it reinforces interpretive questions raised in a traditional analytic context, but in an alternative forum for reflection and discussion. I have found that having students listen to certain popular songs enhances their understanding of Petrarch's poetry, not only through collective examination of the words of popular songs but also in the very act of students' bringing to class recordings of songs they view as reelaborating Petrarchan tropes. The Petrarchan themes I outline here are quite general and (for the most part) widely accepted, and so I refer less to criticism on Petrarch than to scholarship on teaching methodology. This essay seeks, therefore, to demonstrate how certain key themes, tropes, or images conceived or reinvented by Petrarch are reworked in other, subsequent texts, in particular modern and contemporary musical compositions.

That notions should travel across genres and through centuries is by no means a novel idea; indeed, theories of intertextuality have shown that texts are relational and that the reworking of common themes across even wildly diverse works can serve to deepen the interpreter's knowledge of these very themes or concepts and can result in new meanings.[1] In her *Travelling Concepts in the Humanities*, Mieke Bal reminds us that concepts "are not fixed. They travel—between disciplines, between individual scholars, between historical periods, and between geographically dispersed academic communities. Between disciplines, their meaning, reach and operational value differ" (24). And while Bal is arguing for an interdisciplinary approach to major theoretical concepts in the humanities, her general statements ring true for comparable conceptual travels between such genres as poetry and music and between epochs such as the late Middle Ages and contemporary society. My analysis, however, is not meant to provide simply a summary of Petrarchan echoes in a variety of modern contemporary song; instead, it illustrates how these concepts traverse genres and, in exploring these cross-disciplinary journeys, equip students with a means of gaining greater critical understanding of the *Canzoniere* and, ideally, the contemporary musical pieces studied.

The twelve one-hour weekly classes on Petrarch in the second-year course I teach revolve around selected poems from the *Canzoniere*. The twenty to twenty-five students enrolled have had only one year of (albeit intensive) Italian language preparation, and, since the texts are studied in the original Italian, much time is perforce dedicated to careful reading and content analysis. Inevitably, we also pay attention to form, along with an exploration of Petrarch's thematic concerns and classical allusions. The techniques I describe here are derived from my own experience in the delivery of the course and are—I would argue—easily transferable to other contexts of the teaching of Petrarch. Popular music has helped me, in my role as instructor, underpin Petrarchan topoi, as well as the poet's imagery and the forms he adopted. Furthermore, and most importantly, the insertion of musical "interludes" in the curriculum assists me in clarifying just how much students have absorbed in the class and to what extent they have been able to make the material "their own," so to speak.

This exercise is derived in part from a pedagogical philosophy (developed in the Project Zero Classroom workshop of the Center for Teaching and Learning at Harvard) of student-centered learning, namely, the practice of "teaching for understanding" (see Wiske), whereby students are encouraged to give "performances of understanding" that "ask the learner to stretch" and demonstrate his or her comprehension of an issue through a reflective, adaptable process, since "understanding performances are activities which go beyond the rote and the routine" (D. Perkins 43, 43, 42). Understanding, explains David Perkins, "is the ability to think and act flexibly with what one knows" (40). In addition, Perkins argues that "[a]ttaining understanding is less like acquiring something and more like learning to act flexibly. Such a stance casts teachers less in the role of informers and testers and more in the role of facilitators or coaches" (52). Obviously in a course such as the one I teach on Petrarch, standardized, routine forms of lecturing (e.g., on linguistic or metrical features) and assessment (essays, final examination, and so on) are difficult to avoid, but the notion of asking students to give evidence in alternative ways of what they have understood can also constitute a stimulating mode of teaching and learning that can be adopted to complement more traditional, transmission-based modes of instruction.

The philosophy of teaching for understanding also underscores the concept—as formulated by Howard Gardner in his *Frames of Mind: The Theory of Multiple Intelligences*—that many different types of intelligence exist and promotes a teaching practice that attempts to address these various modes of intelligence instead of catering solely to the more conventional categories (i.e., linguistic and mathematical). Martha Stone Wiske elucidates, "[r]ich performances of understanding allow students to learn and express themselves through multiple intelligences and forms of expression; they both develop and demonstrate understanding" (Introduction 4).

Drawing on popular song to discover what students know and understand about Petrarch thus capitalizes in part on what Gardner classifies as musical intelligence. Lois Hetland and Shirley Veenema's *The Project Zero Classroom* supplies a concise definition of this type of intelligence as it applies to an educational context:

> Musical intelligence allows people to create, communicate, and understand meanings made out of sound. While composers and instrumentalists clearly exhibit this intelligence, so do the students who seem particularly attracted by the birds singing outside the classroom window or who constantly tap out intricate rhythms on the desk with their pencils. (67)

Using popular song in the classroom as a means of understanding Petrarch obviously does not stem from my or my students' ability (or presumed lack thereof) to compose or perform music, but nonetheless it falls under the label of musical intelligence in that it constitutes an act of what Gardner, citing Edward Cone, refers to as "active listening" (103). Moreover, using music as an aid to understanding Petrarch's poetry (especially in the context of a course called The Italian Lyric Tradition) also reinforces another important notion: that lyric poetry's origins lie precisely in the setting of verse to music.[2] Musical rhythm can also serve as a tool to reinforce the idea of verbal rhythm, a crucial notion in the reading of poetry.

The phenomenon of adopting a musical approach to Petrarch originated in a class in which a student remarked on the mythological imagery used in canzone 23 as being especially beautiful but nonetheless presenting an idealized concept of woman. Another student then commented that the poet's own presentation of himself as weeping for Laura was somehow not very manly or plausible and seemed rather self-indulgent. This sparked a lively discussion about gender roles in the Middle Ages and how even today there is a stigma attached to the notion of men crying. Students talked about present-day society's stereotyping of sex roles, and I remarked that many modern popular songs represent love, women, and men in modes that might seem like clichés but that in Petrarch's time were innovations, or at the very least rich reworkings of key concepts found in the courtly love tradition, such as those delineated by Andreas Capellanus in his treatise *De amore*. Rather offhandedly, I said to the group that, if they wished, they could bring to class some songs that they thought contained ideas found originally in Petrarch and in the courtly love tradition. The following week I brought a CD player to class with a couple of CDs I had picked for their Petrarchan themes, not imagining that my students might have taken up my suggestion. But one student arrived with recordings she had made for this purpose, and so during that class we listened to two songs and then briefly analyzed the lyrics and imagery that reminded us of Petrarch's poetry.

Over subsequent weeks I was pleasantly surprised to see that different students continued to bring recordings of popular music that for them evoked

Petrarchan thematics and imagery, often making sure to photocopy the lyrics ahead of time so as to facilitate our collective analysis of the Petrarchan echoes, an activity that took place in the last ten or fifteen minutes of each class. The gesture of a student's sharing a song with his or her fellow classmates and instructor, without being obliged to do so, indicates to me a certain initiative that in turn encourages spontaneous dialogue and provides valuable clues as to what the student has been able to comprehend in the course. A further breakthrough occurred a couple of weeks after the first song was introduced, when a student offered a recording of a song in Italian after having gone to the effort of writing out the lyrics himself, thus illustrating that another linkage, in this instance linguistic, had been effected between the standard Italian of today and Petrarch's medieval Italian. On the few occasions when students did not bring songs themselves, I supplied examples I had previously selected, so as to ensure that the activity could continue.

What follows are some examples of pieces that were proposed either by students or by me and that stem from a variety of genres, some of which might seem to share obvious thematic affinities with the *Canzoniere*, and others where the linkages might seem random. That said, two Italian music traditions emerged quite prominently in the classes, namely, classic operatic arias and songs (in particular ballads) by late-twentieth-century *cantautori* ("singer-authors"); this is unsurprising, perhaps, since both genres are frequently centered on the representation of amorous relationships. In addition, these pieces furnish an excellent opportunity for students to learn more about these Italian musical genres and about cultural production. Among the English-language songs selected, a genre that frequently surfaced was American blues and, to an extent, pop country; again, fitting choices, given the songwriters' foregrounding of love unrequited or gone wrong. The remainder of the songs derive from mainstream, English-language pop music and are indicators of students' musical tastes and of their efforts to form a connection between Petrarch's lyrics and the content of the songs.

The themes and images covered in the musical selections intersect primarily with notions such as the poet's love for Laura and his weeping over her unresponsiveness, along with his idealized description of her as beautiful but distant. Clearly, relations between the sexes, expectations about gender roles, and the similarities and differences in outlook between the fourteenth century and contemporary society thus took prominence in many of the class discussions. We also explored the parallels that can be drawn between contemporary song and Petrarch's *Canzoniere* regarding style and form; notions such as the *locus amoenus* or such devices as the personification of the canzone—techniques honed by Petrarch—rematerialize in contemporary lyrics.

The pivotal class discussion about crying and masculinity was sparked by canzone 23, in which the poet is portrayed as weeping: "a le lagrime triste allargai 'l freno, / et lasciaile cader come a lor parve" 'I loosed the rein to sad tears and let them fall as they willed' (lines 113–14).[3] This prompted one student to bring songs revolving around tears, including the legendary American country-rock singer Roy Orbison's 1961 ballad "Crying," which depicts a man who weeps inconsolably over unrequited love:

> I love you even more
> than I did before,
> but, darling, what can I do?
> For you don't love me,
> and I'll always be
> crying over you.

This much more recent example of a man unabashedly referring to his tears as he declares his undying love, along with the fact that Orbison's musical production consistently displayed an unapologetic sense of vulnerability precisely during the rise of rock and roll (a genre often marked by displays of "virile" tough-guy sexuality and rebellion), serves to render Petrarch's apparently "unmasculine," highly introspective behavior all the more current and, I would argue, accessible to today's readers.

Other poems of the *Canzoniere* insist even more on the poet's tears, as is the case of sonnet 216:

> Tutto 'l dì piango; e poi la notte, quando
> prendon riposo i miseri mortali,
> trovomi in pianto, et raddopiarsi i mali:
> così spendo 'l mio tempo lagrimando. (lines 1–4)

> All day I weep; and then at night, when miserable mortals take rest, I find that I am in tears and that my pains are doubled; thus I spend my time weeping.

In 234 the solitary poet weeps in the seclusion of his room:

> O cameretta che già fosti un porto
> a le gravi tempeste mie dïurne,
> fonte se' or di lagrime notturne,
> che 'l dì celate per vergogna porto. (1–4)

> O little room that used to be a port from my fierce daily storms, now you are a fountain of nocturnal tears, which in the daytime I keep hidden for shame!

Similar images can be traced in the British rock stars Jeff Beck and Rod Stewart's "Blues Deluxe" of 1968 (which owes much to the African American "King of the Blues," B. B. King), in which the artist, alone in his room, also weeps over his unresponsive lady love:

> As I'm sittin' here . . . in my lonely room,
> You know the tears flowin' all down my god-darn eyes
> I wonder how you could treat me so low down and dirty, ha-ha,
> You know what? Your heart must be made out of iron.

The beloved's heart being likened to iron evokes Laura's hardened heart, frequently compared with stone, a leitmotiv that is part of a continuum originating in Dante's *rime petrose*.[4]

The cardiac symbology resurfaces in yet another piece chosen by a student: the Neapolitan song by Salvatore Cardillo, "Core 'ngrato" ("Ungrateful Heart"), as performed by José Carreras, and written originally for Enrico Caruso in 1911. In this song—which forms part of the noted Italian repertoire for tenors and has been performed by the likes of Luciano Pavarotti and Andrea Bocelli, among others—the desired Catarì has caused the singer pain, because of her ungrateful heart:

> Tu nun'nce pienze a stu dulore mio,
> tu nun'nce pienze, tu nun te ne cure.
> Core, core 'ngrato,
> t'aie pigliato 'a vita mia.
>
> You don't think of my pain,
> you don't think of it, you don't care.
> Ungrateful heart,
> you have taken possession of my life.[5]

The uncaring Catarì elicits sorrow in her scorned admirer, something the singer attributes to her hard heart, a reaction not dissimilar to that of the poet Petrarch to the seemingly unsympathetic Laura, whose callous heart is frequently mentioned throughout the corpus. That the *Canzoniere* hinges on the extolling of unrequited love is, of course, well-known, and critics such as Aldo Scaglione have analyzed just how the notion of frustrated desire was perfected by Petrarch and adopted by many after him. Indeed, Scaglione concludes his intertextual analysis of the poetics of Platonic love by saying:

> [Petrarch's] deep theme was the impossibility of satisfying our inner urges, since the satisfaction of the sexual instinct is nothing but a dangerous and unworthy delusion. In a subtle way it is perhaps this inner motif that, somewhat unconsciously, underlies much of the literary representation of unfulfilled love, and Petrarch has been a master transmitter of this message. Concomitantly, Petrarch's embrace of the Augustinian heritage of total introspection contributed to the establishment of the concentration on the inner experience. ("Love" 572)

Thus Scaglione posits Petrarch, in his literary homage to unrequited, platonic desire, as an innovator who influenced subsequent poetry on frustrated romantic relationships that focus on self-reflection and unrequited passion.

Woman's indifference—above all, in the first part of the *Canzoniere* (i.e., Laura *in vita*)—is undoubtedly one of the principal traits defining Laura's attitude toward the poet, who is regularly rebuffed, as exemplified in sonnet 21, where the haughty female beloved looks down on the poet's heart, an organ repeatedly described (and in some instances even personified):

> Mille fiate, o dolce mia guerrera,
> per aver co' begli occhi vostri pace
> v'aggio proferto il cor; m' a voi non piace
> mirar sì basso colla mente altera. (1–4)
>
> A thousand times, O my sweet warrior, in order to have peace with your lovely eyes, I have offered you my heart; but it does not please you to gaze so low with your lofty mind.

Thus, several popular songs offered by students replicate the image of the unfeeling woman who breaks the artist's heart, indicating that situations such as Petrarch's expressing his pain over his apparent rejection continue to characterize texts concerning romantic love. In "Tristesse"—based on Frédéric Chopin's étude, with lyrics by Francis Giacobetti—Carreras sings:

> È triste il mio cuor senza di te
> Che sei lontana e più non pensi
> A me, dimmi perché
> Fai soffrir quest'anima che t'ama
> E ti vuole vicin.
>
> My heart is sad without you;
> You are far away and no longer think
> Of me, tell me why
> You make this soul suffer, this soul which loves you
> And wants you near.

The song evokes the kind of physical distance between the lover and the female object of desire found in sonnet 21 and again stresses the image of the heart.

In the 1980s mainstream hit "Every Breath You Take," Sting, the lead vocalist for the British rock group the Police, bemoans his beloved's unresponsiveness (and, like Petrarch, he sheds tears):

> Since you've gone I been lost without a trace
> . . . .
> I look around but it's you I can't replace

I feel so cold and I long for your embrace
I keep crying baby baby please . . .
Oh, can't you see
You belong to me
How my poor heart aches
With every breath you take.

In this instance, too, the singer's heart suffers because of an uncaring woman.

In the *Canzoniere* woman is depicted as not only indifferent but also fickle; in sonnet 183, the poet fears that Laura's unusual responsiveness is but temporary, declaring in line 12, "Femina è cosa mobil per natura" 'a woman is a changeable thing by nature.' Given this proclamation, one student's offering of a classic in the Italian operatic tradition—namely, the Duke of Mantua's aria "La donna è mobile" ("Woman Is Fickle"), from Giuseppe Verdi's *Rigoletto* (1851)—would seem to have some relevance, along with the warning it provides, where cardiac imagery resurfaces in the tenor's words (by the librettist Francesco Maria Piave):

È sempre misero
Chi a lei s'affida
Chi le confida
Mal cauto il core!

Always miserable
Is he who trusts her,
He who entrusts her
His incautious heart!

Thus, the female beloved's inconstant heart is also the cause of sorrow for the man, although in this particular instance, the aria plays on the fact that it is the duke who is unreliable and unfaithful.

In addition to the metaphor of the heart that runs throughout the *Canzoniere* (and is a stock metaphor in modern popular song), another recurrent trope employed by Petrarch is the flame as an expression of his desire, as in sonnet 19, "Son animali al mondo" ("There are animals in the world"), where the moth (and in turn the poet) is drawn to the fire by its ardor:

et altri, col desio folle che spera
gioir forse nel foco, perché splende
provan l'altra vertù, quella che 'ncende:
lasso, e 'l mio loco è 'n questa ultima schera. (lines 5–8)

and others, with their mad desire that hopes perhaps to enjoy the fire because it shines, experience the other power, the one that burns; alas, and my place is in this last band.

The 1993 Grammy Award–winning hit "That's the Way Love Goes," by the American pop and R & B icon Janet Jackson, begins with images that find parallels in these and other lines of the *Canzoniere*:

> Like a moth to the flame
> burned by the fire
> my love is blind
> can't you see my desire

Jackson's moth, destroyed by desire, can be compared with the same insect present in 141:

> Come talora al caldo tempo sòle
> semplicetta farfalla al lume avezza
> volar negli occhi altrui per sua vaghezza,
> onde aven ch'ella more, altri si dole
> così sempre io corro al fatal mio sole (lines 1–5)

> As sometimes in the summertime the simple butterfly, seeking the light, will in its desire fly into someone's eyes, whereby it dies and the other is pained: so always I run to my fated sun.

Here the poet goes on to liken himself to the moth inasmuch as he is fatally attracted to Laura's eyes. Jackson's track—and indeed the entire album—signals a shift in the artist's production in her assuming a role of sexual agency and presenting a woman-centered perspective on intimacy. It is interesting, therefore, to see how in the late twentieth century a metaphor employed by Petrarch (and others before him) has been reappropriated to express female desire.

The contemporary Welsh pop singer Duffy has also emphasized the notion of female desire in her 2008 hit "Mercy," in which she exhorts her beloved to release her as their relationship compromises her morals, a plea found frequently in Petrarch:

> I love you
> But I gotta stay true
> My moral's got me on my knees
> I'm begging please
> Stop playing games
> . . . .
> I'm under your spell
> You got me begging you for mercy
> Why won't you release me?

This kind of plea for pity on the part of the beloved resonates with Petrarch's repeatedly voiced regret and his begging Laura to show mercy, as when he reproaches his tongue for not helping him "dimandar mercede" 'ask for mercy' (49.6) or seeks Laura's "pietà" 'pity' or bemoans her lack of it (e.g., poems 23 and 44). Whereas Duffy feels that she is ethically tarnished in her role as her man's "thing on the side" and implores him to set her free, Petrarch repeatedly wishes for Laura to demonstrate pity for him and sympathy for his feelings. Yet he also expresses regret over his romantic relationship—despite its chasteness—because in loving the mortal Laura instead of devoting himself to his salvation, he is compromising his moral standing.

Laura's eyes, as I repeatedly point out to the students, are undoubtedly a key feature of her idealized portrait and constitute an image to which Petrarch returns obsessively throughout the entire collection. In class I explain how the medieval love lyric, from the *stilnovisti* onward, relies heavily on this trope and on the belief that love enters the heart through the gaze of the beloved and through the eyes of the beholder. In addition to expounding on the beauty of Laura's eyes, Petrarch repeatedly compares them with the sun and with light. The Italian *cantautrice* Elisa Toffoli, in her song "Luce (Tramonti a NordEst)," which won first prize at the San Remo popular music competition in 2001, also links light with the eyes: "Siamo nella stessa lacrima, come un sole e una stella / Luce che cade dagli occhi, sui tramonti della mia terra" 'We are in the same teardrop, like a sun and a star / light falls from your eyes, on the sunsets of my land.' Here, too, the figure of the teardrop is foregrounded, and yet the song presents a female voice that attempts to speak to an apparently indifferent man, reversing the gender roles that characterize the *Canzoniere*.

When discussing Laura, I raise the fundamental issue of the real/ideal debate regarding her existence and, along with the students, analyze her physical description, which is consistently maintained along very generic lines, as are the locales in which she is found. J. B. Trapp remarks:

> Her true loveliness, according to Petrarch—like the beauty envisaged by later Petrarchism—lay in the ideal of beauty, beauty wrought up to its highest pitch, which reflected the beauty of her nature. Such inward grace, he allows, has an outward expression. . . . [H]e descants often upon her golden hair, pale and beautiful face, dark eyebrows, shining eyes. (66)

One of the more famous portraits of Laura places her in the *locus amoenus* in canzone 126, "Chiare, fresche et dolci acque" ("Clear, fresh, sweet waters"), where she sits amid the trees and is covered in flowers:

> Qual fior cadea sul lembo
> qual su le treccie bionde,
> ch'oro forbito et perle
> eran quel dì a vederle. (lines 46–49)

> this flower was falling on her skirt, this one on her blond braids, which were burnished gold and pearls to see that day

This picture of canonical female beauty prompted one student to share a recording of a classic from one of the foremost Italian *cantautori*, Lucio Battisti. His number-one hit of 1971, "La canzone del sole" begins with the words "Le bionde trecce gli occhi azzurri" 'Blond braids, blue eyes,' which draw on the classic imagery to describe the singer's beloved. The song also depicts the two lovers in a field, recalling the pastoral setting and floral imagery found in Petrarch:

> Le biciclette abbandonate sopra il prato e poi
> Noi due distesi all'ombra
> Un fiore in bocca può servire, sai
> Più allegro tutto sembra
> E d'improvviso quel silenzio fra noi
> E quel tuo sguardo strano
> Ti cade il fiore dalla bocca e poi . . .
>
> Our bicycles abandoned on the field and then,
> the two of us lying in the shade,
> a flower in your mouth can be useful, you know
> everything seems more beautiful
> and suddenly silence falls between us
> and that strange look of yours
> the flower drops from your mouth and then . . .

The song then proceeds to lament innocence lost in the *cantautore*'s female object of desire. Battisti's song also illustrates that idealized portraits of women, such as that constructed by Petrarch for his Laura, have endured up until today.

One song that some students provided—"La giarrettiera rosa" ("The Pink Garter"), by the legendary Italian singer-songwriter Paolo Conte, whose compositions frequently avail of humor as he sings to his own accompaniment on the piano—initially seemed not to have anything in common with Petrarchan thematics, until the students explained that for them it was parodic of the male gaze in the *Canzoniere*, as witnessed, for example, in poem 52. In this madrigal the poet refers to the myth of Actaeon spying on Diana as she bathes in the water, likening his watching a "pastorella" 'shepherdess' (presumably Laura) washing her veil, her blond hair uncovered, to this mythological precedent (line 4). In Conte's song, a dark-haired curvaceous woman walking along is followed by the man's eye, and to his delight a gust of wind raises her skirt and reveals a pink garter, a much more explicit scenario than that painted in Petrarch's madrigal.

Another highly successful *cantautore*, Lucio Dalla, is the composer of the generically entitled "Canzone" (from his 1996 album *Canzoni*). I selected this song because it furnishes an excellent illustration of the rhetorical devices of the form of the canzone with which Petrarch experimented, in particular, the practice of the poet addressing the composition directly, as often occurs in the *congedo* of poems in the *Canzoniere*. Canzone 126, for example, concludes with the stanza, "Se tu avessi ornamenti quant'ài voglia, / poresti arditamente / uscir del boscho, et gir in fra la gente" 'If you had as many beauties as you have desire, you could boldly leave the wood and go among people' (lines 66–68). Dalla makes a similar exhortation in his song:

> Canzone trovala se puoi
> Dille che l'amo e se lo vuoi
> va per le strade tra la gente
> diglielo veramente
> non può restare indifferente
> e se rimane indifferente non è lei.
>
> Please find her if you can
> and tell her that I love her and, if you wish
> go in the streets, amidst all the people
> and tell her
> she can't remain indifferent
> and if she is indifferent, it can't be her.

Dalla's song presents a woman who clearly does not reject the lover's advances, and it portrays a more graphic sexual relationship in its other verses, and in this sense it can be considered very much a product of our epoch.

Yet despite the radical changes across the centuries in relations between the sexes and in socially accepted discourses on sexuality, much can be gained from employing modern and contemporary music when teaching and studying Petrarch. This musical modernization of Petrarchan tropes should not be viewed as a potentially negative practice because of contemporary song's often less elegant style, frequent lack of grammatical rules, and sometimes crass language, for it is precisely the engagement of these musical pieces with contemporary culture that ensures a certain accessibility to our students and spurs them to conduct their own search for Petrarchan links. The repertoire outlined in this essay is meant to present a springboard from which others can then go on to assemble their own musical portfolio for teaching Petrarch or even encourage their students to propose songs, an exercise that can help students recognize and identify important thematic and stylistic aspects of Petrarch's poetry and reflect on parallels between medieval poetry and contemporary song. Thus students and teachers of Petrarch can explore further resonances of his themes and stylistic techniques in musical motifs and genres not addressed in this essay. Moreover, this cross-cultural, transmedial, and intertextual activity can also enable instructors to ascertain what their students have understood and learned about the *Canzoniere*. Indeed, by carefully examining, within an informed context, the transposition of such themes and concepts across periods, genres, and media, new analytic insights and further opportunities for student understanding may find fertile terrain from which to emerge.

NOTES

[1] "Every text has its meaning, therefore, in relation to other texts. . . . [T]his relationality can itself be figured in various ways: it can involve the radical plurality of the sign, the relation between signs and texts and the cultural text, the relation between a text and the literary system, or the transformative relation between one text and another text. However it is used, the term intertextuality promotes a new vision of meaning, and thus of authorship and reading: a vision resistant to ingrained notions of originality, uniqueness, singularity and autonomy" (Allen 6).

[2] In her review of *Francesco Petrarca, Citizen of the World*, Smarr refers to Petrarch's singing his own compositions: "Although Villani says that Petrarch sang his own poems, accompanying himself on the lute, almost no settings have come down to us from Petrarch's time, possibly because contemporary composers preferred the madrigal and ballate forms to Petrarch's sonnets and canzoni" (264).

[3] All quotations from the *Canzoniere* are from Manica's edition and Durling's translation.

[4] Critics such as Fornasiero have pointed out, for example, "Nella prima zona del macrotesto Laura è l'oggetto irraggiungibile di un desiderio perennemente inappagato; ha un potere di seduzione che le deriva dall'eccellenza dell'aspetto fisico. . . . È remota, insensibile alla sofferenza amorosa del protagonista, protetta da una dura corazza: i suoi tratti distintivi la accomunano in qualche misura alla Petra dantesca, che soggioga l'amante senza nulla concedergli" 'In the first zone of the macrotext Laura is the unreachable object of a constantly unsatisfied desire; her powers of seduction derive from her outstanding physical appearance. . . . She is distant, indifferent to the poet's suffering for love, protected as she is by a hard casing: her distinctive traits liken her to a certain extent to Dante's Petra, who enslaves her lover while conceding him nothing' (92; my trans.).

[5] All translations of song lyrics from the Italian are mine.

Petrarch's Lyric Progeny

Michael Sherberg

> Se tu avessi ornamenti quant'ài voglia,
> poresti arditamente
> uscir del bosco, e gir in fra la gente. (*Canzoniere* 126.66–68)
>
> If you had as many beauties as you have desire, you could boldly leave the wood and go among people.[1]

As we all know, Petrarch's famous, beautiful, mean-spirited canzone did in fact leave the woods, helping him become the most influential poet in the Western tradition. So great is Petrarch's reach and so abundant the lyric—and narrative—production that gazes back at him that the topic of Petrarchism can be as knotty as Laura's windblown hair. Petrarchism often receives scant attention in the classroom because it seems like Petrarch all over again and because other Renaissance texts, deemed more important, crowd it out. Nevertheless, the narrative of Petrarch's reception and the imitative school that his lyric spawned discloses a great deal about the pathways of Renaissance culture. Students should not think of Petrarch monolithically, and they can benefit from a more nuanced understanding of how and why he mattered and how and why later poets paid tribute to him.

The well-documented linguistic heterogeneity of the early quattrocento, which produced a poetic corpus not only in multiple vernaculars—Florentine, Emilian, Neapolitan, and so forth—but also of diverse registers, ranging from the high register of the Petrarchan love lyric to the low register of burlesque, was largely unmoored from a linguistic normativism rooted in the vernacular

Petrarch. That linguistic heterogeneity also ran alongside the rise of a humanism that took cautious note of the *tre corone* (Dante, Petrarch, and Boccaccio) in general and of Petrarch in particular. In his biography of Petrarch, for example, Leonardo Bruni praises the poet principally for his singular rediscovery of Cicero (57–58). Bruni also assesses the respective careers of Dante and Petrarch, judging the latter to surpass Dante in his Latin writings and as a sonneteer but finding the Dante of the *Commedia* to trump anything Petrarch wrote (61–65). While Renaissance intellectuals would continue to debate the merits of the two poets, the affirmation of the vernacular Petrarch would only come about thanks to the sustained support of his fans and some luck.

Interest in the vernacular Petrarch persisted almost from the time of his death, as a rich manuscript tradition demonstrates. Early manuscripts often pair the *Canzoniere* with the *Trionfi*, the latter judged by Paola Vecchi Galli to be "forse, con la *Commedia*, il più importante libro di poesia del Quattrocento" 'perhaps, with the *Comedy*, the most important book of poetry of the fifteenth century' ("Petrarca nel Cinquecento" 331; my trans.). These manuscripts circulated despite the hegemonic thrust of Latin humanism, suggesting the challenges humanists faced in dictating the cultural agenda. Petrarch's affirmation as a model for other poets follows a lengthy argument, begun in the middle of the quattrocento, that the vernacular enjoyed the same status as classical Latin. In his *Grammatichetta*, for example, Leon Battista Alberti defended contemporary Tuscan as meritorious of its own *grammatica*, a term previously reserved for Greek and Latin. The proem to book 3 of Alberti's *Libri della famiglia* also contains an important defense of "la nostra oggi toscana [lingua]" 'our Tuscan language of today' as capable of rising to the level of classical Latin through its use by contemporary writers (188; my trans.). By the final decades of the quattrocento, in fact, the vernacular Petrarch had become the centerpiece of a program of Florentine cultural promotion led by Lorenzo il Magnifico. Cristoforo Landino's public readings of the *Canzoniere*, held at the Studio Fiorentino in 1470 and surely organized with Boccaccio's public lectures of Dante in mind, laid claim to Petrarch as a son of Florence, and Lorenzo's *Canzoniere*, deeply indebted to Petrarch's, affirms the significance of Petrarch's achievement.

Even before Landino, however, others commentaries were circulating. The humanist Francesco Filelfo began a commentary of the *Canzoniere* between 1444 and 1447, which Girolamo Squarzafico completed some forty years later. There were as well a number of other commentaries dedicated to the *Trionfi* (Vecchi Galli, "Petrarca fra Tre e Quattrocento" 183–84), beginning with the one by Jacopo di Poggio, published sometime between 1476 and 1478. Following the publication of Pietro Bembo's *Prose della volgar lingua* in 1525, a new spate of commentaries appeared, and by mid-century members of Cosimo I's Accademia Fiorentina were delivering public lectures on single lyrics in homage to Landino and to Lorenzo.

Quattrocento and cinquecento Petrarchisms differ principally in their mode of organization. While the trecento already witnessed significant manifestations of Petrarchism, as the movement gathered steam in the quattrocento, it took the form of a so-called Petrarchism *d'intarsio*, or inlay, consisting of the isolated borrowing of Petrarchan imagery or phrasing. Also common was the composition of entire *canzonieri* based on the Petrarchan model (Mutini 172–73), as undertaken by Giusto de' Conti's *La bella mano*, Matteo Maria Boiardo's *Amorum libri*, and Lorenzo il Magnifico's *Canzoniere*. The aulic lyric production exemplified in these poets and many others contrasts sharply with popular currents, particularly those that rely on Florentine jargon: Burchiello's lyrics, the *canto carnascialesco*, or carnival song tradition, even Luigi Pulci's *Morgante*. Burchiello can be a surprisingly accessible poet for instructors who wish to highlight the contrast between high and low registers in quattrocento lyric. The banality of economic pressures, clearly expressed in his tail sonnet "La poesia combatte col rasoio" ("Poetry does battle with the Razor"), is wholly antithetical to the ethereal Petrarchan experience and demonstrates the vivacity of voices that situate themselves outside the courtly setting. In this regard it bears note that Lorenzo il Magnifico was practiced in both the high and the popular styles, penning his own Petrarchan lyrics as well as a number of *canti carnascialeschi*.

This binary development of court poetry and street poetry in the fifteenth century also generated some of the normative force of sixteenth-century Petrarchism, the need to reconstitute lyric in a courtly context, to reclaim it from those who would appear to debase it by exploiting the genre as a repository for discourses that do not rise to the dignity of poetry. This reaction, which Bembo incarnates, was not wholly one of taste, however: it also reflected the growing insularity and autocracy of the Italian court. Bembo's abandoning the Venetian republic for the hermetic life of Urbino was at once a move that would influence his future writing as well as a measure of the attitudes already in place in him.

The cinquecento offers a much more homogeneous lyric model than does the quattrocento. The development of lyric in the cinquecento owed much to Bembo, though it was a Bembo attuned to the prevailing cultural winds. Amedeo Quondam writes of the vast reach of Bembo's Petrarchism, specifically within the context of the relation of mass and elite culture:

> [Petrarchismo] diventa nel Cinquecento *il* sistema linguistico, *egemone*, pertanto, che emargina nettamente esperienze di scrittura esterne ad esso se non antagoniste e controlla l'intero ambito delle pratiche discursive, sia private che sociali. (*Petrarchismo mediato* 212)
>
> It becomes in the sixteenth century *the hegemonic* linguistic system, which clearly marginalizes experiences of writing that are external to if not antagonistic to it, and it controls the entire sphere of discursive practices, both private and social.

Bembo's proposal, codified in the *Prose*, succeeds because it responds to an urgent need for order that characterizes the early cinquecento. In part that need is practical. As the vernacular continued to extend its reach and earn recognition as a legitimate substitute for Latin, discussions ensued about how best to regularize language so as to facilitate communication, particularly between courts. The advent of printing and the expansion of readership across the peninsula as books became more readily available had likewise redoubled the need for linguistic norms. Bembo capitalized on printing as a tool of cultural hegemony by publishing in 1501 a handy pocket edition of Petrarch's Italian lyrics with Aldo Manuzio in Venice. In this important edition, Bembo curiously corrected some of the forms he found in Petrarch's autographs that failed to match the linguistic norms he was developing (Bologna 329). The edition is noteworthy as well for Bembo's indifference to the quattrocento commentary edition; in effect, with the 1501 Aldine edition, Bembo restarts the culture of Petrarch.

The cultural politics implicit in Bembo's work extend beyond questions of linguistic norms, however. The *Prose* is more than just a grammar; it is also, as Claudio Mutini has argued (159), a manual of rhetoric, though not necessarily in the modern sense. The treatise proposes a way of representing culture as an elite phenomenon, exploiting the models of Petrarch and Boccaccio as the modern answers to Vergil and Cicero to identify a classicism that would rival Rome's and would make Italy the purveyor and arbiter of Renaissance literary culture. Coming at a time when Italian culture had reached the vanguard in the visual arts, Bembo's treatise offered a complementary solution for literature. The Petrarchan model specifically, which was already enjoying considerable success in courtly circles, thus afforded the opportunity to consolidate cultural production in a single idiom, with Italian lyric speaking in a single voice.

Much of that single voice comes in the form of the sonnet, which became for some the singular Petrarchan form. In the cinquecento there appeared *canzonieri* consisting entirely of sonnets, an exacerbation that verges on parody. Gordon Braden attributes the triumph of the sonnet over other lyric forms to Bembo, whose *Rime*, which privileges the sonnet, was the second-most-published lyric collection after Petrarch's in the cinquecento ("Applied Petrarchism" 400). But to limit any study of Petrarchism to the example of the sonnet distorts the historical record: there are likewise Petrarchan canzoni and madrigals and even extraordinary examples of the infusion of the Petrarchan model in narrative poetry. Ariosto's *Orlando furioso* constitutes a singular example of the latter. Not only did Ariosto famously revise the 1532 *Orlando furioso* to align it more closely with the linguistic standards established in Bembo's *Prose*, he also borrowed Petrarchan language and narrative motifs with startling results, as in the narrative of Orlando's pursuit of Angelica and her love story with Medoro.

Bembo emerged as the paragon of classical Petrarchism for two reasons. First, he sought to furnish a new reading of Petrarch, one that excluded the readings implied in late-quattrocento lyric; he went directly to the source rather than to mediations on it. Second, consistent with the proposals in his famous 1512 letter on imitation addressed to Giovanni Francesco Pico, Bembo sought to provide a complete reading of Petrarch, one that included not just the erotic Petrarch but the spiritual Petrarch as well (Pico and Bembo 39–61). As Luigi Baldacci puts it, Bembo sought to rediscover "la *struttura* e il *corpus* dello stile, recuperare l'esempio in tutta la sua estensione e in ogni senso" 'the *structure* and the *corpus* of the style, to recover the example to its full extent and in every sense' (*Petrarchismo* 116). The exercise is thus antithetical to the more superficial *d'intarsio* tendencies that preceded it and to the slavish imitation that followed, an imitation that Bembo had ironically facilitated by writing the *Prose della volgar lingua*.

Instructors wishing to introduce the topic of Petrarchism, seen in its practical applications, can do so easily enough by presenting sonnets by some key figures. Lanfranco Caretti's anthology, *Antichi e moderni*, provides many useful examples, and I derive my recommendations from it (Caretti and Bruscagli; Caretti and Fedi). Boiardo's "Il canto de li augei de fronda in fronda" ("The song of the birds from branch to branch") exemplifies the late-quattrocento assumption of the Petrarchan reverie of nature in the context of the beloved while still referencing earlier poetic models, specifically *dolce stil novo*. The same phenomenon presents itself in Lorenzo il Magnifico's "Belle, fresche e purpuree viole" ("Beautiful, fresh and purple violets"), whose first line echoes Petrarch's canzone 126, "Chiare fresche e dolci acque" ("Clear fresh and sweet waters"), as well as its theme of the sacrality of objects of nature touched by the beloved, while the sonnet elsewhere shows some debt to the *stilnovo*. Both poems thus show how the Petrarchan model must contend with others before achieving exclusivity. Bembo's "Crin d'oro crespo e d'ambra tersa e pura" ("Frizzy hair of gold and amber limpid and pure"), on the other hand, is purely Petrarchan, including the dissection of the beloved into her constituent parts (golden hair, bright eyes, lovely smile) and the invocation of the Petrarchan *senhal* (a code name for the beloved, often involving a play on her name), *l'aura*. Later in the century the example of Michelangelo demonstrates the continuing validity of the Petrarchan model, even at a time when so much slavish imitation of it had degraded it in many sectors. His late sonnet, "Giunto è già 'l corso della mia vita" ("The run of my life has arrived"), recuperates the penitential themes of the *Canzoniere* in a manner reminiscent of Petrarch's late sonnets.

Bembo's achievement was eclipsed by a Petrarchism in which the classical balance between form and content slides into mannerism—the preference for style over substance—so much so that in some ways Petrarchism has come to be seen as a literary example of a much-denigrated mannerism. Here Bembo's best efforts on Petrarch's behalf actually backfired. The publication in 1501 of the commentary-free Aldine, *Le cose volgari di Messer Francesco Petrarca*, had the unintended consequence of showing how Petrarch need not be the object of serious study: the language of Petrarch and his love story were available to one and all. At the same time, the *Petrarchino*, or small volume of Petrarch, became something of a fetish object, appearing in a number of paintings (Bologna 334–35). In an era that valued display, Petrarch became part of the show.

The principal accusation against post-Bembist Petrarchists involves their superficial and slavish adherence to Petrarch's style and lexicon and their borrowing from his catalog of metaphors without lending them any corresponding substance. While we may eschew such an approach today, it was an acceptable practice in certain poetic circles in the cinquecento. This poetic production represented a superficial but still valid reading of Bembo's *Prose*, which, after all, had drawn narrow parameters for lyric production around Petrarch's *Canzoniere*, furnishing a handy catalog of tropes and images from which poets could pick and choose. The culture did not necessarily require that poets develop their own lyric voice; rather, it was content to let them copy Petrarch.

So powerful did the cult of Petrarch grow in the sixteenth century that sincere efforts to move beyond it were met with forceful opposition. The institutionalization of Petrarchism, exemplified in the Paduan Accademia degli Infiammati, founded in 1540, and the later Accademia della Crusca (1582), suggests that in some sectors Petrarchism became nearly tyrannical. So when a genius of the level of Torquato Tasso strayed from the norm, he was vilified, particularly by members of the Crusca, who found the language of the *Gerusalemme liberata* (1581) to be too Latinate and too reliant on northern Italian forms. Their attack had deep roots in the opposition to the *lingua cortigiana*, or courtly vernacular, that Bembo and others had mounted earlier in the century, specifically for its overreliance on Latin (Marazzini 131). The language debates acquired a grinding, repetitive quality, with Petrarch serving as the much-exploited benchmark on all sides of the question.

Throughout its history, however, one element in Petrarchism remains constant: it requires the poet to invent himself through the lens of Petrarch. Petrarch has a remarkable ability to erase any distinction between the historical poet and his poetic persona; thus students often read the *Canzoniere* as literally autobiographical. The Petrarchan poet faces a rather more daunting challenge: to present his or her own story as simultaneously reminiscent of Petrarch's and unique. The degree to which one succeeds also becomes something of a guarantee of future success; thus we look at Michelangelo's lyric today but ignore the poetry of so many others. The cultural force of Petrarch is something he could not have foreseen, but it remains an important story for students as they come to grips with the multifaceted and tangled history of the Renaissance.

NOTE

[1] This quotation from the *Canzoniere* is from Durling's bilingual edition.

Petrarch's Women

Fiora A. Bassanese

In sixteenth-century Italy, imitation of Petrarch's *Canzoniere* was far more than a literary fashion: the medieval poet's artistic world was assimilated into the very fiber of cultural life, concurrently mirroring it, synthesizing it, and typifying its ideals. Moreover, the convergence of printing, broadening urban education, and the emergence of the vernacular for lyric expression contributed to a swelling cadre of versifiers drawn to the emulation of the sanctioned Petrarchan prototype launched by Pietro Bembo in his treatise *Prose della volgar lingua* (1525). Imitative lyric poetry was also one of the few forms of self-expression open to women; indeed, they were urged to compose in the Petrarchan manner as part of social intercourse in an era when polite exchange included philosophical conversation and versifying, alongside music and witty repartee. It is my policy to integrate lyrics by female petrarchists in any course offering with a Renaissance component, taught in either English or Italian, often by including a handful of poems by Gaspara Stampa and Vittoria Colonna in a survey or period course. Stampa and Colonna lend themselves to such courses because their work is widely available in English translation and because they are acknowledged as significant poets. These two poets provide a starting point for the discussion of both the amatory and spiritual elements found in Petrarchan verse, as well as the social framework in which women write, since they represent different urban environments (Stampa, the social gatherings of the Venetian elite; Colonna, the aristocratic courts of Naples and Rome and the post-Tridentine reformist circles) and social backgrounds. Even a limited selection from Stampa's *Rime* (trans. in *Complete Poems*) and Colonna's *Rime* (trans. in *Sonnets for Michelangelo*) serves to illustrate imitative practice and to present the problems peculiar to women writers operating within the canon.[1] In my course Women in the Italian Renaissance, taught exclusively in English, I undertake a comprehensive exploration of Petrarch, his female disciples, and the questions of authority and authenticity. The official course description reads:

> In the Italian Renaissance (c. 1300–1600), women were visible not only as the subject of male writers, philosophers, and artists, but as writers, philosophers, and artists in their own right. This course considers women as both the object of male works and as active contributors to culture by exploring their depiction in literature and the arts.

Initially conceived as one of the pilot Collegiate Seminars required of all lower-level students at the University of Massachusetts, Boston, the purpose of the course is to introduce freshmen and sophomores to the disciplines of cultural history, women's studies, and Renaissance studies through the reading and discussion of primary works (poetry, stories, theater, tracts) as well as secondary sources (critical essays, historical writings, biographies, documents). Intentionally interdisciplinary, the course involves a mandated skills component and an introduction to research methodologies.[2] The texts—both written and visual—are treated as cultural rather than as exclusively aesthetic artifacts. Nevertheless, reading well is essential, and, while the approach is not focused on stylistics, students are introduced to aspects of literary analysis (metaphors, tropes, imagery, basic prosody, genre, point of view, and so on). By the end of the course, students are expected to understand some basic concepts underlying Renaissance and gender studies, distinguish between the present and the past while recognizing commonalities as well as differences, learn strategies about how to interpret literary texts as sources of historical and cultural information, and begin to evaluate the validity of secondary sources.

The course's principal organizing topic is the artistic representation of women, and the syllabus is carefully structured so that it builds on specific concepts and belief systems relating to the construction of female identity. Gendered definitions of terms such as *honor*, *beauty*, and *virtue*, for instance, are gradually introduced, elaborated on, and deliberated in historical context.[3] Our first examples of femininity are literary: Dante's Beatrice and Pietra and Petrarch's Laura. The exploration of dualism is a secondary unifying principle used to present and interpret all course materials. A series of explicit and implicit comparisons and contrasts are introduced and expanded throughout the semester, including antithetical female archetypes (Eve/Mary; wife/mistress; saint/sinner; lady/courtesan), the gender division of lover and beloved in the lyric tradition, physical versus spiritual love, and male versus female roles and attributes. This contrastive element is also operative in the choice of critical readings (traditional versus feminist points of view) and in the analysis of Petrarch and Petrarchism, which forms a substantial portion of the course syllabus.[4]

Any discussion of female Petrarchism requires some knowledge of the *Canzoniere*. Since Women in the Italian Renaissance focuses on female representation and self-representation, students read some of the famous poems centered on the literary construction of Laura (e.g., 3, 30, 52, 90, 123, 126, and 134).[5] Untutored in Italian literature, the class requires an introduction to Petrarch's volume, its structure, its love story, and the characteristics of Laura, including a discussion on the wordplay surrounding her allusive name. During this introductory phase, we focus on Petrarch's manipulation of the courtly love tradition and to the possible differences between the figure of Laura and that of the *donna angelicata* ("angelic woman"). The class then moves on to close readings and guided textual analysis of the poetry. During this segment, consisting of four or five class meetings, we consider Petrarch's construction of the beloved, including the conflict of physical attraction and spiritual aspiration. The final goal of these discussions is to foster student awareness of the multilayered identity of Petrarch's beloved as a subject, a canonical literary type, a fantasy, an ideal, an icon, a myth, the object of desire, and the other in a condition of alterity. I choose selections from both divisions of the *Canzoniere*, *in vita* and *in morte*, to establish the shift in the connotations of the beloved, elevated by death to the role of heavenly guide and spiritual mentor in the latter part of the work.

While grappling with the definitions and characteristics of the beloved, the class inevitably confronts the lover, the speaking subject of the poetry, and his role in the literary construction of gender. Through the analysis of the figure and perceptions of the lover-poet, the class indirectly confronts the issues of gendered subjectivity and point of view. I design individual lessons to address these themes and instructional goals. After a textual analysis of *Canzoniere* 61 and 62, for example, I ask students to define *love* as depicted in the two sonnets. From there, we move on to discuss the intersection of art and love in 61 and that of sin or vanity and love in 62. Finally, having noted the references to prayer contained in both sonnets, I ask the class to consider the sonnets' placement within the volume: what meaning is the poet eliciting by purposefully coupling such antithetical considerations?[6] Other possible in-class activities may include exploring the possibilities inherent in Laura's multiple textual meanings, such as defining the interrelationship of lover and beloved in each stanza of poem 126 or considering the beloved as a dream or fantasy or projection through a word analysis of the poet's construction of Laura in poems such as 302. For such exercises, I divide students into groups of three or four, and the role of the instructor is that of student resource, one who can clarify semantics or meanings, explain mythological or religious references, note the "mistranslation" of terms, ask leading questions, and so forth.

Once the class has a clear perception of the characteristics of Laura as a female subject, we view her from a cultural perspective, seeking answers to questions like the following: Why is romantic love predicated on an adulterous or distant relationship? How would the historical Laura differ from the literary construction? What role does social class play? What religious beliefs feed the poet's depiction? Finally, to conclude the segment on Petrarch, we read a critical interpretation of one aspect of the poet's construction of the female subject: Nancy Vickers's classic study on the Petrarchan use of the literary blazon and the consequent reification of the female body through its linguistic dismemberment. Vickers's "Diana Described" fits neatly into the structure and strategies of the course and provides students with a solid sampling of feminist scholarship. Since this is the group's first encounter with literary criticism, I prepare a worksheet to serve as a study guide and to clarify and explain any unfamiliar points and terminology.

Petrarch's Laura also spawned an abundance of literary daughters in the 1500s.[7] As the focus of Women in the Italian Renaissance shifts from the section on male perception of women, titled "The Male Gaze" in the syllabus, to the section on the self-construction of a female literary identity, a new—albeit related—series of issues emerges. After a discussion of the hows and whys of a growing female participation in culture and social intercourse as both active and passive actors,[8] students read two ideologically loaded and contrastive interpretations on the status of women in the Renaissance: Jacob Burckhardt's "The

Position of Women," from the 1860 classic *The Civilization of the Renaissance in Italy* (2: 389–95), and Joan Kelly-Gadol's "Did Women Have a Renaissance?" Although Burckhardt's piece is old, it influenced public perception of women's social position for generations, and his book remains one of the essential texts in cultural studies. Kelly-Gadol's polemical article challenges the long-standing belief in feminine progress by indicating, instead, women's declining economic, social, and political power. According to Burckhardt, "Women stood on a footing of perfect equality with men" (2: 389), whereas Kelly-Gadol categorically asserts "there was no renaissance for women—at least, not during the Renaissance" (139). By dissecting the writers' attitudes and meditating on the thought processes expressed in these secondary sources, students begin to look at women from diverse and sometimes conflicting perspectives. The class also discovers the need to read critically and develop some basic tools for dealing with seemingly contradictory data. From the readings on the cultural importance of women's writing, it is natural to segue to the question of female imitation and its inherent ambiguities. If time permits, a reading of Virginia Cox's introduction to her *Women Writers in Italy, 1400–1650* offers a current scholarly response to Kelly-Gadol's famous question and a third point of view (xi–xxviii). Once again, the technique of comparison and contrast underlies my approach to the readings. We address several questions: Can Petrarchan emulation be concurrently empowering and reductive? Does social standing influence creative choices? Does imitation level the literary playing field or does it hinder self-expression?

Since Petrarch's *Canzoniere* remained the universal lyric model for decades, I emphasize that it was a standard for both sexes, not just for women writers. But as a male-authored and male-directed model, Petrarchan discourse posed particular difficulties for women. How did such poets manage the paradox of identifying with the Petrarchan lover—innately gendered male—and retain socially endorsed feminine traits? Is imitation an indicator of patriarchal and linguistic oppression, or is it a viable instrument for female self-affirmation?[9] In class, we deliberate on the pitfalls of imitation, including the tendency of falling back on mechanical reproduction of the model, leading to stylistic mediocrity and repetitive clichés rather than the development of authorial authenticity and originality. But we also consider the potential offered to women by a codified standard. Without a legacy of female-authored texts from which to draw, Petrarchism's hegemonic discourse provided women poets an incontrovertible example of excellence to follow, allowing for a determined effort to be the best by emulating the best. At this juncture in the course, I seek to sensitize students to their historical biases, which tend to judge artistic success on the basis of creativity and novelty. I ask students to consider the power of a norm to validate any artist who accepts the patterns of meaning constructed by his or her society, in keeping with Stephen Greenblatt's suggestion that Renaissance self-fashioning was not a question of autonomy or "an epiphany of identity freely chosen but a cultural artifact," where choice was "strictly delineated by the social and ideological system in force" (*Renaissance Self-Fashioning* 256). Nevertheless, it is evident to the class that female Petrarchan imitation is inextricably concerned with issues of alterity, or otherness, and this topic frames the remainder of the curriculum.

A conscious rereading of Burckhardt's chapter from a feminist viewpoint establishes a starting point for the discussion of alterity. Students quickly take note of deficiencies in his argument: the historian's definition of sexual parity is explicitly limited to the private sphere, where woman's "function was to influence distinguished men and to moderate male impulse and caprice" (2: 391)—namely, to be different and reactive. As for women's lyric in the Renaissance, it is valued precisely because it ignores gender difference: Burckhardt states that both amatory and religious verse "are so precise and definite in their character," so far from "the dilettantism" generally found in female poetry, "that we should not hesitate to attribute them to male authors, if we had not clear external evidence to prove the contrary" (390). The class easily grasps the implications such statements have for the study of *petrarchiste*, whose male-inspired poetry seems to be valued precisely because it can sometimes be interpreted as ungendered or transsexual. The next pedagogical step is to show that women poets were not devoid of individuality and self-awareness but manipulated the Petrarchan subtext, deconstructing and reconstituting the original in their own works, thereby subtly positioning themselves as part of the canon. In Women in the Italian Renaissance, I use three *petrarchiste* to exemplify diverse emulative strategies: the aristocrat Colonna, the *virtuosa* Stampa, and the courtesan Tullia d'Aragona (other options include Veronica Gambara, Laura Terracina, Isabella di Morra, Chiara Matraini, and Laura Battiferri).[10] Theoretically, I am guided by the concepts of agency and empowerment and by the poets' use of negotiation, a Marxist critical term that Ann Rosalind Jones defines as "a range of interpretive positions through which subordinated groups respond to the assumptions encoded into dominant cultural forms and systems of representation" (2).

From a sociohistorical perspective, the course is carefully structured so that students gradually master the era's strict gender-determined codes of appropriate behavior, which stressed feminine virtue, decorum, modesty, chastity, and reticence.[11] Therefore the class readily perceives the conundrum faced by any female writer: as author, she speaks publicly, acknowledging her authority; as woman, she is relegated to silence and private life, devoid of an individual voice. Within the segment on Petrarchism, we discuss varied literary strategies women undertook to resolve this conundrum. Colonna, for example, refused repeated requests to publish her verse, preferring to control its distribution through so-called scribal publication as a way to avoid public display and retain personal decorum.[12] On the other hand, in her *Rime* d'Aragona makes herself part of the text, housing her Petrarchan verse in an unusual structure: a volume in which the courtesan's poems are published alongside a series of sixty-seven laudatory sonnets in her honor composed by her circle of praiseworthy men. In this "collaborative process of fame building" (A. Jones 111), d'Aragona manages to exhibit culturally endorsed attributes, such as modesty and humility, in her own verse while concurrently allowing her male collaborators to praise her in a multiplicity of lyric compliments. By manipulating a popular subgenre of Petrarchism, the epistolary sonnet, d'Aragona presents her literary persona as both a passive and active subject, co-opting the male and female roles within Petrarchan discourse.[13] In class we explore d'Aragona's narcissistic and self-affirming construction, achieved circuitously but shrewdly. While the class may only read two or three of the courtesan's rhymes in translation, they have viewed an inventive strategy for revising the Petrarchan source to the female poet's advantage.

As the theorist Monique Wittig has noted, "in reality, as soon as there is a locutor in discourse, as soon as there is an 'I,' gender manifests itself" (65). This concept drives my reading of the poetry of Stampa and Colonna, spotlighting the centrality of gender within female imitative practice. Since good Petrarchan poetry is not concerned with the duplication of the source but with a creative interaction between texts, I point out echoes and borrowings but also revisions and reinterpretations to my class. Stampa is an ideal choice for such an operation, given her persistent use of the *Canzoniere*'s tropes, imagery, and phrasing and the intentional reproduction of Petrarch's fabula in her own love story, so that her *canzoniere* closely mirrors the medieval prototype. The students' first reading assignment in this part of the course is to compare and contrast Petrarch and Stampa's introductory sonnets, both of which establish themes, a tone, and a message for interpreting the two collections. Stampa's rewriting of the Petrarchan text is evident from the first line of her sonnet—"Voi, ch'ascoltate in queste meste rime" 'You who hear in these troubled rhymes'—and is further manifest in her semantic, linguistic, and phonic borrowings. Initially, students working in small groups are simply asked to excerpt Stampa's superficial Petrarchan assimilations, but, in the second phase of analysis, they focus on differences in tone and attitude, paying particular attention to listing words and expressions that are gender-based. How does Stampa present herself? How do the master and his disciple describe the experience of love? Can these differences be attributed to gender? After this exercise, we discuss possible historical reasons for such differences (e.g., medieval versus Renaissance notions of love and sin), but we also explore the importance of Stampa's awareness of her singularity, determined by her sex, which is a recurring motif in her verse, as noted in this emulative prelude to the *Rime*. From Stampa's first "troubled rhymes," students discover a gender-defined poet, writing within the established code, circumscribed by its language and contents, yet curiously self-aware, as she offers herself as a paragon of femininity and art for other women to envy and imitate.

Continuing with this technique, I then have students compare and contrast the two poets' *innamoramento* ("falling in love") sonnets in a similar fashion, highlighting Stampa's strategy of appropriation and revision.[14] Stampa's sonnet "Era vicino il dì" (*Rime* 2; "It was near the day") reverberates with echoes of Petrarch's "Era il giorno" (*Canzoniere* 3; "It was the day"). Of particular note, the motif of a Christian holiday to memorialize the day of *innamoramento* sets the tone for the poets' love experience. Petrarch's Good Friday contrasts sharply with Stampa's Christmas. The dualities suggested are substantial: death versus birth, mourning versus celebration, conflict versus acceptance, regret versus exaltation, male versus female. Stampa's choice not only indicates an acceptance and welcoming of sensual love but also provides an ideal feminine analogy for the poet in the figure of Mary. Looking at Colonna, we discuss the thematic and metaphoric bonds connecting the section of the *Canzoniere* written after Laura's death and Colonna's love lyric, composed for her dead husband. Here the contrastive technique helps us effectively compare the two female poets' debts to the Petrarchan text by analyzing their rewriting of the celebrated ship metaphor. Stampa discards it, as seen in her poem 72, "La mia vita è un mar" ("My life's a sea"), and 221, "A mezzo il mare" ("To the midst of the sea"), which serve to secularize the Petrarchan conceit. Colonna, however, in "Provo tra duri scogli e fiero vento" ("Between harsh rocks and fierce winds I attempt") and "Mentre la nave mia, lungi dal porto" ("While my ship, far from port"), preserves its religious connotations.

The final aspect of Petrarchism we explore in Women in the Italian Renaissance concerns the construction of the personae of lover and beloved in female-authored lyric. Both Stampa and Colonna are caught in the difficult position of assuming the unfeminine role of praising men in a code based on the elevation of women, thereby overturning established social and gender patterns. I focus on the male beloved as a metamorphosis of Laura into a masculine counterpart, paying only cursory attention to the poets' biographies (Stampa's affair with Collaltino di Collalto or Colonna's marriage to Ferrante d'Avalos) to avoid the pitfalls of "phallic criticism" (a term coined by the feminist scholar Mary Ellmann to refer to the situation in which "books by women are treated as though they themselves were women, and criticism embarks, at its happiest, upon an intellectual measuring of busts and hips" [29]). I wish students to treat the texts as literature, not autobiography, and to understand the difference. Therefore, we explore Collalto not as a historical figure but as a literary construct, whose name is ripe with allusions, as was Laura's for Petrarch. I introduce the class to Stampa's word games and allegorizing of the Collalto name and title (a Petrarchan device) and the sexual and social implications these contain for the nontraditional lover. Stampa's beloved is a height to conquer, a superior being, an icon designated "conte" 'count' or "signore" 'lord' to counter Petrarch's "donna" 'woman.' Both Stampa and Colonna accept cultural conventions regarding femininity, leading to self-representations as inferior, subservient, and dependent beings. Stampa's *Rime* 5, "Io assimiglio il mio signor al cielo" ("Often enough, I'll liken my lord to the sky"), and 7, "Chi vuol conoscer, donne, il mio signore" ("Ladies, if you'd like to know my lord"), are particularly effective examples to demonstrate the elevation of the object of desire only to complete the representation negatively with the archetype of the *crudel amante* ("cruel beloved"). Stampa's female lover is the ever-faithful humble worshipper at the altar of the superior beloved, a self-depiction also found in Colonna's love sonnets such as "Scrivo sol per sfogar l'interna doglia" ("I write only to vent my internal sorrow").

As part of this final segment of the course, the students revisit the literary device of the blazon as discussed in Vickers's article, but from a feminine perspective. Stampa's *Rime* 7 is such a catalog, since she is building a male paradigm to equal Laura. The allusive literariness of the representation is heightened by the construction of masculinity undertaken in the sonnet: besides his Laura-like youth, blondness, and fair complexion, this male paragon is also graced with wisdom, courtesy, heroic bearing, broad chest, and height in a positive blending of endorsed masculine and feminine qualities. In similar fashion, culturally established gender traits are attributed to Colonna's deceased beloved, who is presented in heroic terms (e.g., "Qui fece il mio bel sole a noi ritorno" 'Here my beautiful sun returned to us') in a stockpiling of martial attributes suited to masculine *virtus*.[15] Asked to list and describe the various characteristics that define her beloved, students conclude that Colonna's praise appears hyperbolic, suggesting the construction of a static and symbolic ideal rather than a man. A related assignment asks groups to find feminine equivalencies in the poetry for the masculine attributes given, so that ideal but gendered portraits of lover and beloved can emerge. What the class discovers is that, in their self-representations, Stampa and Colonna identify themselves with the womanly qualities honored by their society: fidelity, submission, chastity, self-sacrifice, humility, and virtue. As writers, however, they reject silence, having chosen to imitate the words, if not the gendered perspective of the only readily available lyric discourse of their day. As sixteenth-century versifiers they themselves embody a Petrarchesque oxymoron: the woman poet.

NOTES

[1] Limiting myself to only a handful of poems, I would choose from Stampa's *Rime* poems 7, 208, and 311 and from Colonna's sonnets "Scrivo sol per sfogar" ("I write only to vent") and "Qual digiuno augellin" ("Like a famished bird"). The University of Chicago Press has published new translations of both poets (the translations used here) in its series The Other Voice in Early Modern Europe: Stampa's *The Complete Poems* (trans. Tylus) and Colonna's *Sonnets for Michelangelo* (trans. Brundin), a manuscript selection prepared by the poet herself as a gift. These volumes contain extensive bibliographies and excellent introductions.

[2] Training in critical reading, thinking, and writing, as well as library research, teamwork, and oral presentation was required in the first incarnation of this course as an offering in the college's core curriculum. Today it serves as a university-wide general education course bearing credit in Italian but still dedicated to developing the aforementioned skills. Students are encouraged to write both formally and informally (e.g., journal entries), and testing is not part of the curriculum.

[3] Readings in cultural history can be useful in providing background. See, e.g., Anderson and Zinser, vol. 1; Bridenthal, Koonz, and Stuard; Plumb; Masson. See King for an

excellent bibliography of primary and secondary sources up to 1990. I have sometimes asked students to undertake independent library research to create annotated bibliographies for research papers or to give oral presentations on specific historical figures or lifestyles, such as nuns or merchants' wives.

[4]The methodology used in Women in the Italian Renaissance can easily be modified for an advanced or graduate course on the early modern lyric tradition in Italy or one specifically on Petrarch or sixteenth-century Petrarchism. Cox's *Women's Writing in Italy* would be an excellent general text for an advanced or graduate course on women writers in early modern Italy.

[5]In a more advanced course, I would add some of the poems to Laura's eyes and hands to accompany our critical reading of Vickers's "Diana Described."

[6]I have used Bergin's and Durling's editions and translations of the *Canzoniere*, but, to sensitize students to the issues innate in using translations, I often distribute the original Italian and occasionally provide two or more English versions of the same composition. The newer translations by Musa (Canzoniere) and by Young are quite readable and vibrant.

[7]Available translations of sixteenth-century Italian women poets include Stortoni (bilingual ed. with brief essays); Wilson, pt. 1 (with introductory essays for Stampa, Colonna, and Gambara); Jaffe and Colombardo (interdisciplinary; accompanied by a CD of readings and inventive biographies). Recommendations for Italian editions include Macchia (with an excellent bibliography); Baldacci, *Lirici*; Ferroni.

[8]I use a slide presentation in our discussion of social and cultural history to reinforce visually and iconographically the themes and ideas developed in "The Male Gaze" segment of the course. For example, we first observe religious representations of Mary from the thirteenth to the sixteenth centuries and "read" the paintings to determine the altering perception of the Madonna and her shift from icon to human being. To demonstrate the Mary/Eve dichotomy, I include depictions of episodes from Genesis and show paintings and sculptures of Mary Magdalene. I use some religious scenes as a means of showing the dress, homes, and social distinctions of fifteenth- and sixteenth-century life. To demonstrate the growing centrality of classical studies, we look first at Raphael's *The School of Athens* and go on to the representations of female nudes in mythological dress; here I discuss the presence of courtesans on the cultural scene. The visual presentation concludes with a series of female portraits, denoting the valorization of women as individuals. Many of the individuals depicted are holding books, an observation that serves as an entrée into the topic of female literacy.

[9]In an advanced course, I would explore these issues extensively, using both primary and secondary texts. Side-by-side comparisons of poems by Petrarch and heavily plagiarized compositions by various women writers would demonstrate the extensive and sometimes impersonal use of borrowings. On the tendency to replicate the prototype, using the examples of Colonna, Chiara Matraini, and Stampa, see Borsetto. To further demonstrate the *petrarchista*'s tendency to replication and repetition, if not exact duplication of the Petrarchan source, I have used two epistolary sonnets from d'Aragona's *Rime*: "Più volte, Ugolin mio" ("Many times, my Ugolino") and "Ho più volte, Signor" ("Lord, many times have I"). These poems are variants of each other, phonically and semantically, so that the two men addressed merge into each other and any individuality is excised in the codified language.

[10]We also read selections from Veronica Franco and Moderata Fonte, although these writers are not traditional Petrarchan imitators.

[11] For a discussion of proper womanhood as described in conduct and marriage books of the time, see the first chapter in A. Jones. Jones also has excellent chapters on d'Aragona's and Stampa's use of negotiation.

[12] See Love for a discussion of the private distribution and copying of works in England. Few Italian women knowingly had their works printed and sold to the general public. Colonna's poetry was issued without her consent and became a Renaissance best seller, with multiple editions appearing in the sixteenth century. The most complete and accurate critical edition is Bullock's. On the history of the survival of texts by women, the role of editors in the production of existing editions, and the conditions surrounding publication (the makings of an interesting graduate course), see Cox, ch. 3; Robin.

[13] D'Aragona's elevation to the literary pantheon is realized both visually and verbally. Dozens of sonnets are addressed to her as "Tullia" so that the name appears repeatedly on the printed page, often in bold face. She is also addressed in traditional Petrarchan vocabulary as "donna" 'lady' or "anima/alma bella" 'beautiful soul' and given the descriptors "gentile" 'noble,' "leggiadra" 'beautiful,' "ninfa bella" 'beautiful nymph,' "miracolo" 'miracle,' and so on. We also discuss the biographical inspiration for the collection, published soon after Cosimo de' Medici excused the courtesan-poet from the required wearing of a yellow veil to signify her profession. D'Aragona and Stampa represent the significant presence of marginal women such as musicians, painters, and mistresses within the cultural community.

[14] For a detailed analysis of this and other anniversary sonnets in the *Rime*, see Bassanese. For further discussion of Stampa's Petrarchism, see Russo; Braden, "Gaspara Stampa"; and Borsetto.

[15] While Colonna's love lyric was greatly influenced by Petrarchism, her poetry is also imbued with the imagery and ideas of Neoplatonism. For a discussion of the poet's philosophical underpinnings, see Brundin; McAuliffe.

Tradition and Imitation in Petrarchan Poetics: The Song of the Nightingale

Elisabetta Properzi Nelsen

Never in the history of Italian literature has a poetic imagination and style such as Petrarch's determined the development of poetry over a period of seven hundred years after the poet's birth. If Dante's *Comedy* was the model for the ethical, prophetic, and didactic message that poetry had to convey, Petrarch's *Canzoniere* became the canonized basis of comparison for the individual poetic voice that, instead of finding answers outside the human world, withdrew into itself in a constant search for its soul's desires and memories. Dante challenged himself and the religious and political ideas of his day by imagining the afterlife as a perfect mixture of classical and theological elements rigorously examined under the endorsement of Catholic orthodoxy. Dante conducted his quest for the meaning of life outside himself: in the society surrounding him; in Florence, the city he loved and hated; in his political commitment; in the suffering condition of the man exiled; in the horrifying circles of Hell, the nostalgic steps of Purgatory, or the mystical spheres of Paradise. Petrarch's investigation of this same meaning was instead directed toward his inner life, through questions more than through answers, using a leitmotiv of discordance between an attachment to the past (the vision of Laura and therefore the sense of fleeting love, youth, and beauty) and a sense of guilt for passionately and continuously desiring what is lost. Dante accomplished his mission to be *scriba Dei*, God's writer; Petrarch instead withdrew in his *nugae*, what he considered his lesser poetic works, to become *scriba ipse eius*, the writer of himself, as well as the writer of Laura, female emblem of his never-reciprocated love. For the first time in almost the entire duration of the fourteenth century, Petrarch analyzed the human psyche, particularly its sense of instability and inadequacy and the resulting alienation in confronting the delicate historical and religious situation of his time. His mind indeed reflected the crisis of the changing times, as the significance of individuality and self-expression slowly became more central. For this reason, the poetic language of his *Canzoniere* was especially effective in offering guidelines for the poetics and stylistic manners that were to follow.

When Gianfranco Contini pointed out the linguistic monotony of the *Canzoniere* versus the pluralistic tones of the *Comedy* ("Preliminari"), he emphasized the Petrarchan ability of insisting on certain themes and words to continue the ongoing process of extracting the most concealed ways of the human heart and its battle between opposite poles of self-consciousness: desire and guilt, youth and senility, fugacity of time and eternity, sensual love and spiritual love, idleness and work, fame and humility.[1] An advanced reading of the *Canzoniere*, both in upper-division classes and graduate seminars, should thus stress Petrarch's lexical repetition as a critical issue in the composition and structure of the *Canzoniere*, focusing in particular on the assiduous presence of select thematic and linguistic elements that signal the author's existential vicissitude.

The metaphor is one of the rhetorical figures most used by Petrarch, diversified in the forms of metonymy, similes, and antitheses. In the sonnets as well as in the canzoni and sestine, Petrarch repeats lexemes extracted from the natural world, such as "candida cerva" 'hind of candid white,' "fera" 'the beast, the wild one,' "stella" 'star,' "foglia" 'leaf,' and all the transformations of "lauro" 'laurel,' in an effort to evoke the female image: "così, lasso, talor vo cerchand'io, / donna, quanto è possible, in altrui / la disïata vostra forma vera" 'Thus, alas, at times I go searching in others, Lady, as much as is possible, for your longed-for true form' (16.12–14).[2] In this way, Petrarch concentrates his poetic imagination on a repetitive series of *senhal*, verbal signs aimed at disguising the true identity of the female object of desire.[3] These images attempt to offer a complete vision of Laura, but because they remain shadows of an elusive figure, they are often expressed through the unique form of synecdoche, the part for the whole, *pars pro toto*.

At the same time, Petrarch's effort to retrieve his most personal reminiscences runs parallel to his attempt to recover a cultural or, rather, classical memory. In the tormented, melancholic process of exhuming the past vision of Laura, Petrarch also intends to reevoke classical culture, particularly that of the Romans, while still keeping in mind that everything disappears—what last are only the ruins of the past. The poet, therefore, becomes the archaeologist who celebrates the remains of personal and cultural memory.

One of the key metaphors Petrarch employs to capture both individual and cultural memory is that of the nightingale. Sonnet 311, memorably centered on this image, represents one of the *Canzoniere*'s most symptomatic compositions. I use the adjective *symptomatic* because it evokes symptoms, if not of an ailment, then certainly of an existential condition that struggles between an attachment to earthly passion and hope for eternal life. In the sonnet, which appears in the second half of the *Canzoniere*, or the poems of Laura's death (*in morte*), the Petrarchan speaker compares himself with the nightingale that mourns the loss of his children and mate. Petrarch draws the motif, rooted in the myth of Philomela, from book 4 of Vergil's *Georgics*: "qualis populea maerens Philomela sub umbra / amissos queritur fetus" 'like Philomela, [who] under the poplar's shade cries her young [whom] she has lost' (lines 511–12).[4] Earlier, in sonnet 10, Petrarch introduces the nightingale's presence in a near paraphrase of the Vergilian quotation: "e 'l rosignuol che dolcemente all'ombra / tutte le notti si lamenta et piagne" 'and the nightingale that sweetly in the shadow every night laments and weeps' (lines 10–11).

In Petrarch's sonnet 311, the lady's death reminds the poet of his own cruel destiny. In his lamentation, it seems that Laura is even more humanized since her physical presence is sorrowfully missed:

> Quel rosignuol, che sì soave piagne
> forse suoi figli, o sua cara consorte,

di dolcezza empie il cielo et le campagne
con tante note sì pietose e scorte,

et tutta notte par che m'accompagne,
et mi rammente la mia dura sorte:
ch'altri che me non ò di ch'i' mi lagne,
ché 'n dee non credev'io regnasse Morte.

O che lieve è inganar chi s'assecura!
Que' duo bei lumi assai più che 'l sol chiari
chi pensò mai veder far terra oscura?

Or cognosco io che mia fera ventura
vuol che vivendo et lacrimando impari
come nulla qua giù diletta et dura.

> That nightingale that so sweetly weeps, perhaps for his children or for his dear consort, fills the sky and the fields with sweetness in so many grieving, skillful notes,
> and all night he seems to accompany me and remind me of my harsh fate; for I have no one to complain of save myself, who did not believe that Death reigns over goddesses.
> Oh how easy it is to deceive one who is confident! Those two lights much brighter than the sun, who ever thought to see them become dark clay?
> Now I know that my fierce destiny wishes me to learn, living and weeping, how nothing down here both pleases and endures!

Here, the speaker's fate is determined by Laura's death, a tragic event rendered even more gruesome by the two lines of the first tercet, in which, in horrid contrast, the lady's fair eyes, "lumi assai più che 'l sol chiari" 'brighter than the sun,' become "terra oscura" 'dark clay.' The final *terzina*, then, ponders the moral issue that nothing in this world "diletta et dura" 'pleases and endures.'

A similar situation emerges in the preceding poem, sonnet 310. Here, Philomela the nightingale weeps during springtime and sings with the swallow (her sister Procne) in laughing meadows that regenerate with new grass under clear skies (line 5). Air, water, earth, and all its creatures are full of love. The conjunction at the beginning of the first tercet, however, points out the negative emotional status of the poet, contrary to the optimistic connotation of the flourishing spring:

Zephiro torna, e 'l bel tempo rimena,
e i fiori et l'erbe, sua dolce famiglia,
et garrir Progne et pianger Philomena,
et primavera candida et vermiglia.
. . . .

Ma per me, lasso, tornano i più gravi

> sospiri, che del cor profondo tragge
> quella ch'al ciel se ne portò le chiavi. (lines 1–4, 9–11)

> Zephyrus returns and leads back the fine weather and the flowers and the grass, his sweet family, and chattering Procne and weeping Philomena, and Spring, all white and vermilion. . . . But to me, alas, come back heavier sighs, which she draws from my deepest heart, she who carried off to Heaven the keys to it.

Hence, the sonnet illustrates a contrast between nature's rejoicing and the poet who instead sighs and weeps because Laura "al ciel se ne portò le chiavi" 'carried off to Heaven the keys' to his heart. The nightingale in 310 foreshadows the poet's lamentation in 311. Petrarch does not establish a direct simile between the nightingale and himself or between the nightingale's crying voice and the speaker's; instead, he prefers to acknowledge the bird's song as a reminder of his difficult life. Because it is performed in the solitude of the night, the song represents his sad, solitary, and hidden voice. In 311, the adverb "soave," translated as "sweetly" or "softly," connotes both music and poetry and evokes the category of the sublime. The adverb also suggests a sense of ineffability, as it remains impossible to explain the blend of sadness, sweetness, and beauty in the bird's singing and the poet's words. In fact, the nightingale's song fills the countryside with "note sì pietose e scorte" 'grieving . . . skillful notes,' reflected in the poet's sorrowful but refined words. The literary binomial poet-nightingale emerges more clearly as the sonnet progresses. Through the humanization of the nightingale, acknowledged in his reappropriation of the Ovidian myth, Petrarch establishes a consistent thematic link between classical poetry and his own. He is both the new Orpheus of *Georgics* 4 and the new nightingale weeping for the loss of his "cara consorte" 'dear consort,' Laura.[5]

Petrarch's nightingale also accompanies the voice of the poets who followed him, seen especially through Pietro Bembo's canonization of Petrarchan stylistic elements during the sixteenth century in the work of poets such as Giovanni della Casa, Luigi Tansillo, Michelangelo, and even Bembo himself. In his influential treatise *Prose della volgar lingua* ("Discussions of the Italian Language"), Bembo was able to determine a veritable cultural revolution in acknowledging Italian literature as a classical literature, therefore proving Petrarch even more worthy of imitation than the Greeks and the Latins. With particular reference to the topos of the nightingale, Bembo's sonnet "Solingo augello, se piangendo vai" ("Solitary little bird, if you fly around"; *Opere*; my trans.) is essentially a reexamination of *Canzoniere* 353, "Vago augelletto che cantando vai" ("Wandering bird that goes singing"), as well as of 226, "Passer mai solitario in alcun tetto" ("No sparrow was ever so alone on any roof"). Bembo, in reemploying the semantic extension of the nightingale in the motif of the "wandering bird" that laments his "perduta dolce compagnia" 'sweet, lost company' (line 2), revisits the nightingale in a decidedly less tragic tone than the one that suffuses Petrarch's sonnet 353. While the Petrarchan speaker is conscious of Laura's death and thus of the irreparable nature of his loss, Bembo asks himself whether he will ever have the possibility of finding his "sweet company" once again, a question that still remains a rhetorical pretext to insist on the conventional representation of the solitary, afflicted lyric subject who flees all human comfort. Petrarch, instead, knows that "Death and Heaven are so stingy" 'Morte e 'l ciel son tanto avari' (353.11), for they greedily keep Laura from the speaker, without allowing her to return to earth. Whereas Bembo's "little bird" remains set apart from the speaker in the lush green wood, Petrarch's is called to return to the inconsolable speaker's bosom "a partir seco i dolorosi guai" 'to share its sorrowing groans' (line 8), to better express the unutterable experience of sorrow for Laura's death through the symbiosis of poet and bird.

The ultimate representation of the nightingale emerges during the seventeenth century, in Giambattista Marino's *Adonis*, a short narrative poem divided into twenty cantos, on the mythological fable in which Venus falls in love with Adonis, provoking the wrath and vengeance of the god Mars.[6] Cantos 6–8 focus on the theme of Adonis's initiation to the knowledge of the senses; the seventh, in particular, recounts Adonis's experiences in the Garden of the Ear and the Garden of the Mouth.[7] In the six introductory stanzas of canto 7, Marino deals with the relation between music and poetry as well as the link between art and nature. The canto revolves around the exaltation of nature and love, with the latter conceived as instinctual force and sensual attraction. Music, meanwhile, exhibits an effective cathartic power, since it comforts the human soul and calms its passions. The ear is the sense organ appointed to receive harmonious musical sound. Marino's choice of the nightingale to characterize a specific natural sound similar to musical notes is determined by a particular interest for a natural phenomenon that is able to capture human curiosity.

It is difficult to say whether Marino revisits Petrarch in his use of the nightingale. The structure of *Adonis* is largely classical; Marino was often called the "new Ovid" for having retold the love story from the *Metamorphoses* (Priest xviii). Perhaps the Petrarchan topos of the nightingale could have resurfaced indirectly in Marino's literary memory. At the same time, Marino was also interested in erotic poetry, a genre he explored at quite a young age. (His first volume of lyrics, published in 1602, included the sensual and voluptuous "Canzone dei baci" ["The Song of Kisses"].) Perhaps some Petrarchan influence may be detected in the genre of erotic literature, since Petrarch was a master in hiding or disguising his eroticism. He employed a repetitive lexicon of veils, flowers, grass, clear and fresh waters, branches of trees, blond braids, pearls, and skirt hems to evoke, but not fully reveal, the desired physical image of his lady.[8] Marino, instead, does not disguise or hide. Marino's "giardino delle delizie," or Garden of Pleasure, as described in canto 6, is visible, diverse, tangible, and alluring; its purpose is to move the physical senses. Motivated by the widespread geographic and scientific discoveries of the seventeenth century, Marino conceives the literary arts as a means of investigating the natural universe with curiosity and enthusiasm. The artist, like the scientist or the naturalist, is amazed by the marvelous variety and complexity of the universe. The introduction of the nightingale thus aims to demonstrate the creative work of nature that generates living beings such as birds, able not only to fly but also to emulate the harmony of human sound.

The nightingale episode covers five *ottave* in canto 7, from stanza 32 to stanza 37.[9] Here, the nightingale is called "la sirena de' boschi" 'siren of the woods' and "maestro dell'alato stuolo" 'master of the winged throng.' It is able to modulate its singing in a thousand tones and transform it in a thousand different tongues. Though the bird is described as tremulous and thin, it is still able to produce a great wave of sound. The antithesis between the bird's smallness and fragility and its musical versatility offers a thematic outline to establish Marino's "poetics of wonder."[10] Marino shifts abruptly from offering a precise indication of an aspect of nature to establishing a strong metaphoric tension. In stanza 33, he offers a more detailed acoustic definition of the nightingale's musical talent through a series of verbs that emphasize the bird's skillful melodic sound:

> Udir musico mostro, o meraviglia
> Che s'ode sì, ma si discerne apena
> Come or *tronca* la voce, or la *ripiglia*,
> Or la *ferma*, or la *torce*, or *scema*, or *piena*,
> Or la *mormora* grave, or l'*assottiglia*,
> Or *fa* di dolci groppi *ampia catena*,
> E sempre, o se la *sparge* o se l'*accoglie*,
> Con egual melodia la *lega* e *scioglie*. (my emphasis)

> Melodius prodigy! How marvelous, that one can hear but scarcely can discern, as he *breaks off* his song, and then *resumes*, now lightly and now full, he *holds*, he *trills*, now *murmurs* grave, now subtly *thinning out*, and now he *forms a chain* of sweet roulades, and always, whether *hushed* or *shrill* the song, he *blends*, *dissolves* with equal melody. (my emphasis)

A Petrarchan reminiscence appears in the same canto in stanza 34, line 3, when the nightingale "flebilmente il suo lamento esprime" 'mournfully . . . utters his lament.' Immediately following, the "canzonet" spreads "or languido, or sublime" 'now languid, now sublime,' while the nightingale imitates the sound of various instruments such as the flute, the lyre, the organ, and the lute. The similes that follow become even more daring and transform the bird into a man-made machine. His throat seems to have a "rapida rota" 'rapid wheel' or a "turbine veloce" 'turbine swift,' and his little tongue vibrates like a fencer's blade. All this mighty force is gathered in this "atomo sonante" 'singing atom' that conceals sweetness. The accumulation of metaphors in Marino's *ottava rima* finally explodes in an escalation of startling effects; the nightingale is ultimately called a "voce pennuta" 'feathered voice,' a "suon volante" 'flying sound,' a "vivo fiato" 'living breath,' a "piuma canora" 'canorous plume,' and finally a "canto alato" 'winged song.'

How, then, can we recapture the Petrarchan *rosignuol* in this baroque image of the nightingale? If in Petrarch the sweet, weeping bird serves to remind him of his painful existential status, here in Marino the same musical skills exist only for the pleasure of Adonis's hearing. Did Marino intentionally forget Petrarch? Or did the influence of the latter, so taken for granted at this point, need to be overcome in the moral and religious message constantly present underneath the poetic line? For Petrarch, the natural landscape was the environment with which the poet established an emotional and educational relationship. Each natural aspect became an emblem of the represented meaning: the nightingale, with its singing, simultaneously signified and reminded the poet of his anguish in solitude. But for Marino, nature accumulates and enumerates the largest number of forms, for the sole purpose of stirring the physical senses and the poet's curiosity through a process of amusement and pleasure.[11]

Marino's baroque poetics established itself on rhetoric alone, shattering the balance of classical poetry and avoiding the lyrical and elegiac tones that suffused Petrarch's *Canzoniere*. Marino's literary discourse is, then, shaped according to the versatility of his *ingegno*, his wit and ability to create an "interpenetration of objects one with the other" (Priest xxxv).[12] In this technique, rhetorical figures are mainly decorative and serve primarily to impress and please readers, as in the song of the nightingale, which is aimed solely at refining Adonis's acoustic abilities.

The comparison between Petrarch's and Marino's nightingale provides an interesting approach to the study of Petrarchan tradition and delineates several paths of investigation, such as the continuity and development of the classical topos and the different stylistic solutions of each poet regarding the use of metaphor. Among the few critical approaches to these issues are Amedeo Quondam's edition *Petrarca in barocco* ("Petrarch in the Baroque"), which includes an in-depth comparative analysis of seventeenth-century baroque authors (with the exception of Marino) in relation to the Petrarchan tradition, and Francesco Guardiani's *La meravigliosa retorica dell'*Adone *di G. B. Marino*, which includes a study of the thematic rapport between Petrarch and Marino, paying special attention to the similarities between the two poets regarding the definition of love (149–58). Further studies might concentrate on the presence of the nightingale in the poetry of the Arcadia and the Romantic period, up to the early twentieth century.[13]

Nightingales are an endangered, if not already extinct, species in the panorama of Italian wildlife. Nevertheless, they remain alive in the centuries of ornithological literature since Petrarch revisited the classical past and drew comparisons between his personal experience and what nature offered him in its most suggestive manifestations. This contribution is thus intended to be a useful tool in offering educators and students of literature an interpretive key and an itinerary of research on how certain characteristic Petrarchan topoi, such as his classical employment of the nightingale, have continued to shape the imagination of poets.

NOTES

[1] Contini's "Preliminari sulla lingua del Petrarca" still represents a fundamental reading for the linguistic and stylistic comparison between Dante and Petrarch. Even if a translation of this milestone essay is not available, it is worthwhile for the instructor to provide his or her own of some excerpts.

[2] I quote from Bettarini's edition of the *Canzoniere* and Durling's English translation, which is meant to be a "literal prose translation" where the "absence of rhyme" structures the English version as "a guide to the original, not an equivalent" (ix). I also recommend Mortimer's translation of the *Canzoniere* (though it is only an anthology), because it succeeds in maintaining Petrarch's nostalgic and elegiac rhythms.

[3] *Senhal* is a Provençal word that denotes the fictitious name behind which the poet would hide the real identity of the woman celebrated in his work.

[4] The Latin text is taken from Thomas's edition of Vergil's *Georgics*; the translation is mine. The most direct source of the Philomela myth is found in book 6 of Ovid's *Metamorphoses*. Philomela, daughter of Pandion, king of Athens, was seduced and raped by her brother-in-law, Tereus, who cut off her tongue and imprisoned her so she could tell no one about his crime. Her sister, Procne, wife of Tereus, fed the latter with the remains of their son, Itys, to avenge Philomela's rape. The gods then transformed Philomela and Procne, respectively, into a nightingale and a swallow, while Tereus was changed into a sparrow-hawk. In the *Odyssey*, Homer compares Penelope's mourning to Philomela (19.518–20). In *Georgics*, book 4, Vergil refers to the Homeric lines, though he alters them by introducing the actual nightingale as a comparison to Orpheus lamenting Eurydice. Vergil also mentions Philomela the nightingale in the sixth eclogue (lines 79–81).

[5] Petrarch's identification with the bird is also visible in sonnet 353 of the *Canzoniere*, in which a "vago augelletto che cantando vai, / over piangendo, il tuo tempo passato" 'wandering bird that goes singing or else weeping for past time' is again invoked as the grieving lover's counselor (lines 1–2). In addition, many birds—not necessarily identified as the nightingale—fill the lexical fabric of the *Canzoniere*, as in sonnets 219, "Il cantar novo e 'l pianger delli augelli" ("The new singing and the weeping of the birds") and 279, "Se lamentar augelli" ("If I hear birds lamenting").

[6] Giambattista Marino (Naples, 1569–1625) was the most renowned poet of the Italian baroque. His poem *Adonis* was completed in Paris in 1623. All quotations from *Adonis* are from Pozzi's edition and Priest's translation.

[7] Priest's informative introduction to his translation can help students understand the structure of Marino's poem.

[8] Only in the penultimate stanza of sestina 22 does Petrarch express his desire to spend at least one night with Laura: "Con lei foss'io da che si parte il sole, / et non ci vedess'altri che le stelle, / sol una nocte, et mai non fosse l'alba" 'Might I be with her from when the sun departs and no other see us but the stars, just one night, and let the

dawn never come!' (lines 31–33). Often this stanza goes unnoticed, since the study of this poem's complex metrics requires more attention than the spontaneous exclamation of the speaker who would like to consummate his love. It seems that Petrarch intentionally hid this stanza in the complex metric structure of his sestina, ashamed for having cried out his sexual passion.

[9] Marino's verse form is *ottava rima*, the traditional meter used by major Italian poets such as Boccaccio, Poliziano, Boiardo, Ariosto, and Tasso. Each stanza has eight hendecasyllabic lines, which conform to the rhyme pattern *abababcc*.

[10] The "poetics of wonder," or "poetica della meraviglia," describes the stylistic feature of baroque literature whereby writers invented original, daring, often surprising metaphors to create a sense of wonder and awe in readers.

[11] Before highlighting the nightingale, in the twelve preceding *ottave* (stanzas 20–31), Marino describes an "uccellaia," a large birdcage in which all the different kinds of birds are seen and heard singing. Marino lists the pheasant, the partridge, the eagle, the pelican, the woodpecker, the heron and the egret, the crane, the magpie, the dove and the peacock, the swallow and the canary, the titlark, the serin, the blackcap and the robin, the horned owl and the siskin, the blackbird, and all other birds named in the jargon of hunters and country people. It seems as if all the unnamed birds of Petrarch's *Canzoniere*, except for the sparrow, the swallow, and the nightingale, present themselves in a musical concert.

[12] Instructors and students may find helpful Tesauro's *Il canocchiale aristotelico*, a fundamental text that outlines baroque poetics and stylistic forms, particularly the choice of metaphor. I also recommend Conte's *La metafora barocca*, an outstanding study of the metaphor and its pervasive usage in baroque poetry and prose.

[13] It is important to remember Leopardi's "mesto rosignol" 'melancholic nightingale' in his poem *Appressamento della morte* ("The Approach of Death") and the variation on the bird motif in *Passero solitario* ("Solitary Sparrow"); see Bettarini, esp. 9–42. Even early-twentieth-century Italian poetry is characterized by the songs of birds, as in the works of Pascoli and Montale, whose realism goes beyond the classical reference to the nightingale to privilege region-specific variations on the metaphor.

Petrarch and the Search for *Antica Virtù*

Elizabeth H. D. Mazzocco

One theme that is consistent throughout Petrarch's body of literary production is *renovatio Romae*, the restoration of Rome to the ancient grandeur that will allow the city to take its place in the modern world. Across the interdisciplinary boundaries of his opus, Petrarch's quest for *antica virtù*, the ancient valor that will make the restoration possible, inspired generations of scholars, artists, and patriots. The interdisciplinarity of his work as well as its multigenerational influence makes "Petrarch and the Search for *Antica Virtù*" a valuable component in a number of courses, taught in either Italian or English. This essay discusses Petrarch's concept of Italy, his views on the rebirth of a powerful Rome, and the birth of a dominant Italian state. It analyzes the notion of *renovatio* in two poems from his *Canzoniere*, "Spirto gentil" (53) and "Italia mia" (128), and ends by identifying echoes of Petrarchan sentiment in later Italian writers.

Although Petrarch was powerfully influenced by the teaching of the church and the medieval church fathers, when it came to his concept of Italy, he concentrated on the glories of Rome and sought to refocus the thoughts of his audience from the afterlife preached by the Middle Ages to the possibility of rebirth of Italian greatness in the here and now. Petrarch's evolving view of the relation of antiquity, the Middle Ages, and his own historical present has been a favorite discussion point since Theodor Mommsen released his seminal study "Petrarch's Conception of the 'Dark Ages,'" in which he makes a powerful argument that it was Petrarch who was the first to speak of the "dark ages." For the present analysis, the salient feature is that Petrarch not only thought about the difference between the two ages but also actively tried to convert other Italians to his way of thinking. Writing to Ugo d'Este in 1369, Petrarch exhorts the marquis to give up the medieval chivalric jousts that he staged and to remember how his noble ancestors had behaved: "[W]hen it is necessary, for your life, your dignity, your fatherland, fight bravely, fight like a man, and I wish you luck; but avoid these jousts that are so dangerous, harmful and childish. . . . We never read that Scipio or Caesar went in for this" (*Seniles* 11.13).[1] Petrarch's antimedieval, proclassical fervor was fed by his desire to see the papacy return to Rome from Avignon and shows itself in his solid, point-by-point argument against those who saw post-Carolingian France as the inheritor of Rome's greatness.[2] In letters to Pope Urban V, Petrarch delineates the reasons that the papacy should return to Italy (e.g., *Seniles* 7.1) and later argues fervently that civilization and valor have not been lost to France but still reside in Italy: "[H]ere all civilization flourished, and if there is any of it left anywhere, it still flourishes in some part of Italy. Here are the two pinnacles of the world, the Papacy and the Empire. . . . And although virtue has diminished throughout the world . . . if there are still any remnants, they are in Italy" (9.1). In Petrarch's eyes, Italy still held the potential for greatness; it needed only to understand that potential to realize his vision.

Petrarch's vision of Italy was pan-Italian. He never fell into the *campanilismo* of other Florentine humanists, probably because he spent much of his early life outside Italy at the court of Avignon and did not identify himself solely with Florence. Even though he did not see Rome until his early thirties, Petrarch was mesmerized by the idea of classical Rome. He was convinced that if Italians learned about their classical heritage and imitated their classical ancestors, they, as the inheritors of Roman civilization and *antica virtù*, could revitalize the country. Toward such an end, Petrarch tried to get leaders to learn through example, using letters, ancient texts, or artifacts to achieve this purpose. He describes, for example, giving Roman coins to the emperor Charles IV in an effort to get him to take on the role as modern-day Caesar:

> I gave him as a gift some gold and silver coins bearing the portraits of our ancient rulers and inscriptions in tiny and ancient lettering, coins that I treasured, and among them was the head of Caesar Augustus, who almost appeared to be breathing. "Here," . . . I said, "are the men whom you have succeeded, here are those whom you must try to imitate and admire, whose ways and character you should emulate: I would have given these coins to no other save yourself. . . . [I]t is up to you not only to know but to follow their example." (*Familiares* 19.3)[3]

Some scholars have criticized Petrarch for his vacillation between allegiance to the idea of a new Roman republic (e.g., his admonitions to the Italian Cola di Rienzo to rejuvenate Rome) and fascination with that of a Roman empire based in Italy (his letters to the Bavarian Charles IV, whom he hoped to see crowned emperor) (see Solmi). For Petrarch, however, Rome and Italy were one and the same (see Mazzocco). Indeed, Petrarch's preoccupation was with the rebirth of Italy in the form of its ancient counterpart; the person who brought about that rebirth—be he senator or emperor—was secondary. Petrarch's desire to awaken Italy to its glorious past and the possibilities for its future manifests itself in both his Latin and Italian works. His two most famous vernacular poems on the subject are "Spirto gentil" and "Italia mia." The former addresses the soul of a much-debated personage who holds the future of Rome in his hands.[4] I argue that the identity of the *cavalier* who appears on the Capitoline at the poem's end is of secondary interest to the reader. The significance of "Spirto gentil" lies in Petrarch's vision of Italy as a united political entity. Indeed, this poem served as the battle cry for Italian rebirth and unification throughout future centuries.

The overriding metaphor in the poem depicts Italy as a sluggish body with Rome as its head buried in mud and in centuries of lethargic, almost anesthetized sleep:

> Che s'aspetti non so, né che s'agogni
> Italia, che suoi guai non par che senta:

> vecchia, oziosa e lenta,
> dormirà sempre, e non fia chi la svegli?
> Le man l'avess'io avolto entro' capegli!
> Non spero che già mai dal pigro sonno
> mova la testa, per chiamar ch'uom faccia,
> sì gravemente è oppressa e di tal soma:
> ma non senza destino a le tue braccia
> che scuoter forte e sollevarla ponno,
> è or commesso il nostro capo, Roma.
> Pon man in quella venerabil chioma
> securamente, e ne le treccie sparte,
> sí che la neghittosa esca del fango. (53.10–23)[5]

> What Italy expects or yearns for I do not know, for she does not seem to feel her woes, being old, idle, and slow. Will she sleep forever, and will no one ever awaken her? Might I have my hand clutched in her hair!
> I do not hope that she will ever move her head from her sluggish sleep for any shouting one can do, she is so heavily oppressed and by such a weight; but not without destiny is our head, Rome, now entrusted to your arms, which can shake her strongly and raise her up.
> Put our hand into those venerable locks confidently and into those unkempt tresses, so that this neglectful one may come out of the mud.

Only an individual possessing *virtù* will have the strength to grab the head, shake the mud from it, and raise it (Rome/Italy) up again to greatness. Throughout the poem, the boundaries between Rome and Italy become ever more blurred while Rome/Italy morphs into one indistinguishable whole, united by the eternally living memory of the Roman world, who cries out for remembrance and action: "Roma . . . / con gli occhi di dolor bagnati et molli, / . . . chier mercé" 'Rome . . . with her eyes wet with tears keeps crying out . . . for mercy' (lines 104–06). Throughout the opus of Petrarch, the road to *renovatio* remains stable. First, one must understand the past, and, second, one must strive to learn from that past and follow its examples. Remembrance plus imitation leads to *renovatio* and to restored greatness. The potential for greatness is still within Rome; it is in the mortar of buildings, the stones of the tombs of deceased heroes, the texts of historians, and the collective memory of the world: "L'antiche mura, ch' ancor teme et ama / e trema 'l mondo, quando si rimembra / del tempo andato e 'ndietro si rivolve" 'The ancient walls, which the world still fears and loves and trembles at when it remembers past time and looks back' (29–31). The world still trembles at the memory of the power of Rome.

Why, then, is Italy in such bad shape, so bad in fact that even Hannibal, Italy's most formidable opponent and Petrarch's most loathed historical personage, could pity the Italians ("ch' Anibale . . . farian pio?" '[what] would make Hannibal . . . pity them' [65])?[6] The problem is that Petrarch's compatriots have lost their focus. Instead of concentrating their efforts on realizing their inborn potential and renewing the greatness of Rome, they are engaging in battles against themselves. The factions of Rome are destroying their city, and it has no one to defend it except the unnamed hero with *antica virtù* who will tame the beasts (i.e., the various Roman political factions) and put Rome back on track:

> Orsi, lupi, leoni, aquile e serpi
> ad una gran marmorea colonna
> fanno noia sovente, ed a sé danno:
> di costor piange quella gentil donna
> che t'à chiamato a ciò che di lei sterpi
> le male piante che fiorir non sanno. (71–76)

> Bears, wolves, lions, eagles, and snakes give frequent trouble to a great marble Column and to themselves do harm; because of them that noble lady weeps who has called you to uproot from her the evil plants that do not know how to flower.

The restoration of ancient grandeur to be accomplished by the valorous knight will be cheered by the famed immortals who set ancient Rome on her path to greatness and by contemporary Romans, once they understand the potential inherent in their own *antica virtù*:

> O grandi Scipioni, o fedel Bruto,
> quanto v'aggrada, s'egli è ancor venuto
> romor là giù del ben locato officio!
> Come cre' che Fabrizio
> si faccia lieto udendo la novella!
> e dice: "Roma mia sarà ancor bella." (37–42)

> O great Scipios, O faithful Brutus, how pleasing to you is the news, if it has come to you down there, of how well the office has been placed! How glad I believe Fabricius is, hearing word of it, and he says: "My Rome shall be beautiful again!"

Petrarch has carefully placed the souls of three revered heroes in this stanza—Scipio, Bruto, and Fabrizio—whom he counterbalances with Hannibal in line 65. That the disarray of Rome would cause Hannibal to pity its citizens is a deep-cutting insult to contemporary Italians. Hannibal was the only true threat to ancient Rome, but now the very people whom Bruto, Scipio, and Fabrizio fought to protect are destroying Rome from within. The time has come for them to wake up, know themselves, and harness their inborn Roman valor, which runs in their blood as an inheritance from the days of antiquity, to bring about a *renovatio*. This topos is underscored in a letter to Giovanni Colonna in which Petrarch writes:

> For today who are more ignorant about Roman affairs than the Roman citizens? Sadly do I say that nowhere is Rome less known than in Rome. I do not deplore only the ignorance involved (although what is worse than ignorance?) but the disappearance and exile of many virtues. For who can doubt that Rome would rise again instantly if she began to know herself? (*Familiares* 6.2)

Whatever the genre, Petrarch's vision of *renovatio* shines through, and the message of "Spirto gentil" is the poetic battle cry for Italian patriotism.

So, too, is "Italia mia." Whereas "Spirto gentil" addresses the *cavalier* with *antica virtù* who will rescue Rome from the factions that are tearing it to bits, "Italia mia" looks at the entire body of Italy and the political rivalries between city-states whose wars are essentially destroying it: "Italia mia, benché 'l parlar sia indarno / a le piaghe mortali / che nel bel corpo tuo sì spesse veggio" 'My Italy, although speech does not aid those mortal wounds of which in your lovely body I see so many' (128.1–3). The "barbarico sangue" painting the countryside ("perchè 'l verde terreno / del barbarico sangue si depinga?" 'Why is the green earth covered with barbarian blood?' [lines 21–22]) is juxtaposed with the "Latin sangue gentile" in which flows the nobility and *virtù* that are the birthright of all Italians ("Latin sangue gentile, / sgombra da te queste dannose some" 'Noble Latin blood: throw off these harmful burdens' [73–74]). Petrarch implores his fellow Italians to stop paying foreigners (the "tedesca rabbia" 'Teutonic rage' [35], against whom Petrarch says the Alps provide natural protection) to enter Italy to fight divisive wars for the city-states. He beseeches them to concentrate, instead, on creating an Italian whole that can again rule the world and prove the valor of the Italian being:

> vertù contro furore
> prenderà l'arme, e fia 'l combatter corto:
> ché l'antiquo valore
> ne l'italici cor' non è ancor morto (93–96)
>
> Ingenuity against rage
> Will take up arms and make the battle short.
> For the ancient valor
> In Italian hearts is not yet dead. (qtd. in Machiavelli 225)

Despite the poem's ending with "Pace, pace, pace" 'Peace, peace, peace' (line 122), this is not a pacifistic poem (see Sasso). Petrarch wants peace among Italians, but he understands that they must take up their swords against foreigners to achieve the *renovatio*. Indeed, not only does their "Latin sangue gentile" make them legitimate inheritors of the power of Rome, but their "antiquo valore," again passed through the blood, gives them the strength that is necessary to assert their legitimacy. The result of a successful *renovatio* would be glory and power for the *patria* (i.e., Italy). It is noteworthy that Petrarch uses the word *patria* to mean Italy as a whole rather than to identify a specific region or city state: "non è questa la patria in ch'io mi fido, / madre benigna e pia" 'Is this not my fatherland in which I trust, and my kind and merciful mother' (84–85).

Petrarch died before seeing his vision of a united Italy realized, but his quest for the rediscovery and appreciation of *antica virtù* passed seamlessly into the minds of his successors. Biondo Flavio, for example, the fifteenth-century historical geographer and humanist who declared Petrarch to be the father of humanism (346E), was influenced by Petrarch's patriotic vision of a renewed Rome and, through Rome, Italy. Throughout his *Italia illustrata* and *Roma triumphans*, Biondo sows the seeds for such a *renovatio Romae*, carefully delineating the triumphs, monuments, and men of valor of Roman times. Biondo also believed, like Petrarch, that by understanding and imitating the past, his contemporaries could revitalize Italy. Moreover, also following in the footsteps of Petrarch, he cautioned his contemporaries to rid Italy of mercenary troops, to heal the wounds that caused Italians to fight internal wars, and to make Italy a great power again by imitating the virtues of the ancients (Mazzocco 22–23).

The humanists were not the only Renaissance inheritors of Petrarch's vision; writers such as Baldassare Castiglione followed his lead and perpetuated his theme of the need for a *renovatio* and his vision of Italian unity. Castiglione, in the sonnet "Superbi colli," writes that the ruins are the only extant things to hold the name of Rome: "Superbi colli, e voi sacre ruine, / che 'l nome sol di Roma ancor tenete" 'Proud hills, and you holy ruins, who alone bear the name of Rome' (6.1–2; my trans.). In a 1519 letter to Pope Leo X, Castiglione reiterates Petrarch's stance that the ruins still evoke the *antica virtù* of Italy's noble ancestors. Speaking of the need to preserve the Roman ruins, he says that the ruins serve as intermediaries, transferring the spirit of greatness from the men of ancient Rome to Castiglione's own contemporaries. The memory conveyed by ruins will spur today's Italians to realize their own potential for greatness.[7] We can see from such passionate references to the ruins of Rome and to the greatness of Italy that Castiglione considers himself an inheritor of the Roman spirit that belongs to all Italians. Castiglione thus fosters Petrarch's cause of the *renovatio Romae*.

The *renovatio* cannot occur, however, if foreigners continue to invade Italy, and invade they do. In the last book of Matteo Maria Boiardo's *L'inamoramento de Orlando* (1494), a fanciful epic deftly infused with historical lessons meant to educate its audience, the foreign monster rears its ugly head again, in the form of Charles VIII, yet another outsider invited into Italy by its natives. Boiardo's narrator explains to his audience that he will pause the writing of the epic because he sees all Italy in flames:

> Mentre che io canto, o Dio redemptore,
> Vedo la Italia tutta a fiama e a foco
> Per questi Galli, che con gran valore
> Vengon per disertar non sciò che loco (book 3, canto 9, 26.1–4)

> While I am singing, O God the Redeemer, I see all Italy in flames and on fire because these Gauls come, with great valor [the narrator shows his irony here], to destroy I don't know which place. (my trans.)

The reader can see through the poetic topos of war interrupting verse to understand that, in Charles VIII, Boiardo had identified a foreign threat to the entire political entity of Renaissance Italy just as the Gauls had been the enemies of Caesar and the Romans. Thus one hundred and twenty years after Petrarch's death, Italy was still threatened by the foreign "rabbia."

Another inheritor of Petrarch's Italian vision was the brilliant political theorist Niccolò Machiavelli. He, too, recognized foreign outsiders as a threat to Italy not only in his role as political theorist but also as an Italian patriot. In chapter 26 of *Il Principe* (*The Prince*), "Exhortatio ad Capessendam Italiam in Libertatemque a Barbaris Vindicandam" ("Exhortation to Take Hold of Italy and Liberate Her from the Barbarians"), Machiavelli presents an argument very similar to Petrarch's: "È necessario, pertanto, prepararsi a queste arme, per potere con la virtù italica defendersi dalli esterni" 'It is necessary, therefore, to provide yourself with troops such as these, so that with Italian strength you will be able to defend yourself from outsiders' (220–21). Even bearing in mind Machiavelli's particular definition of the notion of *virtù*, we understand that in this segment of *Il Principe* the political theorist is referring to the *antica virtù* of Petrarch. If there is any doubt, we need look only so far as the end of the chapter, where Machiavelli chooses to insert four lines of "Italia mia" to end the chapter as well as the entire book. His choice of Petrarch reveals his patriotic sentiments. Directly addressing his patrons, the Florentine Medici family and specifically Lorenzo, to whom the book is dedicated, Machiavelli writes:

> acciò che, sotto la sua insegna [of the Medici], e questa patria [Italy] ne sia nobilitata e, sotto li sua auspizii, si verifichi quel detto del Petrarca:
> Virtù contro a furore
> Prenderà l'arme; e fia el combatter corto:
> Chè l'antico valore
> Nell'italici cor non è ancor morto.
>
> So that, under your banner, this country may be ennobled and, under your auspices, those words of Petrarch may come true:
> Ingenuity against rage
> Will take up arms and make the battle short.
> For the ancient valor
> In Italian hearts is not yet dead. (222–25)

It is easy to see how Petrarch's ideas about *patria*, the ruins, and *antica virtù* would be popular during the ottocento, when writers such as Ugo Foscolo, Giacomo Leopardi, and Alessandro Manzoni gazed back on the past for inspiration.

In "Dei sepolcri," for example, Foscolo emulates Petrarch's vision of the power of the Roman ruins and the tombs of Rome's heroes; for Foscolo the sacred grounds are the tombs in Santa Croce, but the effect of ancient heroes on modern man is the same. Ancestors such as Machiavelli, Michelangelo, and Galileo have become mediators of the *antica virtù* of ancient heroes from which they drew their inspiration. Now from their tombs in Santa Croce, they inspire Foscolo's contemporaries to see themselves as belonging to the circle of inheritors of *antica virtù* (Foscolo's term is "le virtù patrie"), to follow in the footsteps of their ancestors, and to restore Italy to greatness. Speaking of the spirit of the tragic playwright Vittorio Alfieri, Foscolo writes, "Con questi grandi abita eterno: e l'ossa / fremono amor di patria" 'With these great ones [Machiavelli and company] he lives eternal; his bones tremble with love for Italy' (lines 196–97; my trans.). Foscolo's use of the verb "abita" is significant because all the heroes—past and present—are alive through memory.

A unit such as "Petrarch and the Search for *Antica Virtù*" is tailor-made for an introductory course to Italian literature that has thematic components. All the works referred to have good, modern translations, so a Petrarch-based unit could be easily taught in Italian or in English. I always give the students the English translations for Petrarch's Latin works, although I put the Latin on reserve for advanced students. My students and I have had the opportunity to read and discuss Petrarch's letter to Giovanni Colonna as we stood looking into the Roman Forum on our spring semester in Italy. A good *PowerPoint* presentation or Web video has otherwise been quite satisfactory when the Forum itself is not quite so near. Even today, some seven hundred years after Petrarch was struck by the palpable life in those ruins, they still inspire something special in students, and images are essential with this unit. The unit also lends itself to a section on music. We explore the Italian national anthem, "Inno di Mameli," which begins with a direct reference to Scipio's helmet that binds the head of risen Italy: "Fratelli d'Italia, / l'Italia s'è desta, / dell'elmo di Scipio / s'è cinta la testa" 'Brothers of Italy, Italy has awakened, she has bound her head with Scipio's helmet' (my trans.). Giuseppe Verdi's opera *Nabucco* is another natural musical choice, whose stirring chorus "Va' pensier" evokes the glories of Italy. For many students, watching the DVD of *Nabucco* is their first exposure to Italian opera.

The multinational possibilities that this unit raises make it also feasible and profitable for a course in comparative literature. Petrarch's original argument for Italy as the only inheritor of Rome's greatness juxtaposes well with those, such as the pro-Carolingians, who argue that the greatness of Rome had been transferred outside Italy. The same argument holds true with Elizabethan England, which, however, saw itself as a new Roman empire.

As the celebrations of the one hundred fiftieth anniversary of Italy's unification continue, so too do the arguments about Italy's future as a nation. Today more than ever Petrarch's vision is pertinent, and many of the same problems that plagued the Italian city-states in the fourteenth century threaten the modern-day European state. This unit on Petrarch provides an excellent opportunity to show students the continuing relevance of Petrarch and the Italian Renaissance that he engendered.

NOTES

[1] All quotations from Petrarch's *Rerum senilium libri* (henceforth, *Seniles*) follow the translation by Aldo Bernardo, Saul Levin, and Reta A. Bernardo.

[2] Ancel Choquart, for example, was one of those who denigrated Italy to build up France. In *Seniles* 9.1, Petrarch writes to Pope Urban V and mentions the diatribe of Choquart, "who in his address . . . took up the largest part of his oration in elevating his beloved Gaul and disparaging Italy."

[3] All quotations from Petrarch's *Rerum familiarium libri* (henceforth, *Familiares*) follow the translations by Aldo Bernardo.

[4] Critics have spent so much time debating the question of whom Petrarch had in mind when he wrote "Spirto gentil" that they have almost overlooked the more important facet of the poem: what is the *spirto gentil* supposed to do? Leading contenders for identity of the mysterious *spirto* include Cola di Rienzo (as argued by Musto) and Stefano Colonna.

[5] Italian quotations from the *Canzoniere* follow Ponte's edition; English quotations follow Durling's translation, except where noted otherwise.

[6] Hannibal receives this dubious honor because he was the only serious threat to Rome's existence. The fact that Hannibal was defeated by Scipio Africanus makes Scipio Petrarch's most beloved ancient hero. See Bernardo, *Petrarch, Scipio*.

[7] "[Q]uel poco che resta di questa antica madre della gloria e della grandezza italiana, per testimonio del valore e della virtù di quegli uonimi divini, che pur talor con la loro memoria eccitano alla virtù gli spiriti, che oggidì sono tra noi" (618–19).

Teaching Petrarchism in the Context of Post-Risorgimento Poetry

Andrea Dini

Explanations in textbooks, footnotes, scholarly introductions—all materials we normally assign to students when teaching Italian poetry or refer to for textual explications and analyses—often, if not always, bring up complex poetic legacies, detail intricate heritages, and underline a writer's personal appropriation of poetic languages through borrowed or recurring words, alluding to (stylistic) traditions, canons, or general allegiances to a conceptual matrix of what poetry is. More often than not, even in unsuspecting texts from modern and contemporary poetry, these materials bring up the names of two of the so-called founding fathers of Italian letters, Dante and Petrarch, as if even today, seven centuries later, their poetic influence fuzzily labeled as *dantismo* and *petrarchismo* could not, and should not, be ignored. Why—the students' silent, respectful, yet puzzled gaze seems to ask—is so much value placed on tradition and imitation in Italian poetry? Why is *dantismo* so decidedly associated with Montale and Pasolini? Why is *petrarchismo* associated with Ungaretti and Luzi or with Zanzotto? Is it just a matter of language (of style), or do these critical connections betray a more deep-rooted relation to a way of understanding literature's function and roles through the literary values Dante and Petrarch embodied? What kind of influence is it, and what does it mean?

These legitimate and important questions are seldom addressed head-on in the classroom. Students who enroll in upper-level courses in Italian have not necessarily had much exposure to a chronological history of Italian literature and may be totally ignorant of any history of the Italian language, which is uniquely intertwined with the development of the literature and with the language of the poetry they are studying. Introductory classes on the relation of the history of Italian literature and the history of the Italian language are, in my opinion, key to the students' understanding of how Italian poetry works and to their gaining an appreciation of a poet's lexical legacy. Given the unmistakable role that Petrarchism had in shaping the destinies of Italian as an idiom and of Italian as a poetic language, I would argue that, to teach it, we must frame it within the discourse of language composition, in particular *la questione della lingua* ("the language question") and its related ideological issues. To this end, instructors might want to take the proverbial bull by the horns when teaching poetry and include at the beginning of the semester some discussion of the diachronic evolution of the Italian language as a prelude to the presentation of Petrarchism.

Teaching Petrarchism seems to me the essential condition for understanding Italian poetry from the sixteenth century on and for outlining Petrarch's conspicuous ideological legacy in twentieth-century literature so that students might comprehend how this author's works have been used, appropriated, and possibly twisted to shape the literary debate—and why.

A module on Petrarchism necessarily includes the following steps: a discussion of Italian's history and key characteristics (to understand how the literary language itself was shaped by Petrarch's legacy); a presentation of *la questione della lingua* and an outline of Pietro Bembo's proposed resolution and of its political and ideological corollaries that explain the weight Petrarch's literary model acquired; and a discussion of the modalities through which the Petrarchan model was assessed and either embraced or refused in nineteenth- and twentieth-century Italian literature and what this critical discussion means to us readers, interpreters, teachers, or students of Petrarch today. Anna Laura Lepschy and Giulio Lepschy's overview in *The Italian Language Today* is a good starting point for a historical approach (11–18, 19–40; see esp. 22–23, 35); students can read it before the lecture on the interrelation of Italian's linguistic development, the creation of a national literature, and the establishment of a literary canon. To illustrate Italian's key characteristics, instructors might rely on Tullio De Mauro's *Storia linguistica dell'Italia unita*, which provides an in-depth examination of phenomena like Italian's morphological and lexical polymorphism or semantic hypertrophy that have direct repercussions in the evolution of the poetic language and in the role that Petrarchism played in it by ultimately providing a model for linguistic standardization (29).

It should be emphasized from the start how what we now refer to as Italian essentially developed as a written language that lacked linguistic selection as determined by everyday spoken usage. As a result, when a form had two or more variations, both were often incorporated into the language's vocabulary, becoming part of its thesaurus. Where other Romance languages only had one form (e.g., in French, *rivage* refers to "coast" or "bank," and *ruisseau* to "brook"), Italian had several (*sponda*, *riva*, *ripa*, *lido*, *lito*, for "coast" or "bank"; *ruscello*, *rivo*, *rio*, for "brook") with essentially the same meaning but with a usage that varied according to the poetic or prose context. In fact, this Italian polymorphism could take on a stylistic distinction and become incorporated into the language of prose or poetry depending on the linguistic register (e.g., the use of headwords such as *uccello* ["bird"] in prose versus *augello* in poetry or, similarly, *anima* ["soul"] versus *alma*). Often, however, no distinction was made. Italian, therefore, developed by additions and steady lexical increments rather than by usage-driven substitutions (the norm in spoken languages), where usage alone determines the language's lexical rates of survival. While this hypertrophy contributed on the one hand to the richness and profusion of headwords in certain lexical sectors of the language, on the other hand it also stripped Italian of linguistic immediacy, giving it a bookish, didactic quality. Literary prestige, not concrete spoken usage, determined what words could continue to circulate and at what stylistic register. As a result, the language we refer to as "Italian" became a possession to acquire by literary means, that is, through either the scholastic, imitative, or rhetorical study of models. In this regard, the eighteenth-century

Venetian playwright Carlo Gozzi was right in defining Italian as "una lingua morta" 'a dead language' (qtd. in De Mauro 14), since, like Latin, it had to be learned exclusively through its literature.

To underline the fundamental role that literary tradition played in shaping this Italian idiom across the centuries, instructors can explain how at the time of Italy's unification, in 1861, Petrarch and Boccaccio and other fourteenth-century authors still reigned as the linguistic models for poetry and prose. (The fact that Dante, regardless of his status as the father of the Italian vernacular, was left out, is another by-product of Petrarchism.) According to De Mauro, eighty percent of the Italian vocabulary in 1861 still remained bound to lexemes dating back to the origins of the language (219). Such a high rate of occurrence shows that the most common words from the fourteenth to the sixteenth centuries were passed down (or preserved) after the sixteenth century and that what we call Petrarchism today was directly responsible for an attempt to codify a fixed, conservative, and supermunicipal language (i.e., an idiom that can be adopted as the lingua franca by linguistically diverse municipalities).

Italian Petrarchism, in fact, cannot be understood if it is not primarily seen through the lens of Italian's linguistic development (or lack thereof), which also identifies with the many attempts at controlling the language through the literary medium for political reasons. A contextualized frame of reference is necessary. It is important for students to know that until the late nineteenth century, Italy (a nation that they generally assume to have always been integrated or unified in terms of history and territorial identity) remained politically and linguistically divided and that neither *Italy* nor *Italian* (as concepts referring to a nation or to a people or even to a language) existed as we understand them today. The birth of Petrarchism in Italy—that is, the canonization of Petrarch's vernacular works and their influence on literary tradition—should be introduced at this point with an examination of *la questione della lingua* that is at its core. Instructors should clarify that the phrase refers to the debate over the selection of the literary idiom, that is, of the written language and style that was most suited to intellectuals and the literate of the Italian peninsula in the sixteenth century, and that the focus of such a debate should be considered political as well as literary. A shared idiom (i.e., a national language) came to be seen as the unavoidable, inescapable binding condition for the creation of a homeland (or re-creation of it, as a modern *renovatio imperii*, a rebirth of the Roman Empire), whose leading, authoritative intellectual figures were to be found in a supermunicipal literary tradition to serve as a point of reference, as ancestors who could confer a sense of (linguistic) unity and ultimately provide (ideal) common roots and an inspiration to national rebirth (Risorgimento) for a people who were, as Alessandro Manzoni aptly called them in "Adelchi" (1822), "un volgo disperso / che nome non ha" 'a dispersed people / without a name.' This intrinsic, historical necessity of creating a supermunicipal literary canon must be fully underlined during the preliminary explanation of what Petrarchism became, if we want students to understand, on the one hand, the artificiality of the process of the

Italian linguistic unification and, on the other hand, the political invention of a nation. Once students are provided with an adequate background on this topic, they will begin to see Petrarch's irresistible presence in Italian poetic language in less abstract terms and will be able to assess how Italian literature and its language really are, at least at this point in time, the result of conscious choices of cultural politics.

Bembo's treatise *Prose della volgar lingua* (1525) offered a solution to *la questione della lingua* by choosing Petrarch and Boccaccio as literary models for poetry and prose, a choice Bembo based on the fifteenth-century humanist debate and resulting preference for Vergil and Cicero in the standardized use of Latin. The concept of standardization was of crucial importance in Italy, where linguistic fragmentation called for the adoption (or invention) of a common but highly refined language that was to be mostly closed and impervious to change. Bembo's proposal of a Petrarchan model for language and its subsequent codification (resulting in a linguistic system devoid of the possible contamination of a concrete, spoken everyday language) represented a degree of linguistic dignity that was complete and perfect.

Instructors should remark how Bembo's plan was motivated by cultural politics. The canonization of Petrarch's vernacular works also implied a hegemonic role for literary texts and for those who wrote them, as the adoption of a fixed, Petrarchan idiom had to become the ultimate language for all literary endeavors and, therefore, the sole language of intellectuals and of the ruling classes in a country that, although politically and geographically divided, placed hope for national rebirth and unification in a common language and literature. Thus Petrarchism became an instrument with which to forge a national identity. Bembo's codification of Petrarch's language in his *Prose* and its practical application in his *Rime* (1530) became essential to such a plan, which was favorably received by Italian intellectuals. The rapid dissemination of Petrarchism according to Bembo's plan was, at least on an ideal level, an indication of its success, resulting in the establishment of a transregional (i.e., national) community of letters in Italy and a transnational one throughout Europe—what is commonly referred to as the literary republic (*res publica litteraria*). Bembo's Petrarch must therefore be considered the primary point of reference for the semantic fixity and the conservative course that the poetic lexicon was to take in later years. The Italian poetic language, embalmed in formalistic modes of expression, basically remained the same until at least the late nineteenth century. Petrarch's presence in Italian poetry became so pervasive that it became almost indistinguishable from Petrarch's own original poetic language or poetic imagination.[1]

A backlash was inevitable. The process of national unification of the Italian peninsula, which culminated after 1861 in the adoption of a national language based on Petrarch's Florentine idiom, paradoxically resulted in the bitter rejection and reappraisal of the stagnant poetic Petrarchan model, a decline that was more ideological than linguistic. During the Risorgimento and postunification periods of Italian civic and literary history, Dante, the exiled *poeta cive* ("citizen-poet") and father of the vernacular, reemerged as an instrumental figure to provide for the fictionalized account of a continuous Italian struggle toward independence, of intellectual engagement toward unity, becoming a symbolic, political hero against the compromised intellectuals who (like Petrarch) had chosen instead to collaborate with tyrants. Petrarch was almost immediately shunned from the Risorgimento narrative because of how he had been popularized by sixteenth-century Petrarchist imitators. He had been read almost exclusively as the poet of forms detached from reality and as the inventor of a conservative language now identified with a divided nation governed by aristocratic privilege. Petrarch's relationships with the tyrannical lords was also interpreted as collaboration without any explicit, direct antagonism, and it ultimately undermined his long-standing literary popularity at this pivotal moment of Italian history, at the moment of the creation of an Italian intellectual history.

Instructors may wish to frame Petrarch's misfortunes in post-Risorgimento Italy within a historical and ideological context. To this end, Amedeo Quondam's approachable *Petrarca, l'italiano dimenticato* ("Petrarch, the Forgotten Italian") provides a useful outline of Dante's and Petrarch's ideological polarization, explaining Petrarch's political exclusion from the formation of the Italian literary canon during the Risorgimento. Quondam's chapter on national identity (35–82) is particularly relevant to this debate (see the first summary chart in the appendix). A discussion of this essay in class can help students comprehend the literary and historical-ideological dual identity attributed to Petrarch and Dante by elucidating the stigmatizing and dichotomizing effect that it has had on literature, poetry, and related ideological practices in the late nineteenth and the twentieth centuries. Such a discussion can serve to illustrate how Dante immediately became aligned with the concept of a historically winning, intrinsically necessary *poesia impegnata* ("engaged poetry"), whereas Petrarch remained identified with an aristocratic disengagement from reality and from the evolution of the new nation. Linguistically, Petrarch became a signifier of the resistance to change the status quo of Italian (political) captivity. In-class discussions of Italian poetry's textual references and citations often overlook the fact that, in the context of post-Risorgimento literature, writing poetry implied an indirect, a priori alliance with either Dante or Petrarch and the related traditions, schools of thought, and languages on which their poetics are founded. By association, a poet's choosing Dante's or Petrarch's language underlined an ideological alliance with the founding fathers, with either of the two seemingly, mutually exclusive views to conceive literature and its social (ideological) role.[2] In this context, *dantismo* and *petrarchismo* reveal two divergent ways of understanding history and the role to be played by intellectuals in Italian society. They offer two opposing models of behavior, of which one—Petrarch's—is seemingly uprooted from any relation to history and is only preoccupied with a life of forms, with literature that actually receives its value by its impermeability to reality.

In "Petrarca e i poeti d'oggi," a dense but brief article in Italian, several modern-day Italian poets elaborate on this (damning) interpretation. Andrea

Zanzotto's contribution is a useful complement to Quondam's historiographical position. In Zanzotto's view, Petrarch's proposed formalism is justifiable not only as a psychological defense but also as a conscious intellectual revolt against the horrors of history—a sort of political statement with an apolitical intent. Zanzotto's radical reading serves implicitly to refute the negative connotation of semantic elusiveness established as the defining characteristic of Petrarch's poetry, the idea of an evasion from history or disengagement from reality. Zanzotto argues, instead, that the modern idea of poetry itself can be directly traced to Petrarch as he discovered the "autonomia assoluta del fatto poetico" 'poetry's absolute autonomy' that was in opposition or an alternative to history (193–95): the (alleged) absence of social and political contemporary history from this poetry overall must be considered a default accusation of the horrors that mark that history, an indirect indictment of the political powers with which he, as an intellectual, was forced to contend (194). To Zanzotto, Petrarch's poetic production in the *Canzoniere* must be seen not as an escapist solution but, perhaps paradoxically, as a historical critique.

Also in "Petrarca e i poeti d'oggi," Antonio Porta offers a depiction, akin to Zanzotto's, that explores the issue of Petrarchan formalism in historical terms and blames Petrarch's critical legacy (i.e., what is now known as Petrarchism) for the misunderstandings that have distorted the original meaning of his poetry. He emphasizes the importance of engaging in a reading of Petrarch that goes beyond the clichéd anthologies that are responsible for reinforcing the stereotype of an immobile, poetic form that would rule his work. Porta encourages readers to move beyond issues of language and formal perfection that cast Petrarch as retreating into himself and his poetry. Porta's approach proposes a reading of Petrarch's production as receptive to diverse, mobile forms, or, in other words, forms that must be interpreted as diverse experiences necessarily resulting from Petrarch's skeptical interpretation of the role of history. According to this view, the blood and horror of history is caught, beaten, subdued, and transformed by Petrarch into a (seemingly) safe "universo di forme" 'universe of forms,' whose key and comprehension is offered by a comprehensive reading of the *Canzoniere* (196), not by the readings often presented in anthologies, which typically have any historical and political instances removed.

Both Zanzotto and Porta help Petrarch overcome the estrangement from history caused by the filter of Petrarchism by redirecting interpretations of his poetry back to its original conception. As Quondam suggests, it was Dante's association with a specific intellectual model of poetry (the *poeta cive*, militantly engaged) that denied the field of critical research on Petrarch, who is best understood as a product of rather than as a figure isolated from history. Based on such an observation, it would be misguiding to characterize Petrarch's works as an evasion from or as something impervious to history.

Finally, to further demonstrate to students how specific historical receptions complicate the way Petrarch has been evaluated in more recent times, instructors should propose an examination of Gianfranco Contini's essay "Preliminari sulla lingua di Petrarca" (1951), essential to understanding twentieth-century Italian Petrarchism (see the second summary chart in the appendix). In the light of Quondam's essay, Contini's reading shows how the critical designations of *plurilinguismo* and *unilinguismo*—which have come to embody, respectively, Dante's and Petrarch's stylistic essence—bear strong ideological implications, resulting in negative or positive evaluations of these two authors. Dante's vernacular works are associated with an expressionistic (positive) quality for incorporating a variety of idioms and registers, offering both a mimetic description of reality and theoretical reflections on usage and experimentation. Petrarch's works, on the other hand, are marked by a (negatively evaluated) classical taste and by a fundamental monolingualism based on a unity of tone and lexicon, devoid of theoretical justification and experimentation. In effect, Petrarch's poetry is equated here with the pursuit of an ideal form, as an obsessive, absolute experience. Contini's philological approach therefore pits a linguistically vital and expressionistic *Commedia* against a *Canzoniere* that is defensive and "ermetico—cioè antimimetico . . . antireferenziale e antirealistico per eccellenza" 'hermetic—that is, ultimately antimimetic, antireferential, and antirealistic' (Gardini 16), raising one key aspect of the Petrarchan experience, formal perfection, to the level of critical dogma or paradigm while negating its relation to history. As a result, Petrarch (or, perhaps, Petrarchism) remains ideologically identified with specific (negative) periods of Italian history during which Italian poetry generally embraces an intellectual model of isolation and unadaptability and refuses to engage historical reality as its subject—especially between the seventeenth and the nineteenth centuries, during Italy's captivity in the hands of tyrannical lords or foreign dominators, and between 1922 and 1945, during the fascist dictatorship, its collapse during World War II, and Italy's subsequent foreign occupation in 1943–45. For Italian poetry as deeply rooted as Petrarch's, the determining factor in the process of recognition is, undoubtedly, political (Luti 32): the detachment between Italian intellectuals and Italian society during the fascist era, or even their escape into "hermetic" literature as a way to defend themselves against the literary demands of the fascist regime and its propaganda, has had an unmistakable weight in the evaluation of Petrarch's role within twentieth-century poetry between the two world wars and after 1945.

Petrarchist as an adjective keeps having an implicitly negative (and possibly unfair) stigma. Even with its ideological limitations, Contini's essay remains fundamental to an understanding of the various aspects of Petrarch's language, although I strongly advise instructors to frame it within its historical context. As Adelia Noferi points out, the influence exerted on readings of Petrarch during the 1930s and 1940s came to represent what is still the strongest critical-exegetical tradition (*Poetiche* 227). It is therefore up to us as instructors and readers of Petrarch to correct, historicize, contextualize, and fully explain the singular destiny of an author who now, seven centuries later, paradoxically seems in need of our defense against ideological misinterpretations or exploitations that limit his original and fundamental role in shaping Italian language and Italian literature.

NOTES

This essay—including all quotations—was translated from the Italian by David Del Principe. Revised by the author.

[1] As Leopardi pointed out in the early nineteenth century, Petrarch already appeared to be his own imitator: "quelle tante espressioni racchiudenti un pensiero o un sentimento, bellissime ecc. che furono suoi propri e nuovi, ora paiono trivialissimi, perchè sono infatti comunissimi" 'those many, very beautiful expressions, encapsulating a thought or a feeling which were new and [Petrarch's] own, now appear to be very trivial, because they have in fact become very common' ("Petrarca" 192).

[2] Instructors may wish to reinforce here the notion of how the critical reception of literary works ultimately affect their meaning and the way they are interpreted, emphasizing Guglielmi's relevant observations that all readings are to be considered, intrinsically, "atto di critica" 'a critical reading' and that "i significati di un'opera si producono a livello della ricezione" 'the meanings of a work of art are produced at the level of its reception.' According to Guglielmi, "l'oggetto storico" 'the historical object' (i.e., the text) can always be defined according to two historical perspectives: the one producing the object at the moment and in the context of its inception and the one expressing a critical judgement on it. Thus the meaning of a text, according to the critic, is the primary result of the history of its reception (5).

APPENDIX
SUMMARY CHARTS OF CRITICAL ESSAYS FOR CLASSROOM USE

Ideologization of Dante and Petrarch during the Risorgimento and Post-Risorgimento Periods: Quondam's "A proposito di identità nazionale, di Petrarca e di Dante" (35–82; esp. 57–61)

Dante	Petrarch
Invents Beatrice (a figure capable of taking on philosophical and ideological meaning)	Invents Laura (a figure unsuited to philosophical or ideological interpretation)
Writes a civil, political, prophetic, virile, strong poetry ("poeta di una poesia forte, virile, profetica, politica, civile") Represents the exile poet who will never compromise and thus becomes a model for members of the Italian Risorgimento, who also chose to be exiled	Writes poetry interested in forms and word play ("poeta di forme e di parole") Models the contemplative over the active (politically engaged) life

Lays the foundation for the civic mission of poetry (invents engaged literature, or "letteratura impegnata")	Reinforces the private, elitist, and initiatory mission of poetry (its disengagement, or "disimpegno")
Becomes identified with the "*res publica* reale" (a humanist figure cast in a civic mold)	Becomes identified with a transnational "*res publica litteraria*," a metanation bereft of a local history
Becomes the middle-class symbol for an Italian national identity and for the values of homeland history ("valori profondi della storia patria")	Becomes the model for a closed system of language and poetry, expression of a negative humanism, and symbol of an aristocratic, clerical society
Speaks the language of the people ("lingua del popolo")	Speaks the language of the rulers and courtiers
Becomes the father figure of the Italian people	Becomes a non-Italian

Twentieth-Century Perspectives on Dante's and Petrarch's Poetic Language: Contini's "Preliminari sulla lingua di Petrarca" and Coletti's *Storia dell'italiano letterario*

Dante's Poetic Language	Petrarch's Poetic Language
Multilingualism: the contemporaneous use of Latin and the vernacular; stylistic and genre-related polyglottism ("poliglottia degli stili e dei generi letterari" [Contini 171])	Monolingualism: the distinction in usage between Latin, as the everyday language of communication ("lingua normale anche della comunicazione"), and the vernacular, a language without any practical implication ("non . . . passibile di usi pratici") and only of absolute experiences ("solo . . . di esperienze assolute" [Contini 173])
The coexistence of a plurality of lexical tones and strata ("pluralità di toni e pluralità di strati lessicali" [Contini 171–72]); the mixing of linguistic registers and receptiveness to the practical and communicative basis of language, designated as Dantean realism	The unity of tone and lexicon ("Se non monoglottia letterale, è certa l'unità di tono e di lessico"), removed from linguistic extremes and from a vernacular base that was natural, instrumental, merely functional, communicative, and practical ("naturale, strumentale, meramente funzionale e comunicativa e pratica" [Contini 173–74]); a select vocabulary focusing on a small number of entries designed for specific reference, rendering it ready to be imitated ("pronto per l'imitazione" [Coletti 62])

Theoretical engagement (“interesse teoretico”), constant anxiety of linguistic justification (“ansia di giustificarsi linguisticamente”), and evidence of a linguistic philosophy (“filosofia linguistica” [Contini 172]); clear philosophical and allegorical implications for the discourse on love (Coletti 57)	An absence of a rational process of reflection on language (“razionale opera di riflessione”) and a lack of a theoretical justification (Contini 174); love understood as individual, concrete, private, as a form of psychological or interior exploration (Coletti 57)
Incessant experimentalism (“sperimentalità incessante”) associated with a quick applicability of the new experiences (“rapida derivazione delle esperienze” [Contini 172])	Antiexperimentalism: rejection of experimentalism, with a lifelong work on the same fundamental texts (“Nessun esperimento, ove non sia quello di lavorare tutta una vita attorno agli stessi testi fondamentali” [Contini 174])
Semantic concentration	Semantic elusiveness (“evasività semantica”) associated with a fixed, prevailing pattern of sound (“costante dominante ritmica”), the untranslatability (“intraducibilità”) of his verse (Contini 190)
Allegorical rendering of the love experience; theoretical considerations	Polarity of the verse, use of oppositions, and lexical repetitions by recycling nouns and adjectives (“Dicotomia del verso,” “antitesi,” and “ripetizione per somma di nomi, aggettivi o sostantivi” [Contini 179]); verse whose rhetorical structure is more suited to states of mind and emotions rather than theoretical elaboration (Coletti 57)

On Teaching the *Canzoniere* to Students of Spanish

Leah Middlebrook

Petrarchism existed in Spain before the watershed event of the publication of the collected works of Juan Boscán and Garcilaso de la Vega. Indeed, scholars generally agree that the story of Spanish Petrarchism is inextricable from that of Italian Petrarchism, from the fourteenth century through the seventeenth. Before the joining of Aragon and Castile, Aragonese possession of Naples, among other factors, assured that courtiers, merchants, and diplomats, not to mention soldiers, traveled back and forth from Italy, carrying their cultural and literary discoveries with them. Iñigo López, the marquis of Santillana (1398–1458), is recognized as having written the first Petrarchan sonnets in Spain. However, when Boscán (1493–1542) presented himself to his patron, the duchess of Soma, as "el primero que ha juntado la lengua castellana con el modo de escribir italiano" 'the first to join the Castilian tongue with Italian forms' (117), the reputation stuck. It is with Boscán and his 101-poem Petrarchan sequence (bk. 2) that Spanish Petrarchism, proper, is understood to commence.

Courses I have taught on peninsular lyric take up the story of Petrarchism at the juncture of the publication of the sequence, which appeared, accompanied by an introductory letter defending what Boscán proposed as the "new," Italianate court poetry (115–20), as the second part of a four-book volume whose final book was composed of the collected poems of Boscán's more famous friend Garcilaso de la Vega. The following remarks are directed to two audiences: professors and instructors of Spanish literature who are looking for ways to introduce advanced undergraduates—majors or minors with a reasonable grasp of written Spanish—to the *Canzoniere* and professors and instructors of

Italian who are interested in familiarizing themselves with the canonical texts of the Petrarchan tradition on the Iberian Peninsula. Given the orientation of this volume, I spend more time on the former than the latter, but I do provide at the end a list of poems important to developing a sense of sixteenth- and seventeenth-century Petrarchism in Spain. One preliminary note: much of the material I recommend here is written in Spanish and is not translated into English; the translations from the Spanish appearing in this essay are my own.

Petrarch and Petrarchism

One of the key distinctions to establish from the outset is the difference between the rich and diverse body of work written by Francesco Petrarca, on the one hand, and the tradition of lyric Petrarchism, on the other hand. My courses on Petrarchism generally begin with a series of lectures on the early history of the sonnet and canzone forms as they were developed in thirteenth- and fourteenth-century Italy, their transmission to Spain, and the broader context of European and English Petrarchism. In support of these lectures, I generally assign short readings from Michael Spiller's *Development of the Sonnet* (chs. 2 and 3 provide an overview of the development of the sonnet form, as well as an introduction to the *stilnovisti* poets—particularly Dante and Cavalcanti—and their influence on Petrarch). I also assign pages from the introduction to Antonio Prieto's *La poesía española del siglo XVI*, which explains the difference between Petrarch and the Petrarchisms, making the simple (but important) point that while for Italian writers Petrarch's poetry existed as an integral element of literary tradition, this was not the case for Spanish (or French or English) writers. These readings prepare the way for our discussing the stylistic differences between Petrarch and Boscán, especially. Despite Boscán's call for a move away from the forms and meters traditional to Castilian verse (116–17), his compositional style maintained strong links to this poetry, as is evinced by his reliance on logical argumentation, wordplay, and the intricacies of Renaissance theories of passion and reason, deployed through numerous poetic scenarios of the psychomachia.[1] Prieto's work has the added benefit of providing informed, if occasionally dated, analytic discussions of a good selection of sixteenth-century peninsular poets. On the issue of fifteenth- and sixteenth-century Petrarchism in Italy, many of the points made by William Kennedy in his discussion of Italian Petrarchism in *Jacopo Sannazaro and the Uses of Pastoral* are helpful and can be applied to the Spanish scene, particularly since Sannazaro was an important influence on sixteenth-century Spanish poets such as Garcilaso and Gutierre de Cetina.

In addition to providing background about the tradition of Petrarchism, the initial meetings of my courses are aimed at familiarizing students with the premium that Renaissance writers placed on imitation. Thomas Greene's discussion of sixteenth-century notions of *imitatio* and *translatio* and the "humanist hermeneutic," that is, understanding the present through "recovering" the classical past, are all important concepts to present early on (*Light*, introd. and ch. 5). Anne Cruz, in *Imitación y transformación*, and Maria Menocal, in *Shards of Love*, each provide important contexts for Greene. Cruz adjusts his ideas to the scene of peninsular lyric, in which Provençal writers, especially the famed Catalan poet Ausias March, played a crucial role in Renaissance lyric; Menocal points out that the movement among Spanish humanists to distance themselves from the immediate, medieval past was inextricably linked with the Christian drive for hegemony on the peninsula and the expulsions of the Jews and the Moors (ch. 1). In *Orphans of Petrarch*, Ignacio Navarrete establishes the intellectual and cultural scene in which sixteenth-century Spanish Petrarchism emerges, touching on the differences between fifteenth- and sixteenth-century notions of *translatio imperii* and *translatio studii* and arguing effectively for the impact of *Il Cortegiano* on the lyric sequence as it was interpreted by Boscán (ch. 1).

The clearest way to establish the distinctions between the *Canzoniere* and Spanish Petrarchism, however, is by leading students through readings of a representative selection of the poems of the *Canzoniere* and following these up with a reading of Boscán's lyric sequence and selected poems of the Spanish Petrarchan tradition that foregrounds points of contact with Petrarch's text. By focusing on the poems from the *Canzoniere* listed below, instructors can build toward targeted discussions of Spanish imitative practice while exposing students to some of the central preoccupations and key compositional techniques employed by Petrarch.

The Parts and the Whole

Depending on the level of the course and the skills of the students, I work either with the Italian-Spanish bilingual *Canzoniere* (*Cancionero*) edited and translated by Jacobo Cortines or with Robert Durling's bilingual Italian-English edition, assigning the following selection of poems: 1–5; 11; 12; 23; 34; 35; 52; 55–57; 59–60; 61; 62–65; 67; 70; 72; 74; 85–86; 90; 93; 105; 122; 126; 132; 135; 145; 154; 159; 160; 161; 189; 190; 205; 210; 211; 228; 267–71; 293; 298; 318; 336; 364–66. This list is relatively short, given the breadth of the *Canonziere*, and it is weighted in favor of the poems treating Laura *in vita*. But as a part of a course whose primary theme is Petrarchism (as opposed to Petrarch), it is manageable in size and permits discussion of the major themes Spanish poets adapted from their Tuscan precursor. The list also includes many of the poems that peninsular writers chose as objects of imitation and one or two personal favorites.

The general decreased prominence of literature of all kinds, and perhaps especially in poetry, in United States culture makes it likely that students will arrive at a course like this one with little training in how to read lyric. Daily quizzes on vocabulary help instill the importance of paying attention to each word in a lyric poem and raise levels of student comprehension considerably. Beyond this basic training, two aspects of the *Canzoniere* are initially challenging to undergraduates: the assembly of the figure of the lyric speaker from the fragmented *rime* and the repetition of the theme of unrequited love. On the matter of the lyric sequence, the metaphor of film works well to establish how Petrarch's poems work both as individual fragments, or shots, and as a sustained narrative—scenes that refer backward and forward to each other until they weave a complex, sustained narrative. Durling's overview of Petrarch's lifelong editing of the *Canzoniere* can be helpful in bringing these ideas home to students (Introduction 7–11). In addition, instructors can work with poems 1–5 to accustom students to reading for both the big picture and the pleasing detail. Generally, I have us work through these early poems as a class, tracking how they form a sort of introduction to the sequence by presenting the major tropes and themes to be elaborated over the course of the text. I ask the students to make notes about the following issues: in poem 1, the speaker ("Voi ch'ascoltate"), his sighs, the man transformed ("altr'uom"), the negative example; in poem 2, the assault by Eros; in poem 3, the *possente donna*; in poems 3–4, the month of April, during which watershed events take place, on both the liturgical calendar (the crucifixion, Easter)[2] and the autobiographical one that Petrarch constructs for himself across the spectrum of his writings (his first sighting of Laura [3, 211], Laura's death [336], his crowning as poet laureate). Finally, there are the themes of the lady as a gift from God to nature (4) and of the name Laura, or "LAU-RE-TA" (5), the cascade of syllables that introduces the fragmentation and elaboration by which Laura will be described throughout the text.[3]

Once we have worked together with these poems, I break students into pairs and have them locate as many of these initial themes as they can in poem 93. This exercise delivers quick results. It demonstrates how Petrarch's fragmented expression operates: in poem 93, for example, poem 1 reappears condensed into two lines ("Un tempo fu che 'n te stesso 'l sentivi, / volgare essempio a l'amoroso coro" 'There was a time when you experienced it yourself, a well-known example to the chorus of lovers' [lines 5–6]), and poems 3 and 23 are invoked fleetingly in the reference to the speaker's hardened heart and his conquest through his eyes ("et se' begli occhi ond'io me ti mostrai, / et là dove era il mio dolce ridutto / quando ti ruppi al cor tanta durezza" 'and if those lovely eyes in which I showed myself to you, where my sweet fortress was when I broke all the hardness of your heart' [9–11]) and in Love's triumphant declaration of his powers to effect metamorphosis ("come i miei seguaci discoloro / e 'n un momento gli fo morti et vivi" 'how I change the color of my followers and in one moment make them dead or alive' [3–4]).[4] This exercise also reinforces the idea of a narrative thread that runs through the entire text of the sequence, a thread that weaves together the suffering lover with the successful writer, as in poem 93: "Più volte Amor m'avea già detto: 'Scrivi, / scrivi'" 'Many times had Love already said to me: Write, write' (1–2).[5] From here it is possible to guide students to consider the unifying role played by the songs in punctuating and resuming the shorter poems. We can also begin to move forward through the sequence, examining other poems that mark important elements of the narrative: the theme of time (signaled both through reference to the duration of the speaker's love [74, 118, 122, 364] and through his protestations of eternal passion [55–57, 85–86]), the death of Laura (267–71), the pleasures of erotic obsession (161, 190, 205), the spread of the speaker's fame as a lover and poet (74, 93, 293, 318), and his "conversion" from his idolatrous love (365–66, viewed in the context of 55–57, 59–60, and 70).

Our work with poem 93 also demonstrates how to do a close reading of a poem. Having successfully analyzed that text, it is possible to instruct students to devote the same careful attention to pieces that are not as overtly narrative, so that they can begin to experience the delights of the *rime sparse*. Each reader has his or her own favorites. I enjoy showing students the startling visual effects of poems such as 12, 160, and 190, and two out of three of these poems establish the terms for subsequent Spanish works: the reference to Laura's hair as "l'oro terso et crespo" 'polished, curling gold' (160.14) prepares the way for a later reading of Luis de Góngora's sonnet "En crespa tempestad del oro undoso" ("In a curling tempest of undulating gold"). In poem 12 of the *Canzoniere*, students can uncover the hostility toward Laura that informs the trope of carpe diem and bear it in mind when they encounter sweeter versions of the theme in Garcilaso's sonnet 23, "En tanto que de rosa y azucena" ("While of the rose and the lily"), Góngora's "Mientras por competir con tu cabello" ("While competing with your hair") and "Ilustre y hermosísima María" ("Illustrious and most beautiful Maria"), and Francisco de Medrano's "Veré al tiempo tomar de ti, señora" ("I will see time take from you, my lady"). Poem 190 is not, to my knowledge, an object of direct imitation in the Spanish tradition (although the theme of the wounded deer appears, for example in Boscán's poem "Como el ventor que sigue al ciervo herido" ('Like the hunter who follows the wounded deer'), but it is striking on its own, has left an indelible mark in the English tradition through Sir Thomas Wyatt's "Whoso list to hunt," forms part of the Diana series in the *Canzoniere* (poems 23, 52), and hence merits attention.

Worlds of Difference

My primary focus in teaching the *Canzoniere* is on developing the theme of the "I," the lyric speaker who articulates a self-contained poetic universe that answers "a certain need where lyric and fiction intersect" when it is inherited and adapted by generations of poets to come (R. Greene 1). Speaking generally, our comparative readings of the *Canzoniere* and the Spanish tradition unfold under the rubrics of Roland Greene's "post-Petrarchism" and John Freccero's essay "The Fig Tree and the Laurel." Yet the tension between the "allegorical" and the "auto-reflexive" that Freccero identifies as a structuring element within the *Canzoniere* is far more elaborated in the Italian text than in its Spanish successors, primarily because of Petrarch's success, conditioned by the maturing of Renaissance humanism in the sixteenth century, in creating Laura/*lauro* as a "reified sign" capable of displacing the word as the endpoint of poetic discourse (26–27). For later writers, it is Petrarch's text, and not the Christian logos, that serves as the prop for a tradition of lyric sequences that turn almost exclusively on the elaboration of the self. But as a second qualification to Freccero's thesis, it is important, and profitable, to complicate the notion of Petrarch's speaker's "idolatrous" love. The structural analyses presented by Thomas Roche offer concrete, accessible points of entry into the *Canzoniere* (*Petrarch and the English Sonnet Sequence*), as well as solid platforms from which to think through both "the worlds of Petrarch" (Mazzotta, *Worlds*) and the fragmentation and transformation those worlds undergo as they are adopted into Spanish tradition.

Take, for example, the network of mythological allusion and reference as it is woven into the *Canzoniere* and then into Spanish texts. In explaining the classical mythology that informs both Petrarch and Petrarchism, targeted readings from Ovid, or from any compendium of Greek mythology, provide students with the backstory to how the structuring role played by the Apollo-Daphne-laurel story in the *Canzoniere* makes, on the most elementary plane, intertextual sense (as Petrarch "creates" himself as poet laureate by achieving perfection as the poet of the laurel, in poems such as 1, 5, 30, 34, 74, 293, and 318). By supplementing close readings of the poems with information about the commentaries on Ovid with which Petrarch would have been familiar and drawing on Roche's conception of interpretations by Boccaccio, Bersuire, and Petrarch himself (*Petrarch and the English Sonnet Sequence* 11–28), it is possible to link the poet's brilliant textual self-fashioning with contemporary cultural preoccupations on the Iberian Peninsula in a manner that draws a clearer picture of both Petrarch and his Spanish successors.

As an exercise to this end, I have students consider the similarities and differences between Garcilaso de la Vega's well-known sonnet 13, "A Dafne ya los brazos le crecían" ("Daphne's arms were already growing"), and Petrarch's laurel. As Roche points out, Petrarch's deployment of the Apollo-Daphne myth within the text of the *Canzoniere* inscribes Christian spiritual anguish at the same time that it opens the way toward exalted poetic success on the earthly plane. Building on Ovidian commentaries that link the laurel to the cross (*Petrarch and the English Sonnet Sequence* 21–22), Roche is able to argue that poem 4, which draws Laura together with the crucifixion, works with poem 5 to call attention to the hyperbolic terms in which Laura is praised in the sequence: "the extreme praise of this sonnet worries the poet. . . . He is using the mask of the grieving poet-lover to instruct the reader about the conflicting aims of *caritas* and *cupiditas*" (25). If this is the point of creating a "nexus" of Christ's and Laura's births in the early part of the sequence, as Roche argues, I suggest to my students that this nexus explains the passionate exclamation in the final tercet of Garcilaso's sonnet: "¡Oh miserable estado, o mal tamaño, / que con llorarla crezca cada día / la causa y la razón por que lloraba!" 'Oh miserable state, o great wrong, / that with lamenting her, each day it grows / the cause and the reason for which he weeps!' (lines 12–14). Here, as in the *Canzoniere*, a virtuoso poetic flourish (ending the sonnet with the paradox of the god's tears that water the tree, thereby causing it to grow in size—the Spanish word *tamaño*, in line 12, means "size") attracts and deflects attention to and from the metaphysical problem of the imbrication of sacred and profane love. For Garcilaso, as for Petrarch, the poetry that flows from the tradition of Daphne facilitates and sustains the erotic, as well as the Neoplatonic, gaze—and the vision of Daphne in Garcilaso's poem is markedly erotic, a compendium of golden hair, white feet, and beating "tiernos miembros" 'tender limbs' (line 6) that is rare within nonburlesque sixteenth-century Spanish Petrarchism, in which the technique of blazon is less common than it is in the Italian, French, and English traditions.[6]

It is this painful human truth, as much as it is the rigor of unfulfilled desire, that makes the poet-lover a miserable, wretched man, and in this way Garcilaso is true not only to the letter but also to the spirit of his precursor. At the same time, it is important to point out to students that specific themes and issues in Spanish Petrarchism do not receive the extended treatment that they do in the *Canzoniere*. Myths such as Diana and Actaeon (poems 23, 52) or Medusa (poems 51, 179) or the trope of metamorphoses are woven into the *Canzoniere* in ways that allow them to bear some of its structural weight.[7] In the Spanish tradition, mythological reference most often functions to demonstrate a given poet's knowledge of Ovid, not of Petrarch. (Garcilaso's sonnet 13 provides a possible exception, but we need to bear in mind that he may have learned his Petrarchan Daphne through conversation with Italian contemporaries.) To some extent, this difference has to do with the fragmentary nature of sixteenth- and seventeenth-century *imitatio*. Garcilaso did not write a sequence exploring the further dilemmas of the Christian lover. Boscán did, but his text was aimed at updating Petrarch to accommodate the new courtly vogue for a self-styled, Horatian-Senecan invulnerability—a project that, as interpreted by Boscán, involved replacing imagery with argument, not only because of the traditional Castilian influences mentioned above but also because of a healthy, Stoic suspicion of images as spurs to passion (Middlebrook, ch. 2).

This view did not spread much beyond Boscán. Garcilaso wove dense, evocative visual effects into a number of sonnets, as well as into his famous "Third Eclogue," and both the richly colored, self-consciously aesthetic poetry of Fernando de Herrera and the opulent, nested, encrusted baroque sonnets of Góngora, Francisco de Quevedo, and Medrano made use of Petrarchan topoi such as golden hair, eyes like suns and stars, necks and breasts like marble columns, and cheeks of pink and white like flowers (e.g., Herrera, "El oro crespo al aura desparzido" ["Curling gold, scattered before the dawn"] and "Rojo sol, que con hacha luminosa" ["Red sun, which with a shining brush"], as well as the poems by Garcilaso, Góngora, and Medrano already mentioned). Nevertheless, having introduced students to the problem of the sacred and the profane as it is broached in Petrarch, it is useful to lead them through Boscán's sequence to illustrate the effects of mid-sixteenth-century ideologies of *mediocritas* and courtiership as they condition his view of what Petrarchism should look like in Spain.

Boscán's Sequence

These effects are readily apparent. Boscán's speaker, like Petrarch's, struggles with his passions over the course of an extended lyric sequence made up of sonnets and songs; however, as Petrarchan as Boscán's text is in many respects (it follows a version of the trajectory of the *Canzoniere* and contains several close imitations of *rime*), it splits openly and self-consciously with Petrarch on the matter of erotic desire. In Petrarch's text, carnal desire is damning, even as it is supremely pleasurable; in Boscán's it is licit as long as it is not the stuff of passionate extremes. Hence, the turning point of Boscán's sequence is the juncture at which the speaker abandons the "tyrannical" love of his first mistress to take up with a second woman whose gentle return of his love leads to the shared, moderate joys of mutual sexual fulfillment.

Since Boscán's sequence is carefully crafted, this theme is presented systematically at both the beginning and the end of the text. Poems such as 36, "Quise amaros, Señora, de mi grado" ("I wished to love you, my lady, in my way"),[8] inscribe the theme, after a *Canzoniere*-style introduction to the figure of the speaker and his cautionary tale; two important poems that appear at the end of the text, numbers 115 and 116, "Antes terné que cante blandamente" ("I will maintain that in previous times I sang gently") and "Amor me envía un dulce sentimiento" ("Love sends to me a sweet sentiment" [based on *Canzoniere* 168]), conclude the narrative in the theme of passion transcended. Boscán calls attention to his swerves from both the Petrarchan and the Provençal traditions on which he has been drawing and from which he now wishes to distance himself. When his speaker announces, in poem 115, "sé que'n Amor no es término forzado / sólo escribir aquel que dolor siente" 'I know that in love, it is not a required term / that only he who feels pain may write' (lines 3–4), he is referring not only to the wretched verses of Ausias March but also to Petrarch. The reference becomes apparent when Boscán draws on the theme of eternal song in the shade of "algun" 'some' branch (not the highest or the strongest one that would have been sought by his illustrious precursor):

> Yo cantaré conforme a l'avezilla
> que canta así a la sombra de algun ramo.
> . . . .
> Así yo de ver quien me ama y a quien amo,
> en mi cantar tendré gozo contino (lines 9–10, 13–14)

I will sing in conformity with the little bird
who so sings in the shade of some branch.
. . . .
Thus I, by seeing whom I love and who loves me,
will take continuous joy in my song.

The theme continues in the following poem. Contented recipient of calm, uxorious love, Boscán's speaker concludes his narrative not by turning to the Virgin but instead by celebrating the appropriate minor miracle of harmony between lovers, which he symbolizes as the union of the laurel with the palm:

El milagro fue hecho extrañamente,
porque resucitando el mortal velo,
resucitó también la immortal alma.
Celebrado seré en toda la gente,
llevando en mi triunfo para el cielo,
con el verde laurel la blanca palma. (116.9–14)

The miracle was performed strangely,
because reviving the mortal veil,
the immortal soul, too, was revived.
I will be celebrated among all people,
raising to heaven, in my triumph,
the white palm with the green laurel.

After having worked so carefully with Petrarch's text, students are primed to find Boscán's sequence somewhat bizarre. Not only is the poetic language of the Spanish text devoid of much of the imagery and sensuality that is found in Petrarch, but poems such as 116 inscribe a strange rivalry on the issue of faith. The poem that corresponds to Boscán's 116 is Petrarch's 168, but whereas Petrarch's speaker doubts his redemption, Boscán's accepts it without question ("hace de esto fianza el pensamiento" 'my mind keeps faith on this' [line 5]). The discordant note as one compares the poems is struck by the apparent discrepancy in the stakes: Petrarch's speaker wrestles with the dilemma of the sacred and the profane, while Boscán's seems most desperate for rescue from a bad girlfriend.

What is important to drive home to students is the relative value assigned to earthly life in the two texts. The devotional language that is omnipresent in the Spanish sequence reflects the discourse of the particularly sixteenth-century Stoicism of which Boscán was an adherent. Informed by a modern type of Epicureanism, as well as by Christianity, this philosophy was directed toward living well, securing the good in this life through the practice of continence, moderation, and the avoidance of extremes. Among these extremes can be included profound, metaphysical experiences of conversion such as those that overtake Petrarch's speaker throughout the *Canzoniere*, culminating in the final turn to the Virgin in poems 365–66. With this in mind, my students and I compare Boscán's poems 67–70 with poems 55–65 in Petrarch, to which Boscán's clearly allude. The key to understanding the relation of the two groups, I tell students, lies in Boscán's poem 68, which opens, "Todo es amor en quien de verdad ama, / hasta el mudar que haze es mas firmeza" 'All is love in he who loves in truth / even in his change he is more steadfast.' The insistent repetition of "mudanza" that follows reflects the sort of wordplay that is traditional to Castilian verse, but it also signals the moderation of conversion, the transposition of the higher aims and boons of love into the register of worldly life. Petrarch, conversely, specifically rejects moderation in poem 65.

Building on this interpretation, it is possible to move beyond simple compare and contrast to observe how the different worldviews of Petrarch and Boscán create significantly different meanings for devotional poems such as *Canzoniere* 61, 154, and 159 and the versions of them that appear in Boscán's text, poems 79 and 80. From poem 59, Petrarch's speaker has embraced further spiritual torment by turning from the road to salvation and recommitting to his passion. He flirts with blasphemy when he cries:

> Bendetto sia 'l giorno e 'l mese et l'anno
> e la stagione . . .
> . . . ov'io fui giunto
> da' duo begli occhi. . . . (61.1–4)
>
> Blessed be the day and the month and the year and the season . . . where I was struck by the two lovely eyes. . . .

Boscán's speaker, however, has changed his desire and taken up a mode of loving that will sustain him through the end of the sequence. Hence, his calling down nearly identical blessings in the tercets of poem 79 can be understood as his engaging in a form of Neoplatonism, celebrating the woman who has saved him from peril.

Additional Poems

There are numerous additional points of contact between the *Canzoniere* and the Spanish Petrarchan tradition. The above is not intended as a survey of source poems for the tradition of Spanish Petrarchism; most editions of early modern Spanish writers include that information in footnotes. Rather, I have presented a highly personal view of elements in the *Canzoniere* that teach well in a Spanish classroom. A few additional poems that are important to bear in mind for this enterprise are *Canzoniere* 298; 132; 35, 145, and 126; and 23 and 105. Petrarch's poem 298 is the source for Garcilaso's sonnet 1, "Cuando me paro a contemplar mi estado" ("When I stop to consider my state"); Garcilaso's poem is, in turn, the model for numerous Spanish imitations, including the inaugural poem of Lope de Vega's *Rimas sagradas*. It is worthwhile to alert students to its source, as well as to the centrality of "passos," or steps, to the Spanish tradition. Similarly, *Canzoniere* 132 mirrors the types of wordplay and conundrum popular in traditional Castilian *cancionero* verse, and its theme of "no sé que" ("I know not what") is omnipresent especially in the poetry of Boscán and the Sevillian Cetina. Petrarch's poems 35 and 145 have direct imitations in Boscán, as does poem 126 (Boscán's interest in poem 145 likely derived from the Horace that was Petrarch's source text; 145 also is cited in Garcilaso's "First Song"). Garcilaso's sonnet 22 ends with a version of line 34 of *Canzoniere* 23, "non essermi passato oltra la gonna" 'had [not] gone beyond my garment,' while an otherwise negligible sonnet by Cetina, "Al pie de un monte que divide a España" ("At the foot of a mountain that divides Spain"), concludes with a version of line 17 of *Canzoniere* 105, "intendami chi può" 'understand me who can.' All these Spanish poems are canonical and will likely make an appearance on an undergraduate syllabus. Read in conjunction with the *Canzoniere*, they illustrate the wide range of *conceptos esparcidos* ("scattered concepts") that constitute Petrarch's legacy to Spain.

NOTES

[1]On Boscán and the so-called *cancionero* poetry, see Lapesa.

[2]On the role of the liturgical calendar in the *Canzoniere*, see Durling, Introduction; Roche, *Petrarch and the English Sonnet Sequences*.

[3]On Laura as "scattered woman," see Vickers, "Diana."

[4]All quotations from the *Canzoniere* are from Durling's bilingual edition.

[5]Note that poem 93 is the model for Boscán's song "Gran tiempo ha que amor me dice, 'scrive'" ("For a long time, love has said to me, 'write'").

[6]When blazons do appear in these poems, they tend to be less charged, as in Cetina's "Por esta faz, por esta bella mano" ("By this face, by this lovely hand"); see the excellent anthologies of erotic verse edited by Alzieu, Jammes, and Lissorgues and by Diez Fernández.

[7]On the role of Diana and Actaeon, see Vickers, "Diana"; see also Freccero 30–31. References to the Medusa build up the theme of the speaker's "petrification" and thus offer to link the *rime sparse* with the *rime petrose*.

[8]Note that poem 36 is actually the seventh of the sequence. In most critical editions, Boscán's poems are numbered continuously, beginning with his traditional Castilian verses; for this reason the sequence, which makes up the second book of his collected works, begins with poem 29.

Exploring Petrarchan Subjectivity in the Early Modern French Lyric

Deborah Lesko Baker

Writing about teaching the Petrarchan lyric tradition in early modern French poetry carries a special and paradoxical charge. The seven-hundredth anniversary of Petrarch's birth felicitously coincided with a flourishing of scholarly studies on Petrarchism in male- and female-authored Renaissance texts.[1] At the same time, the realities of the classroom—at least in my experience and at my institution—appear to confirm that poetry in general, and poetry from premodern periods in particular, is increasingly unfamiliar to and holds limited initial attraction for many students. This frequent resistance to the study of poetry and the tendency to embrace the literary production of the present and recent past over that of the more distant past are by no means new phenomena. They have, however, assumed importance over the past twenty years as learning paradigms continue to become more multidisciplinary and technologized and less tied to the culture of reading—especially the close reading and attention to language that remain the keys to unlocking the mysterious and enduring potency of poetic texts. For me, then, the double and ongoing challenge, as a teacher of early modern poetry is to find ways to activate the intellectual excitement that can come from this type of intensive reading and to rediscover the core connections that link the writings of a fourteenth-century Florentine and his French descendants to the inner lives and struggles of individuals in the here and now. I believe, with the late Elaine Marks, that students who commit to embarking on this now less-traveled path will continue to be excited by the magic of words and the inescapable dilemma of mortality—notions that enable them "to engage with beauty, desire, and death" and with "what gives pleasure and what gives pain without rewards and without remedies" (2).

Desire, Gender, and Lyric in Early Modern France

Over the past twenty years I have developed and reworked a French literature course that teaches the sixteenth-century French lyric specifically through the lens of Petrarch's *Canzoniere*. This course has been presented under several titles, partly to reflect refinements in my approach and partly to respond to the growing practical need to interest a student constituency in taking that first uneasy step into the early modern classroom. Although in honor of Petrarch's septicentennial, I offered my course as a senior seminar called The Petrarchan Lyric Legacy in Early Modern France, the title of its more recent iteration, Desire, Gender, and Lyric in Early Modern France, captures the three key notions guiding my approach in a formulation more successful at attracting students' initial curiosity.

In the most overarching terms, I center my semester-long study on Petrarch's innovative articulation of a complex, desiring self in response to the love experience and the adaptations of that self among his French male and female imitators. This focus provides a rich thematic and rhetorical base extending even to modern and contemporary verse, as well as a point of contact with modern psychological or existential perspectives and with conceptions about love in both high and popular culture to which contemporary students can relate. My course aims above all to illuminate the early modern French lyric subject, whether male or female, through a study of the multifaceted phenomenon of desire—and in so doing, to engage students in the powerful process of self-creation and self-representation engendered by poetic writing. A second and no less important goal is to cultivate—through an interactive discussion workshop format—those skills in close reading and textual analysis that will make this illumination and subsequent engagement possible. With the exception of the introductory presentations and occasional synthesizing remarks I make on each author, this sustained guided-discussion format constitutes the base of my teaching methodology.

In advance of specifics on the readings and issues I choose to highlight, the following overview of the course content and its progression may be helpful. We begin with Petrarch himself, prioritizing the development of a privileged, if anguished, selfhood in selected sonnets from the *Canzoniere*. This foundational point of departure then leads to an examination of the ways in which each French poet under consideration defines his or her erotic, artistic, or historical identity and consciousness through the vehicle of the poetic speaking voice. I generally work with the short poetry of the most salient French Petrarchan imitators in the sixteenth century: Maurice Scève, Louise Labé, Joachim Du Bellay, and Pierre de Ronsard; however, one could certainly choose to extend the study to others such as Clément Marot, Pernette du Guillet, Pontus de Tyard, Antoine de Baïf, and Olivier de Magny.

I have found it particularly effective to focus student attention first on the beginnings of the poets' respective lyric sequences and their immediate positioning of the lyric speaker in respect to the tortured, self-turned posture of the Petrarchan lover. Although the lyric speakers in Scève's *Délie* and Labé's *Sonnets* differ sharply in their psychic reaction to the Petrarchan *innamoramento*—the destabilizing onset of love—we discover how they share Petrarch's tendency to give priority to the existential register of their subjective experience. In contrast, we explore how Du Bellay and Ronsard, in the inaugural poems of the *Antiquitez de Rome* and the *Regrets* and of the *Amours de Cassandre*, respectively, resituate their self-absorption—either in response to the love experience (Ronsard) or in response to historical change and succession (Du Bellay)—at the level of the poetic act itself. We then move on to determine in the progression of these poetic sequences the ways and extent to which the selfhood or ontology of the Petrarchan lyric speaker is confirmed, subverted, or transcended. Just as additional writers could be envisioned in this framework, so obviously could other sequences by the core poets I study—most notably Ronsard's *Sonnets sur la mort de Marie* and *Sonnets pour Hélène*, Du Bellay's *Olive*, and Labé's three elegies.

Specific Readings and Discussion Topics

I assign very small amounts of poetry (one or two poems per fifty-minute session) for in-depth analysis in class and more (twenty to thirty additional poems in all) for overview reading, general discussion, and eventual selection of texts for individual papers. Since the course is oriented toward critical thinking, analysis, and imagination and since I teach upper-level undergraduates, I require little secondary reading. But even were I giving the course as a graduate seminar, although I would recommend an extensive bibliography of secondary works as well as a much broader spectrum of poems, my in-class focus would remain on each student's connection to selected primary texts—especially given that many of these texts represent virgin territory for graduate as well as undergraduate students.

Petrarch

For Petrarch's *Canzoniere*, I have typically reproduced and assigned the readings from Robert Durling's classic 1976 edition with prose translations.[2] Mark Musa's 1996 edition with verse translations is another excellent choice and provides contextual and lexical notes for each poem. To supplement the background on Petrarch's life and works provided in class, I recommend the pertinent chapters of Thomas Bergin's concise 1970 critical biography, *Petrarch*.

In our central study of the celebrated inaugural sonnet, "Voi ch'ascoltate in rime sparse" ("You who hear in scattered rhymes"), I prioritize the speaker's renowned focus on the ontology and integrity of his own self by encouraging students to identify the multiple layers of tension and opposition in the poem: the former man versus the new man; the perception of self versus the perception of others; the assertion of powerful and conflicted emotions versus the assertion of clear and rational thinking. In the context of these tensions we examine the key polyvalence of the speaker's self-admitted "errore" 'error' as both moral and spiritual failing and as a more generalized psychic wandering or divagation from a stable path. We then interrogate the rich network of diction that illuminates each of these ontological issues not only as preoccupations of the opening sonnet but as preoccupations played out in a number of settings and at a number of points of his itinerary. Among the stagings of affective conflict, spiritual turmoil, and psychic instability that students enjoy exploring are the first violent presentation of the actual *innamoramento* (*Canzoniere* 2); the speaker's appropriation of an old man's disillusioning Roman pilgrimage to view Veronica's handkerchief (16); the flight of the alienated speaker—"Solo et pensoso" ("Alone and filled with care")—from society (35); the classic presentation of the lover in the prey of oxymoronic vacillations (134); and the explosion of his contradictory emotions into internal war ("guerra è 'l mio stato" 'war is my state') against the backdrop of cosmic nocturnal tranquility—with its inescapable recognition of the beloved's paradoxical power to wound and heal, to destroy and to redeem (164).

In following the speaker's spiritual voyage in the sonnets after Laura's death (*in morte*), we move to investigate stagings of the lover's crushing confrontation with mortality as another catalyst of psychic trauma, as in the metaphoric dramatization of the sea storm and dismasted ship (272) and the poignantly reverent fragmentation and disintegration of Laura's body set against a parallel disintegration of poetic power experienced by the speaker (292). Finally, we evaluate the levels of dynamic displacement in play in the final sonnet (365) and final canzone (366), where the speaker's spatial perspective ascends heavenward, his temporal perspective turns toward a celestial future, and he calls on the figures of Christ and the Virgin Mary to forgive the failings provoked by his indomitable and maligned human desire—and to provide the presence and the responses that the beloved Laura could not. This embrace of a compensatory, overtly religious transcendence as the poet's concluding posture provides a fascinating point of comparison with his French descendants.

Maurice Scève

Scève was the first French poet to undertake Petrarch's global project in the *Canzoniere*: the composition of an entire sequence of love poems to a single deified female figure. Given this important fact of literary history, and because, in my view, Scève remains the closest in temperament to his Italian predecessor among his French peers, I turn to the *Délie* immediately after the unit on Petrarch. The challenge posed by this adherence to chronology is that Scève's poetry is lexically and syntactically much more difficult than that of either his Lyonnais or Pléiade counterparts, and so it is crucial to approach excerpts from his 449 ten-line poems (*dizains*) deliberately, patiently, and with appropriate reference aids. For Scève, as well as for Labé, Du Bellay, and Ronsard, I order the well-known Gallimard-Poésie edition, which features modernized French spellings, a useful glossary, and some helpful, although very limited, notes.[3] In addition, I place I. D. McFarlane's classic 1966 edition of the *Délie* (in the original Middle French) on reserve, requiring students to read the ninety-two-page introduction for basic grounding and strongly encouraging them to consult the substantial notes on problems of allusion, diction, and syntax in each poem. I also place on reserve the 1611 Cotgrave French-English print dictionary (now also available electronically [http://www.pbm.com/~lindahl/cotgrave/]), for particularly thorny lexical questions, as well as several mythological dictionaries and manuals; these items then serve as supports for the study not only of Scève but of Labé, Du Bellay, and Ronsard as well.

The *Délie*'s two-pronged beginning, including the dedicatory *huitain* (eight-line poem) and the opening *dizain*, provides a rich set of similarities and divergences in respect to Petrarch's inaugural sonnet and sonnet 2's announcement of the *innamoramento*. In these two Scève poems I invite the students to explore such issues as the reformulations of Petrarchan *errore*, in both of its semantic dimensions; the revisiting of desire as a mistrusted and victimizing phenomenon; the raising of Love's first attack to a more violent and hyperbolic level; the identification of the beloved with an "Idole," a term infused with multiple and at times contradictory meanings in sixteenth-century French; and, finally, Scève's mysterious invocation of "deaths" catalyzed by the beloved as the subject of his volume.

We then try to situate and understand this figuration of plural deaths in the sequence by exploring such phenomena as the speaker's propensity for repeating the scene of love's onset (in *dizains* such as 6, 212, and 388) and its possible theoretical relationship to the Freudian repetition compulsion, as well as the speaker's unnamed but unmistakable identification with the character of Ovid's Narcissus and his Neoplatonic avatars—an identification reengaging the familiar Petrarchan features of inaccessible love, psychic contradiction, anguished self-absorption, and eventual death (60). Scève's dramatic appropriation in *dizain* 98 of the Petrarchan lover's tortured isolation from the rhythms and harmonies of the external universe provides a useful stepping-stone to poems that paint the affective turmoil and alienation of Scève's speaker in ways even more extreme than the portrayal of instability in the *Canzoniere*. We focus in particular on how the images of the "ténèbres" 'shadows' in *dizain* 129 and the "gouffre" 'abyss' in *dizain* 164 depict a disordering of the self so radical as to figure yet another type of metaphoric death. Yet however visceral these figurations of disorientation and loss may be, they give way to a nonlinear but nonetheless perceptible evolution near the end of the volume toward a more positive reconstruction of the speaker's experience. We analyze markers of this subtle evolution such as the speaker's use of positive metaphors reflecting his grasp of the beloved as an authentic and salutary spiritual presence (378); the affirmation that he can re-create himself out of his suffering (409) and that detachment over time can bring new clarity to the memory of his experience (434); the realization that although emotional wars and suffering will not cease, they can paradoxically coexist with a new sense of peace and moments of joy (446); and the occasional incorporation of first-person plural references (*nous* and *notre*) embracing the beloved and the reader in a dynamic vision of future survival and unification in a higher sphere (449). The goal is to suggest that if the final recourse to the rhetoric of Petrarchan dynamism posits the positive hope for transcendence, it does so not through a plea for any overtly religious intervention or salvation but through a recognition of the paradoxically redemptive power of suffering.

Louise Labé

After the intense representations of male subjectivity in the love poetry of Petrarch and Scève, the progression to the female voice of Labé provides a striking change in perspective. The fundamental question that I ask students to consider throughout their reading of her twenty-four love sonnets is, as Juliana Schiesari puts it, "[W]hat happens . . . if we have a woman writing in the Petrarchan tradition and the roles are reversed, that is, the 'I' that speaks is the 'I' of a woman?" ("Appropriating" 168). The fact that Labé's inaugural sonnet is written in Italian produces an immediate interest in how what seems an overt homage to her Italian predecessor might also introduce a departure from certain elements of his tradition. We examine how the reminiscences of Petrarchan diction in the poem—from the divinization of the beloved, to Cupid's visual attack, to the paradoxical embodiment of the love experience in the wounding and healing powers of the scorpion image—are nonetheless framed by two transgressive suggestions. The opening reference to Ulysses, presented as a negation, provides a rich terrain of discussion in terms of both the hero's arduous but ultimately un-Petrarchan journey back to fulfilled conjugal union and the denial to his male wisdom of any privileged status in the face of what for Labé is the equalizing and universalizing force of love. Likewise, the highlighting of the impassioned negative imperative at the end of the poem—"Non estingua el desir a me si caro, / Che mancar non potrà ch'i' non mi muoia" '[Do not] extinguish the burning I crave to feel, / this desire whose broken life would break my own'—alerts students immediately to Labé's positive validation and embrace of a desire portrayed as dangerous and even sinful by her Petrarchan male model.

I try to increase students' awareness of the various ways that the female subject seeks to empower herself as a desiring subject throughout the sequence: by unashamedly reaching out for the solidarity of her earthly or celestial female counterparts (2, 5, 24); by amusingly turning the tables and invoking praise for the male body through the same fragmentary process (related to the popular Renaissance genre of the *blason*) by which male poets conventionally praise the female beloved (2, 10, 21); and, most of all, by creating scenarios of shared physical and spiritual love—whether envisioned, remembered, or achieved. Here we spend one full class session on close analysis of each sonnet in Labé's famous trilogy—the fantasy in sonnet 13, "Oh si j'etois en ce beau sein ravie" ("Oh, if I were taken to that handsome breast"); the struggle to sustain memory and self-expression in sonnet 14, "Tant que mes yeux pourront larmes espandre" ("While my eyes can still pour out fountains of tears"); and the celebration of mutual love in the here and now in sonnet 18, "Baise m'encor, rebaise moy et baise" ("Kiss me again, rekiss me, and then kiss me again"). We strive in these readings to focus not only on the reversals of Petrarchan self-absorption and attitudes toward desire but also on the clever subversions of Petrarchan and Scèvian diction, including the semantic transformations of the images of storm (sonnet 13), weeping (14), and psychic instability (18); the proliferation of pronouns and verbs reflecting communication and reciprocity (13 and 18); and the systematic and courageous refusal of any transcendent or otherworldly emotional impulse or rhetoric.

Joachim Du Bellay

As seductive as these evolving amatory discourses may be, I find at this point that a hiatus from love poetry is welcome and that the class is mystified but intrigued by how such ostensibly different and austere public lyrics such as Du Bellay's *Antiquitez de Rome* and *Regrets* might share in certain Petrarchan paradigms and obsessions. I ask students to reflect on how, in the broadest sense, Du Bellay's speaker faces a crisis analogous to that of his grieving counterparts. For the *Antiquitez*, the common thematic paradigm is loss, separation, and inaccessibility transposed to the level of cultural displacement and the attendant anachronistic shock of viewing the ruins of Rome against the image of their former grandeur. In the dedicatory poem to King Henry II and the opening sonnet, we examine how the speaker dramatizes this anachronistic shock and posits wishful remedies to resuscitate antique glory by relying on two different artistic strategies. In the prefatory "Au Roy" ("To the King"), I try to communicate how the poet's opening assertion of his inability to transport the vestiges of Roman architecture into the king's Renaissance chateaux might be akin to admitting these days that it would be futile to transport the Pantheon into the Trump Tower. In the face of such disorienting impossibility, we explore how the speaker tries to offer his vernacular poetry as a metaphoric architecture to rebuild and reconstitute the antique past. In sonnet 1, on the other hand, we follow the poet's frustration as he tries to bridge the gap to the past by calling out directly to the "Divins esprits" 'divine spirits of antiquity' and, in so doing, paints a scene of such profound distance and difficulty that we find him literally screaming into the "Abysmes" 'Abysses' in an attempt to make himself heard. Here his only poetic recourse is to pronounce magical incantations and expressions of religious awe through which he pledges to carry onward the glory of the past.

Other fruitful forays into the *Antiquitez* include the anthology favorite sonnet 3, "Nouveau venu qui cherches Rome en Rome" ("Newcomer, you who seek Rome in Rome"), in which the repeated plays on the word "Rome" dramatize the fact that the contemporary signifier is no longer coextensive with its mythical signified. This slippage between desire and reality recalls the Petrarchan speaker's lamentable comparison of himself to the old pilgrim in their common futile search for the Lord's or the beloved's "disiata vostra forma vera" 'longed-for true form' (*Canzoniere* 16.14). More reminiscent still of the Petrarchan *camino* ("path" or "journey") is Du Bellay's recasting in sonnet 5 of Petrarch's widely imitated sonnet "Chi vuol veder" ("Whoever wishes to see"; *Canzoniere* 248), where the exaltation of the female beloved is transposed onto Rome—that is, until the city is shown to be but a shadow of its former self that can only be raised from its tomb, once again, by the magical incantation of its ancient writings "font errer" 'made to wander' as a Scèvian "Idole" ("statue" and "fantasm") throughout the world (line 14). I draw the students' attention to the displacement of *errer*, an ontological term typically used to evoke the psychic instability of the Petrarchan speaker, and try to analyze with them the impact of Du Bellay's projection of this wandering onto the personified "Idole" of his loss.

Finally, this suggestion of a troubled afterlife for classical civilization enables us to see later in the *Antiquitez* that the poet is dealing not only with the past and present Rome but also with his conflicted attitude toward his parent cultures—both classical and Italian—a conflict posed in almost oedipal terms in sonnet 31 as the arming of "le propre gendre encontre son beau-père" 'the son-in-law against his own father-in-law' (line 11). Likewise, this notion provides an excellent segue to a short study of sonnets 1 and 4 of Du Bellay's *Regrets*, where the poet famously expresses his blatant and repeated disdain to continue the filial path of imitation. Here students enjoy identifying how the poet almost systematically subverts and deconstructs the very images through which he majestically fashions his poetics of ruins—most notably in a reversal in which those daunting "Abysmes ouvers" 'opened Abysses' of the *Antiquitez* become sealed over as the "Abysmes couvers" 'covered Abysses' of the *Regrets*.

An important question to pose at this point is whether the poet's open rejection of the fundamental humanist imitative enterprise—which he follows by a lament over lost poetic inspiration—is to be believed. Focusing on the presentation of vanished inspiration in sonnets 6 and 13 of the *Regrets*, we explore how the poetic speaker enters into the paradox of revolting against imitation through the very process of imitating. Moreover, it is once again the Petrarchan intertext that surges into play. For these two poems, I ask students to speak to the proliferation of images and motifs that depict the relationship of the speaker to his own lost muse in terms similar to the relationship of the Petrarchan poet to his inaccessible beloved. These include the "flight" of the female muse beyond the speaker's grasp ("Et les Muses de moi, comme étranges, s'enfuient" 'And the Muses, like strangers, flee from me' [sonnet 6, line 14]), the crisis of self portrayed in terms of erring and storms, the reliance on oxymoronic rhetoric—including a return to the paradoxical wounding-healing image of the scorpion—and the familiar dynamic of mistress and slave. Moreover, the transposition of Petrarchan love paradigms into a figuration of artistic impotence, along with the paradoxical worship and disillusionment in respect to Rome's past, is accompanied by the speaker's bitter sense of exclusion from his mother country and French poetic compatriots, as expressed in the well-known sonnet 9, "France, mère des arts, des armes, et des lois" ("France, mother of arts, of arms, and of laws"). These forms of exile reveal the poignant sense of alienation that we have come to associate with the fundamental Petrarchan mentality of dissatisfaction and loss.

Pierre de Ronsard

A final return to love poetry in the *Amours* of Ronsard often provokes unexpected reactions from students. If they have encountered any early modern poetry, let alone any by Ronsard, usually they have read "Ode à Cassandre" and "Quand vous serez bien vieille, au soir, à la chandelle" ("When you are very old, sitting in the evening by candlelight beside the fire"), from *Amours pour Hélène.* We do study these poems at the very conclusion of the course, along with Andrew Marvell's "To His Coy Mistress," and students enjoy the refiguration of Petrarch's agonizing sense of the passage of time into scenarios of the ephemeral engaging the strategies of seduction and persuasion for which Ronsard is so famous. But the pleasure experienced in these familiar texts is accompanied by a sense of their limited emotional depth and a preference for where and how we can read Ronsard in a more compelling way in respect to the Petrarchan lyric tradition. This sense also comes through at the very beginning of our study of Ronsard, where an analysis of the *Amours de Cassandre*'s prefatory poem, "Voeu" ("Prayerful wish"), reveals not visceral interrogation of internal struggle or existential crisis on the part of the speaker but rather the narcissistic invocation of a partnership with the muses in which he has become their leader and commands them to inscribe his poetic immortality on their altars.

I suggest to my students that it is not uncommon to feel, after reading Petrarch, Scève, Labé, and even Du Bellay, a certain attenuation of emotion or even a certain superficiality in Ronsard and that we will have to look for different modalities through which to understand and evaluate this poet's recasting of the Petrarchan model—at least in the volume to Cassandre. Moreover, since several sonnets early on in the volume tend to rehearse standard Petrarchan motifs without any substantive innovation, I propose that two promising and related registers in which to explore Ronsard's departure from the Petrarchan temperament lie in his use of mythology and in his reworking of the *blason* tradition centering on specific female body parts. One might say of sonnets 41 and 94, for example, that Ronsard's speaker is entranced by his beloved's hair, not as an evocation of distant angelic light, but rather as a sensual, organic, growing, and changing emblem of her erotic body—one that is savored by the speaker with exuberance and without shame. If the description of his own "déesse" 'goddess' wrapping herself in her tresses repaints the Botticellian birth of Venus, the speaker suggests that his appreciation of the female body comes out of an imaginative incorporation of its images in natural, human, and mythological spheres.

Our centerpiece for Ronsard's use of mythology is sonnet 20, "Je voudrais bien richement jaunissant" ("How I wish I could turn a rich yellow"), in which the speaker attempts to evade the reality of Cassandre's unattainability by imaginatively appropriating a series of mythical self-transformations that enable him to unite with her. Students work on examining the tales of Jupiter and Danae, Jupiter and Europa, and Narcissus, as well as the overall rhetoric of metamorphosis in the poem, to appreciate how the speaker once again seamlessly amalgamates the realms of the natural, the erotic, and the cosmic to empower himself and to effectuate an oneiric consummation of passion unmarred by personal psychic rupture. This occurs, however, in a way that maintains the privileging of the male subject and thus diverges from Labé's dream of mutual erotic union and expression. Equally fascinating is sonnet 160, "Or que Jupin espoint de sa semence" ("Now when Jupiter, excited by his virility"), in which cosmic and natural images of fertility, sensuality, and flow are juxtaposed, almost competitively, against allusions to the Petrarchan lover's internal drama of anguish and loss. This juxtaposition can stimulate an awareness that one of Ronsard's richest contributions to his tradition is in proposing an alternative to this conflicted Petrarchan universe, one based on the energizing potential and fertile interconnections between all possible dimensions of being in the world.

Class Work and Independent Work

To accomplish the above itinerary in a format that is predominantly discussion-based, the level and quality of student preparation is clearly crucial—and it weighs heavily (fifty percent) in the final evaluation for the course. But my assigning small numbers of poems for intensive analysis in class does not ensure students' readiness to participate in fruitful dialogue, because the natural tendency, particularly given the complexity of the genre, is to skim fairly passively over the surface of the text. Thus my course has two requirements designed to promote substantive preparation of the one or two poems to be discussed in each class session. First, I ask that students identify and resolve to the fullest extent possible before class all issues of unfamiliar vocabulary, including mythological or other allusions, consulting as necessary not only their French or French-English dictionaries but also the resources on library reserve. Second, to engage students in active rather than passive reading, I require the submission of a journal entry, not to exceed one page, responding to the assigned poems. There are no particular directives for the journal assignments, and I am lenient in my evaluation of them; however, I do write comments and return these reflections on a daily basis and often refer to them in class, so the students know that I am also responding actively to their efforts. My experience has been that the additional work involved for the instructor is more than worth it, simply because one observes from day to day and week to week that students (even the more timid among them) arrive in class with something to say and can move quickly and comfortably to deeper and more sophisticated levels of conversation.

In addition to the regular journals, I ask students to write two formal papers of five or more pages focusing on the intensive analysis of a single poem—generally a *dizain* from Scève's *Délie* at the midterm and a sonnet by Labé, Du Bellay, or Ronsard at the end of the semester. Students choose and submit to me in advance a poem that has not been discussed in class but that has been part of the assigned overview reading. Since I have found, especially in the last several years, that many students have never written an analytic essay on a single poem, I distribute and discuss a set of directives on how they might proceed.

Instead of adhering to any rigid formulas concerning what such an explication de texte must look like, I try to provide some flexible and inclusive guidance on the various stages—prewriting, writing, and postwriting—through which they will work. I suggest that they annotate primary readings (diction and syntax), secondary readings (thematics and rhetorical strategies), and tertiary readings (rhythm, sound, and form) that will best precede the act of writing. I also make recommendations for composing and structuring the paper and offer advice for presenting the best possible final essay through active and productive proofreading of the content (argument and analysis) and the written French. In addition, given what has become the "newness" of this type of assignment and also the extreme difficulty of Scève, a week before submission of the first paper—and after everyone has completed the three sets of preliminary readings mentioned above—I meet for forty-five minutes to an hour with each student to discuss his or her ideas, questions, problems, and an overall drafting plan for the essay. Once again, although time-consuming, these meetings are most often mutually rewarding on the academic and personal levels. In conjunction with the broader dialogue in class, this one-on-one dialogue helps students work toward developing a strong critical voice, both orally and in writing, and enhances their depth of connection with the power of language in the communication of human experience.

NOTES

[1]Among the book-length studies devoted primarily to Petrarch and Petrarchism published since 1990 are Braden, *Petrarchan Love*; Cervigni; Dubrow; R. Greene; Kennedy, *Authorizing* and *Site*; Lesko Baker; Mazzotta, *Worlds*; Moore; Sturm-Maddox, *Ronsard*. Books published after 1990 in which Petrarch and his tradition form a significant component include Enterline; Holmes; A. Jones; Reiss; Rigolot; and Yandell. Thomas M. Greene's groundbreaking *The Light in Troy*, although published in 1982, remains indispensable. I wish to acknowledge here my profound debt both to his work and to his pedagogy in my readings and teaching of the Petrarchan tradition.

[2]I use Durling's bilingual edition for all quotations from Petrarch. Translations of lines by Labé, Du Bellay, and Ronsard are by Annie Finch, Richard Helgerson, and Malcolm Quainton and Elizabeth Vinestock, respectively. Translations of individual words or phrases are my own.

[3]Should the context of the course benefit from accompanying English translations, I recommend the following bilingual editions: Sieburth (for Scève), Lesko Baker (for Labé), Helgerson (for Du Bellay), and Quainton and Vinestock (for Ronsard).

English Petrarchism

William J. Kennedy

Here I suggest strategies for teaching English Petrarchan poetry, whose pleasures in relation to Petrarch's *Canzoniere* may at first elude many if not most undergraduate students. I do not assume students' resistance to this poetry. To the contrary, once students uncover its expansive richness, they become perceptive readers of its paradoxes, ironies, wit, depth of emotion, and dramatic complexity. And if they have at least a nascent sense of history, they can understand how this poetry might express social, cultural, political, economic, and intellectual concerns that ramify even today.

You may be teaching the poetry of English Petrarchism in a survey of British literature, using perhaps anthologies of English literature published by Norton (Greenblatt et al., *Norton Anthology*), Longman (Damrosch and Dettmar), or Oxford (Hollander and Kermode). Or you may be teaching it in a majors' course devoted to the English Renaissance, using an anthology of sixteenth-century English poetry and prose (the separate "period" volume of Norton [Greenblatt et al., *Sixteenth Century*] or Longman [Carroll and Hadfield]; Rollins and Baker) or using individual prose texts alongside an anthology of sixteenth-century English poetry (Braden, *Sixteenth-Century Poetry*; Norbrook and Woudhuysen; E. Jones; Sylvester). From an instructor's perspective, there's a trove of broad surveys, specialized studies, and bibliographic aids too vast to enumerate here. I recommend the following as particularly relevant, accessible, and helpful: Patrick Cheney and Anne Lake Prescott's *Approaches to Teaching Shorter Elizabethan Poetry*; Cheney, Andrew Hadfield, and Garrett Sullivan's *Early Modern English Poetry*; Cheney's *Reading Sixteenth-Century Poetry*; Heather Dubrow's *Echoes of Desire*; Robin Kirkpatrick's *Dante to Shakespeare*; and Alistair Fox's *English Renaissance*, as well as those mentioned below.

Getting Students Started

The story that I like to tell about English Petrarchism concerns the many kinds of Petrarchism available to writers and readers in sixteenth-century England. To students, Petrarchan poetry might seem confined to a limited set of themes and motifs (usually amatory, often moralistic), conveyed through familiar recycled figures and tropes. But I want students to discover that there are multiple Petrarchs and competing forms of Petrarchism. The vehicle for this discovery is the poetry itself, supercharged texts that advertise their uniqueness, as well as quieter texts that, on close reading, reveal exceptional charm. I begin with the notion of multiple Petrarchs because the poet's personae can easily be documented by commentaries framing his vernacular poetry in early printed editions (e.g., Richardson; Pettegree; Kennedy, *Authorizing*). Students are intrigued to learn that Petrarch's *Canzoniere*—highly stylized and, to them, consisting of many poems that may seem indistinguishable among themselves—generated so many controversial interpretations. Students see, however, that an accumulation of ideas about Petrarch and his poetry appealed to readers and poetic imitators in different ways at different times and in different places. These ideas range from Petrarch as the subject of northern Italian despotic patrons to Petrarch as a classical scholar and rediscoverer of classical antiquity, from Petrarch as aggressive lover of Laura to Petrarch as a passive slave to his passions.

In addition to being mediated by critical commentaries, Petrarch's European reception was mediated by both the visual and musical arts. Simone Martini's lost portrait of Laura, recounted in Petrarch's sonnets 77 and 78, stimulated the efforts of such painters as Giorgione (*Laura* [1506], Vienna, Kunsthistorisches Museum) and Titian (*La bella* [1536], Florence, Pitti Palace) to render a likeness of the Petrarchan beloved. Raphael, in his idealized version (*La donna velata* [1516], Florence, Pitti Palace), and Agnolo Bronzino, in his portrait of the Petrarchan poet Laura Battiferri (*Portrait* [1555], Florence, Palazzo Vecchio), depict their subjects holding a slim volume of the *Rime sparse* (see Mirollo). These and other paintings—available for downloading and presenting on *Web Gallery of Art*—influenced the engravings of Laura, and of Petrarch, that began to appear in printed editions of the *Canzoniere* published in Venice by Gabriel Giolito in 1538 and 1544–60 and by Jean de Tournes in Lyon in 1545 (Fowler 96–99). The resulting profusion of illustrations shaped readers' ideas about Laura and Petrarch and, in turn, their reception of the poetry.

The same goes for sixteenth-century music. Beginning in Venice in the 1540s with the madrigals of Cipriano da Rore and Adrian Willart, Petrarchan poems lent themselves to musical settings that express sentiments of longing, fulfillment, or mourning in imitative styles (Feldman; L. Perkins). English Renaissance music developed these styles, offering competing forms of expression in madrigals, songs, and airs for single- or multivoice performance (Donington; Fischlin). (Students can listen to digital recordings of compositions by John Dowland, Thomas Ravenscroft, Henry Lawes, and others on Naxos's Web site.) Petrarch's love lyrics emerge from these performances as an object of highly variable interpretation, whether chaste or lascivious, sensual or ennobled, faithful or promiscuous; as a model for style that projects on other styles its aspirations toward craftsmanship and skill; or as a model whose propensity toward extravagance and exaggeration inspires anti-Petrarchan parody and satire.

Thomas Wyatt and Henry Howard, Earl of Surrey

My starting point for close readings of English Petrarchan poetry is Sir Thomas Wyatt (1503–42), whose diplomatic missions to France and Italy in 1526–27 likely exposed him to the *Canzoniere*, and his younger, more deeply pedigreed friend Henry Howard, earl of Surrey (1517–47), whose verse dates from the mid-

1530s. Their imitations of Petrarch at the court of Henry VIII anticipated the tidal wave of Petrarchism that would break in the century's last decade. Both poets experimented with translating, adapting, and imitating several dozen of Petrarch's sonnets. I begin by asking students to extract stylistic differences between them. These differences imply something of the variety and broad range of responses in Petrarch's verse as well as something about those qualities in later English verse.

The anthologies edited by Stephen Greenblatt and others (*Sixteenth Century*), by Clare Carroll and Andrew Hadfield, and by Gordon Braden (*Sixteenth-Century Poetry*) enable this comparison by printing all or part of Petrarch's sonnet 140 with Robert Durling's literal translation of it alongside Wyatt's and Surrey's versions of the poem. Wyatt's version opens with jagged trochaic rhythms, abrupt turns of phrase, and provincial Kentish verb endings in *-eth* that express his lack of shame or embarrassment about social status or cultural origins: "The longe love that in my thought doeth harbar / And in myn hert doeth kepe his residence." The personified "long love" (in Petrarch's poem, "Amor" is the mythological Cupid) goads Wyatt's speaker "with bold pretence" until the beloved "with his hardiness taketh displeasure." Her rebuke signals a breakdown in their relationship, as the speaker ventures too far in displaying "lust's negligence." Surrey's version, by contrast, begins with a personified "Love, that doth raine and live within my thought" and wittily ends with the same word, *love*, now stripped of personification: "Sweet is the death that taketh end by love." Unlike Wyatt's phallic Cupid, Surrey's deity is stately, aristocratic, and in control, elegantly clad in chivalric "armes" and accustomed to "raine" in the speaker's thought (with a triple pun on "reign," "rein in," and "rain"). Unlike Wyatt's bold lover, Surrey's has learned to cover his "hote desire / With shamefast clooke," measuring his composure in regular iambics until the poem's smoothly resolved final line.

To show students how modern editors have treated these differences, I have drawn up a table of the glosses and footnotes that accompany each poem in various editions. Greenblatt's anthology, for example, describes the first four lines of Wyatt's poem as "introduc[ing] the 'conceit' (or elaborately sustained metaphor) of Love as a warrior who, 'with bold pretense' (i.e., making bold claim), flaunts his presence by means of the 'banner'" and glosses "Cupid's banner" as "the speaker's blush." It then glosses Surrey's "shamefast" as "modest" and "plain" as "complain" so as to emphasize his speaker's subdued manner and compliant demeanor. Carroll and Hadfield's anthology, by contrast, notes that for Wyatt's poem Petrarch's verse "could invest subjects with a spirituality and a seriousness previously attributed to the epic, the ode, and to philosophical poems." In Surrey's poem, it glosses "shamefast" as "ashamed."

For selected poems by Wyatt and Surrey, I have also compiled a table of the headnotes that accompany the texts in their earliest printed edition. As courtly amateurs for whom poetry was an avocation, neither Wyatt nor Surrey felt compelled to publish his work. Their publication came posthumously in an anthology of 271 early Tudor poems assembled at the beginning of Elizabeth's reign by

Richard Tottel, *Songs and Sonnets Written by the Right Honorable Lord Henry Howard Late Earl of Surrey and Others* (1557, with eight further and revised editions through 1587). This collection includes ninety-seven poems by Wyatt, forty by Surrey, and the remainder by Nicholas Grimald, Lord Vaux, John Heywood, John Cheke, Thomas Norton, Thomas Churchyard, and others. Tottel blatantly subordinates the lower-born Wyatt to the higher-born Surrey, featuring the latter's name prominently in the title and, in the preface, commending Surrey's "honorable style" as superior to Wyatt's "deep-witted" poems.

I draw on Tottel's headnotes from his 1557 *Songs and Sonnets*, reproduced digitally in *Early English Books Online* (*EEBO*). The headnote for Wyatt's "The longe love" proclaims, "The lover for shamefastnesse hideth his desire within his faithfull hart" (fol. 19r), thereby emphasizing its speaker's squeamish retreat despite his brash declaration of sexual aggression. Similarly the headnote for Surrey's "Love that doth raine" announces "Complaint of a lover rebuked" (fol. 4v), emphasizing its speaker's blustery protestation in the face of his courtly composure and dry-eyed self-assurance. As students proceed through other poems by Wyatt and Surrey, I provide them with relevant headnotes from Tottel: "The lover showeth how he is forsaken of such as he sometime enjoyed" for Wyatt's "They flee from me that sometime did me seek"; "The frailty and hurtfulness of beauty" for Surrey's "Brittle beauty that nature made so frail"; and "Complaint of the absence of her lover being upon the sea" for Surrey's "Ye happy dames that may embrace." Students enjoy discussing differences between our close readings of the poems and those suggested in Tottel's usually moralizing, often illuminating, and sometimes baffling commentaries.

From Tottel to Thomas Nashe

A different kind of commentary frames Thomas Watson's Englishing of Petrarch in his *Hecatompathia* (1582). This volume offers translations of verse by Petrarch, Ronsard, Serafino, Theocritus, Ovid, Horace, and others in eighteen-line poems called "passions," approximations of the sonnet form with couplets added to each of the two quatrains. For each poem, Watson provides a headnote on its classical and continental sources. From Petrarch's *Canzoniere* Watson translates seven poems, three into English, three into Latin (since the ancient language "commeth somwhat neerer vnto the Italian phrase then the English doth"), and one (sonnet 132) into both languages. A good example is passion 21, on which Watson comments, "In the first staffe of this passion the Authour imitateth *Petrarch sonneto 211, Chi vuol veder quantunque pò natura*" (sig. C3r). (The source is sonnet 248, taken from an Italian edition that renumbered Petrarch's poems.) Watson's translation begins:

> Who list to vewe dame Natures cunning skil,
> And see what Heau'n hath added to the same,

Let him prepare with me to gaze his fill
On her apace; whole gifts exceed the trump of fame:
But let him come a pas before they flye
From hence, to fixe her seate aboue the skye.

In his headnote, Watson acknowledges that his poem's final line, "No bird but Iove's can looke against the sunne," derives from a strambotto by Serafino: "And the very like sense hath *Serafine* in one of his *strambotti.*" The observation enables me to point out that Watson set an example for later Elizabethans to supplement Petrarch's model with others drawn from poets in the Petrarchan canon.

Beyond the commentaries of Tottel and Watson, I mention other representations of Petrarchan love in prose fiction that also expanded the horizons for Petrarch's reception in England. Two particular short novels deserve mention. The first, George Gascoigne's *Adventures of Master F. J.* (1573, rev. 1575), is a cautionary tale that recounts a naive young man's courtly seduction of a married woman and her nonchalance in first indulging and then rebuffing him. The first three of its eight Petrarchan sonnets represent the lover as a trapped mouse, a caught bird, and a singed fly. Its fifth sonnet, "That selfe same day," parodies Petrarch's sonnet 61, "Benedetto sia 'l giorno," and its sixth sonnet is a blazon that epitomizes the form's most lurid features. The second novel, Thomas Nashe's *The Unfortunate Traveler; or, The Life of Jack Wilton* (1595), appeared at the height of the Petrarchan sonnet craze. It recounts the adventures of its narrator, Jack Wilton, as a vagabond soldier hired for Henry VIII's wars against France and ends with an episode in which the hero takes up service with a fictionalized Surrey. Needing to assume a protective disguise, Surrey exchanges identity with Wilton, who plays the role to satiric perfection by taking sexual advantage of his master's mistress, the beloved Geraldine, after wooing her with two Petrarchan sonnets and a ballad. In a brief unit on Renaissance Petrarchism, I simply mention these narratives, but in a full course on Elizabethan literature, I include either or both in the syllabus.

Philip Sidney

The story that I tell about English Petrarchism pivots in 1591, when Thomas Newman published an unauthorized edition of *Astrophil and Stella*, by Philip Sidney (1554–86). Nashe, in an epistle for this edition, comments on Sidney's text as a "theater of pleasure" in which "the tragicomedy of love is performed by starlight" (sig. A3r). Sidney had composed his sequence of 108 sonnets and eleven songs sometime in 1580–81, during his banishment from court after he opposed Elizabeth I's proposed marriage to the duke of Anjou. A year or so earlier he had formulated *The Defence of Poesy* (1595, pub. in two different versions), which urges a literate population to analyze, interpret, and evaluate its reading more deeply, carefully, and persuasively than it has been wont to do.

Among its many literary examples, such "passionate sonnets" as Petrarch's run the risk of "abus[ing] men's wit" unless readers assess them constructively (*Defence* 236). *Astrophil and Stella* affords ample ground to test this theory, since Sidney equips his besotted persona with fleet, funny, and politically pungent indications of his shortcomings.

These shortcomings have a basis in Sidney's lived experience, which I convey to students. Just as Petrarch's Laura refers to a real woman whom the poet purports to have loved, so does Sidney's Stella, though in ways that are both more direct and less obvious. Stella stands in for Penelope Devereux, a daughter of the earl of Essex, to whom Sidney had become engaged in 1576 as part of a deal brokered by their fathers to end political rivalry between their families. Sidney soon reneged on the arrangement, possibly hoping for a more prestigious match. In November 1581 Penelope married Lord Robert Rich, and Sidney came to regret his decision on tactical if not amatory grounds as the Essex fortunes rose. Sonnet 33 intimates as much when his alter-ego, Astrophil, complains:

> I might, unhappie word, o me, I might,
> And then would not, or could not see my blisse
> . . . .
> But to my selfe my selfe did give the blow. (435–36)

Equally to the point, the sequence abounds in puns on Lord Rich's name (see sonnets 35, 37, 78, and 79), not the least of which portray him as sublimely unaware of his wife's proclivity to flirtation ("Rich fools there be" [sonnet 24]).

Sidney composed his sonnets not for publication but for coterie recital among family, friends, and associates who could laugh with him, not at him, as in the voice of Astrophil he recounts his missteps on the road to maturity. The wiser among his listeners could admire his capacity for bemused self-criticism and his potential for growth. Sidney's inventive appropriation of Petrarch's most characteristic tropes helps him achieve these ends. In sonnet 1, for example, Astrophil adduces his reason for writing sonnets to Stella so that "Knowledge might pitie winne, and pitie grace obtaine," explicitly summoning from Petrarch's sonnet 1 the line "Spero trovar pietà, non che perdono" 'I hope to find pity, not only pardon.'[1] The difference is striking, however, because Petrarch seeks from the reader a pity that will soften a harsh moral judgment of him, whereas Astrophil seeks from Stella a pity that will enable him to seduce her. In sonnet 2, Astrophil avows that he fell into love "not at first sight" but "by degrees." This inverts Petrarch's proclamation in his sonnet 2 that he fell "nel primiero assalto" 'in the first assault [of Cupid],' suggesting that, while the Italian poet was the victim of a sudden force beyond his control, Astrophil exults in his gradual, even willing descent into corrupted passion.

I ask students to find other inversions of Petrarch's poetry in Astrophil's sonnets, instantiating a shift from the moral gravity of the *Canzoniere* to a humorous—and in its own way both critical and repentant—expression of Astrophil's self-absorbed persona. In sonnet 47, "What, have I thus betrayed my libertie?," his attempt to distance himself from Stella collapses the moment he sees her: "O me, that eye / Doth make my heart give to my tongue the lie," a cry that hyperbolizes the final line of Petrarch's sonnet 169, "tanto gli ò a dir che 'ncominciar non oso" 'I have so much to say to her that I dare not begin.' In sonnet 64, Astrophil's declaration of remaining constant to Stella in the face of adversity—"Let Fortune lay on me her worst disgrace"—recalls and likewise hyperbolizes Petrarch's confidence in sonnet 145, "Ponmi ove 'l sole occide i fiori et l'erba" 'Place me where the sun kills the flowers and the grass,' itself derived from Horace's ode 1.22. Sidney's apostrophe in sonnet 98 to an empty bed, "Ah bed, the field where joyes peace some do see," evokes Petrarch's sonnet 234, "O cameretta che già fosti un porto" 'O little room that used to be a port.' Sidney's account of sleepless nights in sonnet 99, "When far spent night perswades each mortall eye," parallels Petrarch's account in sonnet 164, "Or che 'l ciel e la terra e 'l vento tace" 'Now that the heavens and the earth and the wind are silent.' Even Sidney's depiction of Stella sailing down the Thames in sonnet 103 brings to mind Petrarch's address to the Rhone River in sonnet 208. I guide students through these pairs of poems while they parcel out subtle differences as well as obvious similarities.

As Sidney reflected on his political discomfiture and marital setback, he came to represent Astrophil as a specifically courtly type of failure (Kennedy, *Site*). Astrophil distances himself from the presumptions of his peers even while he indulges in their worst behaviors. Sidney's imitation of Petrarch's sonnet 248, "Chi vuol veder quantunque pò Natura" 'Whoever wishes to see all that Nature . . . can do,' shows how Astrophil misreads its high moral sentiment through indolence and self-pity:

> Who will in fairest booke of Nature know,
> How Vertue may best lodg'd in beautie be,
> Let him but learne of *Love* to reade in thee
> *Stella*, those faire lines, which true goodnesse show.

Willfully distorting his verse with slant rhymes and mixed meters—"As fast thy Vertue bends that love to good: / But ah, Desire still cries, give me some food"—Astrophil sinks under the weight of his own incomprehension. Amid the competing claims between his behaviors and his critical postulates, he appears to be both courtly and anticourtly (in the satires on social pretensions and sexual hypocrisies). Both pro and con, it displays Sidney as a critic of the Petrarchan poetry that he so brilliantly executes and undermines. I close this unit with a final reminder about Sidney's withholding his text from publication and question why, in the decade that followed, so many aspirants to public office did precisely the opposite with their poetry.

Sidney's Heirs: Samuel Daniel, Henry Constable, Thomas Lodge, Michael Drayton

I draw on the examples of Gascoigne and Nashe to respond to this question, speculating on the increasing efforts of English writers not just to publish their poetry and prose but also to professionalize it. Samuel Daniel provides a case in point. Son of a professional musician and an attendee of Oxford, he came to the attention of Sidney's sister Mary Sidney Herbert, countess of Pembroke, when twenty-eight of his sonnets appeared in Newman's unauthorized edition of *Astrophil and Stella*, under the heading "Poems and Sonets of Sundrie Other Noble Men and Gentlemen, the Author of This Poem SD" (62). Perhaps complicit in this event, Daniel protested it as a betrayal and proceeded to revise, rearrange, and augment these poems in his sonnet sequence *Delia* in 1592, only to republish it with minor corrections later that same year. In 1594 he once more expanded the sequence and revised twenty sonnets. For his first collected works in 1601 he again revised his sonnets and added two new ones. We have here the signs of an emerging professional writer who, like Petrarch in his carefully redacted *Familiares*, *Secretum*, *De Ignorantia*, and other prose works and especially in his autograph workbook (Vatican Latin 3196), displayed unprecedented seriousness about his vernacular literary career. Daniel went on to become a tutor to Pembroke's son, William Herbert, but he focused his energies on writing, above all in his eight books of *ottava rima* verse in *The Civil Wars* (1595–1609) and in his prose *History of England* (1612–18).

I convey a sense of Daniel's revisions in *Delia* by comparing the 1591 version of one of his most widely reprinted poems with its final 1601 version as it appears in the anthologies by Braden (*Sixteenth-Century Poetry*), by John Hollander and Frank Kermode, by Greenblatt and others (*Sixteenth Century*), and by Richard S. Sylvester. Here is the opening of sonnet 22 in Newman's 1591 edition, as drawn from *EEBO*'s digital reproduction (73):

> If this be Love to drawe a wearie breath,
> Paint on fluds till the shore crie to the aire:
> With prone aspect still treading on the earth
> Sad horror, pale griefe, prostrate despaire.

And here is its opening as sonnet 9 in the 1601 edition, as reproduced in Sylvester (579), with revisions marked in italics:

> If this be love, to drawe a wearie breath,
> *Paint on floods, till the shore crie to the air*:
> With *downeward looks,* still *reading* on the earth;
> *The sad memorials of my loves despaire*.

I distribute photocopies of the two versions and ask students to remark on the changes between them. The punctuation of line 2 in the revised version enables us to read the line as an entirely different syntactical construction, in which "till" functions as the verb *plow up* instead of as the conjunction *until*, and the change in line 3 from "treading" to "reading" switches the meaning from "making footprints" to its passive opposite, "gazing on footprints." I point out that the poem is a loose metaphrase of Petrarch's sonnet 224, "S' una fede amorosa, un cor non finto" 'If faithfulness in love, an unfeigning heart,' which ends with Petrarch's speaker assigning culpability to Laura: "Vostro, Donna, 'l peccato et mio fia 'l danno" 'Yours will be the blame, Lady, mine the loss.' Students then discuss various reasons why Daniel withholds this incrimination and softens its effect in his conclusion: "Then do I love, and draw this wary breath." Here I note that the 1601 "wary" introduces a possible ambiguity since it transcribes the 1591 "weary."

Yet another metaphrase of Petrarch's sonnet 224 appears in "To live in hell, and heaven to behold," the second sonnet of the sixth "decade" of a revised and augmented *Diana* (1594), by Henry Constable (1562–1613). This poem (which did not appear in Constable's original 1592 edition) is included in the anthologies by Hyder E. Rollins and Herschel Baker, by Greenblatt and others (*Sixteenth Century*), and by Sylvester. Constable, in contrast to Daniel, was a nobleman who, in further contrast to Wyatt, Surrey, and Sidney, chose to publish his work. Here, for comparative purposes with Petrarch's and Daniel's poems, is its second quatrain:

> To tread a Maze that never shall have end,
> To burne in sighes, and starve in daily teares,
> To clime a hill, and never to discend,
> Gyants to kill, and quake at childish feares. (sig. E2v)

I ask students to compare this poem with Petrarch's and Daniel's poems, noting that although it includes Petrarch's figure of the labyrinth, which Daniel's poem does not, it departs from the Italian model precisely at that point and ends like the English poem by softening its accusation of the beloved. But who might this beloved be? Just before or just after composing his sonnets, Constable converted from the Church of England to Roman Catholicism, and critics have argued whether his poetry reflects this conversion (Roche, *Petrarch and the English Sonnet Sequences*). If so, what might the "Gyants" and "childish feares" represent at the end of the second quatrain? Reformation tracts regularly associated the papacy with a Goliath that the young new church would overcome. Does Constable still accept these associations, or in his convert's zeal does he reassign them to the Protestant monarchs Elizabeth and Henry of Navarre? As a concomitant of the "multiple Petrarchs" recorded in earlier literary history, we find multiple uses of Petrarchan figuration in the service of various causes.

Thomas Lodge (1558–1625) pursued a different route toward publication in his sonnet collection *Phyllis* (1593). Lodge took to composing sonnets evidently under Sidney's influence: in 1580 he had followed Sidney's *Defence of Poesy* against Stephen Gosson with the manuscript "Defense of Plays," and in 1584 he dedicated to Sidney his debut satirical fiction, *Alarum against Usurers*. In *Phyllis*, Lodge expanded the range of English Petrarchism by translating the sonnets of sixteenth-century Italian and French poets such as Ariosto, Pietro Bembo, Ludovico Paschale, Jacopo Sannazaro, Pierre de Ronsard, and Philippe Desportes. In this respect, Lodge's translations "I would in rich and golden coloured raine" (sig. G4r; from "Je voudroy bien richement jaunissant," sonnet 20 of Ronsard's *Amours* [in Quainton and Vinestock]) and "Devoide of reason, thralle to foolish ire" (G2v; from "Franc de raison, esclave de fureur," sonnet 120 of Ronsard's *Amours*) help illustrate the widening sphere of continental influences (Prescott). As for his professional prospects, Lodge abandoned his literary career in the mid-1590s, studied medicine in France, and spent the rest of his life as a London physician.

A yet different literary career took shape in the much-reworked and continually augmented poetry of Michael Drayton (1563–1631). The fifty-three sonnets of his 1594 *Ideas Mirrour* evolved into the sixty-three sonnets of his 1619 *Idea* over the course of six major revised editions (1594, 1599, 1600, 1602, 1605, and 1619). I use these editions as captured on *EEBO* to trace the evolution of separate poems in Drayton's various revisions of them. A particularly good exercise is to trace the first version of sonnet 7 in *Ideas Mirrour* to its final version as sonnet 17 in *Idea*. Drayton's original version abounds in archaizing Spenserian alliteration: "Stay, stay, sweet Time, behold or ere thou passe / From world to world, thou long has sought to see" (*Ideas*, sig. B4r) Its final version includes some alliteration while presenting a more colloquial account: "Stay, speedy Time, behold, before thou passe, / From Age to Age, what thou hast sought to see" (*Poems*, sig. Llv). Its various forms retain the awkward exact rhymes of "see" in lines 2 and 6 and of "Glasse" in lines 4 and 5. The rhyme word "see" recurs in line 10 of the final version, but now with a semantic shift to hortatory address: "Yet see thou tell, but truly, what hath beene." Here "yet" indicates the speaker's caution, and "but truly" sharpens his injunction:

> Say to our Nephewes, that thou once hast seene,
> In perfect humane shape, all heav'nly Blisse;
> And bid them mourne, nay more, despaire with thee,
> That she is gone, her like againe to see.

I point out that the poem's argument and its rhetorical structure bear comparison with Petrarch's sonnet 248 ("Chi vuol veder"), the model for Sidney's deliciously off-rhyme and funny sonnet 71, "Who will in fairest booke of Nature know." A quick recap of that poem shows by contrast how far Drayton's plangent adaptation has departed from it. When I ask students whether Drayton's treatment suggests his direct reading of the Italian poem in its original language, most answer in the affirmative.

Edmund Spenser

Toward the end of my unit on Elizabethan poetry, the multiplicity of approaches to Petrarch's *Canzoniere* appears tangible to students in the sonnets of Edmund Spenser (1554?–99). Assembled late in his career (possibly using some sonnets drafted much earlier) into a sequence called *Amoretti* that concludes with *Epithalamion*, these poems narrate the middle-aged widowed speaker's second marriage to a young bride. The mature product of a seasoned poet, it appeared in 1595 after the decade's sonnet frenzy had peaked. Palpable references identify this speaker with the historical poet. In sonnets 33 and 80 he presents himself as one whose duties as a public official (Spenser was secretary to the queen's governor-general of Ireland) interfere with his completion of *The Faerie Queene*. In sonnet 60 he portrays himself as a forty-year-old lover who has wooed the young woman for more than a year. In sonnet 74 he sketches an analogy linking her name, Elizabeth Boyle, to that of his mother, Elizabeth Spenser, and that of his monarch, Elizabeth Tudor. Spenser's wordplay on these names (like that of Petrarch's on Laura or Sidney's on Penelope Rich) sometimes strikes students as predictable and contrived, but I try to turn this criticism to productive uses by explaining it as part of a drama about affective transformation, accentuating its awkwardness in ways that expose a conflict within Petrarchism (Kennedy, *Authorizing*).

Among other things, I encourage students to view this conflict as the plight of a particular lover caught in the grid of a complex social, political, literary, moral, and religious hierarchy. We note the degree to which the speaker's love becomes a public and hence social and political issue as Spenser advertises it in his verse, as well as his literary and moral or religious bondage to various Petrarchan roles—his as a sexually experienced suitor, his beloved's as a guardian of her virginal chastity. In the beginning of the sequence he registers all the preferences of an old-style Petrarchan lover bent on libidinous satisfaction, as some commentators represent Petrarch. In the end Spenser accedes to a reciprocal relationship with the beloved as his wife, sanctioned by a new-style Protestant ethic. Her virtue tempers his egotism without smothering his desire, while his ardor arouses her interest without damaging her virtue. Spenser's transformational narrative grows out of a bygone Petrarchism as the beloved with her "most goodly temperature" (sonnet 13; 349) begins to instruct the lover to shun his courtly ways and redirect his goals toward marriage.

As I construe the narrative, Petrarchism becomes an instrument by which the beloved's withering disapproval of the speaker's behavior prompts a crisis. Sonnet 34, "Lyke as a ship that through the ocean wyde," for example, draws on the motif of the shipwreck in Petrarch's sonnets 132, 189, 235, 273, and canzone 366 to convey the lover's impasse and the beginning of his introspective journey toward moral recovery. Spenser's sonnet 35, "My hungry eyes through greedy covetize," follows with a reference to the mythic Narcissus: "In their amazement like *Narcissus* vaine / whose eyes him starv'd: so plenty makes me poore." The analogue in the *Canzoniere* is sonnet 45, in which Laura gazes at herself in a mirror that becomes the speaker's adversary, "Il mio adversario in cui veder solete" 'My adversary in whom you are wont to see your eyes.' Italian commentators such as Giovanni Andrea Gesualdo and Lodovico Castelvetro interpreted the beloved's narcissistic gaze on herself as the beginning of self-awareness and hence of self-knowledge that enables one to advance in virtue. Spenser, it appears, has something similar in mind when later in the sequence he repeats the poem as sonnet 83. There, I quiz students about the change of a single word from "having" to "seeing" (line 6). Is this substitution of words merely trivial? Or does it point to a difference between the lover's egotistic possession and his other-directed gaze and, consequently, his acceptance of the beloved as another person distinct from his projection of her?

By sonnet 61, the speaker understands his beloved as a woman who virtuously resists his advances, "My soverayne saynt, the Idoll of my thought." At last, deeply chastened and wholly transformed, he succeeds in sonnet 67, "Like as a huntsman after greedy chace," in winning her hand with a pledge of holy matrimony. Here the unmistakable reference to Petrarch's sonnet 190, "Una candida cerva sopra l'erba" 'A white doe on the green grass,' dramatizes the beloved's assent in terms that figure marriage as a representation of Christ's relation to the church. Neither entirely secular nor entirely sacral (the Reformation disqualified matrimony as a sacrament since non-Christian cultures also practice it), marriage reconciles sexuality to chastity as a redemptive and revivifying act. Sonnet 68 proceeds with its calendrical reference to Easter Sunday to signal the speaker's emergence from bondage of the flesh and his at least tentative steps toward redemption: "Most glorious Lord of lyfe that on this day / Didst make thy triumph over death and sin." It is as though the speaker has tried to redeem a Petrarchism that seems dangerously flawed. To his surprise he finds that it is really a site of multiple interpretations whose possibilities include his own redemption. Whether students view Spenser's speaker as redeeming Petrarchism or Petrarchism as redeeming Spenser depends on which version of Petrarchism gains the upper hand among them.

A Glance at John Donne

It comes as a shock to students when they recognize that John Donne (1572–1631) wrote at least some of his amatory *Songs and Sonnets* during his studies at Lincoln's Inn between 1592 and 1595, exactly when Spenser was assembling his *Amoretti* and completing books 4–6 of *The Faerie Queene*. Donne likely completed most of these poems by 1611, when he decided to seek a career in the

Church of England. Neither entirely Petrarchan nor entirely anti-Petrarchan, Donne's love poetry occasionally deploys Petrarchan figures and tropes. They turn out to accentuate the mutability of the lover's and the beloved's feelings toward each other, or, alternatively, the mutuality of their commitment as a lasting bond. Donne's verses use their share of Petrarchan tears, sighs, glances, and shows, but their shifting contexts attach different valuations of seriousness and sentiment to them. Their most notable feature conveys a variety of dramatic voices and speaking personae that populate the poems. They range from cynical, self-mocking, and ribald to demonstrative, self-assured, and deeply felt. Wyatt's, Sidney's, and Spenser's speakers certainly project strongly defined dramatic voices, but each poet conveys a sense of consistency and assured character development over the corpus of his poetry. With Donne's dramatic speakers, despite the power of individual poems, a disquieting unpredictability and vague anonymity emerge from the whole.

To demonstrate these fluctuating tones and competing moods, I ask students to chart the types of speaking characters that they encounter. Their types range from the lover who is indifferent about his mistress's commitment to him (e.g., in the suggestively titled "Woman's Constancy," "The Indifferent," "Love's Usury," and "Communitie") to the lover who is gleefully pessimistic about it (e.g., "Goe, and catche a falling starre," "The Legacie," "Loves Deitie," and "Loves Diet"), as well as from the lover who is confident about the mutuality of his beloved's devotion (e.g., "The Good-Morrow," "The Sunne Rising," "The Canonization," and "The Extasie") to one who is anxious about their inevitable separation (e.g., "A Valediction: Forbidding Mourning," "Sweetest love, I do not goe," "The Dissolution," and "A Nocturnall upon S. Lucies Day"). There's bound to be a great deal of disagreement about which poems fit into these categories, a conflict the students would not encounter in classifying conventional Petrarchan verse. Far from signaling that Donne's verse is anti-Petrarchan, or even neutrally un-Petrarchan, this disagreement brings us back to the typology of multiple Petrarchs found in Renaissance commentaries on the *Canzoniere*; Donne's voices echo this multiplicity (Dubrow).

There would certainly be little disagreement about the powerful voice of Donne's *Divine Poems*, likely composed after he accepted his call to ordination. The speaker's religious anguish is especially clear in Donne's *Holy Sonnets*, as is the distance of its tone and mood from those of Petrarch's religious verse. In his poems *in morte di Laura*, Petrarch focuses on the speaker's sense of having idolized Laura, of having mystified his love for her in the presence of nothingness, and of having lost himself in the hollows of language. Donne, however, focuses on the speaker's anxiety of separation from God, of breaks and ruptures in his relationship with God, of his creaturely need for repair in acts of near annihilation. Here when I ask students to measure the turns of Donne's sonnets from quatrain to quatrain, octave to sestet, tercet to tercet, they discover the speaker's sudden reversals and counterreversals of thought and feeling that enact their own drama.

Mary Wroth and the End of English Petrarchism

The very last sequence of Petrarchan sonnets published in England is the work of Philip Sidney's niece, Lady Mary Wroth (1586?–1651?). Her prose romance *Urania* appeared in 1621, interspersed with Petrarchan poems; to it is appended a sequence of sonnets, *Pamphilia to Amphilanthus*, named after the main characters of Wroth's narrative.

Early modern women's authorship was not as conspicuous in England as it was in Italy and France, and the sixteenth-century publication of poetry in England by Anne Vaughan Lock (1560), Isabella Whitney (1573), and Aemilia Lanyer (1611) seems nearly anomalous in the English context. But Wroth's poetry and fiction augur a growing trend toward the publication of women-authored texts. Her heroine Pamphilia, queen of Morea, is a paragon of virginal chastity and communal obligation; her beloved Amphilanthus, king of Naples and later Holy Roman Emperor, is a lout. Students enjoy locating in Pamphilia's poems the familiar tropes, rhetorical strategies, and dramatic situations of Petrarchism, now with the gender roles reversed by Wroth's speaker. Their models include not just those in Petrarch's *Canzoniere* but also those in the sonnets of Philip Sidney, whom Wroth consciously echoes, and those of her father, Robert Sidney (whose work appears in the anthologies by Braden [*Sixteenth-Century Poetry*] and by Norbrook and Woudhuysen).

In Wroth's sonnet 10, "The weary traveller who tired sought," provides a good example. It reaches back to Petrarch's sonnet 16, "Movesi il vecchierel canuto et bianco" 'The little white-haired pale old man,' whose speaker travels to Rome and compensates for leaving his beloved by seeking out her likeness among other women. In this poem, Petrarch is desperately trying to refute a rumor that has reached Laura about his affairs with women in Rome. In a similar way, Philip Sidney's Astrophil in sonnet 91 borrows the fatuous defense that Stella's rivals remind him of her: "They please I do confesse, they please mine eyes, / But why? Because of you they models be." Robert Sidney, in his sonnet 17, "The endless Alchemist, with blinded will," bends the trope to show how his speaker "feeds his thoughts with hopes, his hopes on shows." By contrast, Wroth's Pamphilia compares herself with a traveler who attains his end "with joy" when he is "to his home back brought." Refuting some "wrong conseite" of rumor or malicious gossip against her, she enjoys the "greatest happiness" when she receives "beeleefe for faith, while hope in pleasure swimms." Breaking the Petrarchan mold even as she reconstitutes it, Wroth's speaker counters the egotism of her uncle's and her father's personae and offers a positive example of Petrarchan love.

Wroth, in the opening lines of sonnet 14, likewise rewrites the predicament of *Astrophil and Stella*: "Am I thus conquer'd? have I lost the powers / That to withstand, which joy's to ruin mee." This predicament is specifically found in sonnet 47, whose speaker accedes to self-pity as he evaluates his enslavement to Stella: "What, have I thus betrayed my libertie?" In the latter, "libertie" strikes an incongruous off-rhyme with "tyranny" as Astrophil complains "or am I borne a slave / Whose necke becomes such yoke of tyranny." Sidney's lover cannot quite coordinate his impulses, and when in the sestet he vows to strengthen his resolve—"I may, I must, I can, I will, I do"—he immediately slides back into bondage: "O me, that eye / Doth make my heart give to my tongue the lie." I clarify his poem for students as an amalgam of motifs from Petrarch's sonnet 97, "Ahi bella libertà, come tu m'ài, / partendoti da me" 'Ah sweet liberty, how by departing from me,' and sonnet 169, "Pien d'un vago penser che me desvia" 'Full of a yearning thought that makes me stray.' Wroth's sonnet, by contrast, projects a resolution stronger than either Sidney's or Petrarch's, issuing in part from a confident, even defiant, enumeration of impossibilities that must occur before Pamphilia concedes to Cupid: "Love shall loose all his darts, have sight, and see / His shame, and wishings hinder happy howres." When at the end of the poem Pamphilia overturns her resistance—"Butt O my hurt, makes my lost heart confess / I love, and must: So farwell liberty"—she does so by freely giving herself to love. Wroth at once recaptures the Petrarchan model while replacing its abject servitude with a statement of autonomous command.

I conclude the unit by referring to Wroth's and Petrarch's treatments of the Narcissus myth. Petrarch's sonnet 45, "Il mio adversario in cui veder solete" 'My adversary in whom you are wont to see,' identifies its speaker's *adversario* as the reflection of Laura's image in her mirror. This reflection carries positive consequences, however, since it leads to a deepening of her self-awareness and a moral awakening of the lover's self-sacrifice. Wroth's sonnet 46, "Love, thou has all, for now thou hast mee made," likewise brings Pamphilia to a positive encounter with the god of love, who deters her from drinking the waters of self-absorption: "Drinke I could nott, butt in it I did see / My self a living glass as well as shee." Here Pamphilia achieves a measure of transcendence and self-realization by inviting the participation of Love as an effective agent. She sees herself as "a living glass" that reflects her virtues "as well as she"—as vividly embodied, that is, as the real person who enacts those virtues. In doing so, she fulfills the command of John's Gospel to "love one another" (15.12) when she becomes a repository of love, a mirror "[f]or Love to see him self in truly plac'd."

By the end of the unit, I hope that students will have a good sense of the variety that animates English Petrarchism, a lyric mode sometimes thought to recycle stale figures and tropes. More important, I hope that they will gain a better sense of the workings of poetry, a genre that challenges students because they often associate it with obscurity, vapid symbol hunting, and the boredom of ponderous sentiment. I hope that they will learn to feel its pulse, taste its drama, and discover that no two poems—if they are any good—can ever really say the same thing.

NOTE

[1]Italian quotations from the *Canzoniere* are from Santagata's edition; English quotations from the *Canzoniere* follow Durling's translation.

Teaching Petrarch and Shakespeare

Tanya Pollard

Shakespeare's writings, like so much of English Renaissance literature, routinely explore, imitate, and parody Petrarch's poetic conceits. Some plays and poems shape their meanings explicitly through engaging Petrarchan allusions. Giving students an opportunity to explore some of Petrarch's poetry while studying Shakespeare allows them to recognize these motifs and establishes a foundation for exploring what Shakespeare is doing with them. The play *Twelfth Night*, in particular, draws on Petrarch as a basis for much of its humor, as well as for its commentary on love and courtship. Studying Petrarch in this specific context can offer students a window into his powerful influence on English Renaissance literature.

It can be valuable to spend a class session on Petrarch's poetry before introducing Shakespeare's use of Petrarchan motifs, to highlight aspects of Petrarch that Shakespeare typically imitates and parodies. Key Petrarchan tropes that students can easily identify as conspicuous influences on Shakespeare and other English Renaissance poets include preoccupations with a cruel mistress, wounds, attacks on eyes, speechlessness, and the blazon itemizing the beloved's parts. Poems in the *Canzoniere* that illustrate these themes well include 1, 2, 3, 19, 20, 36, 39, 45, 47, 49, 52, 59, 121, 133, 134, 140, 182, 190, 220, and 252; the list can be condensed or expanded depending on the amount of time available for reading and discussion. Robert Durling's bilingual edition of the *Canzoniere*, included in *Petrarch's Lyric Poems*, works especially well, since it juxtaposes the Italian texts with English translations. Having the original language available is useful for those students who are familiar with Italian or another Romance language and makes it possible to discuss significant words, rhymes, and puns in the Italian poems.

It is useful to situate these poems with some historical and biographical information about Petrarch and the popularity of the Petrarchan tradition in the English Renaissance. Students can then discuss what they see in the poems: How do they represent what it is like to be in love? What is the position of the speaker-lover? What do we know about the lady who is the object of the speaker's affections? What are some of the recurring images, and what do they suggest about the nature of erotic desire?

Students often leap right into these questions with responses and examples from the poems; if they hesitate, turning to individual poems can help. Reading aloud poems 1 and 2 of the *Canzoniere*, for instance, raises questions about what it feels like to be in love, about the consequences of falling in love, and about the nature of love. Exploring Petrarch's interest in the myth of Actaeon, alluded to in poems 52 and 23, offers a useful foundation for understanding some of Shakespeare's allusions. What is the significance of Actaeon, and what does the myth imply about the aftermath of his fate? Why does the speaker of the poem compare himself with this figure, and what do they share? What does this poem suggest about the consequences of gazing on the beloved? Students tend to be relatively comfortable making observations about themes and tone; it can be useful to remind them to cite specific language from the poems if their claims become too general. The brevity of the poems helps keep the focus on particular details.

Although these questions are largely general and open-ended, answering them helps students revise their initial assumptions about the poems, as well as about universalizing notions of love as an idyllic state. Many students are surprised at this association of love with suffering—"It's not romantic!"—but others typically point out that this is not entirely strange, given that love, especially unrequited, can feel catastrophic. Students are also often surprised to realize how little the poems tell us about Laura: after a cursory reading, they tend to assume that the poems are all about her, but after being pressed with specific questions about what we know about her, they tend to come up empty-handed and cannot say much more than that she is beautiful and has blond hair.

Writing topics on the board and collectively brainstorming associations with them can help students both organize and remember their ideas; the activity also offers a template for notes that they can revisit when they consider Petrarchan allusions in Shakespeare. Categories can vary, as can answers. Under "Petrarchan lover," for instance, students might volunteer ideas such as "suffering," "wounded," or "self-absorbed." Under "Petrarchan mistress," associations might include "beautiful," "cruel," and "unattainable." "Recurring motifs" might invite "wounds," "burning and freezing," "eyes," and "gold hair." Of course, doing an exercise like this with students is (happily) always unpredictable: although certain themes tend to come up repeatedly, no two groups will ever come up with exactly the same lists, and there are always new and quirky observations to record, discuss, and contemplate further.

Exploring Petrarch's representation of love leads naturally to a discussion of the Petrarchan tradition's popularity. In a course focused on Shakespeare, there will not necessarily be time allocated to reading Petrarchan sonnets by Thomas Wyatt, Henry Howard (earl of Surrey), Philip Sidney, or Edmund Spenser, but students should be aware of the impact of these writers in introducing and developing the Petrarchan tradition in English poetry, so it can be helpful to say a little about them and their translations or reworkings of Petrarch's lyrics. Primarily, though, pointing out Petrarch's popularity in English Renaissance poetry can lead to discussions about why he was popular, through further questions closely related to the earlier ones: Would you like to be a Petrarchan lover? Why or why not? If being a Petrarchan lover is at some level rather miserable, why did so many generations of poets copy Petrarch? What might be appealing about being in this position? What reasons can you imagine for the popularity of Petrarchan forms?

The end of this discussion of Petrarch offers an opportunity to encourage students to keep their eyes open for Petrarchan motifs, echoes, and parodies in Shakespeare. Some moments where students notice blatant Petrarchan echoes typically include *Romeo and Juliet*, where Romeo writes his own forlorn

Petrarchan sonnet to his first love, Rosaline, early in the play, and *As You Like It*, where the shepherdess Phebe is presented as a cruel and unattainable mistress to her lover Silvius. Both episodes, like many other Shakespearean reworkings of Petrarch, offer wry twists on Petrarchan scenarios, using humor and comic inversions to mock both the suffering lover and the cruel mistress. Darker examples, such as Marcus's grotesque blazon of Lavinia after her rape, in *Titus Andronicus*, and Othello's blazon of the sleeping Desdemona, point to the potential violence of this poetic trope. In Shakespeare courses that include the sonnets, their explicit and self-conscious Petrarchan play provides almost endless material for observation and analysis; discussions on this topic could last anywhere from a class session to an entire course.

Among the more frequently taught plays, however, *Twelfth Night* offers a particularly valuable and accessible site for discussing Shakespeare's use of Petrarch. Reading aloud the play's opening exchange between Orsino and Curio, in which Orsino discusses his hapless love for Olivia, leads easily toward discussion of the Petrarchan influence. What sort of a lover is Orsino? What does he suggest it is like to be in love? In particular, why the early allusion to Actaeon? Orsino describes himself in 1.1.18–22 as having been turned into a hart after gazing upon Olivia and subsequently having been hunted by his "desires, like fell and cruel hounds" (line 21).[1] Students may think immediately of Petrarch's interest in this image; if not, a few questions might prompt it: Where have we seen this image before? Where else have we seen the idea that gazing on a beautiful woman could be dangerous and physically painful?

Although these last questions may be somewhat disingenuous, in that they clearly point to a specific answer, the connection is generally striking enough for students to notice it quickly, and it can be satisfying for them to discover it themselves. If they come up with other associations with Actaeon, those can be usefully incorporated into discussion as well. Once students see the link, it leads to other questions: What traits does Orsino share with the Petrarchan lover? How, if at all, does he differ? Students might note Orsino's moodiness, his devotion to contemplating and discussing his love, and his lack of any direct contact with Olivia during the play (they only meet in the final scene) as parallels with the unhappy, introspective, and distant speaker of Petrarch's poems. But what sort of tone does *Twelfth Night* take toward Orsino? How is he treated—with admiration, reverence, concern, mockery? How is he portrayed—heroic, suffering, pathetic? How can we tell? Why does Shakespeare choose to evoke this particular literary stereotype in his depiction of Orsino?

Orsino, despite opening the play and heavily influencing the framework for its plot, ends up being peripheral to much of the action, which takes place primarily at Olivia's house. The play's interest in a Petrarchan model of love, however, is just as important to these scenes. If Orsino is a version of the Petrarchan lover, what does that make Olivia? How well does she fit the model of the Petrarchan mistress? Like Orsino, Olivia matches her Petrarchan counterpart in many respects: she is beautiful, sought after, and (to Orsino, at least) distant and unattainable. But does Olivia share this image of herself? Students often enjoy examining her mocking self-blazon, in which she offers Viola an inventory of her beauty in lieu of creating copies through procreation: "*item*, two lips, indifferent red; *item*, two grey eyes, with lids to them; *item*, one neck, one chin, and so forth" (1.5.216–18). Why does Olivia make fun of this particular poetic tradition? What, exactly, is she mocking, and what does it do to the idealized mistress when she makes jokes about her own beauty? More broadly, what happens when she herself falls into unrequited love, with Viola/Cesario? And what, if anything, is the significance of her falling in love with a woman? As an unrequited wooer of an unattainable beloved, Olivia arguably becomes a type of Petrarchan lover herself. Similarly, Viola could be seen as taking on this role in pining after Orsino. Yet Olivia and Viola are each very different from Orsino, as well as from each other, and all three differ in crucial ways from Petrarch's speaker. What is Shakespeare saying about Petrarch by combining, confusing, and altering these roles? What is he saying about the gendering of lovers and their beloveds? The play's mixed-up courtship scenes tend to be popular with students anyway, but attention to their Petrarchan parodies, both implicit and explicit, can help students appreciate not only their humor but also the sophistication of the questions that they raise. What does Shakespeare gain by framing Petrarch's model of courtship in a comic play? What does the genre do to the bitter, pensive pain of the Petrarchan speaker-lover and to the idealized beauty of the Petrarchan mistress? What sort of a statement (or statements), ultimately, does the play make about both Petrarch and the nature of love?

Petrarch's influence on Shakespeare is evident throughout the latter's works: in the tragedies, the comedies, and especially the sonnets. There are many moments that one could fruitfully examine in detail; *Twelfth Night* serves here as an example because of the range of types of allusions and their centrality to the play's core themes and because students tend to respond well to its combination of playfulness and dark humor. In some ways, studying Petrarch in the context of another writer inevitably limits and distorts the original: it necessarily truncates the time spent on the poems, and it makes some aspects of them loom much larger than others. Similarly, viewing Shakespeare through a Petrarchan lens can lead students to attend to some issues and themes at the expense of others. Overall, though, linking the two together can lead to a whole greater than the sum of its parts. In examining first Petrarch's poetic strategies and then Shakespeare's self-conscious reworkings of them, students can significantly expand their understanding of both writers, as well as of the possibilities of literary imitation and influence.

NOTE

[1]All citations from *Twelfth Night* refer to the version of the play included in *The Norton Shakespeare*.

Petrarch in English after 1750

Edoardo Zuccato

The reception of Petrarch in English-language cultures after 1750 is a strange story of popularity and neglect that has received critical attention only in recent years. Petrarch enjoyed enormous popularity during the Romantic age in England. It was a phenomenon that has no comparison in the rest of Europe, involving a remarkable number of translators, critics, poets, and novelists. It played a decisive role in the revival of the sonnet, the debate on sexual mores, and the definition of the public image of the woman as poet. The Petrarchan revival that took place between 1750 and 1830 offers an exemplary subject for students of British Romanticism, translation studies, and women's studies, at both basic and advanced levels.

British Romantic Petrarchism has remained in the shadow for a long time because the revivals of other writers, such as Dante, Sappho, and Milton, were considered more relevant. In fact, in England the Petrarchan revival preceded and made possible the recovery of Dante and, later, of the native sonnet tradition from Wyatt to Shakespeare. Even Milton the sonneteer was usually read as a Petrarchan poet. For students of Italian, the British Romantic Petrarch is a breath of fresh air. The formalist approach to Petrarch that haunted Italian culture for centuries never convinced British readers. British critics took the content of the *Canzoniere* very seriously, even though their approach was mainly biographical and focused on a limited number of love poems. They admired the texts in which a lovelorn "I" meditates alone while wandering in the countryside. Sonnets like "Solo et pensoso" ("Alone and filled with care" [35]), "Vago augelletto" ("Wandering bird" [353]), "Quel rosignuol" ("That nightingale" [311]), and above all "Zephiro torna" ("Zephyrus returns" [310]) are the core of Romantic Petrarchism, though some political poems and moral meditations like "Voi ch'ascoltate" ("You who hear" [1]) and "La gola e 'l somno" ("Gluttony and sleep" [7]) were widely admired.[1]

The great popularity of Susanna Dobson's *Life of Petrarch* (1775), which marks the real beginning of the revival, shows that the British approach was essentially biographical. Dobson's biography, an abridged version of the abbé de Sade's monumental work, depicted Petrarch as poet and lover rather than scholar and politician. Dobson initiated a debate on the morality of the relationship between Petrarch and Laura that remained alive until the end of the nineteenth century. This criticism must not be judged by twenty-first-century standards. At that time it was a significant part of a discussion on the boundaries of sexual behavior, the meaning of marriage and adultery, and the social role of women. Many women and radical writers appealed to Petrarch to back up their unorthodox views, for this is one of the unexpected sides of British Romantic

Petrarch: he was championed by radicals of various sorts, whereas several conservative authors, from William Gifford to William Wordsworth, had reservations about him. The English Petrarch was not the Jesuit lapdog despised by Ugo Foscolo and other Italian Romantics.

The major historians of that period—Thomas Warton, Edward Gibbon, Charles Burney, Pierre-Louis Ginguené, Jean Charles Léonard de Sismondi, Henry Hallam, and others—discussed Petrarch in their works and made him legitimate reading when he was still unfashionable. But critical analysis was not confined to these historians; rather, the sheer quantity of critical statements on Petrarch is extraordinary and involves all the Romantic writers. Before considering the most original of them, we must discuss the crucial role of the translators.

Like any revival, the Romantic discovery of Petrarch owes a great deal to figures who were later considered minor or obscure. Translations from Petrarch appeared in essays, poetry collections, volumes of translations, and epistolary novels. The range of these translators is impressive and includes authors like Sir William Jones, who read Petrarch in the context of Eastern and Western medieval poetry, and John Nott, an eccentric and innovative translator whose work was focused on lyric poetry as a way of renewing the eighteenth-century hierarchy of genres.[2] Two anthologies, George Henderson's *Petrarch* (1803) and Capel Lofft's *Laura* (1813–14), were the syntheses of five decades of Petrarchan fashion. Besides the Renaissance, the Romantic age was the only time when the sonnet was so deeply identified with Petrarch that publishers used his name as a book title. In Henderson's and Lofft's view, the sonnet tradition was mainly Italian. Even an enormous anthology like Lofft's leaves the reader with the impression that in England there was no real interest in Petrarch and the sonnet before the late eighteenth century, since the English Renaissance sonneteers are given little space. Lofft's first volume includes the longest theoretical discussion of the sonnet—a theme on which most Romantic and Victorian poets expressed their opinions—whereas the other four volumes celebrate the variety of the sonnet. Lofft found the form ideal for themes of love, friendship, morality, and natural description, whereas he excluded grotesque and coarse comedy.

The significant impact of these translators, editors, and essayists was preceded by a noteworthy episode in the mid-eighteenth century: Thomas Gray's seminal "Sonnet on the Death of Mr. Richard West" (1742, pub. 1775). The sonnet is an evident rewriting of "Zephiro torna," a fact that modern critics have stubbornly ignored, though most Romantic readers were aware of it. From his school days, West's nickname was Zephyrus, and Gray mentioned it in several poems and letters. Gray used a Petrarchan theme in a sonnet when the form was extremely rare. The rhyme scheme and the imagery of Petrarch's and Gray's sonnets are identical, though Gray gave the single images a different emphasis. Rewriting an obscure sonnet of a half-forgotten Italian poet, Gray gave vent to his anxiety for both the loss of his beloved friend and the impossibility of expressing homosexual passion fully. Petrarch's influence on Gray extends to other poems, including "Elegy in a Country Churchyard."[3] Together with the sonnet to West, this work was an anticipation of sensibility, since the association between the sonnet and elegiac poetry became central in the following decades.

Nowhere was this association stronger than in the poems of Charlotte Smith, the next protagonist of British Romantic Petrarchism. Her *Elegiac Sonnets* was the most influential of the 1780s poetic novelties and started a vogue for sonnet writing that has continued ever since. Petrarch's central place in her poetics is evident in the first three editions of her collection (1784 and 1786), which contain translations and imitations of Petrarch's sonnets. In other words, Smith began her career like other Petrarchan translators; later, however, she became independent of her model. Smith's elegiac sonnets do not commemorate a departed lover or friend. In fact, they are elegiac because they lament her tragic lot, that of a well-to-do young woman whose life was shattered by a reckless husband who abandoned her and their many children after squandering her fortune. The enormous popularity of Smith's "tragedy of estate" made her for a few decades the supreme master of the English sonnet, well above Shakespeare and Milton in the opinion of her contemporaries.

Smith has recently been reread, against Wordsworth and other high Romantic sonneteers, as a sort of postmodern poet, because her texts echo, cite, paraphrase, and imitate her sources. Nevertheless, her way of writing belongs fully to the main poetic modes of her age: although she may have selected different writers to imitate, the way in which she rewrote them matched the methods of her peers. A formal misunderstanding of her work concerns her metrics. Smith employed an irregular sonnet form, based on the English Renaissance sonnet, and thus her Petrarchism has been judged as partial and superficial, even though her affinity with Petrarch is perhaps the deepest of her time, despite her not using a Petrarchan sonnet form. The poems of *Elegiac Sonnets* sound like variations on an obsessive underground theme—not love, as in Petrarch, but her miserable condition as aristocrat fallen on hard times and a woman who struggled to eke out a livelihood with her pen.

Smith's mournful Petrarchism fed on the *in morte* section of *Canzoniere* and neglected love as a subject, despite the references to Goethe's *Werther* and to Alexander Pope's *Eloisa to Abelard* in some of her sonnets. While this trend continued in Smith's numerous followers, Mary Robinson, perhaps the most talented poet of the next generation, returned to the core of Petrarch's poetry—that is, the psychology of love. Robinson was a famous actress and the mistress of the Prince of Wales, who eventually abandoned her. She ended her life as a social outcast, a poor and crippled woman. Her career began in the 1770s on the pages of the *World*, the journal of the Della Cruscans, a group of fashionable literati, under the pen name of Laura-Maria. Her 1791 collection contains the poem "Petrarch to Laura" (*Poems* 46–51), which appears after several texts signed by Robinson as Laura, thereby creating a complex effect of identification. "Petrarch to Laura" is an Ovidian epistle in which Robinson paraphrased passages from Petrarch's poems and linked them with comments and additions. Her Petrarch is a gloomy lover for whom unreciprocated passion is a hell without consolation, not the bittersweet mixture of pleasure and pain of the *Canzoniere*. Robinson found Petrarch's lifelong passion for Laura dubious: his passion lasted so long because it remained unfulfilled, and Laura was too ignorant a woman to attract a sophisticated man like Petrarch. But however odd their relationship, Petrarch remained a superb love poet, and Robinson explored that contradiction in *Sappho and Phaon*.

Robinson's *Sappho and Phaon* is the only love sonnet sequence of the Romantic age. It is an ambitious work that synthesizes the main trends of the love poetry of her time, which was dominated by three figures: Sappho, Petrarch, and Werther. Another essential component was the tradition of the Ovidian epistles (the *Heroides*), especially as interpreted by Pope in *Eloisa to Abelard*. *Sappho and Phaon* tells Ovid's version of Sappho's story in Petrarchan sonnets, which are written as verse epistles. The preface contains an intriguing defense of regular against elegiac sonnets. It discusses the meaning of form and the social status of women poets, and it shows that Robinson had reread Sappho's story with Petrarchan eyes. Robinson considered Sappho's lesbianism a historical forgery and did not believe in the platonic character of Petrarch and Laura's relationship. Devoid of its bisexual complications, Sappho's life became, for Robinson and for most of her contemporaries, a story of unreciprocated heterosexual passion whose scanty fragments were inevitably put together along Petrarchan lines, though with a tragic conclusion.

Robinson's last statement on Petrarch is the sonnet "Laura to Petrarch," a long-overdue answer of the famous mistress to her would-be lover (*Poetical Works* 3: 119). Robinson's Laura addresses Petrarch the "solitary wanderer," but only to tell him that friendship is better than love and human company better than isolation. The natural sublime is not the climax of creativity but a parasitic condition of sterility that feeds on human relations, however remote. His love was a "sick passion" that lasted so long because it contained an element of pathological immaturity. Robinson's perspective was based on the eighteenth-century tradition of commonsense, laced with ideas of sensibility. It was a call for reason and self-control even in one's sentimental life, and it was at odds with the cult of excess endorsed by Byron and other Romantics. It is not surprising that Robinson's poems have for so long been unread.

A writer who was familiar with excess was Samuel Taylor Coleridge, whose approach to Petrarch was radically different from what we have seen so far. His reading of Petrarch began, conventionally enough, with some scathing statements in the preface to his *Sonnets from Various Authors* (1796). At that time, his view of the sonnet was based on sonneteers like William Lisle Bowles and William Preston and reflected the poetics of sensibility. He believed that the essential traits of the sonnet were organic unity in the structure and empathic sentiment in the content. In an 1810 marginal note to his book he described these views as immature presumption (vol. 1, pt. 2: 1205n).

In the early 1800s, Coleridge studied Italian and traveled to Malta and Italy. His two main literary projects were an essay on metrics and *The Soother of Absence*, a collection of love poems he planned as a reaction to his unreciprocated passion for Sara Hutchinson. Coleridge soon realized that Petrarch had composed the most influential "soother of absence" in the history of Western literature. Coleridge never became a Petrarchist, nor did he idealize his beloved as Petrarchists usually do, but the love poetry of his maturity contains images, concepts, and turns of phrases that can be traced back to Petrarchism. Their form, often epigrammatic and concettistic, is indebted to the same tradition.

Coleridge was an avid and independent reader and did not stop at the *Canzoniere*. He delved into Petrarch's Latin works, which he held in high regard, especially the epistles and some treatises. In his prose works Coleridge quoted Petrarch in support of his opinions and discussed him in the *Philosophical Lectures* (1819). Coleridge understood that, though Petrarch was not a philosopher, the change he brought about in the cultural history of Europe was decisive. Moreover, Coleridge was intrigued by Petrarch's idea of love and his view of the social role of intellectuals. The section of love poems in Coleridge's *Sibylline Leaves* (1817) carries a motto from Petrarch's epistle to Barbato da Sulmona, a paraphrase of "Voi ch'ascoltate," because Coleridge felt a special affinity for Petrarch's philosophy of love, which he saw as the most congenial mixture of Christianity and Platonism he had ever come across in an area he considered of the utmost importance.

Coleridge's relation with the sonnet remains problematic even after—or especially after—he became familiar with the Petrarchan tradition. The sonnets are the most intimate of his poems, but he realized that his planned *Soother of Absence* required a ruthless display of feelings that he found embarrassing. Most love poems in *Sibylline Leaves* conceal their autobiographical origins, which are revealed only by their Latin motto from Petrarch. The motto plays the same role in chapter 10 of his *Biographia Literaria*, where it blatantly contradicts Coleridge's contention that his principles remained unchanged over the years. In any case, Coleridge found consolation for his torments in duty and faith, as the late sonnet "Work without Hope" suggests. Given this association between the sonnet and his existential suffering, he tried to exorcize the form through parody and irony in several texts, carrying his organicist antiformalism to extremes.

From Coleridge, the Petrarchan vogue continued unabated. Poets and critics responded to both Petrarch and Petrarchism, ancient and recent. Just as in the Renaissance, the Petrarchan fashion generated a wave of anti-Petrarchism, whose champion was George Gordon Byron. Byron took an unusual attitude toward Petrarch, embracing the views of both the adversaries and admirers of Petrarch to have them demolish each other. In canto 4 of *Childe Harold's Pilgrimage*, Byron celebrated Petrarch and Arquà, the village where Petrarch died, together with Dante and Tasso, as poet-heroes of an oppressed Italy. John Hobhouse's note to the canto discusses the critical points of Petrarch's life, Laura's identity, and Petrarch's passion for Laura (229–30). Predictably, the note casts irony on the bourgeois strictures put forward by A. F. Tytler and other critics on Petrarch's adulterous love. Later, Byron found inspiration in Petrarch when he lived with Teresa Guiccioli, who admired the *Canzoniere*. To console himself in her absence, Byron wrote "To the Po. June 2nd 1819," which echoes Petrarch's "Rapido fiume" ("Swift river" [208]).

These, however, were occasional episodes. Byron disliked the sonnet, a form he never mastered, and he disliked Petrarch even more: "I would not be the man even to have obtained his Laura, which the metaphysical, whining dotard never could" (*Byron's Letters* 3: 240). His hostility was given poetic form in *Don Juan*. The poem celebrates adultery—including Dante's and Petrarch's—and derides marriage, which is described as the tomb of love. At the same time, Byron attacks the hypocritical sentimentalism of the sonneteers of sensibility and their masters, Plato and Petrarch, who is wittily defined as "the Platonic pimp of all posterity" (5.1.8). The demolition of Petrarchan love was a necessary step in Byron's campaign to speak the truth plainly in matters of love and to invent a new type of lover, the Byronic hero.

The other main player in the anti-Petrarchan faction was William Wordsworth, whose reading of Petrarch was less sensational though more corrosive than Byron's. Like most poets of his generation, the young Wordsworth translated Petrarch occasionally and made his poetic debut in print with a sonnet. In the 1790s he laid the sonnet aside, only to take it up again under Milton's influence in the early 1800s. His mythical account of that afternoon was a biographical fiction that allowed him to present himself as the inventor of the Romantic sonnet. Wordsworth had a generic admiration for Petrarch, and the sonnet he used was a variant of the Petrarchan form based on organicist principles, in which unity of subject and feeling was the sonnet's central feature. The crucial change introduced by Wordsworth, however, concerned not form but content. He turned away from love, traditionally the sonnet's main theme, and replaced it with political and moral subjects. Unlike most poets of sensibility, he believed that Petrarch was a preposterous love poet and a genuine political poet, since, in Wordsworth's view, Petrarch's love poetry was a display of empty rhetoric, whereas his political verse was the work of a sincere patriot.

This interpretation came together with a rejection of the eighteenth-century British Petrarchans, whose achievements Wordsworth downplayed or ignored. His well-known criticism of Gray's sonnet in the 1802 preface to *Lyrical Ballads* is not only a polemic against eighteenth-century poetic diction but also an acknowledgment of a source of Romantic sonnet writing and a dismissal of it and its followers—that is, Smith, Robinson, and the other poets of sensibility (1: 875–76). For example, though Wordsworth knew Smith personally and was reading her poems in 1802, he acknowledged her role in English poetry only late in life, offering only faint praise by establishing his own primacy as a Romantic sonneteer instead of doing justice to Smith's merits. Wordsworth's "Scorn not the Sonnet," one of his masterpieces, has the same hidden purpose:

it outlines a mini-history of major sonneteers, from Dante and Petrarch to Milton, and implies that the last of them is himself.[4]

Byron's demolition and Wordsworth's erasure of Petrarch did not convince all their contemporaries. Even the responses of the greatest Romantic writers do not coincide with the usual alliances described by literary historians. Byron and Wordsworth are indeed a strange couple. Percy Bysshe Shelley's attitude to Petrarch recalled Coleridge's, though Shelley, Leigh Hunt, and John Keats continued in different ways the work that the sonneteers of sensibility had begun, as indeed did the major women poets of the time.

Shelley was one of the few Romantic poets to take a serious interest in Petrarch's philosophy of love, which was usually adjudged baffling or unlikely. In his teens, Shelley began reading Petrarch with Cornelia Boinville and her mother, who considered the Italian the supreme poet of love. This opinion was shared by Shelley, who found nothing equal to Petrarch's chivalric sensibility even in ancient Greek poetry or in Dante. Shelley was aware of the debate on Petrarch's morality, but he ignored it, because he thought it unworthy of Petrarch's idealism. He emphasized the incantatory quality of Petrarch's verse, which he understood better than most English readers thanks to his command of the Italian language.

Shelley's later works contain an original balance of individual love and political expectations, for which he found an ideal poetic form in allegory. Shelley was fascinated not by the sonnets but by Petrarch's work as Latin rhetorician, love philosopher, and politician. These aspects of Petrarch's personality, which remained marginal for most British readers, found their poetic expression in the *Triumphi* (*Triumphs*), which inspired some of Shelley's mature works, such as "The Mask of Anarchy" and "The Triumph of Life." Shelley demonstrated a use of medieval allegory that was doubly original, not only because he revived an outdated form but also because he combined Petrarch's form of allegory with Dante's. T. S. Eliot's influential view of "The Triumph of Life" as the greatest Romantic homage to Dante is misleading. With greater imagination and free from ideological blinkers, Shelley was interested in what united Dante and Petrarch rather than what distinguished them. The result was two memorable poems that, as Peter Vassallo argued, reread Petrarch's *Triumphs* in terms of Dante's *Inferno* ("From Petrarch" 104).

Hunt's and Keats's Petrarchism is directly rooted in the tradition of sensibility, which does not mean that it was banal. Unlike Shelley, their interest focused primarily on the sonnet. After composing a few Petrarchan sonnets, Keats mentioned Petrarch and Laura together with Sappho in a sonnet he wrote after one of his first visits to Hunt's cottage. Most of Keats's early sonnets were conceived during poetic contests or on social occasions, as were those of the Della Cruscans. Unlike Smith and Bowles, he celebrated friendship, sociability, and poetic fame rather than solitude.

By 1818 Keats had grown dissatisfied with the Petrarchan sonnet and turned to the Shakespearean form, which he then quickly abandoned to work out a "better sonnet stanza" for his poems, as he wrote in May 1819 (qtd. in Garrod 82). The most accomplished of his experiments remains "If by dull rhymes our English must be chained," whose irregular rhyme scheme is very close to the stanzas of his odes, which, as H. W. Garrod and Walter Jackson Bate have shown, stem directly from the Petrarchan and Shakespearean sonnet forms (Garrod 82–91; Bate 297–300). Despite the greater formal and thematic range of Keats's mature odes, he never abandoned the sonnet completely. He returned to his old sins when he fell desperately in love with Fanny Brawne. These texts contain the Petrarchan vocabulary of loss and frustration cast in Shakespearean forms and recall Coleridge's problematic attempts to come to terms with sentimental turbulence. Keats took a formal interest in the sonnet, whose main content—love—was kept at a safe distance because he found sentimental intimacy embarrassing. He broke up the sonnet form and invented an ode stanza (Shelley had done the same in his *Ode to the West Wind*), although, strangely, he was not attracted by the many fine examples of complex stanzas in Petrarch's canzoni. His formal interest led him toward metapoetry, and the sonnet or the ode stanzas he developed from it are ideal structures for musing on the nature of rhyme, meter, poetic form, language, and creativity.

Despite Wordsworth's revision, the sonnet still preserved feminine connotations, which caused embarrassment for Coleridge and Keats. Petrarch remained a crucial author for the early-nineteenth-century women writers, who continued to imitate his sonnets and compose fictional versions of his life. Though feminist criticism has emphasized the importance of the Sapphic tradition as an alternative to Petrarchism, they continued to foster each other. The most successful and emblematic work in this respect was Germaine de Staël's *Corinne*, whose protagonist, the most influential image of the woman writer of that time, was a combination of Sapphic and Petrarchan elements. *Corinne* is full of references to Petrarch, from mottoes and quotations of his works to rewritings of episodes like the coronation on the Capitol (ch. 2). Women poets often evoked Petrarch when the meaning of poetry, the social respectability of writers, and the value of fame were at stake.

When in 1824 Letitia Elizabeth Landon (L. E. L.) published her second collection, The Improvisatrice *and Other Poems*, her starting point was Petrarch associated with Sappho. L. E. L. drew on Byron, but she ignored his indictment of Petrarch. Like Staël's Corinne, the protagonist of her poem is a young Italian poet, painter, and musician. Two of her canvasses contain scenes from Petrarch's and Sappho's lives. These paintings introduce a pattern of tragic, unrequited love followed by the other characters in the poem, all women, with one significant exception: Petrarch. She mentioned him in other poems, as well, the most original of which are "Vaucluse" and "Petrarch's Dream." "Vaucluse" (1820) is a description of the River Sorgue in terms of the River Alph of Coleridge's "Kubla Khan." It is an extraordinary text that links two remote traditions, Petrarchism and the Romantic sublime. Her allusions to the demonic sources of creativity make "Vaucluse" the most Romantic rewriting of Petrarch. The same ideas reappear in "Petrarch's Dream," a longer poem in which L. E. L., again like Coleridge, traced the sources of poetry to love, death, and dreaming.

The Victorian age, although a golden age of the sonnet, saw a change in taste that sparked the revival of pre-Raphaelite painting and pre-Petrarchan poetry. Dante Gabriel Rossetti championed Dante and Beatrice as substitutes for Petrarch and Laura, the medieval poetic couple who had haunted British audiences for a century. Rossetti was dissatisfied with both Petrarch as interpreted by the British Romantics and Wordsworth's revision of the sonnet. Therefore he turned to Dante, the other medieval master of the form.

Yet despite the growing influence of Petrarch's detractors, interest in his poetry did not die out. The Victorian views on Petrarch can be understood only as a continuation of the Romantic attitudes, something impossible as long as Romantic Petrarchism remained neglected. The continuity with Romanticism is evident in two anthologies of the 1870s, Charles Tomlinson's *The Sonnet* and David M. Main's *A Treasury of English Sonnets*. Tomlinson, in what was an updated version of Lofft's text, saw the sonnet primarily as an Italian story. Petrarch's sonnets were the supreme masterpieces of the genre, whereas some of Wordsworth's were not even sonnets. Tomlinson included literal versions from Petrarch because he believed that the existing translations gave a distorted idea of Petrarch's verse. Main, on the other hand, offered a proud vindication of the native sonnet tradition in his anthology and gave no space to foreign models.

The Victorian poets were not prejudiced and used what they fancied, be it native or foreign. In particular, some women poets continued the work of their precursors, including their interaction with the Petrarchan tradition. Elizabeth Barrett Browning's *Sonnets from the Portuguese* revived the love sonnet sequence with unprecedented originality. Browning learned a great deal from Wordsworth and Byron, but she understood that the love sonnet tradition could neither be ignored (Wordsworth) nor ridiculed (Byron). Women poets had to go learn from it if they wanted to reshape the image of the ideal woman and relations between the sexes. Her sonnet sequence not only reverses the traditional roles of man and woman but redoubles them, making each character play both Petrarch's and Laura's parts. Since outspoken autobiographical passion was still considered scandalous for a woman poet, she presented her poems as translations from another language. Her work also showed that the strict Italian sonnet form was suited to the English language and that the renewal of the tradition was a question of content rather than mere form.

In the Rossetti household, no one doubted that Italian forms could be used in English. Unlike her brother, Christina Rossetti did not replace Petrarch with Dante as a model for her sonnets. She understood that for a woman Dante and Petrarch were two sides of the same tradition, which was the source of the view of the ideal woman and the conventions of love still dominant in her age. Rossetti wrote *Monna innominata* (*Poetical Works* 58–63), a sonnet sequence that summarizes an interest in Petrarch that began in 1857 with an entry on Petrarch she wrote for John Francis Waller's *Imperial Dictionary of Universal*

Biography. This note contains standard biographical information on Petrarch, followed by a discussion on Laura's identity. Its surprising conclusion affirms that Laura was Rossetti's ancestor—a fictional statement that her biographers have not been able to explain. In the late 1870s Rossetti helped Charles Bagot Cayley with his edition of Petrarch.

Monna innominata does not describe a fulfilled love story, unlike *Sonnets from the Portuguese*. It celebrates the supposed virtues of self-denial, frustration, and impossible love. Rossetti found that the female character of Browning's sequence lacked fantastic idealization, yet she refused the idealization of the love sonnet tradition, which turned women into perfect, lifeless statues. Rossetti's belief that love poetry could be composed only out of unhappiness makes her sonnets more traditional than Browning's. *Monna innominata* reversed the central conventions of the sonnet tradition, but it argued that refusal was the only way of getting rid of them. Her gloomy parody signals the end of an ancient tradition, but it preaches nihilist self-denial as an alternative.

In *Goblin Market* (*Poetical Works* 1–8), Rossetti further disfigured the tradition. The two main characters are Lizzie and Laura, which cannot be a coincidence, since Rossetti was composing the poem while she was writing the Petrarch entry for Waller's dictionary. In the poem, Laura defies conventions, whereas Lizzie embodies order. The Laura of *Goblin Market* is the opposite of Petrarch's mistress: she is all body, and her orgiastic, uncontrolled behavior subverts the delicate literary echoes Laura's name evokes. At last, Laura was given back a physical body, but it was immature and almost repellent.

By the time Christina Rossetti ended her struggle with the sonnet tradition, Petrarch had ceased to be a source of inspiration for the most innovative Victorian writers. Petrarch, no longer the charming lover of Laura, had become the overweight, priestly scholar falling off his horse, as described in Walter Savage Landor's *Imaginary Conversations*. From the late Victorian period onward, few writers took an interest in Petrarch. In the twentieth century, there were only isolated episodes of British Petrarchism.[5] This scarcity has nothing to do with the spirit of the age, since in Italy and France the situation was radically different. Stéphane Mallarmé, possibly the most innovative writer of the late nineteenth century, is simply Petrarch taken a step further. Instead of concentrating on the poet's self, as Petrarch did, Mallarmé focused on language. Mallarmé's poetics can be defined as a metaphysics of formalism—the formalism that is one of the main trends of the Petrarchan tradition. Mallarmé exerted a crucial influence on twentieth-century Italian poetry, where the dominant Dantean trend was counterbalanced by a Petrarchan line that emerged in the late works of Giuseppe Ungaretti, in the early works of Andrea Zanzotto, and in the work of Amelia Rosselli and several younger poets.

English-language writers, on the other hand, found only Dante stimulating. The most obvious reasons for this are Dante's greater variety and concreteness, though English writers used only excerpts from Dante, taking the chunk that suited his or her taste and ignoring the rest. Even the very few who tried to imitate his all-embracing architecture, like Ezra Pound and Derek Walcott, did so fragmentarily. But technical reasons are not enough. The widespread admiration for the most self-assured poet of the Middle Ages in the age of anxiety is striking. From a psychological standpoint, it is easy for us to understand why a latent, intellectual nostalgia for the Europe of theological certainties would thrive in a world dominated by the problematic truths of scientific thought. Petrarch is unattractive because he is more modern than Dante, and Dante is fascinating because he is so radically different from what we are. Petrarch's fragmentation is too familiar to be exotically inspiring. At the same time, his amorous romance, however neurotic, is too sexless to interest readers living after Freud. Unlike the Romantics, twentieth-century Petrarchists focused on the formal aspects of Petrarch rather than his existential torments.

In England, Petrarch's linguistic vagueness, which attracted the Romantics, became a stumbling block, in the first place for the translators. After the complete editions of Petrarch's poems published by Henry George Bohn in 1859, the translations by Romantic and Victorian authors, and Cayley's 1879 *Sonnets and Stanzas of Petrarch*, another complete translation, Robert Durling's bilingual prose edition, did not appear until 1976. Since then, however, several complete or selected verse translations have been published, notably by academics, whereas many leading poets, from Seamus Heaney to Ciaran Carson, from Mark Strand to C. K. Williams, among others, have translated or imitated Dante. As Peter Hainsworth pointed out in a fine article, the recent translators of Petrarch have tried, in different ways, to recast the *Canzoniere* in the languages of contemporary poetry, an undertaking that has proved to be implausible in many cases ("Translating"). The rereading of Petrarch developed by Franco-Italian modernism remained marginal for the anglophone writers, despite noteworthy exceptions such as J. M. Synge (who translated some sonnets), W. B. Yeats's "When You Are Old" (46; possibly the highest homage to the Petrarchan tradition, by way of Ronsard, in the last century), and Geoffrey Hill's *The Triumph of Love*. No one can tell whether this wave of academic translations is a prelude to a renewed interest in Petrarch on the part of poets, as in the Renaissance and the Romantic age. Whatever may happen, any future collection of poems will be yet another version of the *Canzoniere*, the most inescapable book in the history of Western poetry.

NOTES

[1] English translations from the *Canzoniere* follow Durling's bilingual edition.

[2] Nott's was the only bilingual anthology of Petrarch's work available in England for a long time.

[3] Gray translated into Latin "Lasso, ch'i' ardo, et altri non me 'l crede" (*Canzoniere* 203), creating a version in which his troubled feelings are expressed even more clearly.

[4]The poem cannot have been written to defend the sonnet against its detractors, as modern interpreters usually believe. In 1827, the date of its composition, the sonnet's respectability was firmly established, and critics complained about the contemporary "sonnettomania" rather than the nature of the sonnet (see, e.g., "Sonnettomania").

[5]See Manini for a selection of twentieth-century poems inspired by Petrarch and the Petrarchan tradition.

Russian Petrarchism

Tom Dolack

In the strict sense of the term—that is, the direct and indirect imitation of the works of Francis Petrarch (1304–74), especially the sonnets of the *Canzoniere*—there is no such thing as Russian Petrarchism as a coherent movement, mostly because of the peculiar development of Russian literature. It simply comes too late, not until the middle of the eighteenth century, about a century and a half after the last Petrachist poets wrote and a good two centuries after Petrarchism's heyday—Garcilaso de la Vega (1503–36), Thomas Wyatt (1503–42), Joachim du Bellay (1522–60), and Pietro Bembo (1470–1547). By the end of the eighteenth century, there are too many other influences, and Petrarchism gets too watered down to merit the name.

This should not, however, stop us from looking at the rich afterlife Petrarch has enjoyed in Russia and the Soviet Union. In fact, Russia's brand of "post-Petrarchism" (as Roland Greene refers to it) is particularly interesting. The use of Petrarch for broad cultural purposes in the nineteenth and twentieth centuries continues a process begun centuries earlier in other European countries. For this reason the *Canzoniere*'s reception in Russia will be of particular use in teaching Petrarch's legacy, as well as in teaching the sonnet in general and in courses on comparative poetry. The instructor of Russian literature will likely be interested only in specific reincarnations. Petrarch is especially helpful in understanding the work of Konstantin Nikolaevich Batyushkov (1787–1855), Osip Emilevich Mandelstam (1891–1938), and Vyacheslav Ivanovich Ivanov (1866–1949).

Speaking more generally, there is a highly Petrarchan element that runs through all Russian letters. Beginning so late and owing so much to Western models, Russian literature has always had a deep-rooted anxiety about its own belatedness. Much of Russian poetry can be studied in terms of its original appropriation of foreign material. But is this not one of the great inheritances of Petrarchism? The work of Juan Boscán (c. 1492–1542) and Garcilaso de la Vega in Spain is only fully intelligible within the context of the *Canzoniere* and Renaissance theories of *imitatio*, as is the work by Mikhail Vasil′evich Lomonosov (1711–65) and Gavrila Romanovich Derzhavin (1743–1816) and their French and Latin models. The breadth of Petrarch's influence in Russia is best seen in V. T. Danchenko's two-volume edition Петрарка в русской литературе, in my view the best textbook on the topic (the introductory essay by I. A. Pil′shchikov is particularly useful ["Петрарка"]). In addition, the bibliography compiled by Danchenko and others is a helpful general reference.

Russian Petrarchism, if we choose to adopt the term, comes in two often indistinguishable forms: translation and imitation. Unsurprisingly, Petrarchan elements can be observed as far back as Lomonosov. His position in Russian letters is analogous to that of the great European Petrarchists: Boscán and Garcilaso in Spain, Pierre de Ronsard (1524–85) in France, Wyatt in England, and to a lesser extent Martin Opitz (1597–1639) in Germany. Alexander Sergeevich Pushkin (1799–1837), a great reader of eighteenth-century Russian literature, noted that Lomonosov and Petrarch were the founders of their respective tradition, were indebted to the ancients, and both shared a dedication to enlightenment (Пушкин-Критик 114).

Petrarch dots the literary landscape of the late eighteenth and early nineteenth centuries (see Maver Lo Gatto; Mixailov; Lozinskii). He was translated, although only in bits and pieces, by the likes of Vassilii Ivanovich Maikov (1728–78), Ivan Ivanovich Kozlov (1789–1840), Ivan Ivanovich Dmitriev (1760–1837), and Ivan Andreevich Krylov (1769–1844). Particularly worth examining are Dmitriev's "Подражание Петрарку" ("Imitation of Petrarch"), Nikolai Aleksandrovich L′vov's (1751–1803) translation of *Canzoniere* 90, "Ее власы тогда приятно развивали" ("Her hair then pleasantly unwound"), and Krylov's "Сонет к Нине" ("Sonnet to Nina"), essentially a translation of poem 134. The first Russian poet to directly use Petrarch is Gavrila Derzhavin, whose "Задумчивость" ("Reverie") is a translation of Petrarch's sonnet "Solo et pensoso i più deserti campi" ("Alone and pensive, the most deserted fields" [35]). Teachers wishing to place Derzhavin in the context of Petrarchism can point to both his use of classical models as well as his rejection, typical of sentimentalism, of the strict rules of neoclassicism in favor of the dictates of personal experience and the poet's inspiration.

But the nineteenth-century author who took Italian poetry most to heart was Batyushkov. Batyushkov was well-read in the Italian classics and translated Torquato Tasso's *Gerusalemme liberata*. Batyushkov's 1815 essay "Петрарка" ("Petrarch") lays out not only his thoughts on Petrarch but also his reasons for choosing Petrarch as a model. He describes the vastness of the commentary on Petrarch's oeuvre, noting that "только в тех землях, где умеют таким образом уважать отличные дарования, родятся великие авторы" 'only in those lands where such respect is paid to outstanding talents are great authors born' (90; all translations are my own). Such a comment could only come out of Russia (and a Russia where Pushkin is only sixteen years old). Batyushkov's attention to Petrarch is thus an attempt to produce a renaissance of sorts in Russia, to create an atmosphere where great authors can flourish. Batyushkov goes further and follows Petrarch's own poetic process. Just as the humanists attempted to escape the Dark Ages through the imitation and restoration of classical authors, so Batyushkov imitates Petrarch, translating his model's matter and style into his own (Pil′shchikov, Батюшков). Batyushkov then serves as an excellent model for the appropriation of Petrarch throughout Russian literature, as shown with two texts in particular: "На смерть Лауры: Из Петрарки" ("On the Death of Laura: From Petrarch"), a very loose translation of "Rotta è l'alta colonna e 'l verde lauro" ("Broken is the high column and the green laurel" [269]), and "Вечер: Подражание Петрарку" ("Evening: An Imitation of Petrarch"). The two texts can be fruitfully compared, examining, on the one hand, how the translation is shifted by Batyushkov and, on the other hand, how the imitation uses the work of another author as a springboard for an original creation.

Pushkin, the greatest of Russian appropriators, also shows certain Petrarchan elements, but they remain mostly on the level of stylistic or spiritual affinity. The most notable direct reference is, of course, the epigraph to chapter 6 of *Eugene Onegin*, "La, sotto i giorni nubilosi e brevi, / Nasce una gente a cui l'morir non dole" 'There, under brief and cloudy days, / A people for whom dying is not painful is born,' lines 49 and 51 of *Canzoniere* 28 (Собрание сочинений 4.112). Petrarchan elements can also be found in the short story "Метель" ("The Snowstorm"), in which Pushkin cites (probably by way of Batyushkov) the line "S'amor non è che dunque?" ("If this be not love, then what?"), from the opening of 132 (see Shapiro and Shapiro).

As poetry fell out of fashion in favor of the novel during the second half of the nineteenth century, Petrarch's presence in Russian literature also waned. But it would return at the end of the century with the Russian poetic *risorgimento* known as the Silver Age. Many of the major figures of the period have some contact with the *Canzoniere*. This resurgence dates to 1883 with the protosymbolist Vladimir Sergeevich Solovyov (1853–1900). Solovyov translated the final canzone of the *Canzoniere* (366), Petrarch's prayer to the Virgin Mary. This selection does not do a great service to the *Canzoniere*, which is devoted to the poet's love for Laura, but it serves Solovyov quite well. It allows him to turn Petrarch into a fellow worshiper of Sophia, or divine wisdom. Petrarch's first lines provide an easy starting point for Solovyov's translation: "Vergin bella, che di sol vestita, / coronata di stelle" 'Beautiful virgin who, robed in the sun, / crowned with stars.' Whereas Solovyov's formal changes are obvious—the canzone is changed into a sequence of seven sonnets—the thematic changes are at first rather subtle: the more personal references are removed and references to God and his son are toned down, placing Mary on a higher pedestal. But the translation steadily introduces more and more original material from Solovyov. The final lines are entirely his: "ты . . . / Вся озаренная / Светом и словом!" 'you . . . / All illumined / With light and the word!' Instructors may also wish to examine how Petrarch can serve as a springboard for Solovyov's theories of Eros, ideas that inform much of the Silver Age and its preoccupation with life creation, or turning one's life into a work of art.

Valerii Yakovlevich Bryusov (1873–1924) also imitated Petrarch; his translations and imitations represent a significant part of his work. In particular, his translations from the French symbolists, true to the post-Petrarchan tradition, helped give birth to Russia's symbolist movement—a parallel with the Petrarchists of Western Europe. Bryusov wrote two sonnets with Petrarch specifically in mind: "Сонет в духе Петрарки" ("Sonnet in the Spirit of Petrarch") and "Сонет в манере Петрарки" ("Sonnet in the Manner of Petrarch"), both from 1912. Not unlike Solovyov's translation (a direct influence is not out of the question), Bryusov's imitations present a symbolist take on Petrarch's themes.

Bryusov's "Sonnet in the Spirit of Petrarch" borrows a trope from the *Canzoniere*: the lyric speaker gets a visit from Amor. Love, dressed as an indigent religious wanderer, promises to put the poetic speaker's solitude to a "новое служенье" 'new service.' Bryusov's incarnation of love, however, bears more resemblance to Aleksandr Blok's otherworldly harlot from "Незнакомка" ("The Stranger" [1906]) or something out of Émile Verhaeren than to Petrarch's mythological figure. But it is "Sonnet in the Manner of Petrarch" that truly shows off the differences. There is little that ties this sonnet to Petrarch beyond the sonnet form and the theme of love, although it does demonstrate the ways in which the tropes of Petrarchism can be used to very different literary effects. Here the speaker regrets that he "дух бесстрастью предал" 'committed [his] spirit to cold-bloodedness.' Faced with love in the "лабиринт тусклых снов" 'labyrinth of dim dreams,' he remains silent, dooming himself to a life free of love or passion. The poem is too cluttered with symbolist trappings and post-Romantic ego to be mistaken for Petrarch, but it can be productively read in the context of Bryusov's other work, in particular his forays into history such as Огненный ангел (*The Fiery Angel*) and the collection Сны человечества: Лирические отражения всех стран и всех времен (*Dreams of Humanity: Lyrical Reflections of All Countries and All Times*), the collection in which "Sonnet in the Spirit of Petrarch" was included.

No study of Petrarchism in any context would be complete without some female response. Louise Labé (1524–66) and Sor Juana Inés de la Cruz (1651–95) are among the most insightful of Petrarch's commentators. Russia's greatest female poet, the acmeist Anna Andreevna Akhmatova (1889–1966), is not a Petrarchist (or anti-Petrarchist) in the way that Labé and Sor Juana are (Dante is the much greater presence in her work), but she dealt with many of the same issues. Aside from some passing references in her prose, the main Petrarch reference in Akhmatova comes in her 1957 poem "Эпиграмма" ("An Epigram"), given here in its entirety:

> Могла ли Биче словно Дант творить,
> Или Лаура жар любви восславить?
> Я научила женщин говорить...
> Но, Боже, как их замолчать заставить!
>
> Could B[eatr]ice create just as Dante,
> Or Laura praise the ardor of love?
> I taught women how to speak . . .
> But, my God, how can I make them be quiet!

While obviously a bit tongue-in-cheek, the poem betrays a certain anxiety about women's newfound voice in Russian poetry: one cannot be both admired and admirer, the one who raises the beloved into the empyrean and the beloved herself. Akhmatova takes pride in her role in "[teaching] women how to speak," but, as the title of the poem hints, there is much more to be said about the process.

The two greatest torchbearers for Petrarch, and humanism in general, in twentieth-century Russia are Mandelstam and Ivanov. Mandelstam translated four of Petrarch's poems (311, 301, 164, and 319) in late 1933 and early 1934, roughly the same time that he composed his poem about Stalin that led to his arrest that May. He composed these translations during a period when issues of personal freedom and the individual's place in Soviet society were of tremendous moment. The connection lies in his 1923 essay "Гуманизм и современность" ("Humanism and the Present"), where he clearly identifies humanism as a force opposing the use of human beings as so many bricks in the social structure. In the early 1930s, as the cult of personality began to erase all other personalities, Mandelstam tries to bring humanism back by translating its greatest exemplar (Mureddu, "Mandel′štam"; Semenko; Ilyushin; Dolack).

Russian modernism also found a strong proponent of Petrarch and humanism in Ivanov, who lived for many years in Italy and wrote an essay on the poet in Italian, "Il lauro nella poesia del Petrarca" (see Mureddu, "Petrarch"; Venclova). In addition, he translated, together with Mikhail Osipovich Gershenzon (1869–1925), more of Petrarch's sonnets—thirty-three—than any other Russian poet. Both Petrarch's work and his poetics stand as ideals for Ivanov. In Donata Mureddu's words, "Petrarch's poems are viewed as a paradigm of the universal process of artistic creation, as the 'human dream of perfection' invoked in Nietzsche's philosophy and in Ivanov's poetics" ("Petrarch" 81). Undoubtedly Solovyov's influence can be seen here as well.

Instructors may wish to read Ivanov's translations in conjunction with certain portions of his collection *Cor ardens*, a notably Petrarchan title. There are numerous sonnets and canzoni in this collection, including "Канцона I" ("Canzone 1"), a poem in sonnets; "Венок сонетов" ("Crown of Sonnets"); as well as "Голубой покров" ("A Light-Blue Pall"), a cycle of sonnets. The material is too substantial to cover here, but both the translations and the original work can be elucidated by his correspondence with Gershenzon, published as Переписка из двух углов and in English as *Correspondence across a Room*, in which Ivanov discusses humanism, culture, and metaphysics.

Russian Petrarchism did continue beyond the Silver Age. A Petrarchan note rings through the work of Joseph Aleksandrovich Brodsky (1940–96), who was exiled from the Soviet Union in 1972 and later became the United States poet laureate. His "Сонет к Глебу Горбовскому" ("Sonnet to Gleb Gorbovskii"), for example, demonstrates a preoccupation with time and tradition inherent in the sonnet since Petrarch: "вправду мы поэты, / Когда, кропая странные сонеты, / Мы говорим со временем на «вы»" 'Truly we poets, / When, scribbling odd sonnets, / We speak with time in formal terms.'

The *Canzoniere* in a Comparative Literature Curriculum

Christopher Livanos

Petrarch's *Canzoniere* is the most challenging of all the texts I regularly teach. As a comparatist working in poetic traditions of early modern Europe, I teach Petrarch for his impact on subsequent poets throughout Europe. I study and teach the poetry of early modern Spain and England, where an understanding of the Petrarchan tradition is necessary. Comparatists teaching later Petrarchan poetry should be aware of the potential danger in giving Petrarch too cursory a treatment before moving on to his imitators and their detractors and leaving students with the impression that he was merely a model imitated by Philip Sidney and Garcilaso de la Vega and then subverted by John Donne and Francisco de Quevedo.

My approach to teaching the *Canzoniere* focuses on the novelty of Petrarch's autobiographical depth and the combination of passion and irony found throughout the cycle of poems. While I try to be careful not to downplay the emotionally charged quality of Petrarch's verse, I also like to point out to students that Petrarch was capable of self-directed ironic humor in his own right before Renaissance poets began spoofing the Petrarchan tradition. I try to emphasize Petrarch's status as an innovator, whether discussing his influence on humanism, autobiography, or lyric poetry.

Since Petrarch's apparent self-absorption has the ability to grate on a reader unprepared to recognize the originality of the poet's inward journey, it is helpful early on to draw students' attention to the playful and self-effacing elements of the *Canzoniere*. I address poem 5 directly as an example of Petrarch's irony and complexity. Failure to look past the simplistic surface can sour the reader's expectations for the remaining 361 poems. An appreciation of the sonnet's subtlety, however, can help the reader identify with Petrarch as a lover who imagines finding his beloved in the most unlikely places. I like to introduce readers of the *Canzoniere* as quickly as possible to the idea that Petrarch knows his infatuation is absurd and that he does not always take himself completely seriously. Most people can relate to an infatuated lover's tendency to imagine that he finds the object of his desire in everything he sees, hears, and reads. Poem 5 is thus a cleverly ironic and self-deprecating sonnet on the dangers of overinterpretation. It shows that, by looking willfully enough, one can make any text mean anything. If Petrarchism comes to mean the elaboration of precious conceits, Petrarch was the first poet to parody Petrarchism. He says that love had inscribed Laura's name upon his heart (line 2), yet only through outlandish optical contortions can one say it is written anywhere in the poem. When the class later reads in poem 129 how Petrarch sees his beloved's face in water, grass, tree trunks, and clouds, the instructor may recall poem 5 and compare the process of finding someone's name hidden in lines of verse with that of seeing her face revealed in the natural world. As a poem about writing, poem 5 stands at an ironic distance from the empirical world. Poem 129 has the same degree of irony; Laura's face is no more apparent in nature than her name is in the verses of poem 5. Yet the poet's mood has shifted from playful to melancholy. Whereas poem 5 expresses the relief of talking about the world, poem 129 expresses the grief of experiencing it. As the sequence of words "pensi et pianga et scriva" 'thinks and weeps and writes' in line 52 suggests, writing supersedes and temporarily alleviates weeping.

The irony of the third and fourth stanzas of poem 129 is that the poet imagines nature tormenting him with the vision of his beloved, while really he is tormenting himself with the attempt to impose his own artistic vision onto the world. The poem provides a good opportunity to discuss with the class what irony is, since irony is often equated with glibness, but there is nothing glib about poem 129. The ironic double meaning establishes a connection between contemplation of nature and contemplation of the creative process, but the poet's eyes are too full of tears for him to wink at the reader.

We may then look back to poem 119, where Petrarch does wink considerably, and ask if either sonnets 121–24 or canzoni 125–29 have fulfilled poem 119's promise that another canzone would come and deliver a clearer message. The *Canzoniere* is a difficult text, and poem 119 might seem to offer students some consolation when they see that Petrarch anticipates a reader "chi tua ragion chiamasse oscura" 'who call(s) your words obscure' (line 106). But Petrarch is playing with the reader's expectations, and he tells his canzone to respond, "non ò cura" 'I don't care' (line 107).[1] The poet lets the reader down, and the canzone does not care whether anyone understands it. Whatever the "altro messaggio" '[other] messenger' referred to in line 108 may be, at its most basic level the *congedo* of 119 is an ironic echo of poems 71 and 72, both of which deliver on their promise of another canzone to come until the sequence concludes with the poet saying, at the end of poem 73, that he is tired of writing. The reader's desire for "il vero" 'the true' is left as frustrated as Petrarch's desire for Laura.

The quest for certainty reaches its point of crisis in poem 360, only—of course—to be left undecided in a perfect case of the medieval *sic et non*. By the time students have worked their way through the first 359 poems, they are prepared to recognize the self-deprecating humor of the opening line, "Quel antiquo mio dolce empio signore" 'That old and sweet yet cruel master of mine.' When Petrarch begins a poem by referring to his own emotional state, somewhere near the middle of the *Canzoniere* the instructor may find that the students begin to say, "Here we go again." In poem 360 Petrarch is on our side: the incipit also seems to be saying, "Here we go again." The personification of love has become a familiar figure by this point. Students and the instructor will have noted and discussed how varied are Petrarch's mood swings and shifting attitudes toward love. Again in poem 360, Love is *dolce* and *empio* simultaneously. We know that already, so Petrarch slyly tells us that Love is also *antiquo*, an adjective highlighting the shifting states of consciousness Petrarch has gone through in the *Canzoniere*. It is in this poem that Petrarch's indecision about love comes to the fore. When he calls Love to stand against him in the divine court of Reason, Reason refuses to reach a verdict. This prepares us for the radical shift in tone we find in poem 366, where Petrarch finally and decisively renounces his love for Laura.

I use the wit of poem 360 to introduce the philosophical issues and medieval conventions Petrarch addresses. I have taught the *Canzoniere* in a survey course on fourteenth-century European literature in translation that also included Dante's *Inferno*, selections from the *Canterbury Tales*, Juan Ruiz's *Libro de buen amor* (*Book of Good Love*), selections from Boccaccio's *Decameron*, and Julian of Norwich's *Revelations of Divine Love*. Depending on the focus of the course, instructors may wish to discuss the medieval concept of the *sic et non* while teaching poem 360. The students in my survey course read the *Canzoniere* after the *Libro de buen amor*, so they were already familiar with the debate over whether love is good or evil. In this course I related the absence of a conclusive verdict to the growing climate of social, political, and religious uncertainty in fourteenth-century Europe.

In any class where I will be teaching Petrarch's *Canzoniere*, I find it helpful to introduce as early as possible two concepts central to medieval culture. The first is the notion of human love as an ennobling force that can lead to salvation. I do not generally require undergraduate students to do secondary reading on Petrarch, but I would recommend Peter Dronke's *Medieval Latin and the Rise of European Love-Lyric* to instructors who wish to discuss the concept of earthly love as a step toward divine love. Dronke emphasizes aspects of the medieval tradition that corroborate such an optimistic view of love. Petrarch, however, takes a more negative view. Dante is more characteristic than Petrarch of the tradition Dronke discusses, and students may have some familiarity with Dante before they approach the later poet. It is likely that many instructors will teach the *Canzoniere* in the same course as Dante's *Vita nuova* and *Commedia*, and students reading Petrarch after Dante will be familiar with Beatrice as an earthly beloved transformed into a guide on the path to salvation. Petrarch entertains the notion several times in the *Canzoniere* that Laura may be a Beatrice-like figure leading him to heaven; he expresses such a Dantesque hope as early as poem 13: "Da lei vien l'animosa leggiadria / ch'al ciel ti scorge per destro sentero, / sì ch' i' vo già de la speranza altero" 'There comes from her all joyous honesty / that leads you by the straight path up to Heaven— / already I fly high upon my hope' (lines 12–14). Students who have read Dante will also observe, later in the *Canzoniere*, that, like Beatrice, Laura seems to become even more divine after her death: "Piacciale al mio passar esser accorta, / ch'è presso omai; siami a l'incontro, et quale / ella è nel Cielo, a sé mi tiri et chiame" 'Let her watch for the day I pass away / (it is not far from now), let her meet me, / call me, draw me to what she is in Heaven' (333.12–14).

If the class will be reading Petrarch later in the term, I try to prepare students to recognize these allusions to the feminine bestower of grace that will come up as we read the *Canzoniere*. Then I discuss how Petrarch's Laura differs from Beatrice. Beatrice successfully ensures that Dante is led from anxiety at the beginning of the *Inferno* to ecstasy at the end of *Paradiso*, while Petrarch's fixation on Laura causes his mood to vacillate between exaltation and despair several times throughout the *Canzoniere*. Ultimately, Petrarch rejects the idea that his earthly beloved can serve as a vehicle of divine grace, and in the final poem of the *Canzoniere* he calls the Virgin Mary, "vera Beatrice," letting us know that Dante's (*falsa*) Beatrice and his own Laura were idols set up in the Blessed Virgin's place. In classes that go on to read parodies of the Petrarchan tradition, I find it important to point out how Petrarch could be quite subversive of conventions he received from his predecessors.

While Petrarch comes to reject the idea that his love for Laura can save his soul, he grudgingly acknowledges that Laura is not to blame. "Medusa et l'error mio m'àn fatto un sasso" 'Medusa and my sin turned me to stone' (366.111), he says, recognizing that if he had not erred he would not have allowed the sight of her to turn him to stone. All created things are, in themselves, good: "se mortal velo il mio veder appanna / che colpa è de le stelle / o de le cose belle?" 'If mortal veil it is that dulls my sight, / what fault is it of stars / or any lovely thing?' (70.34–36).

The second aspect of medieval thought I always teach my students as soon as possible is the anti-Manichaean view of good and evil. When Petrarch asks in poem 70, "che colpa è . . . de le cose belle?" (lines 36–37), he is referring to the church's teaching that evil is a privation of good. For Petrarch and for all Catholics, evil has no essence of its own. If something causes Petrarch to sin, it cannot be because the thing that leads to sin is evil in its own right. It must be the viewer's own misperception of an object that causes him to sin rather than anything intrinsically evil about the object. Petrarch goes on to explain this in the following stanza:

> Tutte le cose di che 'l mondo è adorno
> uscir buone de man del mastro eterno,
> ma me che così a dentro non discerno
> abbaglia il bel che mi si mostra intorno;
> et s'al vero splendor giamai ritorno
> l'occhio non pò star fermo,
> così l'à fatto infermo
> pur la sua propria colpa, et non quel giorno
> ch' i' volsi in ver l'angelica beltade
> "Nel dolce tempo de la prima etade." (41–50)
>
> All things adorning our world with their beauty
> came forth in goodness from the Master's hand,

> but I, who cannot see so deep in her,
> am dazzled by the beauty on the outside;
> should I ever again see the true light,
> my eyes will not resist,
> so weak have they become
> by their own fault and not by that day's fault
> when I turned them to her angelic beauty
> "In the sweet season of my early age."

A lecture on the traditional Christian view of evil as absence of good can give students a sufficient background to recognize references to medieval theology and philosophy in poem 70. The analogy of hunger as absence of food helps convey what the doctrine must have meant to Petrarch as well as the fact that calling evil a "privation" or an "absence" does not in any way downplay its destructiveness. In classes that read Dante's *Inferno* before the *Canzoniere*, the instructor may wish to point out the many images of absence and want in the lower circles of hell. Darkness, cold, and hunger are all forms of privation the pilgrim witnesses in the circle of the traitors.

How much Augustinian theology I bring into lectures and class discussions depends on the interests of the particular group of students. I do not always discuss religion in much depth except when some theological background is necessary for the understanding of a poem, but I always discuss Augustine's influence on Petrarch's autobiographical project. Students read at least an excerpt from *The Ascent of Mt. Ventoux* to see the mandate Petrarch receives from Augustine to compose an autobiographical work, pulling out his copy of the *Confessions* to read, "And men go about admiring the high mountains and the might waves of the sea and the wide sweep of rivers and the sound of the ocean and the movement of the stars, but they themselves they abandon" (Musa, *Selections* 17).

Another course in which I teach the *Canzoniere*, The Self and the Other in the Renaissance, concentrates on exploration and Western European contact with other cultures, but we discuss inward as well as outward journeys. Petrarch's *Canzoniere* is chronologically the earliest work assigned for the course, and I discuss Petrarch's importance as one of the most significant founders of Renaissance humanism. In discussing Augustine's influence on Petrarch, I emphasize Petrarch's preference for the fathers over the scholastics as an example of the humanist preference for antiquity over the Middle Ages. Another trend in Renaissance thought covered in the course is the development of individualism, especially as it is reflected in the increasing popularity and scope of autobiographical narratives. The *Canzoniere* represents an important milestone in the tendency for autobiographical works to become longer, broader in scope, and more psychologically introspective. While the *Confessions* now ranks alongside the *City of God* as one of Augustine's two most important works, in the Middle Ages it was not cited as frequently as *De doctrina christiana*, *De Trinitate*, and other works by Augustine that are not now so widely read. The *Confessions* was not only the first psychological autobiography but also the only one of comparable length and scope until Petrarch took the cue from Augustine and composed his *Canzoniere* and *Secretum*. Later in the course, we read Teresa of Avila's *Interior Castle* as another example of an inward journey into the human psyche written at the same time as the early modern travel narratives that chronicle outward journeys of discovery. Students generally respond well to the idea that the development of autobiographical writing is similar to the development of the travel narrative in that both genres are concerned with different types of discovery.

Three hundred sixty-six autobiographical poems make for a lot of introspection, and some readers will inevitably object to what they see, perhaps rightly, as Petrarch's self-absorption. A minimum of three weeks, or 450 minutes of class time, are devoted to Petrarch's verse. This allows for close readings of the most famous poems, but many sections must be passed over quickly. In discussing sections that cannot be read in depth, I have found it helpful to lecture on how sonnet sequences and song cycles fit into the broad narrative pattern we see emerging in the *Canzoniere*. Students tend to develop an admiration for Petrarch's influence and originality before an aversion to his self-absorption sets in. Somewhere around the middle of the *Canzoniere*, when observations of the poet's fascination with himself inevitably arise, I try to create an opportunity to discuss the rise of the cult of the artist and the development of the idea of the artist as a visionary social outsider. Petrarch is as responsible as anyone for the popularity of these ideas as they have existed, in various forms, in Western culture since the Middle Ages. His words "dal mondo i' son diviso" 'I am divided from mankind' (17.4) reverberate throughout the history of modern art and literature in stories of creative people struggling to express their visions. In surveys of lyric poetry, the instructor may find it helpful to discuss similarities and differences between Petrarch's concept of the poet's function with the Romantic notion of individual genius (O'Rourke Boyle).[2] Romantic ideas of inspiration owe something to Petrarch's self-portrait in words of a suffering intellectual giant cut off from human society by the depth of his passions and the magnitude of his thoughts, but Petrarch is more aware than the Romantics of the inescapable formative influence of his predecessors. Poem 70, in which Petrarch incorporates verses by earlier poets, is an ideal text for discussion of the anxiety of influence, as Petrarch shows himself superseding his predecessors by closing with a line lifted from his own poem 23.

The *Canzoniere* is a challenging text for students and teachers alike. More than any other text, I find that it requires a carefully thought-out teaching plan. The *Canzoniere* can fit into many different courses in many different ways, but I find it particularly necessary to plan how exactly it will fit into each syllabus and structure the course accordingly. If we are reading Dante earlier in the course, I prepare students to recognize how Laura resembles and significantly differs from Beatrice. If we will be reading *Romeo and Juliet*, *Don Quixote*, or any other texts containing mock-Petrarchan elements, I try to discuss Petrarch in sufficient depth for the class to appreciate such parodies for their humor without developing notions that might prejudice their reading of the *Canzoniere*. Discussions of Petrarch's irony and the originality and influence of his exploration of the human psyche can, in a carefully constructed course, provide one of the most important keys to understanding Renaissance thought and many traditions in Western literature.

NOTES

Preparation of this essay was made possible with the generous support of the Wisconsin Alumni Research Foundation.

[1]All quotations from the *Canzoniere* follow Musa's bilingual 1996 edition and translation. I normally use this edition in class so we can refer to the Italian, and I find that most of Musa's verse translations accurately convey both the sense of the Italian and the sad, pensive tone of most of Petrarch's poems. In some courses, time constraints demand that we read only selections, in which case I use Musa's *Selections from the* Canzoniere *and Other Works*.

[2]For instructors teaching a survey course that moves on to Milton or Blake, O'Rourke Boyle's *Petrarch's Genius* can be particularly helpful in exploring antecedents to the two English poet-prophets.

NOTES ON CONTRIBUTORS

Fabian Alfie, professor, is head of the Department of French and Italian at the University of Arizona, Tucson. He received his PhD in Italian from the University of Wisconsin, Madison. He specializes in medieval Italian poetry and is the author of books on Cecco Angiolieri and on Dante's *tenzone* with Forese Donati.

Fiora A. Bassanese, professor of Italian at the University of Massachusetts, Boston, and former vice president of the American Association of Teachers of Italian, is the author of *Gaspara Stampa* and *Understanding Luigi Pirandello* and more than thirty book chapters and journal articles. Her research focuses on early modern Italian women writers and modern fiction and poetry.

Aldo S. Bernardo, a Fulbright scholar and a Guggenheim fellow, was Distinguished Service Professor Emeritus of Italian and Comparative Literature at Binghamton University, State University of New York. He cofounded and directed the Center for Medieval and Early Renaissance Studies. His many publications include books on Petrarch—*Petrarch, Scipio, and "The Africa": The Birth of Humanism's Dream* and *Petrarch, Laura, and the* Triumphs—as well as translations of Petrarch's Latin letters. He received the Order of Merit from the president of Italy and a gold medal from the Folger Shakespeare Library for organizing a major conference on Petrarch.

Theodore J. Cachey, Jr., is professor of Italian at the University of Notre Dame. He specializes in Italian medieval and Renaissance literature. He is the author and coeditor of several books, including *Petrarch's Guide to the Holy Land* and, with Zygmunt G. Baranski, *Dante and Petrarch: Anti-Dantism, Metaphysics, Tradition*. His essays have appeared in such journals as *California Italian Studies*, *Intersezioni*, and *Modern Language Notes*.

Andrea Dini is associate professor of Italian at Montclair State University. He is the author, with Graziana Lazzarino, of several editions of McGraw-Hill's *Prego!* and the first two editions of *In giro per l'Italia*. His book, *Il Premio Riccione 1947 and Italo Calvino*, is on Calvino's first novel, *The Path to the Spiders' Nests*, and he is completing another volume on Calvino's early work.

Tom Dolack is visiting assistant professor of Russian at Wheaton College. He graduated with a PhD in comparative literature from the University of Oregon, and his research interests include translation studies, theories of imitation, Renaissance and twentieth-century European poetry, and Russian literature. He is working on a book on resurrection in the work of the Russian poet Osip Mandelstam.

William J. Kennedy is professor of comparative literature at Cornell University. His books include *Authorizing Petrarch* and *The Site of Petrarchism*. He is completing a book on professionalism in the poetry of Stampa, Michelangelo, Ronsard, and Shakespeare. He has served on the board of the American Comparative Literature Association and is past president of the Renaissance Society of America.

Christopher Kleinhenz is Carol Mason Kirk Professor Emeritus of the University of Wisconsin, Madison, where he taught medieval Italian literature. Among his publications are *The Early Italian Sonnet* and *Medieval Italy: An Encyclopedia*. A fellow of the Medieval Academy of America, he has received the *Fiorino d'oro* from the Società Dantesca Italiana, as well as awards for distinguished service from CARA, AATI, and the ADFL.

Deborah Lesko Baker is professor and former chair of the Department of French at Georgetown University. She is the author of *The Subject of Desire: Petrarchan Poetics and the Female Voice in Louise Labé* and *Narcissus and the Lover: Recovery and Reinvention in Maurice Scève's* Délie and the editor and cotranslator of the first bilingual critical edition of Labé's *Complete Works*.

Christopher Livanos is associate professor of comparative literature at the University of Wisconsin, Madison. He is the author of *Greek Tradition and Latin Influence in the Work of George Scholarios* and is studying Petrarch's influence in Russian literature and collaborating with Floris Bernard on a bilingual edition of the works of the Byzantine poets Christopher of Mytilene and John Mauropous.

Massimo Lollini is Hatzantonis Distinguished Fellow in Italian and professor of Romance languages at the University of Oregon. He is the author of *Le muse, le maschere e il sublime. G. B. Vico e la poesia nell'età della "Ragione spiegata"* and *Il vuoto della forma. Scrittura, testimonianza e verità*, the principal investigator of the *Oregon Petrarch Open Book*, and the editor in chief of *Humanist Studies and the Digital Age*.

Ilaria Marchesi is associate professor of classics and comparative literature and director of the classics program at Hofstra University. She is the author of *The Art of Pliny's Letters: A Poetics of Allusion in the Private Correspondence* and of several articles on the satire of Horace and Petronius. Her current research focuses on the Roman poet Martial and his role as poetic censor of Flavian Rome.

Simone Marchesi is associate professor of French and Italian at Princeton University. His published work includes *Stratigrafie decameroniane*, *Traccia fantasma. Testi e contesti per le canzoni dei Virginiana Miller*; *Un'America*, an edition and translation into Italian of Pinsky's 1979 long poem *An Explanation of America*; *Dante and Augustine: Linguistics, Poetics, Hermeneutics*; and an edition and translation of Hollander's commentary to Dante's *Commedia*.

Christopher Martin is associate professor of English at Boston University. His published work includes the books *Policy in Love: Lyric and Public in Ovid, Petrarch, and Shakespeare*, *Ovid in English*, and *Constituting Old Age in Early Modern English Literature, from Queen Elizabeth to* King Lear, as well as articles on early modern continental and English literature.

Elizabeth H. D. Mazzocco is professor of Italian in the Department of Languages, Literatures, and Cultures at the University of Massachusetts, Amherst, and director of the Five College Center for the Study of World Languages. She is the producer of *Lang-Media*, a Web resource for language acquisition materials, and the author of articles on Boiardo, the Este court, Boccaccio, and Renaissance women.

Leah Middlebrook is associate professor of comparative literature and Romance languages at the University of Oregon. Her books include *Imperial Lyric: New Poetry and New Subjects in Early Modern Spain* and *Poiesis and Modernity in the Old and New*

Worlds, edited with Anthony J. Cascardi. Her work explores shifting tropes for poetry in the contexts of the book and digital culture.

Elisabetta Properzi Nelsen is professor of Italian literature at San Francisco State University. She has published on Elsa Morante, Dacia Maraini, and Clara Sereni, among others. She is the author of *Literary Florence*, a literary guide and an homage to her native city, and is working on a book on Baroque poetry.

Tanya Pollard is professor of English at the Graduate Center and Brooklyn College, City University of New York. Her publications include *Drugs and Theater in Early Modern England, Shakespeare's Theater: A Sourcebook, Shakespearean Sensations: Experiencing Literature in Early Modern England*, and essays on early modern English plays, medical writings, and classical reception. She is writing a book on sixteenth-century responses to Greek plays and their effects on dramatic genres in early modern England.

Silvia Ross is former associate dean and head of the Graduate School of the College of Arts, Celtic Studies, and Social Sciences at University College Cork, where she teaches in the Italian Department. She is the author of *Tuscan Spaces: Literary Constructions of Place* and the coeditor of *Mediterranean Travels: Writing Self and Other from the Ancient World to Contemporary Society* and *Gendered Contexts: New Perspectives in Italian Cultural Studies*.

Laurie Shepard is associate professor of Italian at Boston College. She is the author of *Courting Power: Persuasion and Politics in the Early Thirteenth Century* and, with Matilda Bruckner and Sarah White, *Songs of the Women Troubadours*. In 2000, she began a public reading of the *Divine Comedy* at Boston College with Emilio Mazzolla that was completed in 2013.

Michael Sherberg is professor of Italian and chair of the Department of Romance Languages and Literatures at Washington University in St. Louis. He is the author of *Rinaldo: Character and Intertext in Ariosto and Tasso* and *The Governance of Friendship: Law and Gender in the* Decameron, as well as of essays on Boccaccio, chivalric narrative, the *canti carnascialeschi* tradition in Florence, Aretino, Machiavelli, *la questione della lingua*, and Carlo Collodi.

Madison U. Sowell is provost of Southern Virginia University and was Karl Maeser Professor of General Education and the Scheuber and Veinz Professor of Humanities and Languages at Brigham Young University. He is the editor of *Dante and Ovid: Essays in Intertextuality*; translator, with Sidney Sondergard, of Giordano Bruno's *Cabala of Pegasus*; and coauthor of *Il balletto romantico*.

Marc Vanscheeuwijck is a baroque cellist and an associate professor of musicology at the University of Oregon, where he is chair of the musicology, ethnomusicology, and historical performance practice area. He is the author of articles for such journals as *Performance Practice Review* and *Early Music* and the book *The Cappella Musicale of San Petronio in Bologna under Giovanni Paolo Colonna (1674–1695): History-Organization-Repertoire*.

Germaine Warkentin is professor emeritus of English at the University of Toronto and a fellow of the Royal Society of Canada. Her interests include the manuscript book, Renaissance literature, early libraries, Canadian exploration writing, and the history of the book, especially the significance of the book as material object in literary and historical culture; her most recent work on Petrarch concerns Ernest Hatch Wilkins and the manuscripts of the *Canzoniere*.

Jobst Welge is a guest professor of literature and cultural theory at the University of Konstanz. He is the author of *Hidden Natures: Early Modern Subjects and Authorities* and the comparative study *Genealogical Fictions: Cultural Periphery and Historical Change in the Modern Novel*. He has taught and published on the modern literatures of Italy, Spain, Portugal, Argentina, and Brazil.

Edoardo Zuccato is associate professor of English literature at Università IULM, in Milan. He is the author of *Coleridge in Italy*, *Petrarch in Romantic England*, and articles on Romantic and contemporary poetry and, with Elinor S. Shaffer, the editor of *The Reception of S. T. Coleridge in Europe*. He serves on the editorial board of *Comparative Critical Studies* and contributes to the journal *Testo a fronte*.

SURVEY RESPONDENTS

Fabian Alfie, *University of Arizona, Tucson*
Fiora A. Bassanese, *University of Massachusetts, Boston*
Aldo S. Bernardo, *Binghamton University, State University of New York*
Theodore J. Cachey, Jr., *University of Notre Dame*
Veena Kumar Carlson, *Dominican University*
Thomas L. Cooksey, *Armstrong Atlantic State University*
Virginia Cox, *New York University*
Jack D'Amico, *Canisius College*
Andrea Dini, *Montclair State University*
Tom Dolack, *Wheaton College*
Christopher Kleinhenz, *University of Wisconsin, Madison*
Deborah Lesko Baker, *Georgetown University*
Reiner Leushuis, *Florida State University*
Jessica Levenstein, *Horace Mann School, NY*
Christopher Livanos, *University of Wisconsin, Madison*
Massimo Lollini, *University of Oregon*
Dennis Looney, *University of Pittsburgh*
Ilaria Marchesi, *Hofstra University*
Simone Marchesi, *Princeton University*
Manuela Marchesini, *Texas A&M University, College Station*
Christopher Martin, *Boston University*
Angelo Mazzocco, *Mount Holyoke College*
Elizabeth H. D. Mazzocco, *University of Massachusetts, Amherst*
Leah Middlebrook, *University of Oregon*
Leslie Zarker Morgan, *Loyola University, Baltimore*
Roberta Morosini, *Wake Forest University*
Elisabetta Properzi Nelsen, *San Francisco State University*
Tanya Pollard, *Graduate Center and Brooklyn College, City University of New York*
Roy Rosenstein, *American University of Paris*
Silvia Ross, *University College Cork*
Silvia Ruffo Fiore, *University of South Florida*
Laurie Shepard, *Boston College*
Michael Sherberg, *Washington University in St. Louis*
Janet Levarie Smarr, *University of California, San Diego*
Madison U. Sowell, *Brigham Young University, UT*
Marc Vanscheeuwijck, *University of Oregon*
Gary Waller, *Purchase College, State University of New York*
Marguerite Waller, *University of California, Riverside*
Germaine Warkentin, *University of Toronto*
Jobst Welge, *University of California, Santa Barbara*
Molly Mezzetti Zaldivar, *University of Texas, San Antonio*

WORKS CITED

Works by Petrarch

Editions of the Canzoniere

Belloni, Gino, ed. Rerum vulgarium fragmenta: *A Facsimile of the Valdezoco Edition (Padova 1472)*. Venice: Marsilio, 2001. Print.

Belloni, Gino, Furio Brugnolo, H. Wayne Storey, and Stefano Zamponi, eds. *Rerum vulgarium fragmenta: Codice Vat. lat. 3195*. 2 vols. Rome: Antenore, 2003–04. Print.

Bettarini, Rosanna, ed. *Canzoniere: Rerum vulgarium fragmenta*. 2 vols. Turin: Einaudi, 2005. Print.

Bezzola, Guido, ed. *Rime*. Milan: Rizzoli, 1976. Print.

Carducci, Giosuè, and Severino Ferrari, eds. *Le Rime*. 1899. Florence: Sansoni, 1984. Print.

Chiari, Alberto, ed. *Il Canzoniere*. Rome: Curcio, 1968. Print.

Chiorboli, Ezio, ed. *Le Rime sparse*. Milan: Trevisini, 1924. Print.

Il Codici Chigiano L. V. 176: Autografo di Giovanni Boccaccio. Introd. Domenico de Robertis. Facsim. Rome: Archivi, 1974. Print.

Contini, Gianfranco, ed. *Canzoniere*. 1964. Notes by Daniele Ponchiroli. Introd. Roberto Antonelli. Turin: Einaudi, 1992. Print.

———, ed. *Canzoniere (Rerum vulgarium fragmenta)*. *Wikisource*. Wikimedia, 24 Nov. 2003. Web. 27 Dec. 2011.

———, ed. *Canzoniere: Rerum vulgarium fragmenta*. *IntraText*. IntraText–Èulogos SpA, 2007. Web. 27 Dec. 2011.

Cudini, Piero, ed. *Canzoniere*. Milan: Garzanti, 1988. Print.

Dolce, Lodovido, comp. *Il Petrarcha corretto da M. Lodovico Dolce et alla sua integrità ridotto*. Venice, 1547. Print.

Dotti, Ugo, ed. *Canzoniere*. 2 vols. Rome: Donzelli, 1996. Print.

Fausto da Longiano, Sebastiano, comp. *Il Petrarcha col comento di M. Sebastiano Fausto da Longiano*. Venice, 1532. Print.

Fenzi, Enrico, ed. Il Canzoniere *e* I trionfi. Rome: Salerno, 1993. Print.

Maffei, Sabrina, ed. *Poesie*. Rome: Bonacci, 1996. Print. Classici italiani per stranieri.

Manica, Raffaele, ed. *Canzoniere*. Florence: Newton, 1997. Print.

Mestica, Giovanni, ed. Le Rime *di Francesco Petrarca*. Florence: Barbèra, 1896. Print.

Modigliani, Ettore, ed. *Il* Canzoniere *di Francesco Petrarca riprodotto letteralmente dal cod. vat. lat. 3195*. Rome: La Società, 1904. Print.

Petrarca, Francesco. *Il Codice vaticano lat. 3196, autografo del Petrarca*. Rome: Biblioteca Apostolica Vaticana, 1941. Print.

———. *L'originale del* Canzoniere. *Codice vaticano latino 3195 riprodotto in fototipia a cura della Biblioteca Vaticana*. Milan: Hoepli, 1905. Print.

Ponte, Giovanni, ed. *Rime sparse*. Milan: Mursia, 1979. Print.

Santagata, Marco, ed. *Canzoniere*. 1996. Milan: Mondadori, 2004. Print.

Savoca, Giuseppe, ed. *Rerum vulgarium fragmenta*. Florence: Olschki, 2008. Print.

———, ed. *Rerum vulgarium fragmenta*. *The Oregon Petrarch Open Book*. Dir. Massimo Lollini. U of Oregon, 2010. Web. 13 Oct. 2013.

Scherillo, Michele, ed. *Il Canzoniere*. Notes by Giuseppe Rigutini. 4th ed. Milan: Hoepli, 1925. Print.

Vellutello, Alessandro, comp. *Le volgari opere del Petrarcha con la espositione di Alessandro Vellutello da Lucca*. Venice, 1525. Print.

Zingarelli, Nicola, ed. *Le rime di Francesco Petrarca*. Bologna: Zanichelli, 1963. Print.

Translations of the Canzoniere

Bergin, Thomas G., ed. and trans. *The Rhymes of Francesco Petrarca: A Selection of Translations*. Edinburgh: Oliver, 1955. Print.

———, ed. *Selected Sonnets, Odes, and Letters*. New York: Appleton, 1966. Print.

———, ed. *The Sonnets of Petrarch, in the Original Italian, together with English Translations*. New York: Heritage, 1966. Print.

Blanc, Pierre, ed. and trans. *Le Chansonnier*. Paris: Garnier, 1988. Print.

Bohn, Henry George, comp. *The Sonnets,* Triumphs *and Other Poems of Petrarch, Now First Completely Translated into English Verse by Various Hands, with a Life of the Poet by Thomas Campbell*. London: Bohn, 1859. Print.

Cayley, Charles Bagot, trans. *The Sonnets and Stanzas of Petrarch*. London: Longmans, 1879. Print.

Conaway Bondanella, Julia, and Mark Musa, eds. *The Italian Renaissance Reader*. New York: New Amer. Lib., 1987. Print.

Cook, James Wyatt, trans. *Petrarch's Songbook:* Rerum vulgarium fragmenta. Binghamton: Medieval and Renaissance Texts and Studies, 1995. Print.

Cortines, Jacobo, ed. and trans. *Cancionero*. 2 vols. Madrid: Cátedra, 1989. Print.

Crespo, Ángel, trans. *Cancionero*. Madrid: Alianza, 1995. Print.

Durling, Robert M., ed. and trans. *Petrarch's Lyric Poems: The* Rime sparse *and Other Lyrics*. Cambridge: Harvard UP, 1976. Print.

Garcés, Enrique, trans. *Los sonetos y canciones del poeta Francisco Petrarcha*. Madrid, 1591. *The Oregon Petrarch Open Book*. Dir. Massimo Lollini. U of Oregon, 1 Oct. 2011. Web. 26 Dec. 2012.

Genot, Gérard, trans. *Le Chansonnier*. Paris: Aubier, 1969. Print.

Gramont, Ferdinand L. de, trans. *Canzoniere*. 1842. Introd. and notes by Jean-Michel Gardair. Paris: Gallimard, 1983. Print.

Henderson, George, comp. *Petrarch: A Selection of Sonnets from Various Authors*. London: C. and R. Baldwin, 1803. Print.

Jones, Frederic J., ed. and trans. *The Canzoniere (Rerum vulgarium fragmenta)*. 2 vols. Market Harborough: Troubador, 2000–01. Print.

Kline, A. S., trans. *Petrarch: The* Canzoniere. *Poetry in Translation*. Kline, 16 June 2002. Web. 23 Dec. 2011.

Lofft, Capel, comp. *Laura; or, An Anthology of Sonnets and Elegiac Quatuorzains*. 5 vols. London: R. Taylor, 1813–14. Print.

Mandelstam, Osip, trans. Собрание сочинений в четырех томах. *The Oregon Petrarch Open Book*. Dir. Massimo Lollini. U of Oregon, 1 Oct. 2011. Web. 26 Dec. 2012.

Mortimer, Anthony, trans. Canzoniere*: Selected Poems*. London: Penguin, 2002. Print.

Musa, Mark, ed. and trans. *The* Canzoniere*; or,* Rerum vulgarium fragmenta. Bloomington: Indiana UP, 1996. Print.

———, ed. and trans. *Selections from the* Canzoniere *and Other Works*. 1985. Oxford: Oxford UP, 1999. Print.

Nichols, J. G., trans. *Canzoniere*. Manchester: Carcanet, 2000. Print.

Nott, John, trans. *Petrarch Translated*. London: J. Miller, 1808. Print. Rev. ed. of *Sonnets and Odes*. London: T. Davies, 1777.

Synge, J. M., trans. *Some Sonnets from "Laura in Death" after the Italian of Francesco Petrarch*. Ed. and introd. Robin Skelton. Dublin: Dolmen, 1971. Print.

Toutes les euvres vulgaires de François Pétrarquet. Avignon: Barthelemy Bonhomme, 1555. *The Oregon Petrarch Open Book*. Dir. Massimo Lollini. U of Oregon, 1 Oct. 2011. Web. 26 Dec. 2012.

Young, David, ed. and trans. *The Poetry of Petrarch*. New York: Farrar, 2004. Print.

Editions and Translations of Petrarch's Other Works

Bernardo, Aldo S., trans. *Letters on Familiar Matters (Rerum familiarum libri)*. 3 vols. New York: Italica, 2005. Print.

———, trans. *Letters on Familiar Matters, IX–XVI*. Baltimore: Johns Hopkins UP, 1982. Print.

———, trans. *Letters on Familiar Matters, XVII–XXIV*. Baltimore: Johns Hopkins UP, 1985. Print.

———, trans. *Rerum familiarum libri, I–VIII*. Albany: State U of New York P, 1975. Print.

Bernardo, Aldo S., Saul Levin, and Reta A. Bernardo, trans. *Letters of Old Age. Rerum senilium libri I–XVIII*. 2 vols. Baltimore: Johns Hopkins UP, 1992. Print.

Bufano, Antonietta, ed. *De vita solitaria*. Turin: UTET, 1977. Print.

Cosenza, Mario Emilio, trans. *Petrarch's Letters to Classical Authors*. Chicago: U of Chicago P, 1910. Print.

Dotti, Ugo, ed. *Secretum*. Rome: Mursia, 1993. Print.

Fenzi, Enrico, ed. and trans. *De sui ipsius et multorum ignorantia / Della mia ignoranza e di quella di molti altri*. Milan: Mursia, 1999. Print.

Mommsen, Theodor E., ed. and trans. *Petrarch's Testament*. Ithaca: Cornell UP, 1957. Print.

Nachod, Hans, trans. *On His Own Ignorance and That of Many Others*. *The Renaissance Philosophy of Man*. Ed. Paul Oskar Kristeller, Ernst Cassirer, and John Herman Randall, Jr. Chicago: U of Chicago P, 1948. 47–133. Print.

Nichols, J. G., trans. *My Secret Book*. London: Hesperus, 2002. Print.

Pacca, Vinicio, and Laura Paolino, eds. *Trionfi; Rime estravaganti; Codice degli abbozzi*. Milan: Mondadori, 1996. Print.

Quillen, Carol E., ed. and trans. *The Secret: With Related Documents*. Boston: Bedford–St. Martin's, 2003. Print.

Robinson, James Harvey, ed. and trans. "To Posterity." Excerpt. *Petrarch: The First Modern Scholar and Man of Letters*. Ed. and trans. Robinson. New York: Putnam, 1898. 59–76. Print.

Rossi, Vittorio, ed. *Le familiari*. Critical ed. 4 vols. Firenze: Sansoni, 1942. Print.

Stoppelli, Pasquale, ed. *Epystolae metrice*. *Biblioteca italiana*. Sapienza Università di Roma, 2003. Web. 15 Oct. 2013.

Villani, Gianni, ed. *Lettera ai posteri*. Rome: Salerno, 1990. Print.

Wilkins, Ernest Hatch, trans. *The Triumphs of Petrarch*. Chicago: U of Chicago P, 1962. Print.

Zeitlin, Joseph, trans. *The Life of Solitude*. Urbana: U of Illinois P, 1929. Print.

Primary and Critical Works by Others

Adorno, Theodor. *Minima Moralia: Reflections from a Damaged Life*. Trans. E. F. N. Jephcott. London: Verso, 1978. Print.

Akhmatova, Anna. "Эпиграмма." Danchenko 2: 153.

Alberti, Leon Battista. *Grammatichetta e altri scritti sul volgare*. Ed. Giuseppe Patota. Rome: Salerno, 1996. Print.

———. *I libri della famiglia*. Ed. Ruggiero Romano and Alberto Tenenti. Turin: Einaudi, 1969. Print.

Alighieri, Dante. *De vulgari eloquentia*. Ed. P. V. Mengaldo. Milan: Ricciardi, 1979. Print. Vol. 2 of *Opere minori*.

———. *De vulgari eloquentia*. Ed. and trans. Steven Botterill. Cambridge: Cambridge UP, 1996. Print.

———. *La Divina Commedia: Inferno*. Ed. Umberto Bosco and Giovanni Reggio. Florence: Le Monnier, 1983. Print.

———. *The Divine Comedy*. Ed. and trans. Charles S. Singleton. Princeton: Princeton UP, 1970–75. Print.

———. *Vita nova*. Ed. Guglielmo Gorni. Turin: Einaudi, 1996. Print.

———. *La vita nuova*. Trans. Barbara Reynolds. Suffolk: Chaucer, 1975. Print.

———. *La vita nuova*. Ed. Michele Barbi. Milan: Hoepli, 1907. Print.

Allen, Graham. *Intertextuality*. London: Routledge, 2000. Print.

Alzieu, Pierre, Robert Jammes, and Yvan Lissorgues, eds. *Poesía erotica del siglo de oro*. Barcelona: Biblioteca del Bolsillo, 2000. Print.

Amaturo, Raffaele. *Petrarca*. Bari: Laterza, 1971. Print.

Anderson, Bonnie S., and Judith P. Zinsser. *A History of Their Own: Women in Europe from Prehistory to the Present*. Vol. 1. New York: Harper, 1988. Print.

Anedda, Antonella, and Corrado Bologna. "Petrarca." *Classici italiani da Francesco d'Assisi a Italo Calvino*. *RSI Rete Due*. RSI Radiotelevisione Svizzera di Lingua Italiana, 30 June and 1 July 2009. Web. 23 Dec. 2011.

Antonelli, Roberto. "*Rerum vulgarium fragmenta* di Francesco Petrarca." *Letteratura italiana. Le opere. I. Dalle origini al Cinquecento*. Ed. Alberto Asor Rosa. Turin: Einaudi, 1992. 378–471. Print.

Antonio da Tempo. *Summa artis rithimici vulgaris dictaminis*. Ed. Richard Andrews. Bologna: Commissione per i Testi di Lingua, 1977. Print. Collezione di opere inedite o rare 136.

Aragona, Tullia d'. *Le Rime di Tullia Di Aragona. Cortigiana del sec. XVI*. Ed. Enrico Celani. Bologna: Commissione per i testi di lingua, 1968. Print.

Ariani, Marco. *Petrarca*. Rome: Salerno, 1999. Print.

Ascoli, Albert Russell. "Petrarch's Middle Age: Memory, Imagination, History, and the 'Ascent of Mount Ventoux.'" *Stanford Italian Review* 10.1 (1991): 5–43. Print.

Augustine. *Les confessions*. Ed. M. Skutella. Paris: Desclée de Brouwer, 1962. Print. Vol. 13 of *Œuvres de Saint Augustin*.

———. *Confessions*. Trans. James J. O'Donnell. Oxford: Oxford UP, 2012. Print.

———. *In Joannis Evangelium Tractatus CXXIV*. *Patrologia Latina*. Ed. J.-P. Migne. Vol. 35: cols. 1379–976. *Documenta Catholica Omnia*. Web. 13 Oct. 2013.

Bal, Mieke. *Travelling Concepts in the Humanities*. Toronto: U of Toronto P, 2002. Print.

Baldacci, Luigi, ed. *Lirici del Cinquecento*. Milan: Longanesi, 1975. Print.

———. *Il petrarchismo italiano nel Cinquecento*. 2nd ed. Padua: Liviana, 1974. Print.

Balsamo, Jean, ed. *Les poètes français de la Renaissance et Pétrarque*. Geneva: Droz, 2004. Print.

Barański, Zygmunt G., and Theodore J. Cachey, eds. *Petrarch and Dante: Anti-Dantism, Metaphysics, Tradition*. Notre Dame: U of Notre Dame P, 2009. Print.

Barnard, Mary E. *The Myth of Apollo and Daphne from Ovid to Quevedo*. Durham: Duke UP, 1987. Print.

Barney, Stephen A. "Allegory." Strayer 1: 178–88.

Barolini, Teodolinda. *Dante's Poets: Textuality and Truth in the "Comedy."* Princeton: Princeton UP, 1984. Print.

———. "The Making of a Lyric Sequence: Time and Narrative in Petrarch's *Rerum vulgarium fragmenta*." *MLN* 104.1 (1989): 1–38. Print.

———. "Petrarch at the Crossroads of Hermeneutics and Philology: Editorial Lapses, Narrative Impositions, and Wilkins' Doctrine of the Nine Forms of the *Rerum vulgarium fragmenta*." Barolini and Storey 21–44.

Barolini, Teodolinda, and H. Wayne Storey, eds. *Petrarch and the Textual Origins of Interpretation*. Leiden: Brill, 2007. Print.

Bassanese, Fiora A. "Gaspara Stampa's Petrarchan Commemorations: Validating a Female Lyric Discourse." *Annali d'italianistica* 22 (2004): 155–69. Print.

Bate, Walter Jackson. *John Keats*. Cambridge: Belknap–Harvard UP, 1963. Print.

Battisti, Lucio. "La canzone del sole." *Gli anni 70*. BMG, 1971. CD.

Batyushkov, Konstantin N. "Вечер." Danchenko 1: 86.

———. "На смерть Лауры: Из Петрарки." Danchenko 1: 87.

———. "Петрарка." Danchenko 1: 90–99.

Beck, Jeff, and Rod Stewart. "Blues Deluxe." *Truth*. Remastered. Sony, 2000. CD.

Becker, Marvin B. *Medieval Italy: Constraints and Creativity*. Bloomington: Indiana UP, 1981. Print.

Beer, Jeanette M. A. "*Roman de la rose*." Strayer 10: 449–52.

Belloni, Gino, ed. *Francesco Petrarca, da Padova all'Europa: Atti del convegno internazionale di studi, Padova, 17–18 giugno 2004*. Rome: Antenore, 2007. Print.

———. *Laura tra Petrarca e Bembo. Studi sul commento umanistico-rinascimentale al* Canzoniere. Padua: Antenore, 1992. Print.

Bembo, Pietro. *Opere in volgare*. Ed. Mario Marti. Florence: Sansoni, 1961. Print.

———. *Prose della volgar lingua*. Ed. Carlo Dionisotti. Turin: TEA, 1989. Print.

Berger, Harry, Jr. *The Absence of Grace: Sprezzatura and Suspicion in Two Renaissance Courtesy Books*. Stanford: Stanford UP, 2000. Print.

Bergin, Thomas G. *Dante*. Boston: Houghton, 1965. Print.

———. *Petrarch*. New York: Twayne, 1970. Print.

Bernardo, Aldo S. "The Crux of Petrarch's Poetic Dilemma." *Mediaevalia* 15 (1993): 145–63. Print.

———. "Dante, Petrarch, and Boccaccio." *Italian Poets and English Critics, 1785–1859*. Ed. Beatrice Corrigan. Toronto: U of Toronto P, 1973. 19–43. Print.

———, ed. *Francesco Petrarca, Citizen of the World: Proceedings of the World Petrarch Congress, Washington, D.C., April 6–13, 1974*. Padua: Antenore; Albany: State U of New York P, 1980. Print.

———. "Laura as a *Nova Figura*." Bernardo, *Francesco Petrarca* 179–92.

———. *Petrarch, Laura, and the* Triumphs. Albany: State U of New York P, 1974. Print.

———. *Petrarch, Scipio, and "The Africa": The Birth of Humanism's Dream*. Baltimore: Johns Hopkins UP, 1962. Print.

———. "Petrarch's Attitude toward Dante." *PMLA* 70.3 (1955): 488–517. Print.

Bertolani, Maria Cecilia. *Il corpo glorioso: Studi sui* Trionfi *del Petrarca*. Rome: Carocci, 2001. Print.

Bettarini, Rosanna. *Lacrime e inchiostro nel* Canzoniere *di Petrarca*. Bologna: CLUEB, 1998. Print.

Biancardi, Giovanni. "L'ipotesi di un ordinamento calendariale del *Canzoniere* petrarchesco." *Giornale storico della letteratura italiana* 172 (1995): 1–55. Print.

Billanovich, Giuseppe. *Il Livio del Petrarca e del Valla, British Library, Harleian 2493 riprodotto integralmente*. Padua: Antenore, 1984. Print.

———. "Petrarch and the Textual Tradition of Livy." *Journal of the Warburg Institute* 14 (1951): 137–208. Print.

———. "Tito Livio, Petrarca, Boccaccio." *Archivio Storico Ticinese* 97 (1984): 3–10. Print.

———. "Tra Dante e Petrarca." *Italia Medioevale e Umanistica* 8 (1965): 1–44. Print.

———. *La tradizione del testo di Livio e le origini dell'umanesimo: Tradizione e fortuna di Livio tra medioevo e umanesimo*. Padua: Antenore, 1981. Print.

Billanovich, Giuseppe, and Giuseppe Frasso, eds. *Il Petrarca ad Arquà: Atti del Convegno di studi nel VI Centenario (1370–1374), Arquà Petrarca, 6–8 novembre 1970*. Padua: Antenore, 1975. Print.

Biondo Flavio. *De Roma triumphante libri decem, Romae instauratae libri tres, Italia illustrata*. Basel: Froben, 1559. Print.

Bishop, Morris. *Petrarch and His World*. Bloomington: Indiana UP, 1963. Print.

Bizzarini, Marco. *Marenzio. La carriera di un musicista tra Rinascimento e Controriforma*. Rodengo Saiano (Brescia): Comune di Coccaglio, Promozione Franciacorta, 1998. Print.

Blanc, Pierre, ed. *Dynamique d'une expansion culturelle: Pétrarque en Europe, XIVe–XXe siècle. Actes du XXVIe Congrès International du Cefi, Turin et Chambéry, 11–15 décembre 1995: À la mémoire de Franco Simone*. Paris: Honoré Champion, 2001. Print.

Bloch, R. Howard. *Medieval Misogyny and the Invention of Western Romantic Love*. Chicago: U of Chicago P, 1991. Print.

Bloom, Harold. *Petrarch*. New York: Chelsea, 1989. Print. Modern Critical Views.

———. *The Western Tradition: The Books and School of the Ages*. New York: Riverhead, 1994. Print.

Boase, Roger, and Diane Bornstein. "Courtly Love." Strayer 3: 667–74.

Boccaccio, Giovanni. *Amorous Fiammetta*. Trans. Edward Hutton. London: Navarre Soc., 1926. Print.

———. *Carmina*. Ed. Giuseppe Velli. *Tutte le opere di Giovanni Boccaccio*. Vol. 5, pt. 1. Ed. Vittore Branca. Milano: Mondadori, 1992. 430–33. Print.

———. *Decameron*. Ed. Vittore Branca. Turin: Einaudi, 1992. Print.

Boiardo, Matteo Maria. *L'inamoramento de Orlando*. 2 vols. Ed. Antonia Tissoni Benvenuti and Cristina Montagnani. Milan: Ricciardi, 1999. Print.

Boitani, Piero. *The Tragic and the Sublime in Medieval Literature*. Cambridge: Cambridge UP, 1989. Print.

Bologna, Corrado. *Dalle origini al Tasso*. Turin: Einaudi, 1993. Print. Vol. 1 of *Tradizione e fortuna dei classici italiani*.

Bondanella, Peter, and Julia Conaway Bondanella, eds. *The Dictionary of Italian Literature*. Westport: Greenwood, 1996. Print.

Bonghi, Giuseppe. *Progetto Petrarca*. Regione Piemonte, 1996. Web. 23 Dec. 2011.

Borsetto, Luciana. "Narciso ed Eco. Figura e scrittura nella lirica femminile del Cinquecento: esemplificazioni ed appunti." *Nel cerchio della luna. Figure di donna in alcuni testi del XVI secolo*. Ed. Marina Zancan. Venice: Marsilio, 1983. 171–233. Print.

Boscán, Juan. *Obra completa*. Ed. Carlos Clavería. Madrid: Cátedra, 1999. Print.

Bosco, Umberto. *Francesco Petrarca*. Bari: Laterza, 1968. Print.

———. "Petrarca e l'umanesimo filologico." *Giornale storico della letteratura italiana* 120 (1942): 43–54. Print.

Braden, Gordon. "Applied Petrarchism: The Loves of Pietro Bembo." *Modern Language Quarterly* 57 (1996): 397–423. Print.

———. "Gaspara Stampa and the Gender of Petrarchism." *Texas Studies in Literature and Language* 38.2 (1996): 115–39. Print.

———. *Petrarchan Love and the Continental Renaissance*. New Haven: Yale UP, 1999. Print.

———, ed. *Sixteenth-Century Poetry: An Annotated Anthology*. Oxford: Blackwell, 2005. Print.

Branca, Vittore. "L'Atteone del Boccaccio." *Studi sul Boccaccio* 24 (1996): 193–208. Print.

———. *Boccaccio: The Man and His Works*. Trans. Richard Monges and Dennis J. McAuliffe. Ed. McAuliffe. New York: New York UP, 1976. Print.

Brand, Peter, and Lino Pertile, eds. *The Cambridge History of Italian Literature*. Rev. ed. Cambridge: Cambridge UP, 1999. Print.

Bridenthal, Renate, Claudia Koonz, and Susan M. Stuard, eds. *Becoming Visible: Women in European History*. 2nd ed. rev. Boston: Houghton, 1987. Print.

Brodsky, Joseph. "Сонет к Глебу Горбовскому." *Stikhotvoreniia i poemy*. Washington: Inter-Lang. Lit. Assocs., 1965. 40. Print.

Browning, Elizabeth Barrett. *Sonnets from the Portuguese*. Aurora Leigh *and Other Poems*. Ed. John Robert Glorney Bolton and Julia Bolton Holloway. Harmondsworth: Penguin, 1995. 377–99. Print.

Brundin, Abigail. *Vittoria Colonna and the Spiritual Poetics of the Italian Reformation*. Hampshire: Ashgate, 2008. Print.

Bruni, Leonardo. *Le vite di Dante e del Petrarca*. Ed. Antonio Lanza. Roma: Izzi, 1987. Print.

Bryusov, Valerii. "Сонет в духе Петрарки." Собрание сочинений. Vol. 2. Moscow: Khudozhestvennaya literatura, 1973. 352. Print.

———. "Сонет в манере Петрарки." Danchenko 1: 188.

Burckhardt, Jacob. *The Civilization of the Renaissance in Italy*. 2 vols. New York: Harper Colophon, 1958. Print.

Byron, George Gordon. *Byron's Letters and Journals*. 12 vols. Ed. Leslie A. Marchand. London: Murray, 1973–82. Print.

———. *Childe Harold's Pilgrimage*. Ed. Jerome J. McGann. Oxford: Clarendon, 1981. Print. Vol. 2 of *The Complete Poetical Work*. 7 vols. 1980–93.

———. *Don Juan*. Ed. Jerome J. McGann. Oxford: Clarendon, 1986. Print. Vol. 5 of *The Complete Poetical Works*. 7 vols. 1980–93.

Cabello Porras, Gregorio. *Ensayos sobre tradición clásica y petrarquismo en el Siglo de Oro*. Almería: U de Almería, 1995. Print.

Cachey, Theodore J., Jr. "Between Dante and Petrarch." Barański and Cachey 3–50. Print.

———. "From Shipwreck to Port: *Rvf* 189 and the Making of the *Canzoniere*." *MLN* 120 (2005): 30–49. Print.

———. "Petrarchan Cartographic Writing." *Medieval and Renaissance Humanism: Rhetoric, Representation and Reform*. Ed. Stephen Gersh and Bert Roest. Leiden: Brill, 2003. 73–89. Print.

———. "The Place of the *Itinerarium*." Kirkham and Maggi 229–41.

Calcaterra, Carlo. *Nella selva del Petrarca*. Bologna: Cappelli, 1942. Print.

Cale, Frano, ed. *Petrarca i petrarkizam u slavenskim zemljama / Petrarca e il petrarchismo nei paesi slavi*. Zagreb: Jugoslavenska akademija znanosti i umjetnosti, 1974. Print.

Calvino, Italo. "Why Read the Classics?" *The Uses of Literature: Essays*. San Diego: Harcourt, 1986. 125–34. Print.

Capellanus, Andreas. *On Love*. Ed. and trans. P. G. Walsh. London: Duckworth, 1982. Print.

Caretti, Lanfranco, and Riccardo Bruscagli, eds. *Dal Cinquecento al Settecento*. Milan: Mursia, 1984. Print. Vol. 2 of *Antichi e moderni: Antologia della letteratura italiana*.

Caretti, Lanfranco, and Roberto Fedi, eds. *Dalle origini al Quattrocento*. Milan: Mursia, 1984. Print. Vol. 1 of *Antichi e moderni: Antologia della lettertura italiana*.

Carreras, José. "Core 'ngrato." *Carreras, Domingo, Pavarotti: The Three Tenors in Concert*. Cond. Zubin Mehta. Decca, 1990. CD.

———. "Tristesse." *Passion*. Elektra, 1996. CD.

Carroll, Clare, and Andrew Hadfield, eds. *The Early Modern Period*. New York: Longman, 2010. Print. Vol. 1B of *The Longman Anthology of British Literature*.

Cassell, Anthony K. "*Il Corbaccio* and the Secundus Tradition." *Comparative Literature* 25 (1973): 352–60. Print.

Castiglione, Baldassare. Il Libro del Cortegiano *con una scelta delle Opere minori*. Ed. Bruno Maier. Turin: UTET, 1964. Print.

Cattaneo, Mariateresa. *Francesco Petrarca e la lirica d'arte del '200*. Turin: Loescher, 1964. Print.

Un CD-Rom per Francesco Petrarca. Biblioteca Nazionale Centrale, 1 Nov. 2008. Web. 23 Dec. 2011.

Celati, Gianni. *Lunario del Paradiso*. Turin: Einaudi, 1978. Print.

Certeau, Michel de. "Walking in the City." *The Practice of Everyday Life*. Berkeley: U of California P, 1984. 91–110. Print.

Cervigni, Dino, ed. *Petrarch and the European Lyric Tradition*. *Annali d'Italianistica* 22 (2004): 1–563. Print.

Ceserani, Remo. "'Petrarca': Il nome come auto-reinvenzione." *Quaderni Petrarcheschi* 4 (1987): 121–37. Print.

Ceserani, Remo, and Lidia De Federicis. *La società urbana*. Turin: Loescher, 1979. Print. Vol. 3 of *Il materiale e l'immaginario. Laboratorio di analisi dei testi e di lavoro critico*.

Cetina, Gutierre de. *Sonetos y madrigales completos*. Ed. B. López Bueno. Madrid: Cátedra, 1990. Print.

Cheli, Giovanni. Illus. Lucia Cheli. *Franciscus, la vita del Petrarca a fumetti*. Montepulciano: Le Balze, 2005. Print.

Cheney, Patrick. *Reading Sixteenth-Century Poetry: An Annotated Bibliography*. Oxford: Blackwell, 2011. Print.

Cheney, Patrick, Andrew Hadfield, and Garrett Sullivan, eds. *Early Modern English Poetry: A Critical Companion*. New York: Oxford UP, 2007. Print.

Cheney, Patrick, and Anne Lake Prescott, eds. *Approaches to Teaching Shorter Elizabethan Poetry*. New York: MLA, 2000. Print.

Cherchi, Paolo. "Petrarca (*Familiares* I, 1) e Plinio il Giovane (*Epistulae* I, 1)." *Rivista Europea di Letteratura Italiana* 24 (2004): 101–05. Print.

Coleridge, Samuel Taylor. *Poetical Works*. Ed. J. C. C. Mays. 3 vols. Princeton: Princeton UP, 2001. Print.

Coletti, Vittorio. *Storia dell'italiano letterario. Dalle origini al Novecento*. Turin: Einaudi, 1993. Print.

Colonna, Vittoria. *Rime*. Ed. Alan Bullock. Rome: Laterza, 1982. Print.

———. *Sonnets for Michelangelo*. Ed. and trans. Abigail Brundin. Chicago: U of Chicago P, 2005. Print. The Other Voice in Early Modern Europe.

Concordanze del Canzoniere *di Francesco Petrarca*. 2 vols. Florence: Accademia della Crusca, Opera del Vocabolario, 1971. Print.

Constable, Henry. *Diana, Augmented with Diverse Quatorzains*. London: Richard Smith, 1595. *EEBO*. Web. 22 Oct. 2013.

Conte, Giuseppe. *La metafora barocca. Saggio sulle poetiche del Seicento*. Milan: Mursia, 1972. Print.

Conte, Paolo. "La giarrettiera rosa." *Gli anni 70*. BMG, 1998. CD.

Conti, Giovanni. "La musica al tempo del Petrarca." *RSI Rete Due*. RSI Radiotelevisione Svizzera di Lingua Italiana, 6 June 2010. Web. 23 Dec. 2011.

Contini, Gianfranco. "Un'interpretazione di Dante." *Un'idea di Dante. Saggi danteschi*. Turin: Einaudi, 2001. 69–111. Print.

———. "Preliminari sulla lingua del Petrarca." *Paragone* 16 (1951): 3–26. Rpt. in *Varianti e altra linguistica*. Turin: Einaudi, 1975. 169–92. Print.

Convegno internazionale Francesco Petrarca: Roma-Arezzo-Padova-Arquà Petrarca, 24–27 aprile 1974. Rome: Accademia Nazionale dei Lincei, 1976. Print.

Cotgrave, Randle. *A Dictionarie of the French and English Tongues*. 1611. Reproduced from the 1st ed. Introd. William S. Woods. Columbia: U of South Carolina P, 1968. Print.

Courcelle, Pierre. Les confessions *de Saint Augustin dans la tradition littéraire: Antécédents et postérité*. Paris: Etudes Augustiniennes, 1963. Print.

Cox, Virginia. *Women's Writing in Italy, 1400–1650*. Baltimore: Johns Hopkins UP, 2008. Print.

Cruz, Anne J. *Imitación y transformación: El petrarquismo en la poesía de Boscán y Garcilaso de la Vega*. Amsterdam: Benjamins, 1988. Print.

Culcasi, Carlo. *Il Petrarca e la musica*. Florence: Bemporad, 1911. Print.

Dalla, Lucio, and Samuele Bersani. "Canzone." *Canzoni*. BMG, 1996. CD.

D'Amico, Jack. *Petrarch in England: An Anthology of Parallel Texts from Wyatt to Milton*. Ravenna: Longo, 1979. Print.

Damrosch, David, and Kevin H. J. Dettmar, gen. eds. *The Longman Anthology of British Literature*. 4th ed. New York: Longman, 2010. Print.

Danchenko, V. T., ed. Петрарка в русской литературе. 2 vols. Moscow: Rudomino, 2006. Print.

Danchenko, V. T., et al., eds. Франческо Петрарка: Библиографический указатель русских переводов и критической литературы на русском языке. Moscow: Kniga, 1986. Print.

Daniel, Samuel. *Delia*. Sylvester 577–81.

Del Puppo, Dario, and H. Wayne Storey. "Wilkins nella formazione del canzoniere di Petrarca." *Italica* 80 (2003): 295–312. Print.

De Mauro, Tullio. *Storia linguistica dell'Italia unita*. Bari: Laterza, 1986. Print.

Denomy, Alexander Joseph. *The Heresy of Courtly Love*. New York: McMullen, 1947. Print.

De Robertis, Domenico. "Petrarca interprete de Dante (ossia leggere Dante con Petrarca)." *Studi danteschi* 61 (1989): 307–28. Print.

Derzhavin, Gavrila P. "Задумчивость." Danchenko 1: 81.

Diez Fernández, J. Ignacio. *La poesía erotica de los siglos de oro*. Madrid: Laberinto, 2003. Print.

Dmitriev, Ivan Ivanovich. "Подражание Петрарку" Danchenko 1: 70.

Dobson, Susanna, trans. *Life of Petrarch*. 2 vols. London: James Buckland, 1775. Print.

Dolack, Tom. "Mandelstam's Petrarch Translations and His Humanist Archaeology." *Annali d'Italianistica* 26 (2008): 187–201. Print.

Dolla, Vincenzo. "Echi properziani nella cultura e nella poesia dei secoli XIII e XIV." *Properzio nella letteratura italiana. Atti del Convegno Nazionale (Assisi, 15–17 novembre 1985)*. Ed. Silvio Pasquazi. Rome: Bulzoni, 1987. 21–40. Print.

Domański, Juliusz. *La Philosophie, théorie ou manière de vivre? Les controverses de l'antiquité à la Renaissance*. Fribourg: Universitaires; Paris: Cerf, 1996. Print.

Donington, Robert. *The Interpretation of Early Music*. New York: Norton, 1992. Print.

Dotti, Ugo. *Vita di Petrarca*. Rome: Laterza, 1992. Print.

Drayton, Michael. *Ideas Mirrour: Amours in Quatorzains*. London: Nicholas Linge, 1594. *EEBO*. Web. 22 Oct. 2013.

———. *Poems*. London: John Smithwicke, 1619. *EEBO*. Web. 22 Oct. 2013.

Dronke, Peter. *Medieval Latin and the Rise of European Love-Lyric*. 2 vols. Oxford: Clarendon, 1965–66. Print.

Du Bellay, Joachim. Les Regrets *précédé de* Les Antiquités de Rome *et suivi de* La Défense et Illustration de la Langue Française. Pref. Jacques Borel. Ed. S. de Sacy. Paris: Gallimard, 1967. Print.

———. The Regrets, *with* The Antiquities of Rome, Three Latin Elegies, *and* The Defense and Enrichment of the French Language. Ed. and trans. Richard Helgerson. Philadelphia: U of Pennsylvania P, 2006. Print.

Dubrow, Heather. *Echoes of Desire: English Petrarchism and Its Counterdiscourses*. Ithaca: Cornell UP, 1995. Print.

Dufay, Guillaume. "O Vergine bella." *The Pleasures of the Royal Courts*. The Early Music Consort of London. Cond. David Munrow. Elektra Asylum Nonesuch Records, 1976. CD.

Duffy. "Mercy." *Rockferry*. A&M–Mercury, 2008. CD.

Durling, Robert M. "The Ascent of Mt. Ventoux and the Crisis of Allegory." *Italian Quarterly* 18.69 (1974): 7–28. Print.

———. "Boccaccio on Interpretation: Guido's Escape. *Decameron* VI.9." *Dante, Petrarch, Boccaccio: Studies in the Italian Trecento in Honor of Charles S. Singleton*. Ed. Aldo S. Bernardo and Anthony L. Pellegrini. Binghamton: Medieval and Renaissance Texts and Studies, 1983. 273–304. Print.

———. Introduction. Durling, *Petrarch's Lyric Poems* 1–33.

———. "Petrarch's 'Giovene donna sotto un verde lauro.'" *MLN* 86 (1971): 1–20. Print.

Dutschke, Dennis. "The Anniversary Poems in Petrarch's *Canzoniere*." *Italica* 58 (1981): 83–101. Print.

———. *Francesco Petrarca: Canzone XXIII from First to Final Version*. Ravenna: Longo, 1977. Print.

Einstein, Alfred. *The Italian Madrigal*. 3 vols. Princeton: Princeton UP, 1949. Print.

Eisaman Maus, Katharine. *Inwardness and Theater in the English Renaissance*. Chicago: U of Chicago P, 1995. Print.

Eisner, Martin. "Petrarch Reading Boccaccio: Revisiting the Genesis of the *Triumphi*." Barolini and Storey 131–46.

Eliot, T. S. *The Waste Land*. Ed. Michael North. New York: Norton, 2000. Print.

Ellmann, Mary. *Thinking about Women*. New York: Harcourt, 1968. Print.

Enenkel, Karl A. E., and Jan Papy, eds. *Petrarch and His Readers in the Renaissance*. Leiden: Brill, 2006. Print.

Enterline, Lynn. *The Rhetoric of the Body from Ovid to Shakespeare*. Cambridge: Cambridge UP, 2000. Print.

Ezust, Emily. "Francesco Petrarca." *The Lied, Art Song, and Choral Texts Archive*. Ezust, 1 Jan. 2011. Web. 23 Dec. 2011.

Fedi, Roberto. *Francesco Petrarca*. Florence: La Nuova Italia, 1975. Print.

Feldman, Martha. *City Culture and the Madrigal at Venice*. Berkeley: U of California P, 1995. Print.

Fenlon, Iain, and James Haar. *The Italian Madrigal in the Early Sixteenth Century: Sources and Interpretation*. Cambridge: Cambridge UP, 1988. Print.

Fenzi, Enrico, ed. *Saggi petrarcheschi*. Florence: Cadmo, 2003. Print.

Feo, Michele. "Petrarca." *Enciclopedia dantesca*. Vol. 4. Rome: Istituto dell'Enciclopedia Italiana, 1973. 450–58. Print.

———. "Petrarca ovvero l'avanguardia del Trecento." *Quaderni Petrarcheschi* 1 (1983): 1–22. Print.

Ferroni, Giulio, ed. *Poesia italiana: Il Cinquecento*. Milan: Garzanti, 1978. Print.

Fineman, Joel. *The Subjectivity Effect in Western Literary Tradition: Essays toward the Release of Shakespeare's Will*. Cambridge: MIT P, 1991. Print.

Fischlin, Daniel. *In Small Proportions: A Poetics of the English Ayre, 1596–1622*. Detroit: Wayne State UP, 1998. Print.

Fornasiero, Serena. *Petrarca: Guida al* Canzoniere. Rome: Carocci, 2001. Print.

Forster, Leonard. *The Icy Fire: Five Studies in European Petrarchism*. London: Cambridge UP, 1969. Print.

Foscolo, Ugo. *Opere*. 2 vols. Ed. Franco Gavazzeni. Turin: Einaudi, 1994. Print.

Foster, Kenelm. "Beatrice or Medusa." *Italian Studies Presented to E. R. Vincent on His Retirement from the Chair of Italian at Cambridge*. Ed. C. P. Brand, Foster, and Uberto Limentani. Cambridge: Heffer, 1962. 41–56. Print.

———. *Petrarch: Poet and Humanist*. Edinburgh: Edinburgh UP, 1984. Print.

Fowler, Mary, comp. *Catalogue of the Petrarch Collection Bequeathed by Willard Fiske*. London: Oxford UP, 1916. Print.

Fox, Alistair. *The English Renaissance: Identity and Representation in Elizabethan England*. Oxford: Blackwell, 1997. Print.

Francesco da Barberino. *I documenti d'amore*. 2 vols. Ed. Marco Albertazzi. Lavis: La Finestra, 2008. Print.

Frasso, Giuseppe. "Recensione a J. Petrie, *Petrarch: The Augustan Poets, the Italian Tradition and the* Canzoniere." *Studi Petrarcheschi* 3 (1986): 280–83. Print.

———. *Travels with Francesco Petrarca*. Trans. Nicholas Mann. Pref. Giuseppe Billanovich. Photographs by Lorenzo Capellini. Padua: Antenore, 1974. Print.

Frasso, Giuseppe, Giuseppe Velli, and Maurizio Vitale, eds. *Petrarca e la Lombardia: Atti del convegno di studi, Milano, 22–23 maggio 2003*. Rome: Antenore, 2005. Print.

Freccero, John. "Autobiography and Narrative." *Reconstructing Individualism: Autonomy, Individuality, and the Self in Western Thought*. Ed. Thomas C. Heller et al. Stanford: Stanford UP, 1986. 16–29. Print.

———. "The Fig Tree and the Laurel: Petrarch's Poetics." *Literary Theory / Renaissance Texts*. Ed. Patricia Parker and David Quint. Baltimore: Johns Hopkins UP, 1986. 20–32. Print. Rpt. of *Diacritics* 5 (1975): 34–40.

Fucilla, Joseph. *Estudios sobre el petrarquismo en Espana*. Madrid: Consejo Superior, 1960. Print.

———. *Oltre un cinquantennio di scritti sul Petrarca (1915–1973)*. Padua: Antenore, 1982. Print.

Gagliardi, Roberto, and Mirko Locatelli, eds. "Petrarca, Francesco." *Liber Liber*. Liber Liber, 3 Aug. 2007. Web. 23 Dec. 2011.

Garcilaso de la Vega. *Obras completas con comentario*. Ed. Elias L. Rivers. Columbus: Ohio State UP, 1974. Print.

Gardini, Nicola. *Breve storia della poesia occidentale*. Milan: Mondadori, 2002. Print.

Gardner, Howard. *Frames of Mind: The Theory of Multiple Intelligences*. London: Fontana, 1993. Print.

Garin, Eugenio. *Studi sul platonismo medievale*. Florence: Le Monnier, 1958. Print.

Garrod, H. W. *Keats*. Oxford: Clarendon, 1926. Print.

Gascoigne, George. *Adventures of Master F. J.* 1573. Rev. ed. London, 1575. Print.

Gentile, Giovanni. "Le traduzioni medievali di Platone e Francesco Petrarca." *Studi sul Rinascimento*. Florence: Vallecchi, 1923. 5–66. Print.

Gidino da Sommacampagna. *Trattato dei ritmi volgari*. Ed. Giovanni Battista C. Giuliari. Bologna: Commissione per i Testi di Lingua, 1968. Print. Scelta di curiosità letterarie inedite o rare 105.

Giunta, Claudio. "Memoria di Dante nei *Trionfi*." *Rivista di letteratura italiana* 11.3 (1993): 411–52. Print.

Gmelin, Hermann. "Das Prinzip der *imitatio* in den romanischen Literaturen der Renaissance." *Romanische Forschungen* 46 (1932): 85–360. Print.

Góngora, Luis de. *Sonetos completos*. Ed. Biruté Ciplijauskaité. Madrid: Castalia, 1982. Print.

Goring, Paul, Jeremy Hawthorn, and Domhnall Mitchell. "Guide to the Use of Electronic Media." *Studying Literature: The Essential Companion*. London: Arnold, 2001. 101–32. Print.

Gorni, Guglielmo. "Metamorfosi e redenzione in Petrarca: Il senso della forma Correggio del *Canzoniere*." *Lettere italiane* 30 (1978): 3–16. Print.

Gray, Thomas. "Sonnet on the Death of Mr. Richard West." *The Poems of Thomas Gray, William Collins, Oliver Goldsmith*. By Gray, William Collins, and Oliver Goldsmith. Ed. Roger Lonsdale. London: Longmans, 1969. 64–68. Print.

Greenblatt, Stephen. *Renaissance Self-Fashioning: From More to Shakespeare*. Chicago: U of Chicago P, 1980. Print.

Greenblatt, Stephen, et al., eds. *The Norton Anthology of English Literature*. 9th ed. New York: Norton, 2012. Print. 2 vols.

———, eds. *The Sixteenth Century / The Early Seventeenth Century*. 9th ed. New York: Norton, 2012. Print. Vol. B of *The Norton Anthology of English Literature*.

Greene, Roland A. *Post-Petrarchism: Origins and Innovations of the Western Lyric Sequence*. Princeton: Princeton UP, 1991. Print.

Greene, Thomas M. "The Flexibility of the Self in Renaissance Literature." *The Disciplines of Criticism: Essays in Literary Theory, Interpretation, and History*. Ed. Greene, Lowry Nelson, and Peter Demetz, Jr. New Haven: Yale UP, 1968. 241–64. Print.

———. *The Light in Troy: Imitation and Discovery in Renaissance Poetry*. New Haven: Yale UP, 1982. Print.

———. "Petrarch and the Humanist Hermeneutic." T. Greene, *Light* 81–103.

———. "Petrarch: Falling into Shadow." T. Greene, *Light* 127–46.

———. "Petrarch: The Ontology of the Self." T. Greene, *Light* 104–26.

Grendler, Paul F., ed. *Encyclopedia of the Renaissance*. 6 vols. New York: Scribner, 1999. Print.

Guardiani, Francesco. *La meravigliosa retorica dell'* Adone *di G. B. Marino*. Florence: Olschki, 1989. Print

Guglielmi, Guido. *Ironia e negazione*. Turin: Einaudi, 1987. Print.

Guinizzelli, Guido. *Rime*. Ed. Luciano Rossi. Turin: Einaudi, 2002. Print.

Hadot, Pierre. *Philosophy as a Way of Life: Spiritual Exercises from Socrates to Foucault*. Trans. Michael Chase. Oxford: Blackwell, 1995. Print.

Hainsworth, Peter. *Petrarch the Poet: An Introduction to the* Rerum vulgarium fragmenta. London: Routledge, 1988. Print.

———. "Translating Petrarch." Martin, Panizza, and Hainsworth 341–59.

Hanna, Ralph, III, and Traugott Lawler. "Antigamous Ideologies." *Jankyn's Book of Wikked Wives: The Primary Texts*. Ed. Hanna and Lawler. Vol. 1. Athens: U of Georgia P, 1997. 8–31. Print

Hanson, Elizabeth. *Discovering the Subject in Renaissance England*. Cambridge: Cambridge UP, 1998. Print.

Hardie, Philip R. *The Epic Successors of Virgil: A Study in the Dynamics of a Tradition*. Cambridge: Cambridge UP, 1993. Print.

———. "Ovid into Laura: Absent Presences in the *Metamorphoses* and Petrarch's *Rime sparse*." *Ovidian Transformations: Essays on the* Metamorphoses *and Its Reception*. Ed. Hardie, Alessandro Barchiesi, and Stephen Hinds. Cambridge: Cambridge Philological Soc., 1999. 254–70. Print. Supplementary vol. 23.

Hempfer, Klaus W., Gerhard Regn, and Sunita Scheffel, eds. *Petrarkismus-Bibliographie, 1972–2000*. Stuttgart: Steiner, 2005. Print.

Herrera, Fernando de. *Poesía castellana original completa*. Ed. Cristóbal Cuevas. Madrid: Cátedra, 1985. Print.

Hester, Nathalie, Massimo Lollini, and Leah Middlebrook, eds. *Proceedings of the International Symposium, "Francesco Petrarca: From Manuscript to Digital Culture," 3 April 2010. Humanist Studies and the Digital Age* 1.1 (2011): 1–222. Web. 31 Dec. 2012.

Hetland, Lois, and Shirley Veenema, eds. *The Project Zero Classroom: Views on Understanding*. Cambridge: President and Fellows of Harvard Coll., 1999. Print.

Hill, Geoffrey. *The Triumph of Love*. London: Penguin, 1998. Print.

Hinds, Stephen. *Allusion and Intertext: Dynamics of Appropriation in Roman Poetry*. Cambridge: Cambridge UP, 1998. Print.

Hollander, John, and Frank Kermode, eds. *The Literature of Renaissance England*. New York: Oxford UP, 1973. Print. Vol. 2 of *The Oxford Anthology of English Literature*.

Hollway-Calthrop, H. C. *Petrarch, His Life and Times*. New York: Putnam, 1907. Print.

Holmes, Olivia. *Assembling the Lyric Self: Authorship from Troubadour Song to Italian Poetry Book*. Minneapolis: U of Minnesota P, 2000. Print.

Homer. *Odyssey*. Trans. Rodney Merrill. Ed. Thomas R. Walsh and Merrill. Ann Arbor: U of Michigan P, 2002. Print.

Howard, Henry, earl of Surrey. "Love, that doth reign." Sylvester 185.

Ilyushin, A. A. "Данте и Петрарка в интерпретациях Мандельштама." Жизнь и творчество О.Э. Мандельштама: Воспоминания, материалы к биографии, "новые стихи," комментарии, исследования. Ed. O. G. Lazunskii et al. Voronezh: Izdatel'stvo voronezhskogo universiteta, 1990. 367–82. Print.

In Morte di Madonna Laura: Madrigal Cycle after Texts of Petrarca. Cond. Paul van Nevel. Perf. Huelgas Ensemble. Sony Vivarte, 1991. CD. SK 45942.

Ivanov, Vyacheslav. *Cor ardens*. Ivanov, Собрание сочинений 2: 221–533.

———. "Il lauro nella poesia del Petrarca." Danchenko 2: 21–32.

———. Собрание сочинений. 4 vols. Brussels: Foyer Oriental Chrétien, 1971. Print.

Ivanov, Vyacheslav, and Mikhail Gershenzon. *Correspondence across a Room*. Trans. Lisa Sergio. Marlboro: Marlboro, 1984. Print.

Jackson, Janet. "That's the Way Love Goes." *Janet*. Virgin, 1993. CD.

Jaffe, Irma B., and Gernando Colombardo, eds. and trans. *Shining Eyes, Cruel Fortune: The Lives and Loves of Italian Renaissance Women Poets*. Bronx: Fordham UP, 2002. Print.

Jauss, Hans Robert. *Alterität und Modernität der Mittelalterlichen Literatur: Gesammelte Aufsätze, 1956–1976*. Munich: Fink, 1977. Print.

Jones, Ann Rosalind. *The Currency of Eros: Women's Love Lyric in Europe, 1540–1620*. Bloomington: Indiana UP, 1990. Print.

Jones, Emrys, ed. *The New Oxford Book of Sixteenth-Century Verse*. Oxford: Oxford UP, 1991. Print.

Jones, Frederic J. *The Structure of Petrarch's* Canzoniere*: A Chronological, Psychological, and Stylistic Analysis*. Cambridge: Brewer, 1995. Print.

Jones, Randall L., and Steven P. Sondrup. "Computer-Aided Lexicography: Indexes and Concordances." *Computational Linguistics: An International Handbook on Computer Oriented Language Research and Applications*. Berlin: de Gruyter, 1989. 490–509. Print.

Kahn, Victoria. "The Figure of the Reader in Petrarch's *Secretum*." *PMLA* 100.2 (1985): 154–65. Print.

Kaster, Robert. "Servius and *idonei auctores*." *American Journal of Philology* 99 (1978): 181–209. Print.

Kelly-Gadol, Joan. "Did Women Have a Renaissance?" Bridenthal, Koonz, and Stuard 138–64.

Kennedy, William J. *Authorizing Petrarch*. Ithaca: Cornell UP, 1994. Print.

———. *Jacopo Sannazaro and the Uses of Pastoral*. Hanover: UP of New England, 1983. Print.

———. *The Site of Petrarchism: Early Modern National Sentiment in Italy, France, and England*. Baltimore: Johns Hopkins UP, 2003. Print.

Kerrigan, William, and Gorden Braden. *The Idea of the Renaissance*. Baltimore: Johns Hopkins UP, 1989. Print.

King, Margaret. *Women of the Renaissance*. Chicago: U of Chicago P, 1991. Print.

Kirkham, Victoria, and Armando Maggi, eds. *Petrarch: A Critical Guide to the Complete Works*. Chicago: U of Chicago P, 2009. Print.

Kirkpatrick, Robin. *Dante to Shakespeare: A Study of Source, Analogue, and Divergence*. London: Longman, 1995. Print.

Kleinhenz, Christopher. *The Early Italian Sonnet: The First Century (1220–1321)*. Lecce: Milella, 1986. Print.

———, ed. *Medieval Italy: An Encyclopedia*. 2 vols. New York: Routledge, 2004. Print.

———. "Petrarch and the Art of the Sonnet." Scaglione, *Francis Petrarch* 177–91.

Koubourlis, Demetrius J. "On Concordances and Their Uses." *Slavic and East European Journal* 19.2 (1975): 246–53. Print.

Krylov, Ivan Andreevich. "Сонет к Нине." Danchenko 1: 60.

Kuon, Peter. *L'Aura dantesca: Metamorfosi intertestuali nei "Rerum vulgarium fragmenta."* Florence: Cesati, 2004. Print.

Labé, Louise. *Complete Poetry and Prose: A Bilingual Edition*. Ed. and trans. Deborah Lesko Baker; trans. Annie Finch. Chicago: U of Chicago P, 2006. Print.

———. Œuvres Poétiques *précédées des* Rymes de Pernette du Guillet *avec un choix de Blasons du corps féminin*. Ed. Françoise Charpentier. Paris: Gallimard, 1983. Print.

Landon, Letitia Elizabeth. *The Improvisatrice*. 1825. Ed. Jonathan Wordsworth. Poole: Woodstock, 1996. Print.

Landor, Walter Savage. *Imaginary Conversations*. Ed. Charles G. Crump. 6 vols. London: Dent, 1891. Print.

Lapesa, Rafael. *La trayectoria poetica de Garcilaso*. Madrid: Revista de Occidente, 1948. Print.

Larner, John. *Culture and Society in Italy, 1290–1420*. London: Batsford, 1971. Print.

———. *Italy in the Age of Dante and Petrarch, 1216–1380*. London: Longman, 1980. Print.

Lepschy, Anna Laura, and Giulio Lepschy. *The Italian Language Today*. 2nd ed. New York: New Amsterdam, 1988. Print.

Lesko Baker, Deborah. *The Subject of Desire: Petrarchan Poetics and the Female Voice in Louise Labé*. West Lafayette: Purdue UP, 1996. Print.

Levinas, Emanuel. *Time and the Other*. Trans. Richard A. Cohen. Pittsburgh: Duquesne UP, 1987. Print.

Lewis, C. S. *The Allegory of Love*. Oxford: Oxford UP, 1936. Print.

———. *The Discarded Image: An Introduction to Medieval and Renaissance Literature*. Cambridge: Cambridge UP, 1964. Print.

Lodge, Thomas. *Phyllis: Honoured with Pastoral Sonnets*. London: John Busbie, 1593. *EEBO*. Web. 22 Oct. 2013.

Lollini, Massimo. "Return to Philology and Hypertext in and around Petrarch's *Rvf*." *Humanist Studies and the Digital Age* 1.1 (2011): 66–79. Web. 29 Sept. 2011.

Love, Harold. *The Culture and Commerce of Texts: Scribal Publication in Seventeenth-Century England.* Amherst: U of Massachusetts P, 1998. Print.

Lozinskii, Grigorii. "Петрарка и ранние русские петраркисты." Danchenko 2: 118–22.

Luti, Giorgio. *Introduzione alla letteratura italiana del Novecento*. Rome: La Nuova Italia Scientifica, 1985. Print.

L'vov, Nikolai Aleksandrovich. "Ее власы тогда приятно развивали." Danchenko 1: 52.

Macchia, Giovanni, ed. *Poetesse italiane del Cinquecento*. Milan: Mondadori, 2003. Print.

Mace, Dean T. "Pietro Bembo and the Literary Origins of the Italian Madrigal." *Musical Quarterly* 55 (1969): 65–86. Print.

Machiavelli, Niccolò. *Machiavelli's* The Prince*: A Bilingual Edition*. Ed. and trans. Mark Musa. New York: St. Martin's, 1964. Print.

Main, David M., ed. *A Treasury of English Sonnets*. New York: Little, 1879. Print.

Malato, Enrico, ed. *La critica letteraria dal Due al Novecento*. Rome: Salerno, 2003. Print. Vol. 11 of *Storia della letteratura italiana*.

Mandelstam, Osip. "Гуманизм и современость." Собрание сочинений в четырех томах. 4 vols. Moscow: Terra, 1991. 2: 352–54. Print.

Maniates, Maria Rika. *Mannerism in Italian Music and Culture, 1530–1630*. Chapel Hill: U of North Carolina P, 1979. Print.

Manini, Luca, ed. "Presenze petrarchesche nel Novecento inglese." *Testo a fronte* 19.39 (2008): 194–239. Print.

Mann, Nicholas. "The Making of Petrarch's *Bucolicum carmen*: A Contribution to the History of the Text." *Italia medioevale e umanistica* 20 (1977): 127–82. Print.

———. *Petrarch*. Oxford: Oxford UP, 1984. Print.

Manzoni, Alessandro. "Adelchi." *Tragedie*. Ed. Giulio Bollati. Turin: Einaudi, 1965. Print.

Marazzini, Claudio. *Breve storia della lingua italiana*. Bologna: Il Mulino, 2004. Print.

Marcozzi, Luca. *Bibliografia petrarchesca: 1989–2003*. Florence: Olschki, 2005. Print.

Marenzio, Luca. *Madrigaux à 5 et 6 voix*. Cond. René Jacobs. Concerto Vocale. Harmonia Mundi, 1988. CD. HMA 1901065.

———. *Madrigali a quatro voci. Libro Primo*. 1585. Cond. Rinaldo Alessandrini. Concerto Italiano. Opus 111, 1994. CD. OPS 30-117.

———. *La Venexiana. Il nono libro de madrigali*. 1599. Glossa, 1999. CD. GCD 920906.

Marino, Giambattista. *Adone*. 2 vols. Ed. Giovanni Pozzi. Milan: Mondadori, 1976. Print.

———. *Adonis: Selections from* L'Adone *of Giambattista Marino*. Trans. Harold Martin Priest. Ithaca: Cornell UP, 1967. Print.

Marks, Elaine. "In Defense of Modern Languages, Literatures, Masterpieces, Nihilism, and Dead European Writers." *MLA Newsletter* 25.3 (1993): 2–3. Print.

Marrone, Gaetana, Paolo Puppa, and Luca Somigli, eds. *Encyclopedia of Italian Literary Studies*. 2 vols. New York: Routledge, 2007. Print.

Marti, Mario. *Cultura e stile nei poeti giocosi del tempo di Dante*. Pisa: Nistri-Lischi, 1953. Print.

Martin, Christopher. *Policy in Love: Lyric and Public in Ovid, Petrarch, and Shakespeare*. Pittsburgh: Duquesne UP, 1994. Print.

Martin, John. "Inventing Sincerity, Refashioning Prudence: The Discovery of the Individual in Renaissance Europe." *American Historical Review* 102 (1997): 1309–41. Print.

Martinelli, Bortolo. "Dante nei *Rerum vulgarium fragmenta*." *Italianistica* 10 (1981): 122–31. Print.

———. *Petrarca e il ventoso*. Bergamo: Minerva Italica, 1977. Print.

Masson, Georgina. *Courtesans of the Italian Renaissance*. New York: St. Martin's, 1975. Print.

Maver Lo Gatto, Anna. "Primi poeti russi traduttori del Petrarca." Cale 327–34.

Mazzocco, Angelo. "Un'idea politica italiana in Petrarca?" *Petrarca politico: Atti del convegno, Roma-Arezzo, 19–20 marzo 2004*. Ed. M. Miglio. Rome: Istituto Storico Italiano per il Medio Evo, 2006. 9–25. Print.

Mazzotta, Giuseppe. "Antiquity and the New Arts in Petrarch." *The New Medievalism.* Ed. Marina S. Brownlee, Kevin Brownlee, and Stephen G. Nichols. Baltimore: Johns Hopkins UP, 1991. 46–69. Print. Rpt. as "Antiquity and the New Arts." Mazzotta, *Worlds of Petrarch* 14–32.

———. "The *Canzoniere* and the Language of the Self." *Studies in Philology* 75 (1978): 271–96. Print. Rpt. in Mazzotta, *Worlds of Petrarch* 58–79.

———. *The Worlds of Petrarch.* Durham: Duke UP, 1993. Print.

McAuliffe, Dennis. "Neoplatonism in Vittoria Colonna's Poetry: From the Secular to the Divine." *Ficino and Renaissance Neoplatonism.* Ed. Konrad Eisenbichler and Olga Zorzi Pugliese. Toronto: Dovehouse, 1986. 101–12. Print.

McFarlane, I. D., ed. *The* Délie *of Maurice Scève.* Cambridge: Cambridge UP, 1966. Print.

McLaughlin, Martin L. *Literary Imitation in the Italian Renaissance: The Theory and Practice of Literary Imitation in Italy from Dante to Bembo.* Oxford: Clarendon, 1995. Print.

———. "Petrarch: Between Two Ages, between Two Languages." *Italy's Three Crowns: Reading Dante, Petrarch and Boccaccio.* Ed. Zygmunt G. Barański and McLaughlin. Oxford: Bodleian Lib., 2007. 17–33. Print.

McLaughlin, Martin, and Letizia Panizza, with Peter Hainsworth, eds. *Petrarch in Britain: Interpreters, Imitators, and Translators over Seven Hundred Years.* Oxford: Oxford UP for the British Acad., 2007. Print.

Medrano, Francisco de. "Veré al tiempo tomar de ti, señora." *Golden Age Sonnets.* Sweet Briar Coll., 1995. Web. 26 Feb. 2014.

Menocal, Maria Rosa. *Shards of Love: Exile and the Origins of the Lyric.* Durham: Duke UP, 1994. Print.

Mezzadroli, Giuseppina. "Virtues and Vices." *The Dante Encyclopedia.* Ed. Richard Lansing. New York: Garland, 2000. 866–71. Print.

Middlebrook, Leah. *Imperial Lyric: New Poetry and New Subjects in Early Modern Spain.* University Park: Penn State UP, 2009. Print.

Migraine-George, Thérèse. "Specular Desires: Orpheus and Pygmalion as Aesthetic Paradigms in Petrarch's *Rime sparse.*" *Comparative Literature Studies* 36 (1999): 226–46. Print.

Milde, Wolfgang. "Petrarch's List of Favorite Books." *Res publica litterarum* 2 (1979): 229–32. Print.

Minnis, Alastair J. "Authors in Love: The Exegesis of Late-Medieval Love-Poets." *The Uses of Manuscripts in Literary Studies: Essays in Memory of Judson Boyce Allen.* Ed. C. Cook Morse, P. Reed Doob, and M. Currie Woods. Kalamazoo: Medieval Inst., 1992. 161–91. Print.

Minta, Stephen. *Petrarch and Petrarchism: The English and French Traditions.* Manchester: Manchester UP, 1980. Print.

Mirollo, James V. *Mannerism and Renaissance Poetry: Concept, Mode, Inner Design.* New Haven: Yale UP, 1984. Print.

Mixailov, A. D. "L'œuvre de Francesco Petrarca et la science philologique russe." Cale 335–44.

Mommsen, Theodor E. "Petrarch's Conception of the 'Dark Ages.'" *Speculum* 17 (1942): 226–42. Print.

Monteverdi, Claudio. *Selva Morale et Spirituale*. 1640. Cond. Conrad Junghänel. Cantus Cölln, Concerto Palatino. Harmonia Mundi, 2001. CD. 901718.20.

———. *Il sesto libro de madrigali*. 1614. Cond. Rinaldo Alessandrini. Concerto Italiano. Arcana, 1992. CD. A 66.

———. *La Venexiana. Concerto: Settimo libro de madrigali*. 1619. Glossa, 1998. CD. GCD 920904.

Moore, Mary B. *Desiring Voices: Women Sonneteers and Petrarchism*. Carbondale: Southern Illinois UP, 2000. Print.

Mortimer, Anthony, ed. *Petrarch's* Canzoniere *in the English Renaissance*. Rev. and enlarged ed. Amsterdam: Rodopi, 2005. Print.

Multilingual Bibles. Latin Vulgata and King James Version. Ed. Mark Olsen. ARTFL Project, U of Chicago, 1 Oct. 2011. Web. 30 Dec. 2011.

Mureddu, Donata. "Mandel'štam and Petrarch." *Scando-Slavica* 26 (1980): 53–84. Print.

———. "Petrarch and Vjačeslav Ivanov." *Scando-Slavica* 30 (1984): 73–101. Print.

Musa, Mark. Preface. Musa, Canzoniere ix–x.

Musto, Ronald G. *Apocalypse in Rome: Cola di Rienzo and the Politics of the New Age*. Berkeley: U of California P, 2003. Print.

Mutini, Claudio. *L'autore e l'opera: Saggi sulla letteratura del Cinquecento*. Rome: Bulzoni, 1973. Print.

Nardone, Jean-Luc. *Pétrarque et le pétrarquisme*. Paris: PU de France, 1998. Print.

Nashe, Thomas. *The Unfortunate Traveler; or, The Life of Jack Wilton*. London, 1595. Print.

Navarrete, Ignacio. *Orphans of Petrarch: Poetry and Theory in the Spanish Renaissance*. Berkeley: U of California P, 1994. Print.

Newman, F. X., ed. Preface. *The Meaning of Courtly Love*. Albany: State U of New York P, 1968. v–x. Print.

Noferi, Adelia. "Da un commento al *Canzoniere* del Petrarca: Lettura del sonetto introduttivo." *Lettere italiane* 26 (1974): 165–79. Print.

———. *Frammenti per i* Fragmenta *di Petrarca*. Rome: Bulzoni, 2001. Print.

———. *Le poetiche critiche novecenteche*. Florence: Le Monnier, 1970. Print.

Nohrnberg, James C. "The Inferno." *Homer to Brecht: The European Epic and Dramatic Traditions*. Ed. Michael Seidel and Edward Mendelson. New Haven: Yale UP, 1977. 76–104. Print.

Nolhac, Pierre de. *Le* Canzoniere *autographe de Petrarque*. Paris: Klincksieck, 1886. Print.

———. *Pétrarque et l'humanisme*. 2nd ed. Paris: Champion, 1907. Print.

Norbrook, David G., and H. R. Woudhuysen, eds. *The Penguin Book of Renaissance Verse, 1509–1659*. Harmondsworth: Penguin, 1992. Print.

O'Keeffe, Anne, and Fiona Farr. "Using Language Corpora in Initial Teacher Education: Pedagogic Issues and Practical Applications." *TESOL Quarterly* 37.3 (2003): 389–418. Print.

Orbison, Roy. "Crying." *"Pretty Woman": The Best of Roy Orbison*. Columbia, 1996. CD.

The Oregon Petrarch Open Book. Dir. Massimo Lollini. U of Oregon, 1 Oct. 2011. Web. 23 Dec. 2011.

Orelli, Giorgio. "Dantismi del *Canzoniere*." *Accertamenti verbali*. Milan: Bompiani, 1978. 67–81. Print.

———. "Orelli legge Petrarca." *RSI, Rete Due*. RSI Radiotelevisione Svizzera di Lingua Italiana, 22 Oct. 2004. Web. 23 Dec. 2011.

O'Rourke Boyle, Marjorie. *Petrarch's Genius: Pentimento and Prophecy*. Berkeley: U of California P, 1991. Print.

Ovid. Amores*: Text, Prolegomena, Commentary*. Ed. J. C. McKeown. 4 vols. Liverpool: Cairns, 1987–99. Print.

———. *Metamorphoses*. Trans. Stanley Lombardo. Introd. W. R. Johnson. Indianapolis: Hackett, 2010. Print.

Padoan, Giorgio, ed. *Petrarca, Venezia e il Veneto*. Florence: Olschki, 1976. Print.

Parker, Patricia A. "Virile Style." *Premodern Sexualities*. Ed. Louise Fradenburg and Carla Freccero. New York: Routledge, 1996. 201–22. Print.

Peperzak, Adriaan T., ed. *Ethics as First Philosophy: The Significance of Emmanuel Levinas for Philosophy, Literature, and Religion*. New York: Routledge, 1995. Print.

Perkins, David. "What Is Understanding?" Wiske, *Teaching* 39–57.

Perkins, Leeman L. *Music in the Age of the Renaissance*. New York: Norton, 1999. Print.

"Petrarca e i poeti d'oggi (Vittorio Sereni, Andrea Zanzotto, Andrea Porta e Maria Corti)." *Petrarca e il petrarchismo. Un'ideologia della letteratura*. Ed. Marziano Guglielminetti. Turin: Paravia, 1977. 191–96. Print.

Petrarch. Beinecke Rare Book and Manuscript Lib., Yale U, Sept. 2004. Web. 23 Dec. 2011.

Petrarch: Catalogue of the Petrarch Collection in Cornell University Library. Introd. Morris Bishop. Millwood: Kraus, 1974. Print.

Petrarch at 700. Penn Libs., U of Pennsylvania, 10 Jan. 2008. Web. 23 Dec. 2011.

Il Petrarchismo: Un modello di poesia per l'Europa. Ed. Loredana Chines (vol. 1) and Floriana Calitti and Roberto Gigliucci (vol. 2). 2 vols. Rome: Bulzoni, 2006. Print.

Petrie, Jennifer. *Petrarch: The Augustan Poets, the Italian Tradition and the* Canzoniere. Dublin: Irish Acad., 1983. Print.

Petrini, Mario. *La risurrezione della carne. Saggi sul* Canzoniere. Milan: Mursia, 1993. Print.

Petrucci, Armando. *La scrittura di Francesco Petrarca*. Vatican City: Biblioteca Apostolica Vaticana, 1967. Print.

Pettegree, Andrew. *The Book in the Renaissance*. New Haven: Yale UP, 2010. Print.

Pico della Mirandola, Giovanni Francesco, and Pietro Bembo. *Le epistole "De Imitatione" de Giovanfrancesco Pico della Mirandola e di Pietro Bembo*. Ed. Giorgio Santangelo. Florence: Olschki, 1954. Print.

Picone, Michelangelo, ed. *Il* Canzoniere*: Lettura micro e macrotestuale*. Ravenna: Longo, 2007. Print.

———. "Riscritture dantesche nel *Canzoniere* di Petrarca." *Rassegna europea di letteratura italiana* 2 (1993): 115–25. Print.

Pieretti, Piero. "Bibliografia petrarchesca 1964–1973." *Studi petrarcheschi* 9 (1978): 203–46. Print.

Pigman, G. W., III. "Versions of Imitation in the Renaissance." *Renaissance Quarterly* 33 (1980): 1–32. Print.

Pignatti, Franco. *Antichi e moderni. Italica*. Dir. Daniele Maria Renzoni. RAI Intl., 2001. Web. 2 Jan. 2013.

———. *L'imitazione nel Quattrocento e nel Cinquecento. Italica*. Dir. Daniele Maria Renzoni. RAI Intl., 2001. Web. 2 Jan. 2013.

Pil'shchikov, I. A. Батюшков и литература Италии: Филологические разыскания. Moscow: Yazyki slavyanskoi kul'tury, 2003. Print.

———. "Петрарка в России: Очерк истории восприятия." Danchenko 1: 15–40.

Plato. *Complete Works*. Ed. John M. Cooper. Indianapolis: Hackett, 1997. Print.

Plumb, J. H. *The Italian Renaissance*. Boston: Houghton, 1987. Print.

Pontiggia, Giuseppe. *I contemporanei del futuro*. Milan: Mondadori, 1998. Print.

———. "La contemporaneità dell'antico." *Il residence delle ombre cinesi*. Milan: Mondadori, 2004. 101–35. Print.

Porcelli, Bruno. *Petrarca volgare e la sua fortuna sino al Cinquecento*. Pisa: Istituti Editoriali e Poligrafici Internazionali, 2004. Print.

Pötters, Wilhelm. *Chi era Laura? Strutture linguistiche e matematiche nel* Canzoniere *di Francesco Petrarca*. Bologna: Il Mulino, 1987. Print.

Praloran, Marco, ed. *La metrica dei* Fragmenta. Rome: Antenore, 2003. Print.

Prescott, Anne Lake. *French Poets and English Poetry*. New Haven: Yale UP, 1978. Print.

Priest, Harold Martin. Introduction. Marino, *Adonis* xi–lvii.

Prieto, Antonio. *La poesía española del siglo XVI*. Madrid: Cátedra, 1984. Print.

Pulsoni, Carlo. *La tecnica compositiva nei* Rerum vulgarium fragmenta. *Riuso metrico e lettura autoriale*. Rome: Bagatto, 1998. Print.

Pushkin, Alexander S. "Метель." Pushkin, Собрание сочинений 5: 71.

———. Пушкин-Критик. Moscow: Academia, 1934. Print.

———. Собрание сочинений. 10 vols. Moscow: Khudozh. Lit., 1959. Print.

Quaglio, Antonio Enzo. *Francesco Petrarca*. Milan: Garzanti, 1967. Print.

Quarta, Nino. *Di alcuni nuovi studi sull'ordinamento del canzoniere petrarchesco*. Naples: Maria Viscatale de Losa, 1938. Print.

Quondam, Amedeo. *Petrarca, l'italiano dimenticato*. Milan: Rizzoli, 2004. Print.

———, ed. *Petrarca in Barocco. Cantieri petrarcheschi: Due seminari romani*. Rome: Bulzoni, 2004. Print.

———. *Petrarchismo mediato: Per una critica della forma "antologia."* Rome: Bulzoni, 1974. Print.

———. "Ritorno agli antichi. Petrarca scrive a Cicerone." *Italica*. RAI Intl., 1996. Web. 23 Dec. 2011.

———. "Ritorno agli antichi. Petrarca scrive a Omero." *Italica*. RAI Intl., 1996. Web. 23 Dec. 2011.

Raben, Joseph. "Computer Applications in the Humanities." *Science* 26 Apr. 1985: 434–38. Print.

Rafti, Patrizia. "Alle origini dei *Rerum vulgarium fragmenta*." *Scrittura e civiltà* 19 (1995): 199–212. Print.

Reiss, Timothy J. *Mirages of the Selfe: Patterns of Personhood in Ancient and Early Modern Europe*. Stanford: Stanford UP, 2003. Print.

Richardson, Brian. *Print Culture in Renaissance Italy*. Cambridge: Cambridge UP, 1994. Print.

Rico, Francisco. "Francesco Petrarca." *Italica*. RAI Intl., 1996. Web. 23 Dec. 2011.

———. "*Rime sparse, Rerum vulgarium fragmenta* para el titulo y el primer soneto del *Canzoniere*." *Medioevo Romanzo* 3 (1976): 101–38. Print.

———. *El sueño del humanismo: De Petrarca a Erasmo*. Madrid: Alianza, 1993. Print.

———. *Vida u obra de Petrarca. I: Lectura del* Secretum. Chapel Hill: Dept. of Romance Langs., U of North Carolina, 1974. Print. North Carolina Studies in the Romance Langs. and Lits.: Essays 33.

Rigolot, François. *Louise Labé Lyonnaise ou la Renaissance au féminin*. Paris: Honoré Champion, 1997. Print.

Rizzo, Silvia. "Petrarca, il latino e il volgare." *Quaderni petrarcheschi* 7 (1990): 7–40. Print.

Robbins, Jill. "Petrarch Reading Augustine: *The Ascent of Mont Ventoux*." *Philological Quarterly* 64 (1985): 533–53. Print.

Robertson, D. W., Jr. *A Preface to Chaucer: Studies in Medieval Perspectives*. Princeton: Princeton UP, 1962. Print.

Robin, Diana. *Publishing Women: Salons, the Presses, and the Counter-Reformation in Sixteenth-Century Italy*. Chicago: U of Chicago P, 2007. Print.

Robinson, James Harvey. *Petrarch, the First Modern Scholar and Man of Letters*. 2nd ed. New York: Putnam, 1914. Print.

Robinson, Mary. *Poems, 1791*. Ed. Jonathan Wordsworth. Oxford: Woodstock, 1994. Print.

———. *The Poetical Works of the Late Mrs. Mary Robinson*. Introd. Caroline Franklin. 3 vols. London: Routledge, 1996. Print. Facsim. ed.

———. *Sappho and Phaon. Selected Poems*. Ed. Judith Pascoe. Peterborough: Broadview, 2000. 144–80. Print.

Roche, Thomas P., Jr. "The Calendrical Structure of Petrarch's *Canzoniere*." *Studies in Philology* 71.2 (1974): 152–72. Print.

———. *Petrarch and the English Sonnet Sequences*. New York: AMS, 1989. Print.

———, ed. *Petrarch in English*. London: Penguin, 2005. Print.

Rollins, Hyder E., and Herschel Baker, eds. *The Renaissance in England: Non-dramatic Prose and Verse of the Sixteenth-Century*. Lexington: Heath, 1954. Print.

Ronsard, Pierre de. *Les Amours*. Pref. Françoise Joukowsky. Ed. Albert-Marie Schmidt. Paris: Gallimard, 1974. Print.

———. *Selected Poems*. Ed. and trans. Malcolm Quainton and Elizabeth Vinestock. London: Penguin, 2002. Print.

Rossetti, Christina. "Petrarca." *The Imperial Dictionary of Universal Biography*. Ed. John Francis Waller. Vol. 3, pt. 14. London: W. Mackenzie, 1863. 542–44. Print.

———. *The Poetical Works of Christina Georgina Rossetti*. Ed. William Michael Rossetti. London: Macmillan, 1904. Print.

Russo, Luigi. "Gaspara Stampa e il Petrarchismo del '500." *Belfagor* 13.1 (1958): 1–20. Print.

Sadlon, Peter, ed. *Francesco Petrarch and Laura de Noves*. Sadlon, 10 Sept. 2007. Web. 23 Dec. 2011.

Santagata, Marco. *Dal sonetto al* Canzoniere. *Ricerche sulla preistoria e la costituzione di un genere*. Padua: Liviana, 1979. Print.

———. *I frammenti dell'anima. Storia e racconto nel* Canzoniere *del Petrarca*. Bologna: Il Mulino, 1992. Print.

———. Introduzione. Santagata, *Canzoniere* xiii–xcvi.

———. "Il Naufragio dei simboli (*R.V.F.* 323)." *Chroniques italiennes* 41 (1995): 19–41. Print.

———. *Per moderne carte: La biblioteca volgare di Petrarca*. Bologna: Il Mulino, 1990. Print.

———. "Petrarca e Arnaut Daniel." Santagata, *Per moderne carte* 157–211.

———. "Presenze di Dante 'comico' nel *Canzoniere* del Petrarca." *Giornale storico della letteratura italiana* 146 (1969): 163–221. Print.

———. "Le redazione." Santagata, *Canzoniere* ccv–ccxii.

Sasso, G. "Sul ventiseiesimo del *Principe*. L'uso del Petrarca." *La cultura* 33 (1995): 183–215. Print.

Savoca, Giuseppe, and Bartolo Calderone, eds. *Concordanza del* Canzoniere *di Francesco Petrarca*. 2 vols. Florence: Olschki, 2011. Print.

Scaglione, Aldo, ed. *Francis Petrarch, Six Centuries Later*. Chapel Hill: Dept. of Romance Langs., U of North Carolina; Chicago: Newberry Lib., 1975. Print.

———. "Love and the Pleasures of Frustration." *Journal of the History of Ideas* 58.4 (1997): 557–72. Print.

———. "The Structure of the *Canzoniere* and Petrarch's Method of Composition." Bernardo, *Francesco Petrarca* 301–13.

Scève, Maurice. *Délie objet de plus haulte vertu*. Ed. Françoise Charpentier. Paris: Gallimard, 1984. Print.

———. *Emblems of Desire: Selections from the* Délie. Ed. and trans. Richard Sieburth. Philadelphia: U of Pennsylvania P, 2003. Print.

Schalk, Fritz, ed. *Petrarca, 1304–1374: Beiträge zu Werk und Wirkung*. Frankfurt: Klostermann, 1975. Print.

Scherillo, Michele. "Petrarca e i trovatori." *Il Canzoniere.* By Franceso Petrarca. Notes by Giuseppe Rigutini. Ed. Scherillo. Milan: Hoepli, 1925. 41–77. Print.

Schiesari, Juliana. "Appropriating the Work of Women's Mourning: From Petrarch to Gaspara Stampa, and from Isabella di Morra to Tasso." *The Gendering of Me-*

lancholia: Feminism, Psychoanalysis, and the Symbolics of Loss in Renaissance Literature. Ithaca: Cornell UP, 1992. 160–90. Print.

Segre, Cesare. "I sonetti dell'aura." *Lectura Petrarce* 3 (1983): 57–78. Print.

Semenko, I. "Мандельштам – переводчик Петрарки." Вопросы литературы 14.10 (1970): 153–69. Print.

Shakespeare, William. *Twelfth Night*. *The Norton Shakespeare*. Ed. Stephen Greenblatt, Walter Cohen, Jean E. Howard, and Katharine Eisaman Maus. New York: Norton, 1997. 1683–1744. Print.

Shapiro, Marianne. *Hieroglyph of Time: The Petrarchan Sestina*. Minneapolis: U of Minnesota P, 1981. Print.

———. "Petrarch, Lorenzo il Magnifico and the Latin Elegiac Poets." *Romance Notes* 15 (1973): 172–75. Print.

Shapiro, Marianne, and Michael Shapiro. "Pushkin and Petrarch." *American Contributions to the Eleventh International Congress of Slavists, Bratislava, August–September 1993: Literature, Linguistics, Poetics*. Ed. Robert A. Maguire and Alan Timberlake. Columbus: Slavica, 1993. 154–69. Print.

Sidney, Philip. *Astrophil and Stella*. Sylvester 417–96.

———. *The Defence of Poesy*. *The Major Works*. Ed. Katherine Duncan-Jones. Oxford: Oxford UP, 1989. 212–51. Print.

———. *Sir Philip Sidney: His* Astrophel and Stella. London: Thomas Newman, 1591. *EEBO*. Web. 22 Oct. 2013.

Sidney, Robert. *Poems*. Ed. P. J. Croft. Oxford: Clarendon, 1984. Print.

Singleton, Charles S. *An Essay on the* Vita nuova. Cambridge: Harvard UP, 1949. Print.

Sini, Carlo. *Etica della scrittura*. Milan: Il Saggiatore, 1996. Print.

Smarr, Janet L. Rev. of *Francesco Petrarca, Citizen of the World: Proceedings of the World Petrarch Congress*, ed. Aldo S. Bernardo. *Renaissance Quarterly* 35.2 (1982): 261–65. Print.

Smith, Charlotte. Elegiac Sonnets *and Other Poems*. *The Poems of Charlotte Smith*. Ed. Stuart Curran. New York: Oxford UP, 1993. 2–130. Print.

Soldani, Arnaldo. *La sintassi del sonetto. Petrarca e il Trecento minore*. Florence: Del Galluzzo, 2009. Print.

Solmi, Arrigo. "Francesco Petrarca e l'Italia." *Annali della cattedra petrarchesca* 6 (1935–36): 3–21. Print.

Solovyov, Vladimir Sergeevich. Trans. of *Canzoniere* 366. Danchenko 1: 166–68.

"Sonnettomania." *New Monthly Magazine and Literary Journal* (Amer. ed.) 1.6 (1821): 652–56. Print.

Sowell, Madison U. "'The Jingling Sound of Like Endings': Genesis and Evolution of the *Grembo-Nembo-Lembo* Rhyme." *Studies for Dante: Essays in Honor of Dante Della Terza*. Ed. Franco Fido, Rena Syska-Lamparska, and Pamela D. Stewart. Fiesole: Cadmo, 1998. 487–500. Print.

Spagnoletti, Giacinto. *Il Petrarchismo*. Milan: Garzanti, 1959. Print.

Spenser, Edmund. *Amoretti*. Sylvester 343–408.

Spiller, Michael R. G. *The Development of the Sonnet: An Introduction*. London: Routledge, 1992. Print.

Staël, Germaine de. *Corinne, or Italy*. Trans. and ed. Sylvia Raphael. Oxford: Oxford UP, 1998. Print.

Stampa, Gaspara. *The Complete Poems*. Ed. Troy Tower and Jane Tylus. Trans. Tylus. Chicago: U of Chicago P, 2010. Print. The Other Voice in Early Modern Europe.

———. *Rime*. Ed. Rodolfo Ceriello. Milan: Rizzoli, 1976. Print.

Stierle, Karlheinz. *Francesco Petrarca. Ein Intellektueller im Europa des 14. Jahrhunderts*. Munich: Hanser, 2003. Print.

Sting. "Every Breath You Take." The Police. *Synchronicity*. Remastered. Interscope Records, 2003. CD.

Stock, Brian. "Reading, Writing, and the Self: Petrarch and His Forerunners." *New Literary History* 26 (1995): 717–30. Print.

Storey, H. Wayne. "Doubting Petrarca's Last Words: Erasure in MS Vaticano Latino 3195." Barolini and Storey 67–91.

———. *Transcription and Visual Poetics in the Early Italian Lyric*. New York: Garland, 1993. Print.

Stortoni, Laura Anna, ed. *Women Poets of the Italian Renaissance: Courtly Ladies and Courtesans*. New York: Italica, 1997. Print.

Strayer, Joseph R., ed. *Dictionary of the Middle Ages*. 13 vols. New York: Scribner, 1982–89. Print.

Struever, Nancy S. *Theory as Practice: Ethical Inquiry in the Renaissance*. Chicago: U of Chicago P, 1992. Print.

Sturm-Maddox, Sara. *Petrarch's Laurels*. University Park: Penn State UP, 1992. Print.

———. *Petrarch's Metamorphoses: Text and Subtext in the* Rime sparse. Columbia: U of Missouri P, 1985. Print.

———. *Ronsard, Petrarch, and the* Amours. Gainesville: UP of Florida, 1999. Print.

Suitner, Franco. *Petrarca e la tradizione stilnovistica*. Florence: Olschki, 1977. Print.

Sylvester, Richard S., ed. *English Sixteenth-Century Verse: An Anthology*. 2nd ed. New York: Norton, 1984. Print.

Tarrant, Richard. "Ovid and Ancient Literary History." *The Cambridge Companion to Ovid*. Ed. P. R. Hardie. Cambridge: Cambridge UP, 2002. 13–33. Print.

Tatham, Edward H. R. *Francesco Petrarca, the First Modern Man of Letters, His Life and Correspondence: A Study of the Early Fourteenth Century (1304–1347)*. 2 vols. London: Sheldon, 1925. Print.

Taylor, Charles. *Sources of the Self: The Making of the Modern Identity*. Cambridge: Harvard UP, 1989. Print.

Tesauro, Emanuele. *Il canocchiale aristotelico*. 1663. Savigliano: Artistica Piemontese, 2002. Print.

Thompson, David, and Alan F. Nagel, eds. and trans. *The Three Crowns of Florence: Humanist Assessments of Dante, Petrarca, and Boccaccio*. New York: Harper, 1972. Print.

Toffoli, Elisa, and A. Fornaciari. "Luce (Tramonti a NordEst)." *Asile's World*. Sugar, 2001. CD.

Tomlinson. Charles. *The Sonnet: Its Origin, Structure, and Place in Poetry*. London: J. Murray, 1874. Print.

Tottel, Richard. *Songs and Sonnets Written by the Right Honorable Lord Henry Howard Late Earl of Surrey and Others*. London, 1557. *EEBO*. Web. 22 Oct. 2013.

Trapp, J. B. "Petrarch's Laura: The Portraiture of an Imaginary Beloved." *Journal of the Warburg and Courtauld Institutes* 64 (2001): 55–192. Print.

Trinkaus, Charles. *The Poet as Philosopher: Petrarch and the Formation of Renaissance Consciousness*. New Haven: Yale UP, 1979. Print.

Tripet, Arnaud. *Pétrarque ou la connaissance de soi*. Genève: Droz, 1967. Print.

Trottmann, Christian. *La vision béatifique: Des disputes scolastiques à sa définition par Benoît XII*. Rome: Ecole Française de Rome, 1995. Print.

Trovato, Paolo. *Dante in Petrarca. Per un inventario dei dantismi nei* Rerum vulgarium fragmenta. Florence: Olschki, 1979. Print.

Ullman, Berthold Louis. "Petrarch's Favorite Books." *Transactions and Proceedings of the American Philological Association* 54 (1923): 21–38. Print.

Vassallo, Peter. "From Petrarch to Dante: The Discourse of Disenchantment in Shelley's *The Triumph of Life*." *Journal of Anglo-Italian Studies* 1 (1991): 102–10. Print.

Vecchi Galli, Paola. "Petrarca fra Tre e Quattrocento." Malato 161–88.

———. "Petrarca nel Cinquecento." Malato 325–51.

Velli, Giuseppe. "La memoria poetica del Petrarca." *Petrarca e Boccaccio: Tradizione, memoria, scrittura*. 2nd ed. Padua: Antenore, 1995. 1–73. Print.

Venclova, Thomas. "Вячеслав Иванов И Осип Мандельштам – переводчики Петрарки (на примере сонета CCCXI)." Собеседники на пиру: Статьи о русской литературе. By Venclova. Vilnius: Baltos Lankos, 1997. 168–83. Print.

Verdi, Giuseppe. "La donna è mobile." *Rigoletto*. Cond. Carlo Maria Giulini. Deutsche Grammophon, 1980. CD.

Vergil. *Eclogues*. Ed. and trans. Guy Lee. New York: Penguin, 1984. Print.

———. *Georgics*. Ed. Richard F. Thomas. 2 vols. Cambridge: Cambridge UP, 1988. Print.

Vickers, Nancy J. "Diana Described: Scattered Woman and Scattered Rhyme." *Critical Inquiry* 8 (1981): 265–79. Print. Rpt. in *Writing and Sexual Difference*. Ed. Elizabeth Abel. Chicago: U of Chicago P, 1982. 95–109.

———. "Re-membering Dante: Petrarch's *Chiare, fresche et dolci acque*." *MLN* 96 (1981): 1–11. Print.

Wack, Mary Frances. *Lovesickness in the Middle Ages: The* Viaticum *and Its Commentaries*. Philadelphia: U of Pennsylvania P, 1990. Print.

Warkentin, Germaine. "*Infaticabile maestro*: Ernest Hatch Wilkins and the Manuscripts of Petrarch's *Canzoniere*." Barolini and Storey 45–65.

———. "'Love's sweetest Part, variety': Petrarch and the Curious Frame of the Renaissance Sonnet Sequence." *Renaissance and Reformation* 11 (1975): 14–23. Print.

Watson, Thomas. *The Hekatompathia; or, Passionate Centurie of Love*. London: Gabriel Cawood, 1582. *EEBO*. Web. 22 Oct. 2013.

Web Gallery of Art. Created by Emil Krén and Daniel Marx. Web Gallery of Art, 1996. Web. 31 Dec. 2011.

Wilkins, Ernest Hatch. *A History of Italian Literature*. Cambridge: Harvard UP, 1954. Print.

———. *"The Invention of the Sonnet" and Other Studies in Italian Literature*. Rome: Storia e Letteratura, 1959. Print.

———. *Life of Petrarch*. Chicago: U of Chicago P, 1961. Print.

———. *The Making of the* Canzoniere *and Other Petrarchan Studies*. Rome: Storia e Letteratura, 1951. Print.

———. *Petrarch's Eight Years in Milan*. Cambridge: Mediaeval Acad. of Amer., 1958. Print.

———. *Petrarch's Later Years*. Cambridge: Mediaeval Acad. of Amer., 1959. Print.

Wilson, Katharina M., ed. *Women Writers of the Renaissance and Reformation*. Athens: U of Georgia P, 1987. Print.

Wilson, Katharina, and Elizabeth M. Makowski. *Wykked Wyves and the Woes of Marriage: Misogamous Literature from Juvenal to Chaucer*. Albany: State U of New York P, 1990. Print.

Wiske, Martha Stone. Introduction. Wiske, *Teaching* 1–10.

———, ed. *Teaching for Understanding: Linking Research with Practice*. San Francisco: Jossey, 1998. Print.

Wittig, Monique. "The Mark of Gender." *The Poetics of Gender*. Ed. Nancy K. Miller. New York: Columbia UP, l986. 63–73. Print.

Wojciehowski, Dolora A. *Old Masters, New Subjects: Early Modern and Poststructuralist Theories of the Will*. Stanford: Stanford UP, 1995. Print.

Wordsworth, William. *The Poems*. Ed. John O. Hayden. 2 vols. Harmondsworth: Penguin, 1977. Print.

Wroth, Mary. *The Poems of Mary Wroth*. Ed. Josephine A. Roberts. Baton Rouge: Louisiana State UP, 1983. Print.

Wyatt, Thomas. "The longe love." Sylvester 130.

Yandell, Cathy. *Carpe Corpus: Time and Gender in Early Modern France*. Newark: U of Delaware P, 2000. Print.

Yeats, William Butler. *Collected Poems*. 1933. London: Macmillan, 1987. Print.

Zamponi, Stefano. "Il libro del *Canzoniere*: Modelli, strutture, funzione." *Rerum vulgarium fragmenta*. By Francesco Petrarca. Ed. Gino Belloni, Furio Brugnolo, H. Wayne Storey, and Zamponi. Vol. 2. Rome: Antenore, 2004. 13–57. Print.

Zanato, Tiziano. "San Francesco, Pier delle Vigne e Francesca da Rimini nei *Rerum vulgarium fragmenta*." *Filologia e critica* 2 (1977): 177–216. Print.

Zenari, Massimo. *Repertorio metrico dei* Rerum vulgarium fragmenta *di Francesco Petrarca*. Padua: Antenore, 1999. Print.

INDEX

Modern Language Association of America

Approaches to Teaching World Literature

Achebe's Things Fall Apart. Ed. Bernth Lindfors. 1991.
Arthurian Tradition. Ed. Maureen Fries and Jeanie Watson. 1992.
Atwood's The Handmaid's Tale *and Other Works*. Ed. Sharon R. Wilson, Thomas B. Friedman, and Shannon Hengen. 1996.
Austen's Emma. Ed. Marcia McClintock Folsom. 2004.
Austen's Pride and Prejudice. Ed. Marcia McClintock Folsom. 1993.
Balzac's Old Goriot. Ed. Michal Peled Ginsburg. 2000.
Baudelaire's Flowers of Evil. Ed. Laurence M. Porter. 2000.
Beckett's Waiting for Godot. Ed. June Schlueter and Enoch Brater. 1991.
Behn's Oroonoko. Ed. Cynthia Richards and Mary Ann O'Donnell. 2014.
Beowulf. Ed. Jess B. Bessinger, Jr., and Robert F. Yeager. 1984.
Blake's Songs of Innocence and of Experience. Ed. Robert F. Gleckner and Mark L. Greenberg. 1989.
Boccaccio's Decameron. Ed. James H. McGregor. 2000.
British Women Poets of the Romantic Period. Ed. Stephen C. Behrendt and Harriet Kramer Linkin. 1997.
Charlotte Brontë's Jane Eyre. Ed. Diane Long Hoeveler and Beth Lau. 1993.
Emily Brontë's Wuthering Heights. Ed. Sue Lonoff and Terri A. Hasseler. 2006.
Byron's Poetry. Ed. Frederick W. Shilstone. 1991.
Works of Italo Calvino. Ed. Franco Ricci. 2013.
Camus's The Plague. Ed. Steven G. Kellman. 1985.
Writings of Bartolomé de Las Casas. Ed. Santa Arias and Eyda M. Merediz. 2008.
Cather's My Ántonia. Ed. Susan J. Rosowski. 1989.
Cervantes' Don Quixote. Ed. Richard Bjornson. 1984.
Chaucer's Canterbury Tales. First edition Ed. Joseph Gibaldi. 1980.
Chaucer's Canterbury Tales. Second edition. Ed. Peter W. Travis and Frank Grady. 2014.
Chaucer's Troilus and Criseyde *and the Shorter Poems*. Ed. Tison Pugh and Angela Jane Weisl. 2006.
Chopin's The Awakening. Ed. Bernard Koloski. 1988.
Coetzee's Disgrace *and Other Works.* Ed. Laura Wright, Jane Poyner, and Elleke Boehmer. 2014.
Coleridge's Poetry and Prose. Ed. Richard E. Matlak. 1991.
Collodi's Pinocchio *and Its Adaptations.* Ed. Michael Sherberg. 2006.
Conrad's "Heart of Darkness" and "The Secret Sharer." Ed. Hunt Hawkins and Brian W. Shaffer. 2002.
Dante's Divine Comedy. Ed. Carole Slade. 1982.
Defoe's Robinson Crusoe. Ed. Maximillian E. Novak and Carl Fisher. 2005.

DeLillo's White Noise. Ed. Tim Engles and John N. Duvall. 2006.
Dickens's Bleak House. Ed. John O. Jordan and Gordon Bigelow. 2009.
Dickens's David Copperfield. Ed. Richard J. Dunn. 1984.
Dickinson's Poetry. Ed. Robin Riley Fast and Christine Mack Gordon. 1989.
Narrative of the Life of Frederick Douglass. Ed. James C. Hall. 1999.
Works of John Dryden. Ed. Jayne Lewis and Lisa Zunshine. 2013.
Duras's Ourika. Ed. Mary Ellen Birkett and Christopher Rivers. 2009.
Early Modern Spanish Drama. Ed. Laura R. Bass and Margaret R. Greer. 2006.
Eliot's Middlemarch. Ed. Kathleen Blake. 1990.
Eliot's Poetry and Plays. Ed. Jewel Spears Brooker. 1988.
Shorter Elizabethan Poetry. Ed. Patrick Cheney and Anne Lake Prescott. 2000.
Ellison's Invisible Man. Ed. Susan Resneck Parr and Pancho Savery. 1989.
English Renaissance Drama. Ed. Karen Bamford and Alexander Leggatt. 2002.
Works of Louise Erdrich. Ed. Gregg Sarris, Connie A. Jacobs, and James R. Giles. 2004.
Dramas of Euripides. Ed. Robin Mitchell-Boyask. 2002.
Faulkner's As I Lay Dying. Ed. Patrick O'Donnell and Lynda Zwinger. 2011.
Faulkner's The Sound and the Fury. Ed. Stephen Hahn and Arthur F. Kinney. 1996.
Fitzgerald's The Great Gatsby. Ed. Jackson R. Bryer and Nancy P. VanArsdale. 2009.
Flaubert's Madame Bovary. Ed. Laurence M. Porter and Eugene F. Gray. 1995.
García Márquez's One Hundred Years of Solitude. Ed. María Elena de Valdés and Mario J. Valdés. 1990.
Gilman's "The Yellow Wall-Paper" and Herland. Ed. Denise D. Knight and Cynthia J. Davis. 2003.
Goethe's Faust. Ed. Douglas J. McMillan. 1987.
Gothic Fiction: The British and American Traditions. Ed. Diane Long Hoeveler and Tamar Heller. 2003.
Poetry of John Gower. Ed. R. F. Yeager and Brian W. Gastle. 2011.
Grass's The Tin Drum. Ed. Monika Shafi. 2008.
H.D.'s Poetry and Prose. Ed. Annette Debo and Lara Vetter. 2011.
Hebrew Bible as Literature in Translation. Ed. Barry N. Olshen and Yael S. Feldman. 1989.
Homer's Iliad *and* Odyssey. Ed. Kostas Myrsiades. 1987.
Hurston's Their Eyes Were Watching God *and Other Works*. Ed. John Lowe. 2009.
Ibsen's A Doll House. Ed. Yvonne Shafer. 1985.
Henry James's Daisy Miller *and* The Turn of the Screw. Ed. Kimberly C. Reed and Peter G. Beidler. 2005.
Works of Samuel Johnson. Ed. David R. Anderson and Gwin J. Kolb. 1993.
Joyce's Ulysses. Ed. Kathleen McCormick and Erwin R. Steinberg. 1993.
Works of Sor Juana Inés de la Cruz. Ed. Emilie L. Bergmann and Stacey Schlau. 2007.
Kafka's Short Fiction. Ed. Richard T. Gray. 1995.
Keats's Poetry. Ed. Walter H. Evert and Jack W. Rhodes. 1991.

Kingston's The Woman Warrior. Ed. Shirley Geok-lin Lim. 1991.
Lafayette's The Princess of Clèves. Ed. Faith E. Beasley and Katharine Ann Jensen. 1998.
Works of D. H. Lawrence. Ed. M. Elizabeth Sargent and Garry Watson. 2001.
Lazarillo de Tormes *and the Picaresque Tradition*. Ed. Anne J. Cruz. 2009.
Lessing's The Golden Notebook. Ed. Carey Kaplan and Ellen Cronan Rose. 1989.
Works of Naguib Mahfouz. Ed. Waïl S. Hassan and Susan Muaddi Darraj. 2011.
Mann's Death in Venice *and Other Short Fiction*. Ed. Jeffrey B. Berlin. 1992.
Marguerite de Navarre's Heptameron. Ed. Colette H. Winn. 2007.
Works of Carmen Martín Gaite. Ed. Joan L. Brown. 2013.
Medieval English Drama. Ed. Richard K. Emmerson. 1990.
Melville's Moby-Dick. Ed. Martin Bickman. 1985.
Metaphysical Poets. Ed. Sidney Gottlieb. 1990.
Miller's Death of a Salesman. Ed. Matthew C. Roudané. 1995.
Milton's Paradise Lost. First edition. Ed. Galbraith M. Crump. 1986.
Milton's Paradise Lost. Second edition. Ed. Peter C. Herman. 2012.
Milton's Shorter Poetry and Prose. Ed. Peter C. Herman. 2007.
Molière's Tartuffe *and Other Plays*. Ed. James F. Gaines and Michael S. Koppisch. 1995.
Momaday's The Way to Rainy Mountain. Ed. Kenneth M. Roemer. 1988.
Montaigne's Essays. Ed. Patrick Henry. 1994.
Novels of Toni Morrison. Ed. Nellie Y. McKay and Kathryn Earle. 1997.
Murasaki Shikibu's The Tale of Genji. Ed. Edward Kamens. 1993.
Nabokov's Lolita. Ed. Zoran Kuzmanovich and Galya Diment. 2008.
Works of Ngũgĩ wa Thiong'o. Ed. Oliver Lovesey. 2012.
Works of Tim O'Brien. Ed. Alex Vernon and Catherine Calloway. 2010.
Works of Ovid and the Ovidian Tradition. Ed. Barbara Weiden Boyd and Cora Fox. 2010.
Petrarch's Canzoniere *and the Petrarchan Tradition*. Ed. Christopher Kleinhenz and Andrea Dini. 2014.
Poe's Prose and Poetry. Ed. Jeffrey Andrew Weinstock and Tony Magistrale. 2008.
Pope's Poetry. Ed. Wallace Jackson and R. Paul Yoder. 1993.
Proust's Fiction and Criticism. Ed. Elyane Dezon-Jones and Inge Crosman Wimmers. 2003.
Puig's Kiss of the Spider Woman. Ed. Daniel Balderston and Francine Masiello. 2007.
Pynchon's The Crying of Lot 49 *and Other Works*. Ed. Thomas H. Schaub. 2008.
Works of François Rabelais. Ed. Todd W. Reeser and Floyd Gray. 2011.
Novels of Samuel Richardson. Ed. Lisa Zunshine and Jocelyn Harris. 2006.
Rousseau's Confessions *and* Reveries of the Solitary Walker. Ed. John C. O'Neal and Ourida Mostefai. 2003.
Scott's Waverley Novels. Ed. Evan Gottlieb and Ian Duncan. 2009.
Shakespeare's Hamlet. Ed. Bernice W. Kliman. 2001.

Shakespeare's King Lear. Ed. Robert H. Ray. 1986.
Shakespeare's Othello. Ed. Peter Erickson and Maurice Hunt. 2005.
Shakespeare's Romeo and Juliet. Ed. Maurice Hunt. 2000.
Shakespeare's The Taming of the Shrew. Ed. Margaret Dupuis and Grace Tiffany. 2013.
Shakespeare's The Tempest *and Other Late Romances.* Ed. Maurice Hunt. 1992.
Shelley's Frankenstein. Ed. Stephen C. Behrendt. 1990.
Shelley's Poetry. Ed. Spencer Hall. 1990.
Sir Gawain and the Green Knight. Ed. Miriam Youngerman Miller and Jane Chance. 1986.
Song of Roland. Ed. William W. Kibler and Leslie Zarker Morgan. 2006.
Spenser's Faerie Queene. Ed. David Lee Miller and Alexander Dunlop. 1994.
Stendhal's The Red and the Black. Ed. Dean de la Motte and Stirling Haig. 1999.
Sterne's Tristram Shandy. Ed. Melvyn New. 1989.
Works of Robert Louis Stevenson. Ed. Caroline McCracken-Flesher. 2013.
The Story of the Stone (Dream of the Red Chamber). Ed. Andrew Schonebaum and Tina Lu. 2012.
Stowe's Uncle Tom's Cabin. Ed. Elizabeth Ammons and Susan Belasco. 2000.
Swift's Gulliver's Travels. Ed. Edward J. Rielly. 1988.
Teresa of Ávila and the Spanish Mystics. Ed. Alison Weber. 2009.
Thoreau's Walden *and Other Works.* Ed. Richard J. Schneider. 1996.
Tolstoy's Anna Karenina. Ed. Liza Knapp and Amy Mandelker. 2003.
Vergil's Aeneid. Ed. William S. Anderson and Lorina N. Quartarone. 2002.
Voltaire's Candide. Ed. Renée Waldinger. 1987.
Whitman's Leaves of Grass. Ed. Donald D. Kummings. 1990.
Wiesel's Night. Ed. Alan Rosen. 2007.
Works of Oscar Wilde. Ed. Philip E. Smith II. 2008.
Woolf's Mrs. Dalloway. Ed. Eileen Barrett and Ruth O. Saxton. 2009.
Woolf's To the Lighthouse. Ed. Beth Rigel Daugherty and Mary Beth Pringle. 2001.
Wordsworth's Poetry. Ed. Spencer Hall, with Jonathan Ramsey. 1986.
Wright's Native Son. Ed. James A. Miller. 1997.